Black Power, Inc.

POLITICS AND CULTURE IN MODERN AMERICA

Series Editors: Keisha N. Blain, Margot Canaday,
Matthew Lassiter, Stephen Pitti, Thomas J. Sugrue

Volumes in the series narrate and analyze political and
social change in the broadest dimensions from 1865 to
the present, including ideas about the ways people have
sought and wielded power in the public sphere and the
language and institutions of politics at all levels—local,
national, and transnational. The series is motivated by
a desire to reverse the fragmentation of modern U.S.
history and to encourage synthetic perspectives on
social movements and the state, on gender, race, and
labor, and on intellectual history and popular culture.

BLACK POWER, INC.

Corporate America and the Rise of
Multinational Empowerment Politics

Jessica Ann Levy

PENN

UNIVERSITY OF PENNSYLVANIA PRESS

PHILADELPHIA

Published by
University of Pennsylvania Press
Philadelphia, Pennsylvania 19104–4112 USA
www.pennpress.org

EU Authorized Representative: Easy Access System
Europe—Mustamäe tee 50, 10621 Tallinn, Estonia,
gpsr.requests@easproject.com.

Printed in the United States of America on acid-free paper
10 9 8 7 6 5 4 3 2 1

A Cataloging-in-Publication record for this book
is available from the Library of Congress.

Hardcover ISBN 978-1-5128-2857-3
Ebook ISBN 978-1-5128-2858-0

For my dad, my first history teacher,
and for Paulina and Julia, my loves

CONTENTS

LIST OF ABBREVIATIONS

African-American Institute (AAI)
African Chamber of Commerce (ACOC)
African National Congress (ANC)
African National Congress's Black Economic Empowerment (BEE)
Area Redevelopment Association (ARA)
Black Economic Development Conference (BEDC)
Black Enterprise Network (BEN)
Communist Party of South Africa (CPSA)
Community Action Councils (CAC)
Congress of Racial Equality (CORE)
Congressional Black Caucus (CBC)
East Side Voice of Independent Detroit (ESVID)
Empowerment Zones and Enterprise Communities (EZ/EC)
Equal Opportunity Fund (EOF)
Federation of African Business and Consumer Services (FABCOS)
First National Bank of Boston (FNBB)
Foreign Assistance Act (FAA)
General Electric (GE)
General Motors (GM)
Greater New York Co-ordinating Committee for Employment (GNYCC)
Harlem Commonwealth Council Inc. (HCC)
Harlem Youth Opportunities Unlimited (HARYOU)
Industry Support Unit Inc. (ISU)
International Business Machines (IBM)
International Council of Equal Opportunity Principles (ICEOP)
International Monetary Fund (IMF)
Moral Re-Armament Movement (MRA)
National Black Independent Political Party (NBIPP)
Nation of Islam (NOI)

National African Chamber of Commerce (NACOC)
National African Federated Chamber of Commerce (African Chamber)
National Association for the Advancement of Colored People (NAACP)
National Industry Advisory Council (NIAC)
North Philadelphia Youth Employment Service (NPYES)
Office of Economic Opportunity (OEO)
Operation People United to Save Humanity (Operation PUSH)
Opportunities Industrialization Centers Inc. (OIC)
Opportunities Industrialization Centers International (OICI)
Organization of African Unity (OAU)
Organization of Afro-American Unity (OAAU)
Pan African Congress (PAC)
Pan-African Skills Project (PASP)
Patrice Lumumba Coalition (PLC)
Philadelphia Anti-Poverty Action Committee (PAAC)
Philadelphia Citizens Committee Against Juvenile Delinquency and Its
    Causes (CCAJD)
Polaroid Revolutionary Workers' Movement (PRWM)
Progress Aerospace Enterprise (PAE)
Project for Corporate Responsibility (PCR)
Securities and Exchange Commission (SEC)
South African Institute of Race Relations (SAIRR)
Southern Christian Leadership Conference (SCLC)
Student Nonviolent Coordinating Committee (SNCC)
US Agency for International Development (USAID)
US Department of Housing and Urban Development (HUD)
United States-South Africa Leadership Exchange Program (USSALEP)
Universal Negro Improvement Association (UNIA)
Volta Aluminum Company (VALCO)
Zion Investment Associates (ZIA)
Zion Non-Profit Charitable Trust (ZNPCT)

"Build, Brother, Build"

I t was a beautiful Sunday in May 1965 when supporters of Opportunities Industrialization Centers Inc. (OIC) gathered to witness the launch of the West Philadelphia OIC, a new job-training and Black economic development center, the third such center of its kind. Thousands of Black Philadelphians lined 52nd Street, known as the city's "Black Main Street," to see OIC's founder, Reverend Leon Howard Sullivan, cut the ribbon for the center's opening. In its coverage of the event, the city's daily newspaper, *The Philadelphia Inquirer*, insinuated a protest, describing the attendees as "a throng of some 7,000 Negroes."[1] Yet the celebration of OIC's launch was a far cry from the historic civil rights marches undertaken by Black Americans that year, as evident by the presence of multiple city officials and businessmen. At the ceremony, someone read a telegram from President Lyndon B. Johnson. It read, in part: "This new facility should brighten the employment prospects of a large number of disadvantaged Philadelphians so that they may lead useful, rewarding lives." Sullivan echoed Johnson's emphasis on productivity when he exhorted the crowd, "we [Black Americans] must continue to protest when that is needed, but we must also prepare . . . we must also produce."[2]

Several years later, Sullivan's rhetoric sounded bolder, yet his message remained largely the same. Responding to a journalist's inquiry regarding the phrase that had recently captivated the nation, Sullivan proudly declared: "I am Black power—six feet, five inches of Black power. I believe in the ability of the Black man to do what any other man can do." Unlike other invocations of Black Power encouraging Black people to rise up in a global revolution against imperialism and racial capitalism, Sullivan frequently touted the benefits of working within the system. Black Power on its own was not enough. Rather, in Sullivan's words, "Black power and white power must put their strength together to build American power."[3]

What it meant to build Black power—to build American power—during the 1960s was widely contested. Joining others in questioning some of the key tenets of the civil rights movement and mid-century liberalism, Sullivan advocated for Black people's liberation through their inclusion in a reimagined American free enterprise system. Payrolls, not welfare rolls, were what Black Americans wanted, Sullivan told Congress amid hearings discussing the US government's funding of OIC.[4] Nor was Sullivan alone. Over the years, others joined Sullivan in soliciting government and business support for things like job training, Black entrepreneurship, corporate-community partnerships, and various other initiatives designed to cultivate Black buy-in—literally and figuratively—in global capitalism. This approach is what I call Black empowerment politics.

From Black Power to Black Empowerment

Today, references to Black empowerment are ubiquitous. A Google search for the term returns millions of results. While varied, reflecting its diverse meanings, there is a surprising amount of consistency to the uses of Black empowerment, with many of these results including references to job-training, entrepreneurship, corporate social responsibility, and other kinds of private enterprise. This includes the African-American Empowerment Network, focusing on "cradle-to-career opportunities, improving wages, business development, and home ownership"; Black Empowerment Works, a grant program sponsored by the United Way of Greater Cincinnati promoting "Black self-determination, social mobility, and economic prosperity;" and the National Black Empowerment Council, whose mission includes "increas[ing] African American financial literacy, empower[ing] entrepreneurs, and elevat[ing] Black leaders into corporate governance."[5] Black empowerment twice featured in Donald Trump's efforts to curry Black votes during the 2020 and 2024 presidential elections. Titled the Black Economic Empowerment Platinum Plan, Trump's 2020 initiative, while never really making it off the ground, remains noteworthy for its promise to invest nearly $500 billion in Black communities, much of it geared toward job-training and Black entrepreneurship.[6] Despite its widespread usage and seeming malleability in the hands of various actors across the political spectrum, there has been relatively little attention paid to the history of this ideology.

What began as a little-noticed appropriation of the term Black Power subsequently emerged as a popular way for civil rights leaders, politicians, corporate executives, and others to describe a series of programs and policies promoting job-training, entrepreneurship, corporate social responsibility, and other kinds of private enterprise among Black and other marginalized people. One of the first references to the term appeared in 1969 in a Methodist Church program launched in the wake of the Black Manifesto. Drafted by Student Nonviolent Coordinating Committee (SNCC) leader and Black Power activist James Forman, the Black Manifesto demanded, among other things, that white churches and synagogues pay $500 million in reparations for the slave trade.[7] Side-stepping this call, the United Methodist Board of Missions instead announced a $1.3 million grant supporting what they called "Black empowerment," including donations to several Black, Mexican-American, and Indian-American religious and civil rights organizations, along with $550,000 to Black colleges.[8] Subsequently, Black empowerment gained prominence in association with a variety of government and private initiatives at the local, national, and international level, including Bill Clinton's Empowerment Zones/Enterprise Communities and the (South) African National Congress's Black Economic Empowerment program.

Exceeding and frequently preceding the emergence of Black empowerment as a discourse, Black empowerment was also a politics, one that played a crucial role shaping Black struggles across the United States and sub-Saharan Africa during the second half of the twentieth century. Combining aspects of racial uplift, self-help, Black capitalism, Pan-Africanism, and the social gospel, Black empowerment politics positioned private enterprise—broadly conceived—as key to Black people's economic, political, social, and moral salvation. Testifying in 1974 to the success of OIC—by that point, one of the largest Black empowerment programs in the world, with over one hundred chapters in the US and Africa—Sullivan boasted about the impact of having trained more than two hundred thousand people, fifty thousand of whom had previously been on government welfare, and having placed them in jobs, where they contributed an estimated $4 billion to the US economy via new income, new taxes paid, and money saved in relief checks. "All of this," Sullivan stated, "does not include the additional unmeasured benefits on which no dollar value can ever be placed—in human terms—of lives made more useful, homes brought together, families saved . . . [and] a new spirit of hope for the poor in communities across the country whose OIC slogans of 'we help ourselves' and 'build, brother, build,' have replaced the cries of 'burn, baby, burn.'"[9] Hope, self-worth, community: In addition to dollars and cents, these were the dividends championed by proponents of Black empowerment politics.

As Sullivan's juxtaposing of "build, brother, build" with "burn, baby, burn," invoking the ongoing Black rebellions taking place in US cities and towns, suggests, Black empowerment politics evolved in a complex and dynamic relationship with other forms of Black politics, including Black Power. Operating in tandem in the post–World War II Black metropolis, proponents of Black empowerment politics frequently positioned themselves and their programs as an alternative to the most radical aspects of the Black Power movement. Where Black Power activists tended to lionize Black militants and revolutionaries, proponents of Black empowerment instead championed Black entrepreneurs and corporate executives as the embodiment of success.

Frequently differing in terms of rhetoric, imagery, and the instruments they employed, Black Power and Black empowerment politics nevertheless shared a certain set of beliefs, including an emphasis on Black pride, diasporic consciousness, and community control—the idea that local residents should shape the institutions governing their communities. Indeed, it was, in part, Black empowerment's proximity to Black Power that helps explain its popularity among a growing swath of Black people in the US and Africa during the late twentieth century. Echoing popular depictions of the movement, early scholarship on Black Power frequently centered on a handful of individuals and organizations—Stokely Carmichael, Malcolm X, the Black Panther Party—whose ideas and actions have often stood in for the broader Black Power movement.[10] Speaking to a packed auditorium at the University of California, Berkeley, in October 1966, Carmichael, whose impromptu declaration—"We been saying freedom for six years and we ain't got nothin.' What we got to start saying now is Black Power! We want Black Power"—earlier that year set off a nationwide firestorm, characterized Black Power as a distinctly anti-American and anti-imperial politics. "[The United States] is a nation of thieves," declared Carmichael. "It stole everything it has, beginning with black people. . . . I do not want to be a part of the American pie. The American pie means raping South Africa, beating Vietnam, beating South America, raping the Philippines, raping every country you've been in. I don't want any of your blood money. I don't want to be part of that system."[11] Complementing Carmichael, the Black Panther Party heralded anti-imperialism and anti-capitalism, alongside self-determination, as key tenets of Black Power. In the party's Ten-Point Program, party cofounders Huey P. Newton and Bobby Seale demanded "an end to the robbery by the white man of our Black community," a guaranteed income, and socialized housing, among other things.[12] Newton later expanded on what he saw as a fundamental link between Black Power and international socialism, or what he called intercommunalism, in his speeches and writings.[13]

Beyond these well-known figures and their pronouncements, recent scholarship has revealed the Black Power movement functioned as a broad tent containing contradictions.[14] While employing revolutionary rhetoric, and occasionally revolutionary means, many Black Power activists, including those engaged in struggles for affordable and quality housing, healthcare, and education, believed in American liberalism and, indeed, sought its expansion through their engagement with Lyndon B. Johnson's War on Poverty.[15] Elsewhere, Black Power activists, including Black Panthers Bobby Seale and Elaine Brown, pursued electoral politics in an effort to transform American politics from the inside.[16] The relationship between Black Power and American liberalism, moreover, was far from monolithic. While the Black Power movement was certainly not lacking in indictments of the American political and economic system—indictments like Angela Davis's 1972 call to "seize" the power "from the Standard Oils, the General Motors and all the giant corporations, and of course from their protectors, the government," who kept Black and Brown people locked out of the American dream—one also finds self-proclaimed Black Power activists engaged in more moderate efforts to reform American liberalism and American capitalism.[17] In the cases of those I call Black empowerment activists, Black activists and entrepreneurs were some of the loudest proponents of liberalism's transformation into what scholars and pundits have called neoliberalism.[18] They did so by incorporating Black Power, melding it to a free market politics that celebrated the liberatory potential of Black business, as well as corporate America, locally and globally.

Efforts to wield the power of private enterprise to serve the race have long existed within the Black freedom struggle and, occasionally, proved a common cause between Black Power and Black empowerment activists, such as when Stokely Carmichael and Charles V. Hamilton called on Black people to boycott businesses that refused to reinvest a portion of their profits back into the Black community, echoing Sullivan's earlier promotion of selective patronage (discussed below).[19] Over time, Black empowerment politics developed into a distinct ideological and political vision, distinguishable from Black Power politics through its emphasis on individual, as opposed to collective, responsibility, and Black progress through integration into an

American capitalism system, a process capped off by the appointment of Black Americans like Sullivan to managerial and director positions in corporate America.[20] The evolution of Black empowerment politics away from Black Power was encouraged and aided by the US government, which, starting in the mid-1960s, emerged as a major supporter of Black empowerment programs like OIC and Harlem Youth Opportunities Unlimited (HARYOU), the latter of which received $5 million from the Johnson administration to support its job-training program.[21] Located primarily in Black urban communities and led by local civil rights leaders, ministers, and/or businessmen, Black empowerment programs received significant financial and political support from Democratic and Republican administrations—from Nixon to Clinton—as part of a bipartisan trend of using private enterprise to combat poverty and unemployment, especially in US cities.[22]

While heavily reliant on government funding, Black empowerment activists spent the bulk of their energy focused on private-sector solutions to the problems facing Black communities, underscoring a defining feature of Black empowerment politics. This included cultivating close relationships with corporate America. Such relationships frequently had their birth in moments of conflict, such as Leon Sullivan's decision to wage a city-wide boycott of Philadelphia-area businesses that discriminated against hiring Black employees in skilled and high-paying positions, a strategy that became known as selective patronage. The boycott, which garnered national attention, helped inspire a number of similar campaigns, including Jesse Jackson's Operation PUSH. Selective patronage, the aim of which, Sullivan noted, "was not . . . to destroy a business, but only to awaken it and to get it on the right road as far as the employment of Black Americans was concerned," was typical of civil rights capitalism. Paralleling the movement for civil rights, civil rights capitalism advocated for Black people's inclusion within the broader American capitalist system, not its destruction. "We believed in free enterprise!" declared Sullivan, continuing his reflection on the animus behind selective patronage. "We had no desire to destroy it; we wanted to strengthen it. But we wanted it strong for everybody, so that instead of the Black man's getting the crumbs all the time, he would start baking some of the bread."[23]

Emerging out of civil rights capitalism, Black empowerment politics manifested as a series of new partnerships between Black organizations and corporate America, part of a broader transformation in corporate politics during the late twentieth century. This transformation included corporate America's embrace of what came to be called DEI (diversity, equity, and inclusion). In some cases, US corporations were motivated by a desire to reach what many perceived as a growing Black consumer market.[24] Corporate America likewise embraced Black empowerment politics, including implementing equal opportunity and voluntary affirmative action programs, in an effort to forestall government intervention.[25] Still, a third and significant motivation, beyond expanding their market share and avoiding government regulation, included deliberate attempts to shape the trajectory of Black politics through cultivating support for entrepreneurship.[26]

The interweaving of Black empowerment and corporate politics notably occurred at multiple scales—local, national, and international—reflecting the increasingly global terrain in which American business operated during the 1970s and 1980s. What began as a means of countering the ongoing Black rebellion in urban America quickly found application elsewhere, including in efforts by the US government and US corporations to promote American-style free enterprise in sub-Saharan Africa. Starting in the 1960s, the US government, prompted by the Kennedy administration, and followed by US corporations, increasingly touted Africa as the next frontier for American business. As in other parts of the Global South, both the US government, including US international development programs, and US corporations faced resistance from African socialists and Third World critics for their role engendering inequality and global white supremacy. One of the sharpest critiques came in the form of the Declaration on the Establishment of a New International Economic Order. Adopted by the United Nations General Assembly in 1974, the declaration called for a complete overhaul of the international systems of trade and finance, and reasserted the rights of individual nations to control their own natural resources and other economic activity, including that undertaken by transnational corporations, within the country.[27] In response, US government officials in the Department of Commerce and the US Agency for International Development (USAID) and corporate executives increasingly deployed Black empowerment activists as business ambassadors, touting American-style free enterprise as an engine of Black empowerment.

Black Empowerment Meets Anti-Apartheid

Over time, Black Power and Black empowerment politics increasingly diverged. The differences were particularly stark in relation to the international anti-apartheid movement. For Black youth and their allies, who came of age amid the simultaneous movements for Black Power and decolonization, South Africa's apartheid regime provided an especially glaring example of the failures of post-war liberalism and global capitalism.[28] Instead of gradually fading away, as some predicted, South Africa's commitment to a brutal system of racial segregation intensified during the 1960s and 1970s and became more profitable. One scholar estimates that, by the mid-1960s, investors were averaging a 20.6 percent rate of return—the highest rate in the world. By comparison, the next-highest country, Japan, had a 12 percent average return on investment.[29] South Africa, critics claimed, was a textbook case of racial capitalism, a system in which racism and capitalism are co-constitutive.[30] Building on this analysis, anti-apartheid activists called for an international boycott of South Africa.[31]

Meanwhile, white and Black liberals increasingly proffered an alternative response—namely, US-sponsored Black empowerment. Initially unyielding in the face of the anti-apartheid movement (if not outright dismissive of it), US corporations, starting in the late 1970s, increasingly appropriated Black empowerment politics to rebrand corporate America as heroes, not villains, in the struggle to end apartheid. In doing so, they relied on Black American executives to help them justify their continued and, in some cases, expanded, business dealings in South Africa. Chief among these efforts was the Sullivan Principles. Having joined the board of the world's largest corporation, General Motors, in 1971, in 1977 Sullivan collaborated with executives representing twelve of the largest US corporations, including Ford and IBM, on the Sullivan Principles, a corporate code of conduct for companies doing business in South Africa. The Principles borrowed heavily from existing institutional responses to the civil rights movement in the US, including equal pay for equal work and voluntary affirmative action. By applying these same principles to South Africa, US corporations, Sullivan argued, could empower Black South Africans and help bring an end to South African apartheid, while avoiding what he and others argued would be the devastating effects of a withdrawal of US capital. More investment in Black empowerment, not divestment, was the solution to ending apartheid.

Black empowerment initiatives like the Sullivan Principles went a long way toward reconciling free-market and anti-apartheid politics, melding seemingly contradictory movements together. By the early 1980s, the Sullivan Principles had garnered the support of over 150 US companies and the US government. These and other US-sponsored Black empowerment initiatives would not have succeeded to the extent that they did without support from Black Africans. In South Africa, as in other parts of the continent,

Black empowerment politics found a receptive audience among Black African entrepreneurs, politicians, and activists eager for American capital and business acumen. Among those who benefited from partnering with corporate America to promote Black economic empowerment in South Africa was the National African Federated Chamber of Commerce (African Chamber) and members of the African National Congress (ANC). More than profits were at stake in such partnerships. *Black Power, Inc.* reveals the work Black empowerment politics performed legitimating a new set of actors, including Black and white corporate executives and entrepreneurs, as leaders in the global Black freedom struggle. Black empowerment activists, in turn, played a crucial role in constructing a new post–Jim Crow/post-apartheid capitalist world order through reconciling American-style free enterprise and opposition to apartheid.

A Note on Methodology and Organization

Black Power, Inc. brings together two narratives central to twentieth-century US and international history: the rise and curtailment of the global Black freedom struggle and the post–World War II expansion of US corporate power, locally and globally, and reveals their interconnections within the transnational movement for Black empowerment. Moving across spaces, time, and scale, *Black Power, Inc.* traces Black empowerment's evolution as it made its way up the ladder of US power—from the streets of urban America and into corporate boardrooms and various government offices—and across the Atlantic to Africa. The story culminates in the international movement to end South African apartheid, where Black empowerment activists, corporate executives, and US politicians deployed Black empowerment politics with particular success to oppose divestment and apartheid. By centering private enterprise alongside state policy, *Black Power, Inc.* explains how Black American and African entrepreneurs, corporate America, and government officials reconciled American-style free enterprise with the aspirations of countless Black people in the United States and Africa by branding the former as a vehicle of Black empowerment.

That Leon Sullivan features prominently in the following pages reflects his role as a key proponent of Black empowerment politics, though this is not a biography in the classical sense. Those seeking a detailed description of Sullivan's life are encouraged to consult his multiple autobiographies.[32]

Rather, *Black Power, Inc.* utilizes Sullivan as a guide to explore the conceptual and political relationship between Black Power and Black empowerment politics across multiple contexts and levels of private and public power. Appearing alongside Sullivan, this book features other guides whose life stories and testimonies further elucidate the dynamics of Black empowerment politics. These include Harold Sims, who, in 1972, accepted a role as Director of Social Concerns at pharmaceutical giant Johnson & Johnson, while expressing his desire to help one of the world's largest companies "become the corporate leader in multi-racial employment."[33] Paralleling Sullivan's own trajectory as an international ambassador for Black empowerment politics and corporate America, Sims quickly became involved in encouraging Johnson & Johnson to support Black-American-led job-training and economic development programs in Africa, believing that corporate America had much to offer Africans in terms of capital, technical and managerial "know-how," and experience with racial integration. Sims and Sullivan even partnered on a small-business development center in Johannesburg as part of corporate America's broader efforts to combat divestment and apartheid through supporting Black business development in South Africa. Readers will also meet Samuel Motsuenyane, a Black South African who played a crucial role promoting Black empowerment politics as president of the National African Federated Chamber of Commerce (hereafter the African Chamber). *Black Power, Inc.* situates these and other Black empowerment activists alongside a diverse list of other figures, including Booker T. Washington, Marcus Garvey, and Malcolm X, who informed and contested Black empowerment politics.

Many of the most vocal proponents of Black empowerment politics were business*men*, whose class and gender status reflected and shaped the development of Black empowerment politics. To be sure, countless Black women and working-class Black people served as active participants in the movement for Black empowerment. Many benefited from investments in job-training, Black entrepreneurship, and other kinds of economic development programs. All too often, however, their contributions remained behind the scenes. As a politics, Black empowerment frequently reflected the interests of Christian male elites, who championed job-training and entrepreneurship, in part, as vehicles for Black men to achieve a sense of manhood and authority through accumulating financial and moral capital.[34] Such a call resonated with US government and business leaders, whose investments in Black empowerment programs like OIC and the African Chamber reflected their efforts to stave off the challenges posed by Black (often imagined as male) revolutionaries. In place of the Black (male) revolutionary, proponents of Black empowerment frequently celebrated the Black business*man* as the pinnacle of Black masculinity and Black power.

Following Black empowerment activists like Sullivan, Sims, and Motsuenyane, *Black Power, Inc.* traces Black empowerment's rise across four decades—from the 1960s to the 1990s—and space—from North Philadelphia to Soweto, and various places in between. Part I examines the multiple *roots* of Black empowerment politics in earlier intellectual and political movements. Chapter 1, "Booker T's Ghost," focuses on Sullivan's and Motsuenyane's respective upbringing, including their education and indoctrination into Christianity, to reveal the ideological and institutional linkages connecting racial uplift to Black empowerment politics. Through Sullivan and Motsuenyane, I show how racial uplift politics garnered new life in the post–World War II movement for Black empowerment, which championed industrial education and self-help as key to Black advancement. Engaging the history of the Great Migration, the last third of the chapter shifts locale to the midcentury Black metropolis, paying close attention to Sullivan's and Motsuenyane's encounters with urban apartheid and various Black-led movements, including Garveyism, Don't Buy Where You Can't Work campaigns, and Black Progressivism. In doing so, it illuminates the diverse ideologies and traditions that helped shape Black empowerment politics. Chapter 2 maintains a focus on the post-WWII Black metropolis as a critical site for the development of Black empowerment politics. Situated in North Philadelphia, the chapter illuminates Sullivan's and others' work promoting economic opportunity and job-training in response to multiple crises, including deindustrialization, racism, and the so-called moral and social crisis taking place within Black urban communities.

Focusing on the 1960s and 1970s, Part II traces the various *routes* undertaken by Black empowerment activists amid the era's more well-known movements for Black Power and decolonization and against apartheid. Chapters 3 and 5, in particular, illuminate the process of incorporating Black struggle, first through a close look at the War on Poverty and its facilitating of a series of corporate-community partnerships with Black empowerment organizations like OIC and, later, through corporate America's careful deployment of Black American managers and executives, whose appointments the media variably hailed as symbols of Black Power and corporate racial liberalism. In between, Chapter 4, "Empowering Africa," reveals this process as one that occurred on an international scale, highlighting how US corporations' support for Black empowerment programs and deployment of Black American business ambassadors like Sullivan and US Ambassador to the United Nations Andrew Young helped smooth the way for the expansion of American business on the continent. While focusing on the relationship between corporate America and Black politics, the state is not absent from this history. Indeed, these chapters reveal the US government, including the Departments of Labor (DOL), Health, Education, and Welfare (HEW), and Commerce, as well as the US Agency for International Development (USAID), as crucial financiers of Black empowerment programs at home and abroad, reflecting a broader pattern of utilizing private enterprise to combat poverty and promote economic development, while simultaneously deploying state violence to suppress Black nationalist and left-leaning movements that challenged US imperialism and capitalism. Here and elsewhere, I argue for understanding Black empowerment politics as the flipside of the punitive politics undergirding racialized policing and mass incarceration.[35] Both played important roles in disciplining Black people and incentivizing their participation—on a spectrum from voluntary to coerced—within a post–Jim Crow/post-apartheid global capitalist order. Rather than imprisoning Black people, however, Black empowerment politics encouraged Black people to engage in formal private enterprise in accordance with the law.

The political and financial *returns* gained from investing in Black empowerment politics are further revealed in Part III, examining the complex dealings undertaken by US corporate executives, Black American and African entrepreneurs, and politicians in the years leading up to and immediately following the end of South African apartheid. During the late 1970s and 1980s, facing tremendous pressure from anti-apartheid activists, hundreds of US corporations signed onto the Sullivan Principles (the subject of Chapter 5). Then and since, the Principles have garnered significant criticism for having a negligible effect on the conditions of Black workers in South Africa. In one particularly inflammatory report, activist-turned-historian Elizabeth Schmidt revealed that several signatory companies inflated their progress through grouping Indian, Coloured, and Black South Africans together under the broad category of non-white, while employing relatively few workers from the latter category in managerial and/or other supervisory positions.[36] While Americans and South Africans debated the merits of the Principles—and corporate social responsibility more broadly—in the press and other public venues, Chapter 6 utilizes private records, including organizational ledgers, conference minutes, and other records of the African Chamber, to examine the partnership forged between Black South African businesspeople and US corporations, including the signatory companies. Having previously played a negligible role in South African politics and the economy, the African Chamber, with the help of international business, emerged as a major proponent of Black empowerment politics, melding free-market and anti-apartheid politics. Both the Sullivan Principles and efforts by the African Chamber and others championing free-market politics ran counter to the divestment and sanctions movement, which saw major victories in the form of various divestment and sanctions legislation and institutional policies implemented in the 1980s. Rather than a culmination, Chapter 7 shows how "divestment" frequently functioned as a starting point for a new wave of corporate-sponsored Black empowerment initiatives and diplomatic efforts, including a rather surprising partnership between the Coca-Cola Company and the ANC.

Finally, Chapter 8 analyzes the fruits of these efforts. The 1990s and early 2000s—what I call the Black empowerment decade—witnessed a wave of government and private initiatives promoting Black economic empowerment. This chapter focuses on three in particular: Leon Sullivan's continued efforts to promote entrepreneurship and corporate social responsibility through the African-African American Summit (later renamed the Sullivan Summits) and the Global Sullivan Principles; President Bill Clinton's Enterprise Zones/Empowerment Communities; and the ANC's Black Economic Empowerment program. By the early twenty-first century, the idea that private enterprise, including small entrepreneurs and large multinational corporations, should play a leading role in combatting poverty and empowering Black and other marginalized people had become a hallmark of US policy at local, national, and international scales, as well as South African policy.

Over the span of several decades, from the 1960s through the 1990s, Black empowerment activists, aided by government officials and corporate executives, constructed a new politics, one that championed private enterprise as a vehicle of Black empowerment and racial equality while, intentionally and unintentionally, expanding US and corporate power, locally and globally.

PART I

Roots

CHAPTER 1

Booker T's Ghosts

J ust over four years apart in age, Leon Sullivan and Samuel Motsuenyane, two leading proponents of Black empowerment politics, grew up on opposite sides of the Atlantic in the years between World War I and II. It would be many decades before the two men crossed paths, joining forces to promote private enterprise, including Black entrepreneurship and corporate social responsibility, as a key tool in the struggle against apartheid. When they did, they found they had much in common, including the experience of having grown up under segregation and strategies they learned to combat it. Especially important for Sullivan's and Motsuenyane's development were lessons they learned about the importance of hard work, industriousness, faith, and racial uplift. Passed down from parents and grandparents, teachers and preachers, many of these lessons bore the mark of Black intellectual and leader Booker T. Washington, whose legacy Sullivan and Motsuenyane honored as they rose to international prominence in the late twentieth century for championing Black economic empowerment in the United States and Africa.[1]

Born in 1856 in Virginia, Washington was one of the most influential Black intellectuals of his time. His famous "Atlanta Compromise" speech, in which Washington touted Black industriousness to a primarily white audience at the 1895 Cotton States and International Exposition in Atlanta, Georgia, made him a household name in the homes of many Americans. Many more encountered Washington through his autobiography, *Up from Slavery*, which chronicled his journey from slavery to head of the Tuskegee Normal and Industrial Institute.[2] In the book, Washington outlined his views on racial uplift politics, a popular ideology that encouraged educated Black people to take responsibility for uplifting the race. "The happiest individuals are those who do the most to make others useful and happy," wrote Washington.[3] For Washington, service aimed at improving the material conditions of the community, including through educational programs designed to promote industriousness, vocational skills, and Black entrepreneurship, was particularly valuable. This work should be pursued "not for . . . financial value [alone], but" in connection to Black people's struggle "for . . . independence and self-reliance."[4] Black enterprise, in other words, was the key to Black people's moral, as well as their economic, salvation.

During the late nineteenth and early twentieth centuries, racial uplift politics, of which Washingtonian uplift formed one part, influenced countless Black people across the diaspora.[5] Transmitted through spirituals and reinforced by a wave of Black schools established to educate people of African descent about the values of Christianity, industriousness, and Victorian morality, racial uplift politics proved a powerful force—one that attracted Black participation on both sides of the Atlantic. Like dozens of other institutions, Sullivan's and Motsuenyane's respective alma maters, West Virginia State in Charleston, West Virginia, and Wilberforce Institute, in Evaton, South Africa, paid homage to the "Wizard of Tuskegee" with instruction in agricultural science and personal hygiene alongside the liberal arts.[6] Decades later, Sullivan and Motsuenyane put their education to work establishing vocational and managerial training programs as the heads of Opportunities Industrialization Centers Inc. (OIC) and the National African Federated Chamber of Commerce (African Chamber), respectively.

These organizations (discussed in detail in later chapters), and Black empowerment politics more broadly, benefited from the mid-twentieth-century mass migration of Black people to cities. Once conceived as a largely US phenomena, the Great Migration is recognized today as a transnational event involving hundreds of thousands of African-descended people across the Caribbean and Latin America.[7] A parallel demographic shift occurred on the African continent, including in South Africa, which witnessed a dramatic rise in the numbers of Black Africans living and working in large cities starting in the 1930s and 1940s.[8]

The mass urbanization of Black people gave rise to a wide range of political and cultural movements during the mid-twentieth century that challenged and, in some instances, reinforced the status quo of Jim Crow/apartheid. Arriving in New York City and Johannesburg in 1943 and 1946, respectively, Sullivan and Motsuenyane encountered Black people advocating for Black nationalism and socialism. Like many Black people, both also had run-ins with law enforcement, albeit with differing results. Whereas Motsuenyane was the victim of racialized policing and incarceration in Johannesburg,

Sullivan avoided jail time and even joined forces with the New York City police to combat juvenile delinquency. Alongside Washingtonian uplift, these and other movements helped shape the emergence of Black empowerment politics, which combined and reworked aspects of racial uplift politics, Black economic nationalism, respectability politics, and the social gospel, among other traditions, to promote Black enterprise—broadly conceived—as the next stage of the global Black freedom struggle.

The Making of a Modern-Day Booker T. Washington

When Jane, an African-descended woman and Booker T. Washington's mother, heard the news of her and her family's emancipation in April 1865, she immediately began making plans for the family to move to Kanawha Salines (later renamed Malden) in southwest West Virginia to be with her husband, Booker's stepfather, Washington Ferguson. Once home to Cherokee and Shawnee people, by the mid-nineteenth century the Kanawha Valley had emerged as a crucial node in the ongoing mineral revolution that fueled industrialization. Between 1867 and 1887, the amount of coal produced in West Virginia increased tenfold, from 489,000 tons to 4,882,000.[9] By 1910, coal production in the region had reached nearly forty million tons annually, accounting for 70 percent of the state's total output.[10] Like Jane and Washington Ferguson, the Sullivans and Truehearts, two Black American families similarly making their way in the post-emancipation South, relocated to the Kanawha Valley, settling in the county seat of Charleston, located seven miles northwest of Malden. It was there, on October 16, 1922, that Helen Terrell Trueheart and Charles Sullivan had a son, Leon Howard Sullivan. At the time, the city directory listed Charles as an employee of the West Virginia Sand & Gravel Company and the family as residing at 1331 Washington Court.[11]

Born over six decades apart and destined to never meet—Booker T. Washington died seven years prior to Leon Sullivan's birth—the two, nevertheless, remained connected through their shared role of promoting racial uplift and Black empowerment politics. Following Washington, whose Tuskegee Institute served as a symbol of Black achievement for people across the diaspora, Sullivan went on to launch multiple Black empowerment initiatives, starting in the 1960s and continuing until his death in 2001. Among these were OIC, Progress Enterprises, and the Sullivan Principles, which together promoted job training, Black entrepreneurship, and corporate social responsibility as key vehicles for racial uplift and Black empowerment across the United States and Africa. Such were the similarities between Sullivan's and Washington's approaches, the former earned a reputation as a modern-day Booker T. Washington.[12]

Washington's and Sullivan's visions of racial uplift, which shared a commitment to hard work, discipline, and Christian faith, took shape and were influenced by the political and material changes unleashed by emancipation and the rise of industrial capitalism. The Kanawha Valley, where Washington and Sullivan spent many formative years breathing in soot and the explosive energy created by the coal mines, formed one node in a global circuit of financial capital that helped to usher in the hydrocarbon age and, with it, new ways of organizing social relations.[13] Central to this new capitalist order was the construction of an apartheid system of labor. Mirroring the practices of industrial capitalists in places like California, South Africa, and Panama, mining companies in the Kanawha Valley during the late nineteenth and early twentieth centuries pitted workers against one another on the basis of race, underscoring corporations' role as coauthors with the state in constructing the global color line.[14]

As part of this emerging global apartheid labor regime, Black miners in the Kanawha Valley often found themselves relegated to the most grueling and dangerous jobs in an industry known for its violence and disregard for human (and nonhuman) life.[15] Given this, one might expect to find Black miners at the forefront of the era's militant labor struggles. In many cases, they were. At the infamous Battle of Blair Mountain, which occurred between August 25 and September 2, 1921—one year prior to Sullivan's birth—Black and white miners joined forces against the mine owners. The battle would go down in history as the largest armed uprising since the Civil War, resulting in the deaths of approximately one hundred people—mostly miners—and the arrests of many more.[16]

Threatened with violence, and even death, for rebelling against capitalism, other Black miners dug their boots in—literally and figuratively—committing themselves to the Protestant work ethic and the hope that solid performance on the job would eventually "topple the racial ceiling on occupational mobility."[17] This was the lesson Washington hoped to teach readers in a section of Up from Slavery detailing his childhood in Malden. Following a brief period working in the mines with his father, Washington found refuge as a domestic laborer in the home of a mine owner's wife. For the countless Black women for whom domestic labor was frequently the only option available, working in white folks' homes proved a thankless and frequently dangerous occupation.[18] Eliding this reality, Washington recalled favorably his time working as a domestic, remarking on the many "valuable . . . lessons" he learned.[19] Washington reiterated the importance of hard work in narrating his admission to the Hampton Normal and Agricultural School. As part of his admission, a white head teacher, Miss Mary F. Mackie, requested he sweep the recitation-room as demonstration of his willingness to perform manual labor. "The sweeping of that room was my college examination, and never did any youth pass an examination for entrance into Harvard or Yale that gave him more genuine satisfaction," wrote Washington.[20] Washington's words were less an accurate description of his experience than a lesson on the dignity of labor and the importance of hard work as a vehicle for individual and community uplift.

By comparison, Sullivan's recollections of his early experiences with wage labor appeared less rosy. Raised in "an unpaved alley" behind Washington Court apartments in Charleston's predominately Black Block District, Sullivan's mother worked long hours as a waitress and later an elevator operator in downtown Charleston.[21] As a result, Sullivan spent much of his time with his grandmother, who, like many Black women in the post-emancipation South, took in washing and ironing to help the family make ends meet.[22] Sullivan later recalled the hard work of scrubbing boards and helping his grandmother deliver clothes "across town to great big houses" owned by Charleston's white elite. Sullivan noted that the work was made more bearable by the hymns sung by his grandmother and the other women of Washington Court. "They would sit out and they would sing these hymns and through my life I still was inspired by the singing of the hymns and the idea that God was with us," stated Sullivan.[23] In the process, Sullivan, like Washington, learned to associate hard work with being a good Christian, a central theme among proponents of racial uplift politics and, later, Black empowerment politics.

The importance of Christian faith notwithstanding, Black people, Washington counseled, must not depend solely on God to deliver them from drudgery. Rather, they must invest in education. Washington's own education took place at Hampton, where his admission, following an arduous 500-mile journey that included nights spent sleeping in a ditch after being denied accommodations on the basis of his race, proved cause for his "[becoming] one of the happiest souls on earth."[24] For three years, between 1872 and 1875, the young Washington imbibed lessons about the importance of industry, personal hygiene, and Christian duty consistent with the teachings of General

Samuel Chapman Armstrong, the school's founder and president. Following a brief stint teaching back in Malden and eighteen months attending Wayland Seminary in Washington, DC, Washington received an invitation from Armstrong to oversee the newly created Tuskegee Normal School in Alabama.

As head of the prestigious Tuskegee Institute, Washington played a central role shaping post-emancipation Black education locally and globally.[25] In 1862, the Morrill Act enabled eligible states to use the proceeds from sales derived from the sale of federally-owned land—much of it obtained through dubious treaties with Native Americans—to fund the establishment of public institutions of higher education dedicated to agriculture, home economics, mathematics, English, and the mechanical arts. Responding to protestations over the exclusion of Black Americans from many land-grant institutions, the Second Morrill Act in 1890 required each state to show that race was not a criterion for admission. An exception was made for those states that established a separate college for "colored students."[26] At the time, Washington used his influence to lobby for the West Virginia Colored Institute's location in his home county of Kanawha. He subsequently recommended the school's fourth president, Byrd Prillerman, and he himself served as a frequent guest lecturer. Washington's imprint on the school was so great that at one point some briefly considered renaming the school Booker T. Washington State College. Instead, in 1927, the school became West Virginia State College.[27] It was there that Sullivan obtained a college education, earning an athletic scholarship to play basketball and football starting in 1940.

Sullivan's arrival at West Virginia State College occurred at an important moment in the school's history. In 1919, John Warren Davis succeeded Byrd Prillerman as the school's fifth president. As West Virginia State's longest serving president, Davis oversaw a number of key changes at the school, including its accreditation by the North Central Association of Colleges and Schools—the first of seventeen original Black land-grant schools to gain regional accreditation—the launching of several vocational programs, including a civilian pilot training program; and the recruitment of prominent Black faculty, including historian Carter G. Woodson.[28] In 1952, toward the end of his tenure at West Virginia State, Davis was appointed to oversee a technical training program in Liberia, part of Truman's Point Four program, a role that later earned him the Order of the Star of Africa from the Liberian government.[29]

Davis's example, including his emphasis on technical training and US-Africa relations, made a noticeable impression on the young Sullivan, who, decades later, garnered international recognition for his work championing

Black economic empowerment in Africa. As a student, Sullivan formed a close bond with the president, who, in Sullivan's words, ensured that West Virginia State proved a "mecca of opportunity." Alongside a missionary sensibility, Davis instructed Sullivan in "race leadership," advising Sullivan, "there [will] always [be] those who for whatever reasons . . . will not agree with the positions you take . . . a lot of self interests around everything, but if you believe your cause is right stand by it."[30] Going forward, faith and moral conviction performed crucial work, inspiring others to believe in Sullivan and his approach, and explaining the success of various Black empowerment initiatives.

Part of what made Sullivan such a compelling figure was his speaking ability. Sullivan's penchant for words was on display early on, including in a collection of poems he published, titled *America Is Theirs and Other Poems*.[31] His real talent, however, was in oration. During his senior year at Garnet High School, Sullivan was selected to serve on a small delegation to participate in a mock government. Groups of students were selected from each of the schools across the state. These groups then traveled to the state capital, where they elected a white governor and a Black governor. The students elected Sullivan as the Black governor, whence he had an opportunity to meet the actual Governor and Secretary of State. The honor also came with an opportunity to work in the state government. This greatly excited Sullivan, who may have harbored ambitions of holding public office one day. Such aspirations were soon quashed after learning of his job assignment. While the white student governor was offered a position as a page in the state legislature, Sullivan's reward for participating in this exercise in electoral politics involved "digging a hole and cleaning out sewers" in a housing project they were building in the Black section of town.[32] Needless to say, the incident left a bad taste in Sullivan's mouth and may have influenced his subsequent decision to eschew formal politics in favor of private initiatives.

Racial prejudice and injustice were regular occurrences throughout Sullivan's childhood, as they were for countless Black people living under segregation. Still, at times, in his later writings and speeches, Sullivan exhibited what Michelle Boyd has called Jim Crow nostalgia, sentimentalizing the Black community of his childhood—one forged, at least in part, through segregation.[33] Sullivan attended all-Black schools, including Garnet High School, named after Henry Highland Garnet, a former slave who went on to become the US consul to Liberia.[34] Sullivan later recalled with pride that "all the children in my school . . . [as well as] the great teachers were all Black."[35] Echoing Washington's famous proclamation—"in all things . . . purely social we can be as separate as the fingers"—OIC later employed an all-Black, and primarily female, staff to instruct students in its Feeder Program during the early years of the organization's existence. The move was part of a broader effort on Sullivan's and OIC's part to engender a sense of racial pride and Black unity, which Sullivan felt had been lost amid the transition from Jim Crow.

For Sullivan, one of the key indicators of Black community decay was the "decline" of the Black family. Denied full citizenship, upwardly mobile Black Americans frequently embraced Victorian norms as a means of performing class. This included maintaining heteronormative, patriarchal, nuclear families. Those who failed to achieve such standards were often blamed for bringing down the race.[36] Relocating from Charleston to Harlem in the 1940s, Sullivan derided the kinship arrangements of the other Black migrants he encountered, noting: "I . . . could see, particularly in the Black community, that there was lacking a unified, cohesive home experience. Often there was no father at home at all. The mother had to work in order to keep the family together. The children therefore were left to roam the streets to take care of themselves."[37]

Championed by proponents of racial uplift as key to Black people's advancement, the heteronormative, patriarchal, nuclear Black family frequently proved more of an ideal than a reality for many Black Americans.[38] Sullivan's own parents, Helen Terrell Trueheart and Charles Sullivan, divorced when he was still a young child. Helen later remarried a man by the name of Henry Parsons, in 1932.[39] Raised by his grandmother in a matrifocal household, Sullivan spoke very little, if ever, about his father or stepfather, suggesting they played a minimal role in his upbringing. In spite of or, perhaps, because of this, Sullivan spent much of his career endeavoring to serve as a role model to Black male youth. In the process, he frequently touted job-training and Black entrepreneurship as vehicles for Black men to become breadwinners and create "traditional" Black families.

Another way Sullivan embraced "tradition" was through religion. Sullivan credited two figures as inspiring him to become a Baptist minister. The first was his grandmother. While in his sophomore year of college, Sullivan received news that his grandmother was dying. Sullivan recalled his final visit to his grandmother's house, where he observed "wallpaper that had been plastered up layer over layer" and rooms sparsely furnished. As she lay dying, surrounded by "the misery of poverty," the old woman leaned over and spoke to Sullivan. Sullivan later recalled the impact his grandmother's dying words had on him: "Leonie, help your people . . . don't let this kind of thing happen to anybody else." Around the same time, Sullivan befriended a young Black minister, Moses Newsome, who came to Charleston to pastor the First Baptist Church. Newsome "became [Sullivan's] closest friend and . . . teacher."[40] Among the things that attracted Sullivan was Newsome's preaching style. "He would get out on what we call the block street corner and he'd talk to the fellas." Sullivan later claimed, "he taught me about the Bible, he taught me about Jesus, more than what I learned in churches."[41]

Ministry proved more than a calling. It was also Sullivan's ticket out of West Virginia to bigger and better things. With Newsome's help, Sullivan secured his first two preaching jobs. The positions were located at two churches, the first in Vandalia, located across the river from Charleston, where, in Sullivan's recollection, the people were so poor they could only afford to pay Sullivan in fuel, eggs, and the occasional dinner. The second was located in Montgomery, a coal-mining town located thirty miles down the Kanawha River.[42] It was there that Sullivan met Adam Clayton Powell Jr., who was in the area visiting family. The latter quickly took a liking to Sullivan, who perhaps reminded him of his younger self—Powell Jr. was fourteen years Sullivan's senior. Powell Jr. invited Sullivan to come to New York City, where the former suggested the latter might find employment at Abyssinian Baptist Church, in Harlem, the church of Powell Jr.'s father, Adam Clayton Powell Sr.[43]

Sullivan departed for New York sometime in 1943, leaving West Virginia, as Washington had, with aspirations of a better life elsewhere. While leaving the coal-infused air of the Kanawha Valley behind, only returning to visit, Sullivan never relinquished the lessons he learned growing up there: lessons that included the importance of industriousness, Victorian morality, and Christian faith. Going forward, Sullivan combined these lessons with ideas and strategies he imbibed in the post–World War II Black metropolis in helping to give rise to the transnational movement for Black empowerment.

From Alabama to South Africa

At the same time that Sullivan was gaining an education in racial uplift politics in Booker T. Washington's home county, Kanawha County, West Virginia, Washingtonian uplift was likewise making an impact on the lives of Black people across the diaspora. Transported on boats carrying Black migrants and transmitted via an internationalizing Black press, racial uplift crisscrossed the Black Atlantic, sewing a web of Black intellectual exchange that would one day help give rise to a transnational politics of Black empowerment. As it did, racial uplift politics intersected with and, at times, contributed to the late nineteenth and early twentieth century consolidation of Euro-American imperialism. In Washington and Tuskegee, Euro-American colonial officials and capitalists saw a solution to the perpetual "negro problem"—how to turn colonial subjects into productive wage-laborers. Convinced that the "American Negro" possessed a particular, even natural, ability to pick cotton, in 1900 the German colonial government persuaded Washington to send an expedition comprised of faculty and students from Tuskegee to the German colony of Togo. Subsequently, the government established a model cotton plantation in Tove, approximately sixty miles inland from the German colonial capital city of Lome, alongside a school to train local Africans to produce cotton for export and modeled on the Tuskegee Institute.[44] Elsewhere, Washington lent his support to efforts by a group of Americo-Liberian elite to establish a major Firestone Tire and Rubber Company plantation in Liberia, the terms of which required the Liberian government to borrow five million dollars from the Finance Corporation of America—a Firestone subsidiary—in an effort to stave off British and French incursions. As part of the agreement, Firestone agreed to contribute to the establishment in 1929 of the Booker T. Washington Agricultural & Industrial Institute in Kakata, Liberia, modeled on Tuskegee.[45]

Colonial entanglements notwithstanding, Washington remained a hero, revered by many Black people across the diaspora as a symbol of political and economic self-determination. Among those taken with the Black American and his ideas about industrial education was a Black South African named John Dube. Dube first learned of Washington and Tuskegee while studying in the United States. Addressing members of the South African National Native Congress—the predecessor organization to the African National Congress (ANC), of which Dube served as a founding member—back in South Africa, Dube declared "Booker T. Washington . . . [his] guiding star," and called on his fellow Black South Africans to follow his lead in seeking "mental, moral, material and political betterment."[46] In 1900, having previously corresponded with Washington, Dube founded the Zulu Christian Industrial Institute, later renamed the Ohlange Institute, on land donated by Chief Mqhawe of the AmaQadi. Like Tuskegee, Ohlange relied, in part, on white American philanthropy, including philanthropist Anson Phelps Stokes and the wife of a Chicago millionaire, Emaroy June Smith.[47] The school also employed a number of Black Americans, including several Tuskegee graduates.[48]

Ohlange's founding took place amid a series of social, political, and economic changes taking place in and around the southern tip of Africa. Building
on their victories against the Zulu and Boers, the British looked to consoli-
date their hold in the region with the unification of four colonies, including
the former Boer Republics, into a single country, the Union of South Africa,
which became a self-governing dominion of the British Empire in May 1910.
Among some of the first pieces of legislation passed by the Union parliament were a series of laws excluding South Africa's non-white population
from full citizenship, including denying them the right to vote and significantly restricting their access to land via the 1913 Natives Land Act. The latter appropriated 90 percent of the country's territory for white people, who
constituted approximately 20 percent of the population, while creating native
reserves out of the remaining 10 percent of the land for the country's Black
African population. Lacking access to land, a growing number of Black South
Africans were forced to enter the wage economy, laboring for artificially sup-
pressed wages and under dangerous and exploitative conditions in the country's mining, industrial, and/or commercial agricultural sectors.[49]

Among those caught up in the upheavals engendered by the expansion of
colonialism and industrial capitalism was the Motsuenyane family. Descended
from the Bakwena ba Modimosana, the Motsuenyanes traced their roots to
Molokwane in the Magaliesberg Valley in what is today part of South Africa's
Gautang Province. During the 1820s, the Bakwena were forced to flee their
ancestral homelands amid an invasion led by Mzilikazi of the Ndebele. Subsequently, many Bakwena, including the Motsuenyanes, settled in what became
the Orange Free State, where they rented and, eventually, bought land from
white Afrikaners.[50] It was here that Samuel (Sam) Motsuenyane was born, on
February 11, 1927, on a farm called Eignaarsfontein, located approximately
120 kilometers (74 miles) from Johannesburg.

Years later, as president of the National African Federated Chamber of
Commerce, Sam Motsuenyane joined Leon Sullivan as one of the key figures in forging a transnational politics of Black empowerment. Like Sullivan, Motsuenyane's subsequent role championing Black empowerment drew
on his earlier exposure to and engagement with racial uplift. Reflecting the
political milieu in which he grew up, in Motsuenyane's case, racial uplift
was closely associated with access and ownership of land. Eignaarsfontein, where Motsuenyane was born, was located in South Africa's Highveld,
a fertile region on South Africa's central plateau. Unlike Africans forced to
reside in the newly created native reserves, the Highveld continued to offer

Africans some opportunities for land cultivation, fostering, in some cases, a sense of Black independence and entrepreneurship. As a result of the Anglo-Boer wars, many white landowners in the area struggled to make ends meet. This resulted in a situation whereby a growing number of white landowners rented land to displaced Africans in a sharecropping arrangement.[51] In some instances, destitute white landowners sold their land to those Africans able to pay higher prices amid the postwar economic downturn.[52]

Eignaarsfontein was owned by a white Afrikaner named Herklaas Malan, who resided elsewhere a majority of the time. In his absence, Malan hired "a tall slender man with a prominent moustache" named Mr. Piet Mabe to oversee the farm.[53] It was to Mabe that the farm's tenants, including the Motsuenyanes, paid one third of their crop, in accordance with the family's sharecropping agreement.[54] Such a system proved onerous for the Africans whose labor was exploited to enrich South Africa's white settlers. In other instances, Motsuenyane noted, "the system" also benefited Black Africans, some of whom became "very rich."[55]

The Motsuenyanes followed a path pursued by many of South Africa's Christian-educated Black elite. When Sam was thirteen, his parents moved to Krugersdorp, where his father secured employment as a laborer for a timber merchant and his mother as a domestic worker.[56] With the money that they saved from working, the Motsuenyanes were able to acquire land in Wallmansthal, north of Pretoria, and send their children to a nearby American missionary school.[57] It was there that Motsuenyane first learned about the Wilberforce Institute.

Founded in 1905 by African Methodist Episcopal (AME) missionaries, the Wilberforce Institute in South Africa, like Ohlange, was the product of a wave of Black (inter)nationalism promoting racial solidarity and Black pride that occurred alongside and, in many ways, was facilitated by the rise of European colonialism and industrial capitalism. This wave encouraged Black South Africans and Black Americans to view their destinies as interconnected, if not one and the same. One of the first recorded instances of Black Americans to visit South Africa occurred when the Virginia Jubilee Singers, a group of Black American minstrels, visited South Africa on a fin de siècle tour promoting Christianity and good will between the United States and the British Empire. While on tour, troupe leader Orpheus McAdoo and the other Black Americans forged relationships with Black South Africans.[58] Thereafter, a growing number of Black Americans traveled to South Africa as missionaries, intersecting with and lending support to the ongoing Ethiopian movement to establish separate Black churches.[59]

By the time of Motsuenyane's arrival in the 1940s, Wilberforce had grown significantly from its origins as a single "mud hut building," becoming the largest school operated by the AME in southern Africa and the largest independent African school in the Transvaal. Keeping with the spirit of Black internationalism that encouraged African-descended people to come together, literally and figuratively, in a common struggle against white supremacy and for Black advancement, the school attracted students from across South Africa and others from outside the country, including as far as Nyasaland (present-day Malawi) and Northern Rhodesia (present-day Zambia).[60] The diversity of the school, at a time when colonial authorities looked to conquer and divide Africa through fomenting tribalism, could not have failed to make an impression on the young Motsuenyane, who subsequently made a point of resisting the South African government's attempts to divide the African Chamber along ethnic lines.

Once there, students and teachers benefited from Wilberforce's location, situated in the small town of Evaton, in between the rapidly industrializing centers of Johannesburg and Vereeniging. A number of students, including Motsuenyane, found their way to the Black townships surrounding Johannesburg and Pretoria following graduation, where they joined a growing class of English-speaking, educated Black urban professionals. This role, as a training ground for Black professionals, was reflected in the school's curriculum, which included a renowned teacher-training program and seminary, alongside courses in leatherwork, tailoring, and masonry.[61]

Established as a freehold settlement in 1905, Evaton offered its Black African residents a relative degree of autonomy compared to bigger cities like Johannesburg, where Africans faced an expanding surveillance state organized to control and restrict their mobility. Urban apartheid in South Africa gained particular credence following the passage of the 1923 Natives (Urban Areas) Act, which defined Black people as "temporary sojourners," welcome in urban areas only insofar as they ministered "to the wants of the white population."[62] By contrast, Evaton and Wilberforce evolved as a model of self-help with residents and students providing much of the labor necessary to construct and maintain the school. This, combined with Evaton's distinctiveness as one of the few areas where Africans could own land, helped give rise to an entrepreneurial spirit reflected in the number of Black businesspeople with connections to the town, including Motsuenyane.[63]

Given Wilberforce's rural location, it is somewhat surprising the school did not initially develop an agricultural program. Instead, the school's founders, several of whom were graduates of Wilberforce University in Ohio, set about constructing an independent African school on par with white schools in the country, with an emphasis on reading, writing, and arithmetic. A pamphlet advertising the school sent to W. E. B. Du Bois, accompanied by a letter encouraging him to lend his support, explained the Institute's mission as preparing young Africans "to take active part in improving the Moral, Educational, Industrial, and Civic conditions of the communities into which they will go."[64] The leaflet was sent to Du Bois by Reverend Dr. Francis Herman Gow, appointed by the AME church as the school's fourth president in 1925. The son of Francis McDonald Gow, a Black West Indian–born AME priest prominent in the development of the AME church in South Africa and educated at Tuskegee, Wilberforce, as well as Morris Brown and Allen universities in the United States, Gow formed part of a wave of Black American missionaries who traveled to South Africa in the late nineteenth and early twentieth centuries "motivated by a desire to uplift Africa."[65] It was not just Christianity that these Black American missionaries preached. Many carried messages of racial pride and Black liberation. In some instances, particularly amid the rise of Garveyism—a global movement for Black self-determination and Black nationalism inspired by Jamaican-born Marcus Garvey—this transnational dialogue gave rise to popular ideas of Black Americans as liberators, coming to save Black South Africans from white settler colonialism.[66]

In addition to reading, writing, and arithmetic, at Wilberforce Black Americans, following Washington's example, promoted industrial education. Shaped by his time at Tuskegee, Gow placed a greater emphasis on practical education, reflected in the addition of a printing department at Wilberforce.[67] This emphasis continued under the subsequent administrations of Dr. Amos White and Reverend Dr. Josephus Roosevelt, who, together, helped revive the school following its near collapse during the Great Depression.[68] Reflecting on his time at Wilberforce, Motsuenyane noted the curriculum "[catered to] the needs of the head, the heart and the hand" through courses in religion, masonry, carpentry, agriculture, "and home economists for female students." He added, "with such a comprehensive educational programme the institution was truly geared and meant to deliver a service that met the widest needs of [the Black] community."[69]

As Motsuenyane's comments suggest, Black South Africans drew a distinction between the kind of industrial education promoted by white missionary schools and that at Wilberforce. Whereas the former aimed to produce a cheap, pliable labor force for white industry, Wilberforce, following historically Black colleges in the US, many of which combined aspects of Washington's and Du Bois's teachings, strived to provide its students with the tools necessary to become race leaders. Many of the parents who sent their children to Wilberforce and other schools viewed education as a vehicle for "escaping from the ranks of labourers and poor peasants into those of the salariat and successful self-employed . . . [and] evading politically coercive measures such as passes" associated with the former.[70] The school emphasized service to one's community, with students regularly participating in the maintenance of the school, planting and harvesting vegetables from the school's garden, and/or building chairs and desks.[71]

This sense of service, shared by many African people throughout the diaspora, was later channeled into a number of ventures aimed at combating white supremacy and promoting racial uplift in South Africa. Alongside Motsuenyane, Wilberforce functioned as a meeting place for a number of Black South African leaders. This included people like Charlotte Maxeke, who, after receiving her bachelor's from Wilberforce University in Ohio, returned to South Africa in 1901, where she and her husband helped establish the Wilberforce Institute. A champion of Black women's rights and Black liberation, Maxeke went on to play a crucial role in South Africa's nascent anti-apartheid movement, including as the founder of the Bantu Women's League in 1918.[72] Other prominent Black South Africans associated with the school included Jacob Nhlapo, a prominent organizer of the Industrial and Commercial Workers' Union and principal at Wilberforce.[73] For Motsuenyane, like Sullivan, school served as a stepping stone to bigger and better things, not least of which was his selection, in 1968, as president of the National African Federated Chamber of Commerce, a position that ultimately brought him into conversation with Sullivan.

Great Migrations

The 1940s witnessed both Motsuenyane and Sullivan swept up in a global migration that saw hundreds of thousands of Black people moving to cities in search of new opportunities and a better life. In Motsuenyane's case, the young Tswana man's move was prompted by a change in his family's financial circumstances. Toward the end of 1946, Motsuenyane's studies at Wilberforce were cut short, when his aging parents found themselves no longer able to pay his tuition. Subsequently, Motsuenyane ventured to Johannesburg seeking employment. Around the same time, Sullivan met Powell Jr. and embarked on his fateful journey north from Charleston to Harlem, arriving in 1943.

Like many Black migrants, Motsuenyane and Sullivan hoped the city might serve as a respite from the racism they encountered growing up on the Highveld and in West Virginia, respectively. Sullivan, for his part, frequently recounted a particular episode as an example of the humiliation endured by Black Americans in the Jim Crow South. One day, while visiting his mother at work downtown, Sullivan attempted to purchase a Coke at a drugstore. As he approached the counter, "a large white man with his neck red and his face tense and eyes burning said to [Sullivan], 'Black boy, stand on your feet. You can't sit down here.'"[74] The encounter stuck with Sullivan, who vowed to contest apartheid, wherever it existed.

To their dismay, such mistreatment, not to mention outright hostility, followed Black people to the big city, illuminating apartheid's global reach.[75] Arriving in Johannesburg in the late 1940s, Motsuenyane recalled the verbal and physical harassment he received at the hands of multiple white people, including one incident in which his employer falsely accused him of stealing a pair of scissors, resulting in his incarceration. "The worst thing that can ever happen to a young man is to be incarcerated," Motsuenyane stated, recalling the fourteen days he spent imprisoned as "the most traumatic and painful days of [his] entire life." Thereafter, Motsuenyane vowed to "never . . . work for a white person again," enrolling in the Jan H. Hofmeyer School of Social Work to pursue a career as a social worker.[76] Meanwhile, across the Atlantic, Sullivan recalled the disapproving looks he received stepping off the train at Pennsylvania Station, his first indication that things in the north might not be as sanguine as he may have hoped.[77]

Excluded and/or displaced from other parts of the city, many Black migrants took up residence in burgeoning Black neighborhoods like New York's Harlem and Johannesburg's Soweto, which, while products of urban apartheid, also served as places of respite and resistance. In Harlem, Sullivan encountered a northern variant of Black politics—one more militant and influenced by Black nationalism and Marxism, in comparison to that in West Virginia.[78] Home to the New Negro movement and the Harlem Renaissance, mid-twentieth century New York City, as one historian described it, served as "a backdrop to the [movement for] Black Power" that subsequently emerged there and in other northern cities, setting the terms of "the modern Black political agenda," with its residents' "demands [for] criminal justice reform [and] affirmative action."[79] Sullivan's own first forays into this northern Black politics included his involvement with the March on Washington Movement (MOWM), which he joined after seeing a flyer at the Harlem YMCA.

First launched in January 1941, the MOWM was a product of several earlier campaigns channeling Black frustrations into a nationalist politics focused on building Black political and economic power. Many of these efforts were inspired by Marcus Garvey, whose Universal Negro Improvement Association attracted tens of thousands of members, and millions more admirers, in the US and around the globe.[80] Styling himself after Garvey, in 1929, Reverend J. C. Austin, a popular minister in Chicago, lent his support to a campaign targeting white-owned businesses that refused to employ Black people in what became known as "Don't Buy Where You Can't Work." Soon, "Don't Buy Where You Can't Work" movements sprang up in other cities, including Cleveland, Washington, DC, Baltimore, and Newark. Initial efforts to launch a "Don't Buy Where You Can't Work" campaign in New York were led by Effa Manly and the Citizens League for Fair Play before being taken over by Adam Clayton Powell Jr. and the Greater New York Coordinating Committee for Employment (GNYCC).[81]

Garveyism, "Don't Buy Where You Can't Work," and other mid-century Black movements helped to set the stage for Black Power and Black empowerment politics' subsequent rise. In the process, Black Power and Black empowerment politics attracted followers, whose dynamism as political individuals meant that many participated in multiple movements and/or articulated commitments to competing political ideologies at various points throughout their lives. This dynamism and intermingling of multiple agendas was present in the GNYCC. First launched in 1938, the GNYCC brought together a diverse group of two hundred organizations, including social clubs, fraternities and sororities, churches, professional groups, Black nationalists, communists, socialists, and liberals, to combat employment discrimination in Harlem.[82] Wielding the power of the boycott, the GNYCC brought the city's business owners to the negotiating table; Black Power. Once at the table, however, GNYCC's leaders, including Powell Jr., pivoted somewhat, displaying tactics that became more closely associated with Black empowerment politics, namely relying on voluntary negotiations with private entities to secure Black people a piece of the capitalist pie. On July 20, 1938, these negotiations yielded a "Memorandum of Agreement" signed by the GNYCC and the Uptown Chamber of Commerce. Under the terms of the agreement, "stores not already employing between 33 1/3 and 40 per cent colored workers in so-called white-collar positions agree[d] to do so as speedily as possible by making replacements with qualified Negroes as white employees resign or are discharged for cause." Further, "stores agree[d] not to limit the opportunities of Negro workers for advancement," meaning that "Negro workers may aspire to the same executive positions as white employees," and submit "all disputes arising in connection with the employment of Negroes" to a Job Arbitration Committee comprised of four representatives chosen by the Chamber of Commerce and four by the GNYCC.[83]

In Powell Jr. Sullivan found both a patron and role model, someone whose tactics of combining mass mobilization with private negotiation served as a template for the young minister in his dealings with the white power structure. With Powell's help, Sullivan secured a job as a coin-box collector at the Bell Telephone Company, a position held by few, if any, Black people before him.[84] He also joined the local leadership of the MOWM, where he had the opportunity to work alongside prominent civil rights and labor leaders, including Bayard Rustin and A. Philip Randolph. Sullivan later credited Randolph in particular with teaching him "the art of massive community organization," including "the meaning of nonviolent direct action." MOWM gave Sullivan his first experience with community organizing. "On Friday and Saturday evenings . . . [he] and a close friend . . . Dr. Lawrence M. Ervin . . . [took] a ladder and an American flag and [stood] on street corners delivering rousing speeches on civil rights . . . throughout Harlem."[85] In between stump speeches, Sullivan and other MOWM leaders met with city officials, including New York City Mayor Fiorello LaGuardia.[86]

Despite occupying rival positions, sitting on opposite sides of the table, Sullivan and LaGuardia forged a partnership of sorts. Indeed, Sullivan later referred to LaGuardia as "one of the greatest mayors in [New York's] history."[87] Mirroring similar Black-white governing coalitions in other cities, the relationship between Sullivan and other members of the city's self-proclaimed Black leadership and the mayor revolved around an informal agreement, one in which LaGuardia agreed to support expanded opportunities for Black professionals—including in teaching, the building trades, and policing.[88] In exchange, these same Black elites assisted the mayor in managing local "race relations."

The coalition between the mayor and Black community members faced its biggest test with the 1943 Harlem uprising, which began, like many similar uprisings, following word that a white police officer, James Collins, had shot and killed a Black soldier, Robert Bandy. Reports of Bandy's death turned out not to be true. In reality, Bandy had only been wounded. The rumor, however, which spoke to the experiences of Black and Brown Harlemites with police brutality, proved enough to provoke widespread outrage among residents. The ensuring revolt lasted two days and resulted in six deaths and nearly six hundred arrests.[89]

Immediately following the unrest, the city was besieged with calls for law and order. Drawing on popular stereotypes that equated Blackness with deviance and sexual predation, white New Yorkers demanded Mayor LaGuardia take steps to prevent lawlessness in the city.[90] This included expanding the New York Police Department's ongoing crackdown on poolrooms, dancehalls, and clubs.[91] For Black New Yorkers, particularly poor and working-class ones, these places were not just sites of leisure, but often served as a crucial economic resource.[92] During the 1920s and 1930s, for example, numbers games and policy rackets, an illicit form of gambling, emerged as important sources of finance for Black businesses—the venture capital of Black communities—helping fund everything from nightclubs to insurance to the Negro National (Baseball) League.[93] In the aftermath of the riot, they became targets for racialized policing and the disciplining of Black New Yorkers into submission.

Calls for law and order could also be heard coming from Black New Yorkers. Their calls, however, were frequently accompanied by calls for community policing. Years later, community policing emerged as a hallmark of the Black Panther Party, who took it upon themselves to defend Black neighborhoods from the police, whom they decried as an occupying force. No such movement existed in 1944. Instead, LaGuardia responded to the demands of Black New Yorkers by appointing Sullivan to recruit one hundred Black policemen, who were assigned to police the city's Black neighborhoods, including Harlem, reflecting a trend that saw Black professionals benefiting from integration.[94] More than individual gain, Sullivan's involvement in the initiative was in keeping with his and other Black Progressives' commitment to upholding a Victorian morality, which put the blame for social unrest, in part, on the shoulders of Black working-class families who failed to provide proper supervision for their children, producing what Sullivan referred to as large numbers of "latchkey children."[95] These children, according to Sullivan, "[carried] keys about their necks [to] let themselves out in the morning and let themselves in at night. Daddy was off to the war, or working on staggered shifts, and Mama was working too—or if not working, often out somewhere anyway." Some of them had formed themselves into "gangs" and "were terrorizing the community," stated Sullivan.[96]

Like other Black champions of community policing, Sullivan's support for law-and-order politics was not without qualification.[97] In an unusually contentious meeting, reflective of the fissures within New York City's Black-white governing alliance, Sullivan and others pushed back on accusations coming from white residents about Black lawlessness, complaining to the mayor that the media was perpetuating stereotypes about "Negro crime." LaGuardia, for his part, dismissed these complaints. Instead, the mayor appealed to the group's class aspirations by stating: "*decent* Negroes should not be too sensitive about the matter" (emphasis added). "The Italian race had received the same type of abusive treatment in years past," continued LaGuardia, suggesting that Black New Yorkers should suck it up and accept prejudice as an unfortunate, if sometimes necessary, step on the road to social advancement. Shifting responsibility from the state to Black people themselves, LaGuardia insisted it was the responsibility of the self-proclaimed community leaders to "crack down hard" on Black misconduct, lest it tarnish the "Negro race," and encouraged the committee to use their connections to launch a campaign in the Black press with the slogan: "crime does not pay from boys at Sing, E[l]mira," referring to prisons upstate.[98]

Heeding the mayor's call for Black self-reliance, Sullivan increasingly turned away from working with city hall and toward community uplift and anti-juvenile-delinquency programs. Much of this work involved efforts to recruit local Black youth into athletic leagues. Known to carry around a basketball, "a relic of [his] college days" as a college athlete, Sullivan struck up conversations with the Black boys and girls he encountered on the streets of Harlem.[99] "I came to know the leaders of the gangs, acquainted myself with their hangouts, and learned to speak their language." At this time, with Powell's help, Sullivan was serving as a supply minister to the Rendall Presbyterian Church on 137th Street, near Lenox Avenue, in Harlem. Using the church as his base, Sullivan invited the "gangs" to "play . . . stickball." "Instead of fighting, the gangs began to rival each other in athletic activities."[100] This was racial uplift politics.[101]

Sullivan still relied on local government, however, including enlisting the support of the mayor in organizing community councils to help promote an expanded youth development program. The mayor supported the program, stating, "he [did] not want children to feel that they are being forced off the streets." Comprised of "responsible parents, business people . . . and others residing within each district," the councils "work[ed] with the police to ferret out undesirable places where children congregate." Thereafter, the councils focused on enrolling the Black youth they encountered in various community programs, such as Big Brothers, founded in 1909 to address the increase in youth in the legal system.[102]

Throughout the spring and summer of 1944, Sullivan thrust himself into combating juvenile delinquency and uplifting Harlem's youth, joining the Juvenile Welfare Council as the chairman of the Harlem Coordinating Committee.[103] He refused to become discouraged when Mayor LaGuardia, reneging on a previous agreement, denied a request to provide $120,000 in funding to support the community program. Instead, in a precursor to the kind of community-finance model employed by Sullivan and other proponents of Black empowerment politics during the 1960s and 1970s, the minister joined with other members of the committee in fundraising money from the community, including local businesses. A supporter of the program, National Association for the Advancement of Colored People head Walter White suggested that residents contribute between fifty cents and a dollar in order that they "might feel that they were contributing to something that was theirs."[104]

White's comments evoked a long history of community finance. During the early-to-mid-twentieth century, various Black leaders imbued Black enterprise with different meanings and political agendas. Garvey, for one, promoted community finance as a part of his broader program engendering Black nationalism and Black separatism. Following the example set by Washington and other champions of racial uplift, Sullivan increasingly employed community finance as part of a nascent politics of Black empowerment—one that encouraged Black people, including Black youth, to see lawful private enterprise as a vehicle for individual and community uplift, alongside economic development.

*   *   *

The 1930s and early 1940s witnessed Sullivan and Motsuenyane each taking steps to launch their careers, including investing in their educations and pursuing opportunities in the post–World War II Black metropolis. As they did, they both carried with them ideas they had learned growing up in the South. More than a geographic designation, the South is a place constructed in relation to systems of political, economic, and cultural power.[105] During the late nineteenth and early twentieth centuries, the US South and the Global South underwent a process of reconstruction, remade into sites of racialized labor and colonial extraction with the help of northern capital, reformers, and state violence.

Black people did not suffer this assault on their citizenship lying down. Rather, they fought back. In the United States, South Africa, and, indeed, across the Black world, Black people contested the consolidation of racial capitalism and apartheid. Some of the most radical challenges came from the Caribbean, where Black migrants, responding to a wave of racialized violence and legal restrictions, turned to unorthodox religious movements, including Rastafarianism, and Black nationalism in their efforts to break free from the chains of Euro-American empire.[106] Many of these ideas found echoes in the dynamic movement initiated by Marcus Garvey, whose call for "Africa for the Africans" drew admiration from Black people across the Atlantic, including South Africa.[107] Occurring simultaneously and frequently overlapping with various movements championing Black (inter)nationalism and Afrocentrism, Black socialists and those engaged in the labor movement contested a political economic system built on the exploitation of Black and other non-white people.[108] Still others championed industriousness, self-help, Christian faith, and Victorian morality as Black people's salvation. Out of this milieu emerged Sullivan and Motsuenyane, whose encounters with racial uplift, Black/African nationalism, racialized policing, and more shaped their respective worldviews. Going forward, and drawing on these experiences, they joined others in reconfiguring racial uplift politics, infusing it with new ideas, tactics, and rhetoric, in response to multiple crises unfolding in the post–World War II Black metropolis. In time, their efforts helped give rise to Black empowerment politics.

CHAPTER 2

More Than Protest

During the 1940s, Leon Sullivan and Samuel Motsuenyane joined a tidal wave of Black migrations remaking cities in and around the Americas and Africa. Thanks to the Great Migration, the Black world itself expanded during this period, giving rise to new Black metropolises like Watts (Los Angeles, California) and Soweto (Johannesburg, South Africa), and augmenting already established Black urban communities in places like Harlem. We will return to South Africa and Motsuenyane, who went on to lead the National African Federated Chamber of Commerce, representing Black business during apartheid, in subsequent chapters. This chapter focuses on the Black metropolis of Philadelphia, where Sullivan accepted a position pastoring Zion Baptist Church and where he launched several Black empowerment organizations, including Opportunities Industrialization Centers Inc.

One of the first people to study Black urbanity, including its material dimensions, was W. E. B. Du Bois, in *The Philadelphia Negro: A Social Study*, first published in 1899. Reflecting on the circumstances facing Black Philadelphians at the turn of the twentieth century, the eminent scholar and activist wrote: "For a group of freedmen the question of economic survival is the most pressing of all questions. . . . [H]ow, under the circumstances of modern life, any group of people can earn a decent living . . . is not always easy to answer."[1] Yet an answer Du Bois proffered anyway, emphasizing the importance of industriousness and cooperation for Black urbanites. "Every Negro [to] make the best of himself" so that "they may . . . become a source of strength and help instead of a national burden," wrote Du Bois. This included rejecting "idleness" and engaging in "co-operation . . . to open many chances for employment . . . in trades, stores and shops, associations and industrial enterprises."[2] Many Black Philadelphians arriving in the city a half century later would have found much to admire in Du Bois's words, including Sullivan, who, echoing

Du Bois, championed industriousness and cooperation in announcing a new job-training and economic development program, Opportunities Industrialization Centers Inc. (OIC). "The day has come when we must do more than protest—we must now also PREPARE and PRODUCE!" declared Sullivan to a crowd of supporters.[3] Not long after, OIC opened its doors to the first class of trainees, who, in addition to vocational courses in mechanical engineering and garment manufacturing, underwent mandatory behavioral and attitudinal instruction, something Sullivan touted as beneficial, if not necessary, for trainees to reach their full potential.

First launched in January 1964, OIC joined a wave of Black experimentation with job-training, community economic development, and other kinds of Black entrepreneurship that occurred in the 1960s and 1970s in response to deindustrialization, white (capital) flight, and racism. Many of these initiatives touted private enterprise as a means of achieving social, as well as economic, goals. "We are a profit making operation and we hope to make a profit," stated Floyd McKissick in reference to Soul City, "but . . . we have social goals that loom higher than the profit motive."[4] Having previously served as national director of the Congress of Racial Equality (CORE), where he led the organization in embracing Black Power and Black nationalism, McKissick left CORE in 1969 to found Soul City, a planned community, constructed on five hundred acres of former farmland in Warren County, North Carolina. Elaborating on his vision for Soul City, McKissick later stated, "There are too many people who still have that image of the Black man on the corner with his fist in the air and nothing in his head or in his pocket."[5] With Soul City, a private community owned and operated by Black people, McKissick hoped to change that image, turning a once-poor rural area into a symbol of hope and Black empowerment. Elsewhere, Black Americans engaged in franchising, community development corporations, and what Joshua Clark Davis calls "activist entrepreneurship," using business to promote political and social change.[6]

Many of these initiatives had their roots in the ongoing struggle for civil rights and Black Power. Building on his previous work with the March on Washington Movement (MOWM), in 1960, Sullivan joined other civil rights ministers in launching the selective patronage movement in Philadelphia. Using the organizing vehicle of the Black church, the ministers boycotted area businesses that refused to employ Black people in skilled, good-paying jobs. The movement was so successful that it inspired other civil rights activists to launch similar campaigns, including Operation Breadbasket by the Southern Christian Leadership Conference.

Emblems of direct action, selective patronage and Operation Breadbasket are also examples of what I call civil rights capitalism, a politics that fused civil rights activism with a commitment to expanding, as opposed to eradicating or even curtailing, capitalism.[7] Emerging alongside the movement for civil rights and access to public amenities, civil rights capitalism utilized boycotts, or sometimes simply the threat of boycotts, to create opportunities for Black people to participate in the for-profit private sector. In doing so, civil rights capitalism helped pave the way for the emergence of Black empowerment programs like OIC and Soul City later in the decade. Where civil rights capitalism wielded direct action to pressure business from the outside, the latter sought to empower Black Americans within the private sector by turning them into productive capitalists.

The Philadelphia Negro

While still living in Harlem, Leon Sullivan met his future wife, Grace Banks, on a blind date.[8] Grace was born to Julia and George (Carter) Banks in Baltimore in 1924. For unknown reasons, Grace spent a portion of her childhood living in Philadelphia in the home of Edward and Maude Washington.[9] By 1940, at the age of fifteen, Grace had relocated to New York City, where the US Census listed her residing with her mother and several siblings on St. Nicholas Place in Harlem.[10] It was there that she met Sullivan. The couple married on August 5, 1944, in Philadelphia, at the home of her older sister, Virginia (Banks) Cannady.[11]

According to Sullivan, it was Grace who convinced him to leave New York, out of fear that "the big cit[y] [was] doing more harm than good," causing them to "los[e] contact with God."[12] The couple settled first in New Jersey, where Sullivan pastored the First Baptist Church in South Orange. The location, approximately twenty miles west of the city, allowed Sullivan to continue taking courses at Union Theological Seminary and Columbia University, where he received a master's degree in 1948.[13] Not long thereafter, Sullivan accepted an appointment to lead the prominent Zion Baptist Church in Philadelphia. Like many decisions, Sullivan narrated this move as part of God's plan, writing, "after five years [in South Orange] God called me to Philadelphia."[14] That same year, Sullivan's mother, Helen Terrell Parsons (Trueheart), passed away in what was sure a blow to the young minister.[15]

The Philadelphia Sullivan encountered when he arrived in 1950 was noticeably different from the one Du Bois observed in the late 1890s. And yet, in many ways it was similar. Fleeing white supremacy and lured by the promise of jobs, Black people made Philadelphia an important destination amid the Great Migration. In the two decades following Du Bois's publication of *The Philadelphia Negro*, Philadelphia's Black population more than doubled, from 63,000 in 1900 to 134,000 in 1920. Following a temporary slowdown during the Great Depression, Black migration to Philadelphia continued to grow. By 1950, the city's Black population stood at some 375,000 residents.[16] The arrival of Black migrants, combined with insufficient efforts to house them, pushed Black Philadelphians to seek accommodations outside the city's Seventh Ward—the historic heart of the Black community and the site of Du Bois's study—expanding into other neighborhoods in the north, west, and south of the city.

Black mobility was a dangerous undertaking. In an all-too-common experience, Black Philadelphians faced stiff resistance in their struggle for accommodation. On Friday, July 26, 1918, Adella Bond, a "short, young woman of light brown color," was at her home, 2936 Ellsworth Street in South Philadelphia, when a crowd of "about 100 white men and boys" began gathering outside. Aware of incidents of violence targeting Black people in South Philadelphia, Bond had thought carefully before purchasing the home several days before. The Black real estate agent who showed her the house and another unnamed individual, who claimed the home had previously been occupied by another woman of color, a Mrs. Giddings, convinced Bond that the 2900 block of Ellsworth was safe, even "welcom[ing]" of "colored people." They were mistaken. That Friday evening, as the crowd outside continued to grow, someone threw a rock into Bond's parlor. Fearing the worst, she grabbed her revolver and fired a warning shot in an effort to call the police, but unintentionally hit and injured Joseph Kelly, a white man in the crowd.[17] A Black woman defending her home, and injuring a white man in the process, proved the last straw with the crowd. A riot ensued. For four days, white mobs rampaged through the city, attacking Black Philadelphians at random. In the end, over sixty Black and three white residents were arrested. Four others—three white and one Black—died, while many more were injured.

White resistance to Black mobility proved a defining feature of mid-twentieth century American society, affecting Black communities in both the north and south.[18] Faced with growing numbers of Black migrants, many white Philadelphians opted to leave the city, joining a nation-wide trend.[19] Arriving in Philadelphia in 1950, Sullivan recalled seeing "For Sale" signs everywhere, signs of "the white exodus. . . . I was flabbergasted." Meanwhile, in their wake, white residents fleeing the city left Black arrivals with little to work with. "I had heard a great deal about Philadelphia's Black society and the good life of the Philadelphia colored man, but I had never seen so many dilapidated houses, row upon row, in my life," noted Sullivan. In North Philadelphia, where German, Irish, Russian, and other European immigrants had previously built a thriving community amid factories that gave Philadelphia the nickname the "workshop of the world," many of which now stood idle, Sullivan saw only urban decay. "Bad conditions jumped out and hit me in the eyes wherever I looked."[20]

The situation that Sullivan and others observed was the result of more than the individual choices of white homeowners and businesses. Government policy likewise played a crucial role in facilitating white flight and gutting urban America, starting with the New Deal. Between 1935 and 1940, the Home Owners' Loan Corporation (HOLC) undertook a massive reevaluation of US cities, in a process known as redlining. Relying on real estate professionals, the HOLC graded urban neighborhoods according to the perceived mortgage security of properties in that neighborhood. These assessments did more than simply reflect an existing reality; they also shaped investment practices for decades to come. A "D" or "Hazardous" rating, like the one received by areas 11–15, covering North Philadelphia, was shaded red on HOLC maps—hence the term redlining. These ratings made it very difficult for both residents and businesses in redlined neighborhoods to acquire credit. At the same time, a series of legal and extralegal measures, including deed restrictions and physical violence, kept many Black people from moving into higher rated "A" (green) and "B" (blue) neighborhoods, many of which obtained such ratings due to their racial and class exclusivity.[21]

The pattern of redlining, combined with other exploitative real estate practices, resulted in many Black people paying more than their white counterparts to live in overcrowded, dilapidated, inner-city neighborhoods. These practices did not go unnoticed by Black reformers like Sullivan, who noted in regard to the conditions he observed in North Philadelphia: "There was a tendency to put all the blame for the deterioration on the incoming Blacks. [Yet] not much, if anything, was done about the greedy tenant owners' procedure of cutting up single-family houses into three and four apartments, thereby packing the neighborhoods with three or four times the number of people who ordinarily would live there." As a result, "more and more rubbish and unmoved garbage accumulated" in the streets, ignored by the city. "Obstructed sewers also became commonplace nuisances, causing flooded cellars that were perfect for fly-breeding . . . and, of course, for mosquito-breeding too."[22]

In some cases, the neglect proved too much for Black residents to bear. In 1956, following the tragic death of her niece in a tenement fire, community activist Alice Lipscomb joined fellow Seventh Ward resident George Dukes to form the Rittenhouse and Hawthorne community councils, to address the issue of housing. Unlike similar campaigns waged by organizations like the NAACP to open up space for middle-class Black residents to move into formerly whites-only neighborhoods, Lipscomb and Dukes represented the interests of poor and working-class Black residents who desired to remain in the center city. Together, the pair organized a series of rallies and petitions to city government that succeeded in delaying the construction of the Crosstown Expressway through the Seventh Ward.[23]

Campaigns led by poor and working-class Black residents like Libscomb and Dukes were critical in laying bare the role of the local and national government as agents of white supremacist infrastructural violence.[24] Yet, they remained too often fleeting and under-resourced. Meanwhile, many upwardly mobile Black Philadelphians, including Sullivan, elected to invest in strategies that combined contesting urban apartheid with private initiatives promoting self-help and Black economic empowerment.

The Lion of Zion

When Sullivan began his ministry at Zion Baptist Church, he was the seventh pastor to occupy the role. Founded in 1882 by Reverend Horace Wayland, the church held its first prayer meetings in the home of Mr. and Mrs. Lewis Simms in the Seventh Ward. During its early years, the congregation moved several times to accommodate its expanding congregation, eventually settling in the former Spring Garden Baptist Church building at 13th and Wallace streets.[25] Following the northern trajectory of Black migration within the city, in 1955, or thereabout, the congregation entered into negotiations with St. Paul's Reformed Episcopal Church to purchase the latter's building on the corner of North Broad and Venango streets, in the heart of North Philadelphia.

Founded in 1875, as part of the Reformed Episcopal Church that spun off from the Episcopal Church, St. Paul's grew to become a prominent institution within North Philadelphia, serving as a gathering space for the temperance movement.[26] By the 1950s, however, a growing number of the church's members had left the rapidly changing urban neighborhood for whites-only suburbs in Bucks and Montgomery counties. On February 20, 1955, St. Paul's followed suit, purchasing a property at 800 Church Road in Springfield, just outside city lines.[27] The move was part of what one observer described as "the greatest church building boom in history," and paralleled white church flight in other cities, including Chicago and Atlanta.[28] Money for the new church came, in part, from the sale of the old building to Zion Baptist, which paid more than $200,000 for the property.[29]

For Sullivan and members of Zion's congregation, the investment was worth it, enabling the church to expand its foothold in what was quickly becoming a major center of Black life in Philadelphia. The church became Sullivan's base for uplifting Black Philadelphians. "My religious philosophy has always been somewhat unorthodox," said Sullivan. "While some think of the church as a place to get people into heaven. . . . I long to see the kingdom of God a reality in the everyday lives of men."[30] For Sullivan, helping make God's kingdom a reality included addressing the issue of juvenile delinquency. This was a continuation of his work in New York City, where Sullivan had run multiple community programs aimed at getting Black youth off the streets, where they were vulnerable to falling into immoral behaviors, and on track toward a more productive and, in his view, moral life.

Along these lines, in 1953, Sullivan launched the Philadelphia Citizens Committee Against Juvenile Delinquency and Its Causes (CCAJD). Like in New York City, support for action addressing juvenile delinquency was closely associated with a perceived rise in crime. "In March of 1953, a tragic thing . . . occurred. Three boys [were] killed on the steps of the Christian Street YMCA in South Philadelphia," said Sullivan, amid an ongoing "gang war." Subsequently, Sullivan and other "interested citizens" called for a meeting with the mayor at city hall, where the CCAJD was created.[31]

Mirroring the pre-WWII uplift initiatives that preceded it, the CCAJD focused much of its attention on "improving" the moral and social behaviors of poor and working-class Black families. If only parents did their job of rearing Black children properly, then they could eliminate one of "the principal causes of youthful crime," or so claimed the CCAJD, whose members included "P.T.A. officers and members, doctors, lawyers, school teachers,

ministers . . . government workers," and other Black professionals.[32] Alongside
guidance about proper child supervision and programming to keep youth
occupied, the CCAJD paid significant attention to the physical appearance of
Black neighborhoods, reflecting a popular reform discourse that claimed that
"better and cleaner neighborhoods encourage children and helps to inspire
them" to stay out of trouble.[33] Rather than demand the city invest resources
into Black neighborhoods, as it did in white ones, CCAJD celebrated its work
promoting self-help. Working in small teams, CCAJD members patrolled the
neighborhood, identifying and investigating the physical decay of properties
and "crowded housing condition[s]," which they blamed for "fostering juvenile delinquency."[34] Years later, Sullivan employed a similar strategy as part
of the Adult Armchair Education Program, a subsidiary of OIC, offering in-
home instruction focused on personal and community development.

While touting itself as a self-help community organization, the CCAJD
collaborated with several municipal agencies in its effort to rid Black neighborhoods of juvenile delinquency and vice. In doing so, the organization
developed a particularly close relationship with local law enforcement, which
members viewed as a partner to Black progress. "It is the opinion of the
group that for maximum results to be obtained, both the citizen and the law
must work together," stated Sullivan in April of 1953.[35] Following Sullivan,
the CCAJD organized itself into subunits corresponding to police precincts.
Each subunit was assigned a "precinct guide, who established a working relationship with that area's police captain." "All problems in block areas were
reported to division leaders, and then to police headquarters or other departmental agencies for action."[36] Nineteen months later, amid a wave of unrest
blamed on local "youth gangs," Sullivan declared his unequivocal support for
the city's crack down, stating: "I pledge the full manpower of my organization of 5000 members to back the enforcement of this movement to break
up gangs and enforce a curfew, if the police do not have enough manpower
to do it."[37]

Support for expanded policing of Black neighborhoods on the part of
Black liberals was nothing new. Progressive-era Black reformers were well-
known for repeating notions of Black criminality as part of a broader politics
of respectability.[38] In Sullivan's case, his work combating juvenile delinquency
and "community decay" earned the minister accolades from a number of local
Black churches and civic organizations.[39] In 1953, the Philadelphia branch of
the NAACP, which had recently begun working more closely with community leaders in an effort to expand its influence following a period of internal

discord within the organization, invited Sullivan to address local audiences via *The NAACP Reports*, a radio program that aired on Sundays over station WCAM (Camden, NJ), and *The NAACP Forum on the Air*, which aired on WHAT (Philadelphia, PA).[40] In the process, Sullivan joined a small, but growing, number of Black intellectuals, professionals, and performers with access to the kind of platform radio provided.[41]

Where public talks and radio appearances enabled Sullivan to strengthen his connections with Black community organizations and civil rights groups, expanding his audience, other organizations provided Sullivan with access to the exclusive and powerful world of white elite politics. In 1955, in recognition of his work combating juvenile delinquency, Sullivan received the first of several awards from the white business community when he was named one of ten Outstanding Young Men in America by the United States Junior Chamber of Commerce, initiating what would become a long and fruitful relationship between Sullivan and the nation's white business establishment.[42] Other awards included the City of Philadelphia's Good Citizenship Award (1956) and the Boy Scouts of America Silver Beaver Award (1957). In his acceptance speech, Sullivan thanked the Chamber for their recognition, stating, "I am overwhelmed. I appreciate the award particularly from the standpoint of what it means to the Christian church and to the persons of color in the United States. It will point out to them that although at times it appears that what we do is not appreciated, if we work hard enough and fearlessly and without any desire for rewards, we find that compensation comes."[43] Here and elsewhere, Sullivan's trafficking in the trope of Black criminality and the discourse of industriousness garnered white recognition.[44]

At the same time, Sullivan's remarks before the Junior Chamber of Commerce, including his references to hard work and faith, reveal the multiple, sometimes competing, motivations undergirding anti-juvenile-delinquency work. As historians have shown, the midcentury preoccupation with juvenile delinquency gave rise to an intensified racist policing and carceral apparatus targeting Black and Brown people.[45] Building on the ideas espoused by midcentury reformers regarding the connection between physical and moral decay, social scientists James Q. Wilson and George L. Kelling developed the "broken windows" theory, which posited that visible decay in urban neighborhoods like the Bronx and North Philadelphia encouraged crime. This theory was subsequently adopted by police departments as justification for the hyper-policing of Black and Brown neighborhoods, including targeting minor crimes such as vandalism, public drinking, and fare evasion.[46]

Sullivan and his peers in the CCAJD may have supported policing as a means of combating crime in neighborhoods historically neglected by local government. But they did so as part of a broader commitment to racial uplift.[47] Black empowerment, not incarceration, was their goal. This difference was palpable in Sullivan's simultaneous efforts engaging local youth through the church. While the City of Philadelphia, mirroring a national trend in racialized policing, devoted increasing resources to policing Black and Brown communities, Sullivan joined other ministers in launching a new venture to address the material deprivation that had long plagued Black urban communities.[48] "I hoped . . . to develop a program of racial economic emancipation so that the colored man might not only fix up his concentrated communities with flower boxes and clean-street programs but also develop his earning power," stated Sullivan, reflecting on this latest venture.[49] To this end, in 1955, Sullivan announced the launch of a new youth employment center operated out of Zion Baptist.[50] Later, Sullivan partnered with Rev. William V. Ischie, a white minister and rector of Christ Episcopal Church, to expand the program. Together, the two created the North Philadelphia Youth Employment Service (NPYES), a nonprofit, no-fee agency licensed by the state to help secure jobs for youth during their free hours. The program mirrored similar efforts by the Philadelphia Commission on Human Relations, the Philadelphia NAACP, the Committee on Equal Job Opportunity, and the Armstrong Association (Philadelphia's Urban League affiliate), all of which championed job-training and job-placement as part of their broader work contesting Jim Crow.[51]

With Black unemployment at over 60 percent in some parts of the city, the NPYES was quickly flooded with applications.[52] Speaking shortly after the agency's opening in February, Sullivan told reporters that "dozens of boys and girls were lined up outside his church building . . . before the doors of the employment office opened at 9 A.M." It just went to show, stated Sullivan, that "the teenagers of Philadelphia don't want to be delinquent . . . they want to be given an opportunity to go to work, either at part-time or full-time jobs."[53] The claim would soon emerge as a familiar one in Sullivan's and others' efforts championing Black empowerment politics.

Exhibiting a pattern that would become increasingly common with Black empowerment programs in the late 1960s, the NPYES partnered with local businesses looking to demonstrate their commitment to racial liberalism amid a rise in civil rights organizing. Not long after it launched, John J. Kelly, president of local public relations firm Kelly Associates Inc., helped bring the NPYES to the attention of local and national corporations and charities. Subsequently, the NPYES received an anonymous donation of $33,600 to underwrite the project for two years.[54] Honoring the NPYES's success in the official record of the US Senate, Pennsylvania senator Hugh Scott noted that, within a month of its founding, the program had "stimulated 400 job applications, brought inquiries from 150 companies, and led to the placement of 200 teenagers."[55] By November 1960, the NPYES reported having made six hundred placements, putting approximately $250,000 "in the pockets of young people."[56] Here was evidence of a nascent politics of Black empowerment, creating opportunities for Black youth to achieve success in the private sector.

At some point, Sullivan hired Rev. Thomas J. Ritter, pastor of Second Macedonia Baptist Church, to serve as the NPYES's executive director. Like Sullivan, Ritter saw his mission as one of addressing the perceived moral and economic crisis in the Black community. The two pastors shared similar experiences, having revived their congregations following a period of decline, a process that gave both crucial business and community development experience. Ritter famously recalled the "six faithful members" who had attended his first sermon at Second Macedonia.[57] Over the next several years, Ritter had led a campaign to revitalize the church, including initiating an evening bible study, a daycare, and a new building to accommodate the larger congregation. This initiative was supported by contributions from congregation members and businesses, including from the popular Gino's restaurant, which provided the church with a gift of $25,000 of Gino's stock. By the mid-sixties, Ritter had raised over $150,000 from local businesses and foundations, including Girard Bank, Acme Markets, and the Philadelphia National Bank.[58] A number of these businesses subsequently became supporters of Opportunities Industrialization Centers Inc.

OIC borrowed heavily from NPYES, including Sullivan's decision to appoint Ritter as the organization's first executive director. In this sense, civil rights ministers like Sullivan and Ritter provided a bridge between the kind of neighborhood uplift and Black respectability politics of earlier decades and the politics of Black empowerment that emerged in the 1960s and 1970s. Before Black empowerment politics could take hold, Sullivan and others had to contend with a resurgence in Black radicalism, including Black nationalism, which increasingly gained traction during the 1960s among Black Americans disillusioned by the failures of racial liberalism and traditional civil rights tactics.[59]

Competing Visions

The mid-twentieth-century Black political landscape included multiple overlap-ping and, sometimes, competing visions that included various articulations of Black nationalism, Black Marxism, Black feminism, and Pan-Africanism. This multiplicity existed in Leon Sullivan's Philadelphia, as it did across the nation, and was nothing new. Since slavery, Black people have frequently ascribed numerous meanings to freedom and employed different, and sometimes diver-gent, means to achieve it.[60] In the dense setting of the mid-twentieth-century Black metropolis, various organizations holding competing views often existed in close proximity to one another, sometimes even sharing the same build-ing. Less than two miles from Zion Baptist's new home in North Philadelphia existed another religious institution with a radically different vision for uplift-ing the race: the Nation of Islam's Mosque No. 12.

Founded in Detroit in 1930 by Wallace Fard Muhammad, the Nation of Islam (NOI) first gained traction amid the devastation of the Great Depression with its particular blend of Black nationalism, Moorish Science, and ortho-dox Islam. Many of the NOI's early converts were former members of Marcus Garvey's Universal Negro Improvement Association (UNIA), which shared an affinity with the NOI in viewing racial integration as a futile endeavor. Instead, the NOI encouraged its members to develop separate institutions, including daycares, mutual aid societies, and businesses. Following a series of encounters with the police, Fard first fled Detroit for Chicago, where the NOI had recently succeeded in establishing roots, before vanishing entirely in 1933. Subsequently, Elijah Muhammad (formerly Elijah Poole) took Fard's place at the helm of the organization. By 1947, the NOI had established chap-ters in Washington, DC, Detroit, Milwaukee, and Chicago, although their membership remained well below that of other Black Muslim groups, includ-ing the Moorish Science Temple of America and the Ahmadiyya movement, both of which had a presence in Philadelphia. This began to change as a result of NOI's targeting of incarcerated Black Americans, including one by the name of Malcolm Little, later known as Malcolm X.[61]

It is possible that Leon Sullivan encountered a young Malcolm Little. The two both resided in Harlem in the early 1940s. Perhaps they crossed paths at the Harlem YMCA on West 135th Street, where Malcolm sometimes stayed and Sullivan frequented. Or perhaps Malcom heard Sullivan preaching from the street corners in the neighborhood. Had they met, Sullivan would likely have counted Malcolm as one of the many juvenile delinquents he hoped to shepherd off the streets and onto a path toward lawful enterprise and Christian salvation. According to his own account, Malcolm lived a life of vice, illicit drugs, and engaged in multiple illegal activities to make ends meet. Like many young Black men, Malcolm wound up in prison, charged with breaking and entering, larceny, and illegal possession of a firearm.[62] While there, he became radicalized, joining the NOI and adopting the name Malcolm X.

Following his parole in 1952, Malcolm X quickly made his way up the ranks of the NOI, becoming one of the organization's leading spokesmen before splitting with it in the early 1960s over political differences. In March 1954, following his successful effort recruiting new members to the NOI in Boston, Malcolm X was sent by Elijah Muhammad to Philadelphia to "shake things up" in the struggling Temple No. 12, located at 4218 Lancaster Avenue in West Philadelphia.[63] Malcolm, who traveled frequently while ministering at Temple No. 12, was aided by Joseph X Gravitt, a prior convert of Malcolm's and one of his closest confidants. Together, the pair quickly garnered new converts. An FBI informant, who kept tabs on Malcolm's activities at Temple No. 12, described his message as follows: "The white man is the devil and . . . the Black man is God of the earth and the only supreme being."[64] Reinforcing such a view, Joseph told Temple No. 12 members it was their "duty to take the heads of four devils for which they will win a free trip to Mecca." He later clarified that his words should not be interpreted as endorsing murder. Rather, what he meant was "bringing of a lost Muslim into the Nation of Islam and thereby cutting off a devil's head."[65]

Within three months of Malcolm's arrival in Philadelphia, the young minister was reassigned to New York City, where he became minister of Harlem's Temple No. 7. Even though he had been reassigned, Malcolm continued to preach at Temple No. 12 in Philadelphia, where the Nation's influence continued to grow, as it did in other cities. When Elijah Muhammad visited the city on August 14, 1960, *The Philadelphia Tribune* reported two thousand Black Muslims and another fifteen hundred spectators attended the rally.[66] At its peak, in the late 1960s and early 1970s, the NOI operated twelve temples and a number of schools throughout the city, including Mohammad University.[67]

The NOI was not the only radical religious organization with a foothold in Philadelphia at this time. Attesting to the widespread disillusionment of Black Americans with mid-century liberalism and the government's failure to include them in the country's postwar prosperity, the mid-twentieth century witnessed a range of radical Black religious sects take hold across the urban north, including the Moorish Science Temple, Ethiopian Hebrews, and

Father Divine's Peace Mission Movement. While differing in their specific theologies, these groups shared a common distrust of both the US government and mainstream Christianity, the latter of which they believed had been perverted by whites.[68] Frequently existing on the margins of Black political life, these organizations nevertheless played an important role in Philadelphia and other cities as critics of civil rights liberalism and as proponents of Black nationalism and Black separatism.[69] Thus, the NOI, for example, while embracing for-profit enterprise, did so through advocating economic nationalism that encouraged members to save their earnings and invest in a series of NOI businesses. This differed from civil rights ministers like Sullivan, who increasingly demanded inclusion within the US capitalist system through civil rights capitalism.

"We Believed in Free Enterprise!"—Civil Rights Capitalism

The turn to direct action has functioned as a popular trope in histories of the civil rights movement, a catchall phrase for a wide range of actions associated with the rise of Black militancy in the 1960s. Over the years, historians have expanded their lens to reflect more of the diverse actions and actors associated with Black militancy, including highlighting the contributions of Black women and Black queer activists.[70] Scholars have likewise extended the timeline of the movement, reminding us that Black Americans have been engaged in various kinds of direct action since slavery.[71] It is only more recently, however, that historians have begun examining the deeper connections between civil rights and capitalism, revealing how Black activism and the pursuit of profit frequently went hand in hand.[72]

Such was the case for Leon Sullivan, who had the following to say about the selective patronage movement he launched alongside other Philadelphia ministers in 1960: "It was not [our] intention to destroy a business, but only to awaken it and to get it on the right road as far as the employment of Black Americans was concerned. . . . We believed in free enterprise!"[73] Selective patronage marked a turning point in Philadelphia's Black freedom struggle, signaling the turn to direct action and portending the subsequent rise of Black Power in the city.[74] It was also an example of civil rights capitalism.

Like the earlier "Don't Buy Where You Can't Work" boycotts of the 1930s, selective patronage emerged in response to the conditions Black people faced obtaining employment. Between 1946 and 1953, as a consequence of deindustrialization and white flight, Black unemployment in Philadelphia stood between one-and-a-half times and double that of whites.[75] One 1956 study found that 37 percent of Black workers in North Philadelphia were unemployed, while another 42 percent of those surveyed had irregular employment.[76] Those Black Philadelphians who did manage to find steady employment were frequently relegated to low-paying, unskilled jobs. Despite accounting for nearly a third of the city's labor force, in 1960, non-white men comprised 54.8 percent of the city's male unskilled labor force, but only 8.7 percent of male professional and technical positions. The situation was even worse for Black women, who comprised 28.6 percent of the city's labor force, but accounted for 45.9 percent of unskilled female labor and 86.5 percent of female domestic laborers.[77]

Economic conditions alone do not explain why selective patronage emerged when it did. For that, we must look to the shifting landscape of civil rights activism, including student activists, who frequently led the way in pioneering new ideas and tactics, on and off campus.[78] In February 1960, students from multiple Philadelphia schools, including Temple University, the University of Pennsylvania, Lincoln University, Drexel Institute, Swarthmore College, and several area high schools, began picketing two Woolworth stores in West Philadelphia in solidarity with the sit-ins in North Carolina. They succeeded in temporarily halting business activity in both stores.[79] In a move paralleled in other cities, a group of civil rights ministers, including Sullivan, joined the students, who expanded the pickets to four more Woolworth's stores, including the city's largest, located in Center City.[80] While initially supportive of the student-led sit-in, Sullivan moved quickly to launch his own boycott, known as selective patronage, rooted in the church.

Organizing through the church had a number of advantages. For one, the church's economic independence enabled it, in the words of Adam Fairclough, to serve as "an organizational tool [that] was second to none."[81] Joining Sullivan in launching selective patronage was a group of local Black ministers who called themselves the "400 ministers." The group included Thomas Ritter, Reverend Joshua E. Licorish of Zoar Methodist Church, Dr. Noah Moore, Reverend Gus Roman, Reverend William Glenn Jr. and Reverend Henry H. Nichols of Janes Memorial United Methodist Church, Reverend Alfred G. Dunston of African Methodist Episcopal Zion Church, Reverend Jesse Anderson of St. Thomas Episcopal Church, H. J. Trapp of New Thankful Baptist Church, Walter Hazzard of Tindley Temple Methodist, and Clarence L. Cave of Faith Presbyterian.[82] Using the power of the pulpit, the 400 ministers worked to assert their authority as civil rights leaders in Philadelphia over the students, who some worried could damage the cause if left to their own devices. The term selective patronage was chosen over boycott in an effort to avoid potential lawsuits related to restraint-of-trade charges.[83]

The label selective patronage was likewise an early indication of the ways free market ideology shaped the movement, which simultaneously endeavored to change employment practices *and* awaken Black Philadelphians to the economic power they wielded as consumers and business owners. "Nothing influences a company's attitudes or changes its directions more than losing money," explained Sullivan. "In order to hit prejudice where it hurts most, hit it in the pocketbook!"[84] The first company targeted by the campaign was the Tastykake Baking Company, producer of a popular line of baked goods. This required the ministers to work closely with Black businessmen who owned or managed the corner stores in which Tastykake goods were sold. This was not difficult for the ministers, many of whom had close relationships with the city's Black business community. These relationships were part of a longer history linking Black churches and Black businesses. Many of the first Black businesses, including Black-owned insurance companies like North Carolina Mutual, got their start as semi-religious institutions financed with the help of church congregants.[85] In addition to financing the development of Black businesses, Black churches, like their white counterparts, served an important role facilitating knowledge about finance, management, and other practices central to the development of American capitalism.[86] Recall Ritter's work fundraising to rebuild the Second Macedonia Church, including establishing a daycare. In sum, the 400 ministers were well-prepared to think like the business owners they targeted via selective patronage, because they themselves were capitalists.

Capitalists with a captive audience. Getting Black-owned corner stores to stop stocking Tastykake products was the first step in launching a successful boycott. The real success of the selective patronage movement came from the ministers' ability to convince their congregations to change their purchasing behavior. This was no small task. As previously mentioned, many of the "400 ministers," including Ritter and Sullivan, spent the 1950s growing their congregations, including fundraising from local businesses to support building renovations and expanded services. In the case of the latter, Zion Baptist's congregation grew from approximately six hundred members in 1950 to 2,600 members by 1960.[87] Elsewhere, media estimated the number of congregants reached by the 400 ministers as between 250,000 and 300,000.[88]

Underscoring the ministers' central role in the selective patronage movement, each week during the campaign, the 400 ministers met privately to discuss the boycott. Then, on Sunday, the ministers made their decision known to their congregations, including which business to boycott and for how long. In the case of Tastykake, the boycott was drawn out over several weeks. This was what the ministers had expected and hoped for. The strategy behind the decision to target Tastykake went beyond the company's popularity among Black consumers. The choice of Tastykake also presented the 400 ministers an opportunity to assert their leadership within Philadelphia's competitive civil rights landscape. Previously, in 1959, the NAACP had tried and failed to negotiate changes in hiring practices through talks that, while cordial, proved fruitless. As a member of the NAACP board, Sullivan was privy to these efforts. Thus, he knew that Tastykake would not give into the 400 ministers' demands easily. Rather, Sullivan and the other ministers hoped for a protracted, *public* standoff with Tastykake in order to garner media attention.

The media battle began when the 400 ministers publicly announced their demands, including:

1. The assignment of "fixed" routes to three Black salesmen-drivers currently working as substitute drivers;
2. A commitment to hire additional Black salesmen-drivers in the near future;
3. The placement of two "Negro girls" on the company's clerical staff;
4. An end to the company's policy of segregated locker rooms for women workers and a commitment to give Black women workers in the company's production departments the same opportunities for upgrading as white women workers; and
5. The adoption of a written policy of nondiscrimination in employment assignments in all departments.[89]

Numbers three and four, in particular, speak to the pressure the ministers, who were all male, faced from Black women congregants to include them in the spoils of the campaign and not just its enactment.[90]

Tastykake executives quickly fired back, taking out two full-page advertisements in *The Philadelphia Tribune* promoting the company's hiring and treatment of Black employees. In one of the ads, the company deployed colorblind politics to undermine the ministers. "The future would be quite dim for either race or employee relations in any company which would succumb to pressure favoring one group over another."[91] A similar argument was later made by Sears executives in response to a boycott led by Rev. Martin Luther King Jr. and Operation Breadbasket in Atlanta. In the latter case, Sears's attorney, Robert Wood, quoted the 1964 Civil Rights Act to argue that it was the ministers who were in the wrong for seeking employment for persons on the basis of race.[92]

Tastykake's efforts to win the battle with the 400 ministers in the media failed. The boycott continued. After seven weeks of declining sales, company officials caved and agreed to negotiate. On Sunday, August 7, 1960, the ministers announced to their congregants that the company had met their demands and the initial boycott was over. "After the Tasty victory, Black people were walking ten feet tall in the streets of Philadelphia," Sullivan recalled.[93] Going forward, the ministers used their experience with Tastykake to wage successful battles against other local companies, including Sun Oil, Pepsi Cola, and Breyer's Ice Cream. Within several years, the selective patronage movement claimed responsibility for creating an estimated two thousand new jobs for Black Philadelphians.

Along the way, Sullivan and the 400 ministers walked a tightrope, pressuring businesses to hire Black employees in good-paying, skilled positions, without alienating the business owners.[94] Here was an important distinction between civil rights capitalism and left-wing organizations like the Revolutionary Action Movement (RAM), which was also active in Philadelphia at the time. Sometime in late 1962/early 1963, representatives from RAM contacted Sullivan about potentially joining the ministers' selective patronage campaign. Inspired by Black nationalist and revolutionary freedom fighter Robert F. Williams, Malcolm X, and Philadelphia-area Black Marxists calling themselves Organization Alert, RAM emerged as a self-identified Black nationalist and Marxist-Leninist organization committed to shaking up the civil rights movement, which they deemed too "bourgeois." Where RAM and other Black leftists sought the "development of black workers" into a Black vanguard that would ultimately help to lead a socialist revolution overthrowing American capitalism, Sullivan and the 400 ministers sought Black inclusion within an expanded capitalist economy.[95] "We had no desire to destroy it," stated Sullivan. "We wanted to strengthen it. But we wanted it strong for everybody, so that instead of the Black man's getting the crumbs all the time, he would start baking some of the bread."[96] In many cases, following the conclusion of a boycott, the ministers used their pulpits to encourage congregants to patronize the business in question with the same enthusiasm as they had boycotted.[97]

Sullivan's reference to "the Black man . . . baking some of the bread" was likewise revealing of the gender and class politics that permeated much of the movement for civil rights and Black empowerment. Despite the presence of women, who undertook a significant portion of the consumption for their households and thus were frequently on the front lines of the campaign picketing stores, much of the (male) ministers' rhetoric emphasized the importance of empowering Black men to become breadwinners, reflecting patriarchal ideology's influence on the movement.[98] Patriarchy likewise shaped the venues in which Black advancement was negotiated. While the boycott itself was carried out in the streets and in communities, nearly all of the decision-making in the selective patronage movement occurred behind closed doors in exclusively male spaces. This included the private meetings, where the all-male ministers met with company representatives—also all men—to negotiate the terms of desegregation. Indeed, these meetings themselves were a place for the ministers to assert their competence in a prized sphere of male dominance: business.

And competent negotiators the 400 ministers were. Ultimately, selective patronage brought over three hundred Philadelphia-area businesses to the negotiating table. After witnessing the negative publicity against Tastykake, many firms chose to negotiate with the ministers rather than enter a prolonged boycott. Of the three hundred firms, only twenty-nine actually made it to the stage of boycotts.[99] This had important consequences for the movement, namely shifting negotiations over the terms of racial integration from the public—the streets—to the private sphere, including corporate and/or church boardrooms, a pattern repeated countless times amid the subsequent rise of Black empowerment politics.

The private nature of the negotiations gave the ministers significant power to shape the demands, which included the implementation of equal and fair employment policies alongside a commitment to affirmative action in hiring. As Sullivan explained, the ministers did substantial research on each company to determine the "number of job turnovers" each company averaged. "If employers protested" that the ministers' demands were too high, they could respond that they were merely "asking for all of the vacancies" to be given to Black people in an effort to correct past discrimination. "[We] never ask[ed] for more than could be done," stated Sullivan. The point was to get the company moving in the direction of hiring Black "people on an equal-opportunity basis after the campaign was ended," not inhibit profits.[100]

In the case of Gulf Oil Company, the 400 ministers secured a promise from the corporation to implement a policy of "fair job distribution" and hire a dozen or so skilled Black employees, including a Black accountant, a Black sales representative, and several Black oil-truck drivers.[101] The agreement followed a week-long boycott of Gulf by Black Philadelphians, some of whom went without heat in the middle of January.[102] Ultimately, the agreement posed little challenge to the company. A handful of jobs for Black workers was a drop in the bucket for Gulf, which employed hundreds of white workers in its $400 million petrochemical facility just south of Philadelphia.[103] *Philadelphia Courier* editor Bob Queen, who frequently covered the selective patronage movement and offered a favorable view of the ministers, made a similar observation regarding the boycott's impact on Gulf's main competitor, Sun Oil. "It seems hardly likely that the 'selective patronage' program brought Sun Oil to its financial knees, or in any sense endangered the company's pocketbook," wrote Queen.[104] That, as Sullivan readily acknowledged, was not the point. Rather, civil rights capitalism purported that white and Black Americans could profit together.

Selective patronage's limited impact on the companies it targeted notwithstanding, the campaign was hailed nationally as a huge success, inspiring similar selective patronage boycotts in places such as New Haven, Boston, Providence, New York City, Pittsburgh, Detroit, and Baltimore.[105] While Sullivan touted the collective leadership of the 400 ministers, during the campaign, the Lion of Zion was no stranger to the spotlight, frequently providing quotes to the media. In an interview with the *St. Louis Post-Dispatch*, for example, Sullivan explained the movement in terms of "a moral mandate" on the part of the ministers to remedy the "inequality of treatment" received by Black Americans with regard to employment. Going a step further, Sullivan articulated what would become an increasingly important argument—and a key component of Black empowerment politics—about the ability of Black ministers to remedy capitalism's excesses, stating "we . . . ministers are the only morally constituted group . . . best able to reach the most people on a moral issue."[106] In other words: Have faith in us—in me—to deliver you to the promised land.

Sullivan's embrace of civil rights capitalism was replicated by other Black ministers eager to demonstrate the church's relevancy for the ongoing Black freedom struggle.[107] During the early 1960s, Sullivan toured the country, speaking at Black churches and other organizations about selective patronage. In October 1962, Sullivan received an invitation to speak to the Atlanta chapter of the Southern Christian Leadership Conference (SCLC), whose president, Rev. John Middleton, praised Sullivan's work "providing new job opportunities for our people."[108] One month later, under the direction of Ralph Abernathy, John Middleton, and J. D. Grier, SCLC launched its own program, Operation Breadbasket, modeled on the selective patronage efforts in Philadelphia. As its first target, Operation Breadbasket selected Colonial Bakery. One Black minister involved in Operation Breadbasket in Atlanta admitted that the boycott produced limited results in terms of overall jobs won. Like Sullivan, the minister explained this was not necessarily the goal. "We see these [results] as minimal requests. Their fulfillment demonstrates the good-will of the companies."[109] Opportunity and good will likewise featured prominently in Sullivan's next venture, Opportunities Industrialization Centers Inc., whose founding marked an important moment in the history of Black empowerment politics.

The Birth of OIC

On a cold January day in 1964, Sullivan stood before a crowd of over eight thousand Philadelphia residents, government officials, business leaders, and reporters to announce the birth of Opportunities Industrialization Centers Inc. "The day has come when we must do more than protest—we must now also PREPARE and PRODUCE!" declared Sullivan.[110] What did it mean to "do more than protest"? For years following OIC's launch, Sullivan and others like him did not so much abandon direct action as use it strategically to support their broader goal of Black economic empowerment. During the 1970s, for example, Sullivan led thousands of supporters on a "Pilgrimage to Washington" in an effort to pressure policymakers to provide government support for OIC amid growing calls for austerity. In doing so, Sullivan insisted he and his supporters were not after a government handout. "OIC has been phenomenally successful [in making] taxpayers out of tax consumers," Sullivan told Congress in 1970. Channeling the market-logic, which increasingly dominated American politics during the latter part of the twentieth century, Sullivan added that, for every dollar the US government invested in OIC, "the investment would be returned $3 to $1."[111] Here and elsewhere, Sullivan sought to expand American capitalism to create more opportunities for all to profit.

Doing so required making some changes. If selective patronage was about pressuring local businesses to alter their hiring practices to employ more Black people in skilled, high-paying positions, with OIC, Sullivan conceded Black people needed to change, as well. "After we cracked the door of industry

Figure 1. Opportunities Industrialization Center dedication. January 26, 1964. Photographer Rob Clark Jr. George D. McDowell Philadelphia Evening Bulletin Photographs, Special Collections Research Center, Temple University Libraries, Philadelphia, PA.

through selective patronage . . . we began to hear the old excuse 'We would hire him, but he is not prepared.'" Such logic echoed the widespread prejudice of white business owners, who repeatedly deployed racism to resist integration. Yet, similar beliefs could be found among Black Americans demanding increased training and support. In the latter's case, the lack of preparation was inseparable from the history of racialized exclusion from the kinds of institutions and programs that trained white Americans for high-paying, skilled positions in industry. As a result of this exclusion, many Black Americans who managed to find employment in high-skilled, good-paying jobs, found themselves unprepared when entering predominantly white workspaces. "Integration without preparation" proved a recipe for "frustration," stated Sullivan.[112]

During the 1960s, this frustration led a growing number of Black people, including Sullivan, to demand that business and government create and/or expand existing programs to provide job-training for Black Americans as part of a broader movement to remake American liberalism. At a planning meeting for OIC, held in the basement of Zion Baptist church in the summer of 1963 and attended by over one hundred Black technicians, Sullivan alluded to the failure of existing government programs to address the needs of Black Americans when he stated, "We are not waiting any longer for others to train our own people. . . . [W]e have been waiting all these years." "Now we're going to do it ourselves," Sullivan continued, touting the benefits of Washingtonian self-help—a tradition reflected in OIC's motto: "We help ourselves." In doing so, "We hope to prove that genius is color-blind."[113]

Genius took on a particular meaning in the context of OIC. Keeping with the Washingtonian tradition of industrial education, Sullivan called for people with expertise in engineering, drafting, electronics, refrigeration, sheet metal work, chemistry, cabinetmaking and other technical skills. This fit Sullivan's vision of training business owners, as well as employees, in industrial production. "We are now going to be producers. . . . No longer will we merely seek work, but now we will also provide work," stated Sullivan in an interview with *The Philadelphia Inquirer* on OIC's founding.[114] Nor was he alone in championing industrial education as a vehicle for Black empowerment. During the early days of OIC, Sullivan worked closely with Leone H. Chauvet on developing the program. Born in Haiti, Chauvet previously served as a technical advisor to the Haitian delegation to the United States before emigrating to the states, where he served as an industrial consultant in New York City. Chauvet subsequently joined OIC as the organization's technical director.[115]

OIC drew heavily on the NPYES, which by 1963 oversaw job-placement for over seven thousand Philadelphia-area youth and had outgrown its initial home, operating out of local churches.[116] With the launch of OIC, Sullivan and Ritter sought a new home for the operation. At some point, Sullivan eyed an abandoned police station at 19th and Oxford streets in the heart of North Philadelphia. The building was infamous as the former home of the 23rd police district. One local resident, Kenneth Salaam, recalled his experience growing up nearby as follows: "In North Philadelphia . . . it wasn't a good relationship with the police. . . . Nineteenth and Poplar . . . was the police station there. Most African Americans didn't want to go there, you know, because it was you know, definitely a place where you would get your head whipped or, you know, you would be beat up pretty bad."[117] In 1959, the city replaced the station with a new, multistory police station located nearby, at 17th Street and Montgomery Avenue, as part of a citywide campaign to expand the policing

of Black and Brown neighborhoods. The new station was built to accommodate upward of five hundred policemen and sixty detectives.[118]

Viewed by some as a scourge on the neighborhood, an emblem of state
violence, Sullivan saw the old jailhouse as an opportunity. "It was the worst
place in town. If we could change that from a place of despair into a place of
hope, we could change anybody or anything," said Sullivan.[119] Subsequently,
Sullivan enlisted the help of City Councilman Thomas McIntosh, who petitioned the city to have the former station leased to OIC for the bargain price
of one dollar a year.[120] The charge of one-dollar rent was a common tool used
to establish a contractual relationship. The arrangement transferred responsibility and authority for operating the building to OIC, while the city retained
ownership of the land. Subsequently, OIC entered into similar contractual
relationships with other government agencies and corporations to operate
abandoned properties in cities across the US, transforming a deindustrial-
izing landscape into a landscape of Black empowerment, or so they hoped.

Hope played an important role in OIC's founding, which sought to inspire
a change in attitude, as much as economic circumstances, among its trainees.
In order to transform the old police station "from a place of despair into a place
of hope," Sullivan returned to the well-worn tactic of transforming the physical appearance of the building. Touring the site in September 1965, *Christian
Science Monitor* journalist Paul Friggens painted a stirring picture of a former
jail turned empowerment center. "Where once police had booked drunks,
dope addicts, and muggers, I entered a spick-and-span [room], cheerful with
canary-yellow walls, colorful curtains, and modern furnishings," he noted.[121]
Meanwhile, "the old courtroom where prisoners filed from the jail cells down-
stairs was converted into a first-class restaurant," used to train waitresses and
other restaurant workers.[122] The only thing that did not shine with new paint
was one jail cell, which Sullivan intentionally left untouched, claiming, "I want
our trainees to know what it was like—and do better with their lives."[123] The
offhand comment was illustrative of the connection between Black empowerment politics and the carceral state, with supporters of Black empowerment
frequently deploying the threat of incarceration to incentivize Black industriousness and participation in the formal economy; a threat, in OIC's case, made
manifest with the remaining jail cell.

Funding for the renovation came from private donations, revealing a
pattern that would only become more prominent in subsequent years. On
September 25, 1963, Sullivan announced that he had received $50,000 from

an anonymous donor.[124] The donor, according to Sullivan, had previously shown interest in the NPYES.[125] Smaller gifts, including $11,000 from the Philadelphia Foundation; $5,000 from the Smith, Kline, and French Foundation; $2,500 from Scott Paper Company; and donations from individuals brought the total to $75,000. This money was used to renovate the building, in which "over four feet of water had collected in the basement," a sign of neglect.[126] Meanwhile, OIC received over $80,000 in donations and machinery, equipment, and furnishings from local businesses, including the Philco Corporation, General Electric, Bell Telephone, the Sharpless Corporation, and International Business Machines.[127]

Why did businesses aid OIC? Given the history of selective patronage, which pitted Sullivan and other ministers against Philadelphia's white-owned businesses, one might have expected local industry to avoid further dealings with the Lion of Zion. This narrative is supported by scholarship examining the widespread capital flight from cities in the 1960s. In Memphis, for example, civil rights activism contributed to RCA's decision to close their plant there just five years after it had opened.[128] Meanwhile, in Baltimore, a number of businesses located in the popular North Avenue commercial district left the city starting in the early 1960s, fleeing a growing Black population and urban renewal.[129]

Yet other businesses stayed. Why? For some, new programs like the Philadelphia Industrial Development Corporation, a public-private partnership with a mission to forestall the loss of industry in Philadelphia through assistance with financing, proved an incentive.[130] Others sought to buttress declining profit margins by expanding their footprint among urban Black consumers.[131] Still another reason had to do with bolstering business's image amid widespread and growing discontent with corporate America.[132] For those white-owned companies that continued to do business in the Black metropolis, Black empowerment organizations like OIC became fruitful partners in more ways than one.

*   *   *

Despite the efforts of previous generations, apartheid remained very much alive in post-WWII America, where large numbers of white Americans prospered at the expense of Black and other non-white Americans.[133] As white Americans and white-owned businesses moved to the suburbs, Black

residents of cities like Philadelphia and Detroit were left facing the consequences, including crumbling urban infrastructure and growing levels of
unemployment.[134] Black urban residents responded to these developments
in ways that reflected the diversity of Black political and economic thought
in the mid-twentieth century. Indeed, the postwar years saw the flourishing
of multiple, sometimes competing, responses, ranging from the Black Islamic
nationalism of groups like the Nation of Islam to Black labor activism and,
most relevant to our story, civil rights capitalism.

These articulations overlapped in some respects but bore crucial differences. While all sought Black self-determination and an end to white supremacy, the strategies they employed yielded distinct results. Convinced that the
United States was irredeemable, Black nationalists sought to construct self-
sufficient, autonomous communities outside the body politic, with varying
degrees of success. Meanwhile, left-leaning and working-class activists, including working-class Black women like Alice Lipscomb, built vibrant and diverse
coalitions to contest the terms of mid-century American liberalism and
demand government support and accountability to enable people to remain
in their homes and live their lives with dignity.[135] Still another group, which
included people like Sullivan and Ritter, increasingly embraced job-training,
Black entrepreneurship, and corporate-community partnerships—all compo-
nents of Black empowerment politics—as the key to Black advancement and
self-determination.

Already by the mid-1960s there were indicators of the limitations of this
approach. In a widely celebrated example of direct action, the "400 ministers," who organized selective patronage, claimed to have opened roughly two
thousand new jobs for Black Philadelphians. This represented only a small
drop in the bucket, however, in a city where non-white people had an unemployment rate of 10.7 percent, compared to only 5 percent for whites.[136] For
all its success, selective patronage, like similar boycotts at the time, failed to
challenge the spatial inequality of the postwar metropolis. When the ministers negotiated with local businesses, they nearly always were negotiating
for positions within the Black communities in which they lived. Meanwhile,
the bulk of new manufacturing jobs occurred outside the city in whites-only
suburbs beyond the reach of most Black Americans.

Following the rise of civil rights capitalism pressuring businesses to
open their doors to more Black Americans, Sullivan and others turned their
attention to job-training with the founding of OIC. Here, too, the ministers
faced a number of challenges. As previous critics of job-training have noted,

job-training and job-placement programs frequently resulted in trainees being placed in low-wage jobs, while offering tax breaks to businesses.[137] The success and limitations of promoting job-training and Black enterprise more broadly would only become more apparent as Black empowerment programs began to take hold in the late 1960s and 1970s, aided by Johnson's War on Poverty and Nixon's Black Capitalism.

PART II

Routes

CHAPTER 3

Incorporating Struggle

B lack Power! The words resounded like a battle cry. For many they were. Coming of age amid the dramatic movements—deindustrialization, white flight, urban renewal—that transformed US cities in the decades after World War II, making them increasingly uninhabitable for poor and working-class Black and Brown people, and inspired by the ongoing struggles for decolonization in Asia, Africa, and the Caribbean, a new generation of Black activists demanded immediate and dramatic action to dismantle Jim Crow/apartheid and colonialism in and beyond the United States.[1] Alongside Black pride and a diasporic conscience, advocates of Black Power placed a strong emphasis on self-determination. "We are not going to wait for white people to sanction Black Power. We're tired of waiting . . . tired of trying to prove things to white people," declared Stokely Carmichael, in one of many speeches explicating on Black Power.[2] Black people must be able to define their destinies without white people dictating the terms of liberation.

A relatively simple slogan veered in many directions. For some, including the iconic Black Panther Party for Self-Defense (BPP), Black Power connoted militancy, anti-imperialism, and, at times, anti-capitalism. Donning Black berets, leather jackets, and dark sunglasses, in homage to French, African, and Latin American revolutionaries, the Panthers marched through the streets of America's Black metropolises armed with guns, creating a spectacle that shocked many Americans and inspired others. More than an actual armed rebellion, of which there was relatively little, the Panthers' extraordinary display of militancy helped to draw attention to the routine violence enacted against Black Americans.[3] Taking their cue from Frantz Fanon, Che Guevara, and others, BPP cofounders Huey Newton and Bobby Seale claimed Black Americans were an internal colony within the United States and advocated for an anti-imperialist, anti-capitalist revolution. Departing from traditional

Marxism-Leninism, this revolution, they argued, should be led by the lumpen proletariat—what Newton referred to as the "brothers on the block."[4]

Such a revolution appeared to already be occurring in cities and towns across the United States.[5] Like the Panthers' protests, these rebellions frequently began following a confrontation with the police—confrontations like the one that occurred in North Philadelphia, Sullivan's home base, in 1963. On October 26, 1963, John Tourigan, a white police officer, shot Willie Philyaw, a Black man, claiming Philyaw stole a watch—an accusation Philyaw denied—and lunged at Tourigan with a knife when the latter confronted him. Several eyewitnesses contested this account, however, testifying that Philyaw, who was disabled, was attempting to get away from Tourigan when the latter pulled out his gun and shot him. Philyaw later died from the injuries he sustained.[6] News of Philyaw's death elicited widespread anger from residents all too familiar with police violence. As news of Philyaw's murder spread, a crowd gathered outside the police station, demanding to speak with the precinct captain. At one point, the crowd began throwing bricks at the police station. Later that evening, residents, who may or may not have been present at the earlier demonstration, took to the streets and looted stores along North Philadelphia's Susquehanna Avenue retail district. The Susquehanna Avenue rebellion, as it came to be known, mirrored other urban uprisings in which residents targeted businesses, many of which were owned by people from outside the neighborhood, going after credit logs and other emblems of exploitation.[7]

Still, we should be wary of applying a singular meaning to the rebellions, which were diverse in both their causes and forms.[8] The same goes for Black Power. Alongside contesting racialized policing, American imperialism, and racial capitalism, many wielded Black Power as a call for community control, community economic development, and Black capitalism.[9] One such person to associate Black Power with profiteering was Leon Sullivan. Addressing supporters at the launch of Progress Plaza—the first Black-owned shopping center in the United States—Sullivan declared, this here is a "Black power venture."[10] At the time, in November 1968, Sullivan headed what was quickly becoming the largest Black empowerment program in the country, comprised of several interconnected organizations—Opportunities Industrialization Centers Inc. (OIC), Zion Non-Profit Charitable Trust, and Zion Investment Associates, later renamed Progress Investment Associates. All created and led by Black people, these organizations were very much in keeping with Black Power's emphasis on self-determination and Black pride. As Sullivan frequently expounded, these programs were "initiated by the Black community for the Black community."[11] Still, this was a far cry from the kind of participatory democracy championed by many within the movement. Unlike those who sought to harness the energy of Black Power and ignite a revolution or use it at the ballot box, Sullivan sought change in the marketplace through private means, including job-training, Black business development, and corporate-community partnerships.[12] This was Black empowerment politics.

As Sullivan's comments—this is a "Black Power venture"—suggest, the line between Black Power and Black empowerment politics frequently appeared blurry, especially in the early years of their respective development. This slippage was productive, making Black empowerment appealing to self-identified Black Power activists who embraced private enterprise as a vehicle for liberation.[13] Even the Oakland Black Panther Party, known for their revolutionary rhetoric and tactics, attempted to harness the power of profits by soliciting local Black business support for their community survival program, threatening to boycott any businesses that refused to cooperate.[14] During the late 1960s and early 1970s, various politicians, business leaders, and philanthropists played on the overlap between Black Power and Black empowerment politics, mitigating the most radical aspects of Black Power and transforming it into something more compatible with American liberalism and capitalism.[15]

One of the most remarked on efforts in this regard was Richard Nixon's embrace of Black capitalism. Seeking to draw a contrast between himself and Lyndon Johnson, whose War on Poverty conservatives derided as federal overreach and government excess, Nixon claimed during his acceptance speech at the 1968 Republican National Convention, "Black Americans, no more than white Americans . . . do not want more government programs which perpetuate dependency. They don't want to be a colony in a nation. They want the pride, and the self-respect, and the dignity that can only come if they have an equal chance to own their own homes, to own their own businesses, to be managers and executives as well as workers, to have a piece of the action in the exciting ventures of private enterprise."[16] Going forward, Nixon joined others in incorporating Black struggle, making it more compatible with American capitalism.

While rightly credited with giving it a new platform, if not always the corresponding financial backing promised, Nixon did not invent Black capitalism. Indeed, Nixon's touting of Black capitalism in 1968 garnered support, in part, because he tapped into an existing movement within Black America for incorporation and private enterprise. The *Oxford English Dictionary* defines incorporation as "the inclusion of something as part of a whole" and "the process of constituting a . . . legal corporation."[17] Both of these applied to efforts promoting Black empowerment politics during the 1960s and early 1970s, which witnessed hundreds of Black groups incorporate in an effort to take advantage of various government programs and private donations. One particularly popular organizational form was the community development corporation, which exploded during the late 1960s and early 1970s as a vehicle for marrying Black demands for "community control," economic development, and the profit motive.[18] Incorporation, moreover, was not limited to for-profit entities. Black organizations, including OIC, also utilized nonprofits to boost their income, taking in tax-deductible donations from businesses and private individuals. As nonprofits, Black empowerment organizations benefited from the US government's increasing reliance on nonprofits to administer antipoverty programs in poor and marginalized urban neighborhoods.[19]

Founded by Leon Sullivan, the nonprofit Opportunities Industrialization Centers Inc., and for-profit Progress Enterprises were but two of dozens of Black empowerment organizations launched during the 1960s that promoted job-training, Black entrepreneurship, and community economic development in response to multiple crises, including deindustrialization, white flight, and social unrest. In the process of soliciting political and economic support for such efforts, Black empowerment activists forged important relationships with federal, state, and local governments, private philanthropic organizations, and, perhaps most surprisingly, corporate America. This process of incorporation, integrating Black struggle into the broader structure of American capitalism, began prior to Nixon, initially taking shape during the administration of Lyndon Johnson, whose War on Poverty supported Black empowerment programs like OIC as part of a broader effort mitigating urban unrest. In time, the ties binding Black organizations and their political and economic supporters, including corporate America, came to define Black empowerment politics, differentiating it from the better-known radical variants of Black Power espoused by those like Stokely Carmichael and the Black Panther Party.

From Prayer to Progress Plaza

When OIC first opened its doors to the public in the spring of 1964, the center found itself quickly overwhelmed with applications from over two thousand Black Philadelphians.[20] By March, the number of applicants had doubled to four thousand.[21] To meet the demand for training and job placement, OIC relied on a combination of grants from local philanthropies and community donations.[22] Sullivan recalled the time he received "a handkerchief full of pennies totaling three dollars and fifty-one cents" donated by local elementary school children.[23] It was a lovely gesture, but not enough to sustain the program.

In the beginning, OIC operated the way that many Black organizations had functioned for decades, with a staff comprised primarily of volunteers. Sullivan once boasted that those who worked for OIC were "employed on faith." Money was needed, though, to acquire equipment and cover utilities, and to meet the organization's various financial obligations. Not long after OIC's founding, Sullivan took out over $50,000 in loans from Zion Baptist Church and local financial institutions. Still, OIC struggled to make ends meet. At one point, Sullivan was forced to take out a second mortgage on his house. After that, Sullivan recalled, he "got down on [his] knees" and prayed.[24]

Employing a frequent narrative device used by champions of Black empowerment and the prosperity gospel, Sullivan asserted: faith was rewarded.[25] The answer to his prayers came "no more than five minutes later" when the "telephone rang," stated Sullivan. It was the Fidelity Bank letting him know they had approved a $13,000 loan. Sullivan's recounting of his and OIC's "good fortune" only further reinforced the lesson: religious devotion combined with hard work reaped material benefits. Shortly after news of the bank loan, Sullivan received additional good news, namely that the Ford Foundation had awarded OIC a $200,000 grant as part of the foundation's Gray Areas program.[26]

First launched in 1961 and headed by foundation director of public affairs Paul Ylvisaker, the Gray Areas program embraced several ideas that became central to the War on Poverty and the Black empowerment programs it helped to fund. The first was the culture of poverty theory. This theory, promoted by anthropologist Oscar Lewis and widely embraced by social scientists and anti-poverty workers during the 1960s and 1970s, argued that poor people lacked not only material resources, but were also marked psychologically and behaviorally. The theory drew heavily on and replicated racist and sexist ideas, including a fixation with the predominance of single-mother-led households in Black communities to explain the prevalence of poverty in particular communities.[27]

The Gray Areas program also drew on the Ford Foundation's experience promoting international development and modernization of the Third World.[28] Likewise rooted in racist notions of non-white people, modernization theory ranked the world's peoples along a spectrum of "premodern" or "traditional" to "modern" and sought the former's advancement along lines following the latter. Describing America's inner cities as the nation's "Calcutta[s]," Ylvisaker applied a similar logic to the Gray Areas program, the goal of which, he described, was to assist recent arrivals, "the Negroes, the Puerto Ricans, the mountain whites, the Mexicans, and the American Indians . . . climb the totem pole of urban culture."[29] Further underscoring the connection between the "developing" world—America's "Calcutta[s]"—and inner-city Black and Brown neighborhoods, Ylvisaker and his collaborators in the Gray Areas program solicited "indigenous" leaders, in Ylvisaker's words, to help the foundation in its efforts.[30]

As they did, Ylvisaker and the Ford Foundation were forced to confront the rise of Black Power politics in Philadelphia and other cities. Building on selective patronage and other direct-action campaigns earlier in the decade, Black Power activists in Philadelphia contested the foundation's initial preference for controlling the Gray Areas project directly via the foundation-managed Philadelphia Council for Community Advancement (PCCA). Leading the charge was the charismatic and fiery Philadelphia NAACP president Cecil Moore, who helped to revive the local NAACP chapter and turn it into a vehicle for Black Power politics.[31] Criticizing the Ford Foundation, which he claimed did little more than conduct surveys of Philadelphia's Black community while providing the company with a tax-exempt vehicle through which to shield its profits, Moore, echoing other Black Power activists, enacted his own kind of "indigenous leadership" by demanding community control of the anti-poverty program. In doing so, Moore inadvertently helped solidify the foundation's decision to get behind Sullivan.[32]

Having momentarily abandoned direct action following the conclusion of the selective patronage movement and taken to focusing on job-training and economic development, Sullivan appealed to Ylvisaker as the right kind of "indigenous leader" to help the organization—someone whose *past* activism gave him legitimacy within Philadelphia's Black community but also meant he, unlike Moore, did not provide an immediate threat to Ford. Instead, through OIC, Sullivan presented himself as a potential partner. Sensing an opportunity, Ylvisaker arranged for Sullivan to meet the trustees by scheduling a meeting with him just as the trustees were leaving the building. Encountering Henry Ford II and Ford Foundation chairman John J. McCloy in front of the elevator, Sullivan quickly made an impression on the foundation heads. Ford II purportedly exclaimed, "My god, how do we manufacture more of you?" To which Sullivan responded, "By giving me some money."[33] And money Ford gave.

Ford II's inquiry, in which he inquired about how to manufacture more people like Sullivan, rather than jobs, was telling, an indicator of the growing interest in job-training and Black proponents of job-training, in particular. As Tom Sugrue and others have demonstrated, job-training functioned as a hallmark of liberal policy during the mid-twentieth century, despite multiple limitations regarding its efficacy, on its own, as a tool for eliminating poverty and unemployment.[34] Sullivan was aware of these limitations. His efforts focused on job-creation, alongside training. One way he did this was through the 10–36 Plan. Sullivan first introduced the concept of the 10–36 Plan in a sermon at Zion Baptist, in which Sullivan referenced a passage from the bible, Luke 9:10–17, regarding a story about how Jesus fed five thousand people with a few loaves and a few fish. The passage is frequently referenced to illustrate the Christian values of charity and loving thy neighbor. In Sullivan's case, it also served as a model of community finance. Immediately following the sermon, Sullivan called on fifty members of the congregation to invest ten dollars a month for thirty-six months, hence the name: the 10–36 Plan. This, for Sullivan, was another form of community control and Black Power.

Over two hundred people subscribed to the initial 10–36 Plan.[35] The money was subsequently invested in two entities created as part of a series of Black empowerment organizations alongside OIC. The first, Zion Non-Profit Charitable Trust (ZNPCT), took advantage of a long-standing form associated with philanthropy and endowed with tax benefits, including, in many cases, exemption from federal income taxation and local property taxes.[36] The second, Zion Investment Associates (ZIA), later renamed Progress Investment Associates, was a for-profit venture. The 10–36 program was set up so that subscribers spent the first sixteen months contributing ten dollars a month to the nonprofit ZNPCT. For the remaining twenty months, investor contributions went to the for-profit ZIA. At the end of the thirty-six months, subscribers received one share of common voting stock that entitled them to participate in yearly shareholder meetings. Emphasizing the ideological, as well as the material, investment made by participants, Sullivan explained that it was important for people to give (to the nonprofit) before they received (from the for-profit).

The notion that investment reaped rewards—rewards that, in Sullivan's telling, were divinely sanctioned—was further illustrated by what happened next. Using funds collected via the 10–36 program, ZNPCT and ZIA were used to create a number of community development projects, including an apartment complex called Zion Gardens providing affordable housing to seniors in North Philadelphia. In May 1964, two months after the Ford Foundation grant, newspapers reported on a $1.3 million government loan for the project, an early indication of the ways Black empowerment benefited from government investment, including urban renewal.[37]

Initiated under Dwight Eisenhower, urban renewal relied on and augmented practices like slum clearance, neighborhood rehabilitation, and infrastructure development to remake US cities. Elaborating on James Baldwin's famous critique of urban renewal as "Negro removal," scholars have shown the dramatic and disproportionate effects these programs had on Black communities.[38] In Philadelphia, urban planners, led by Edmund Bacon, designated the semirural Eastwick area of Southwest Philadelphia as a relocation site for over two thousand low-income Black residents displaced by the Southwest Temple urban renewal project in North Philadelphia.[39] Similar mass upheavals took place in other cities across the US. By 1967, urban renewal had destroyed an estimated 404,000 housing units, with another 356,000 scheduled for demolition in US cities.[40]

For enterprising Black Americans like Sullivan, however, urban renewal symbolized not so much "Negro removal" but an opportunity for individual and community empowerment.[41] Reflecting a broader pattern of Black urban elites who supported urban renewal, Sullivan partnered with federal and local government officials to secure Zion Gardens space within the Southwest Temple urban renewal zone, as well as funding in the form of the $1.3 million loan from the Federal Housing Administration, part of a new program designed to address redlining and spur Black homeownership, a not insignificant portion of which went to Black churches.[42]

In an article celebrating the July 1965 ground-breaking of the apartment complex, *The New York Times* noted that, when completed, Zion Gardens would offer ninety-six units described as "garden type apartments" to low-income Black and white families.[43] The inclusion of white families in plans for Zion Gardens may have seemed bizarre in the context of promoting Black empowerment, yet it was indicative of a frequent concession on the part of civil rights leaders to the US government's adherence to the ideology of racial liberalism. In order to secure government funding for Black empowerment, Sullivan and others had to adhere to the formula of equal opportunity.

By contrast, the private sector offered more flexibility, as indicated by Sullivan's next project: Progress Plaza. Hailed as the "first shopping center in the

Figure 2. Reverend Leon H. Sullivan at Progress Plaza. October 27, 1969. Photographer Richard Rosenberg. George D. McDowell Philadelphia Evening Bulletin Photographs, Special Collections Research Center, Temple University Libraries, Philadelphia, PA.

US built, owned, and operated by African Americans," Sullivan announced the opening of Progress Plaza at a ceremony on October 29, 1968, attended by over 10,000 people. Standing on a wooden platform, dressed in a grey suit and tie, and surrounded by images of prominent Black Americans, including Frederick Douglass, Benjamin Banneker, and Crispus Attucks, Sullivan proudly proclaimed: "All of this . . . all of these buildings are owned by negroes."[44]

The ceremony at Progress Plaza mirrored similar celebrations by activists, a growing number of whom embraced Black enterprise during the late 1960s and 1970s as part of the broader movement for civil rights and Black Power. Following the assassination of Martin Luther King Jr., Reverend Jesse Jackson took over Operation Breadbasket, which he renamed Operation PUSH following his break with SCLC. In a memo to his staff in 1968, Jackson declared, "building economic viability in the Black community shifts our focus from economic security to economic independence. . . . BLACK COOPERATION

IS THE MOST EFFECTIVE EXPRESSION OF RESPONSIBLE AND MEAN-
INGFUL BLACK POWER that is POSSIBLE FOR BLACK PEOPLE AND
BLACK ORGANIZATIONS" (capitalization in original).[45] Jackson's speech
resonated with people like Floyd McKissick of CORE and members of the
Hough Area Development Corporation in Cleveland, who, like other Black
activists, increasingly gravitated toward Black capitalism in response to white
recalcitrance in employment and housing desegregation and in funding social
welfare.[46]

During his 1968 presidential campaign, Richard Nixon readily touted the
concept of Black capitalism to attack Johnson's War on Poverty. In September 1968, Nixon paid Sullivan a visit in Philadelphia, where he praised the
latter's work promoting Black enterprise and pledged his support for OIC.
His comments in Philadelphia echoed an earlier May radio address, in which
Nixon described Sullivan as one of several "Negro leaders [who] have shown
the way" by "establish[ing] private programs which have opened doors of
opportunity to thousands of Negroes who might never have benefited from a
government program."[47] The irony of Nixon's remarks was that OIC and, to a
lesser extent, Progress Enterprises were major beneficiaries of Johnson's War
on Poverty, which deployed Black empowerment politics as part of a broader
embrace of private enterprise to combat poverty prior to Nixon's rise.[48] Analyzing the intersection between Black empowerment politics and the War on
Poverty helps us better understand the latter's role in the rise of pro-business
or "free-market" politics, revealing its origins in the 1960s, as opposed to the
1970s or 1980s, and its connection to incorporating Black struggle.

Black Empowerment Meets the War on Poverty

First announced during Johnson's inaugural State of the Union address in
January 1964, and reiterated in a speech to Congress in March that year, the
War on Poverty functioned as an umbrella for a wide range of government
programs aimed at addressing poverty in the US.[49] A number of these built
on initiatives begun under John F. Kennedy, including the Area Redevelopment Association (ARA). In November 1964, OIC received its first federal
grant of $50,000 from the ARA to support its job-training and job-placement
program.[50] The ARA grant was part of a broader shift reorienting federal anti-
poverty funding to poor urban neighborhoods and those with a larger share
of non-white residents, in particular. When it was first launched, in 1961,

the ARA focused on addressing deindustrialization and unemployment in rural areas through place-based job-training, business development, and infrastructure improvement.[51] Growing pressure from civil rights activists, however, led the ARA to extend its focus to urban areas. In 1963, the ARA, working with the Department of Labor, expanded its program to eight cities, including Philadelphia.[52]

Relatively small in terms of the overall dollar amount, the ARA grant played a crucial role in getting OIC on the radar of federal government officials, opening the door to other opportunities. The details regarding how the ARA came to select OIC remain somewhat murky. It is possible that the Ford Foundation, many of whose staffers went on to occupy key positions in the Kennedy and Johnson administrations' anti-poverty programs, first brought OIC to the attention of the federal government.[53] Sullivan, however, attributed the government's interest to another midcentury liberal, Dr. Herbert Streiner, a respected Washington, DC, economist and head of the Upjohn Institute for Employment Research.[54] According to Sullivan, Streiner visited OIC and was impressed with the program. Subsequently, Streiner helped arrange a series of meetings between Sullivan and different DC powerbrokers, including ARA director William Batt, in the capital.[55] Batt arranged for Sullivan to speak with officials in the Department of Labor, which awarded OIC $458,000 through its Office of Manpower and Automated Training, $333,000 of which went toward its new pre-vocational Feeder Program.[56] Still, OIC did not reach financial stability until June 1965, at which point the Office of Economic Opportunity (OEO), created in August 1964 to administer the War on Poverty, finally approved $5.9 million in grants for anti-poverty programs in Philadelphia.[57]

The pressure exerted from civil rights and other pro-democracy activists on the ARA to engage the poor only expanded with the Economic Opportunity Act of 1964, one of several key pieces of legislation that comprised the War on Poverty, alongside the Food Stamps Act of 1964, the Elementary and Secondary Education Act, and the Social Security Act of 1965. Countering the top-down approach of other anti-poverty initiatives, Section 202 of the Economic Opportunity Act, on the community action program, called for the "maximum feasible participation of residents of the areas and members of the groups served" by the program.[58] Going forward, the idea of "maximum feasible participation" helped to inspire and reinforce a wave of civil rights and Black Power anti-poverty work in cities and towns across the US.[59]

"Maximum feasible participation" also elicited significant resistance from local governments, which were given the initial authority of administering

OEO funds.[60] In Philadelphia, the administration of Mayor James Tate, a Democrat, initially ignored this particular aspect of the program, leading OEO to reject several earlier proposals from the city. Finally, in February 1965, Tate relented and created the Philadelphia Anti-Poverty Action Committee (PAAC), comprised of representatives from six Community Action Councils (CACs) whose members were elected by residents. This number was later expanded to twelve, to further appease OEO's request for greater community representation on the PAAC.

With the creation of the PAAC and its role overseeing the CACs, it initially appeared that Philadelphia's War on Poverty program would indeed proceed with "maximum feasible participation" from the poor. During the first election, Black women, historically underrepresented in local government, secured 73 percent of CAC seats, which they used to advocate for things like public and affordable housing. Here is where city officials drew the line. Overruling the women's demands, Charles Bowser, an up-and-coming Black politician hand-picked by Mayor Tate to serve as PAAC's first executive director, secured the allegiance of CAC representatives through offering them jobs in city government. Working with city hall, Bowser directed PAAC funding to programs perceived as less disruptive to the status quo. Alongside a nursery school and day care program run by the Board of Education known as "Get Set," OIC emerged as the primary beneficiary of the War on Poverty in Philadelphia. Between 1965 and 1971, the Philadelphia OIC received $14,465,832 in federal grants, far more than other Philadelphia programs.[61]

What led government officials to privilege OIC over other programs? Personal connections certainly played an important role. Reflecting a pattern established in his work combating juvenile delinquency and with selective patronage, Sullivan and OIC benefited from a Black professional network with close ties to the church. This network connected Sullivan to other local Black ministers, including William H. Gray Jr., pastor of Bright Hope Baptist Church and a mentor to Bowser.[62] In 1967, Bowser and Sullivan jointly took part in the installation ceremony of Rev. Gus Roman as pastor of Canaan Church, another Philadelphia Black minister and leading figure within the OIC movement.[63] The two also socialized as members of Kappa Alpha Psi fraternity.[64] These networks, which had long played an important role in governing the Jim Crow city, took on even greater significance with the expansion of Black elected and unelected public officials in the 1960s and 1970s, ensuring open communication and funneling public resources to a relatively small group of Christian Black male professionals like Sullivan.

Still, in the mid-1960s, Black political power remained limited. Sullivan needed more than connections to secure the kind of funding necessary to transform OIC from a local into a national organization. He needed white institutional support, or so he thought. Thus, in December 1966, Sullivan again travelled to Washington, DC, in an effort to persuade the US government to grant OIC even more funding. In the process, Sullivan was forced to contend with growing criticism of Johnson's War on Poverty coming from Congress.

Congressional criticism of the War on Poverty began not long after the program launched. On September 27, 1966, San Francisco's Hunters Point neighborhood, home to many of the city's poor, Black residents, became the latest site to explode in protest, when a white police officer, Alvin Johnson, shot and killed Matthew Johnson, a Black teenager. In the aftermath, a number of conservative politicians blamed the Johnson administration for contributing to the unrest, citing as evidence the fact that several dozen Black youth had gathered at the local OEO headquarters, located at Third and Palou, prior to confronting local police. Among those who blamed the government's anti-poverty program for the unrest was Justin Herman, head of the city's Redevelopment Agency. Herman, notably, had previously advocated for the redevelopment of Hunters Point to exclude social undesirables and "welfare recipients," but had no authority over OEO.[65] In a statement following the rebellion, Herman declared: "This is perhaps the first time in the history of our country that the Federal Government has decided to finance open and overt revolution."[66] His comments were followed by Republican Congressman Paul A. Fino, from New York, who testified before Congress on the "very real danger that Black power is going to ride the demonstration cities gravy train," resulting in further "rioting and . . . anarchy" in US cities.[67]

In response to these and other criticisms of the War on Poverty, Sullivan exhibited pragmatism. While, at times, the civil rights leader readily deployed militant rhetoric in mobilizing Black support for OIC and other initiatives, in 1966, while seeking government funding for OIC, Sullivan chose to employ a more conciliatory approach, including distancing himself from the "controversial phrase 'Black Power.'" "[I would] not have created the term 'Black Power.' I don't need it," Sullivan stated. Instead, Sullivan coined another phrase: "Build, Brother, Build," stating, "with God's help, we are going to change the cries in our streets from 'Burn, baby, burn!,'" invoking the ongoing social unrest, "to 'Build, brother, build!'"[68] The phrase, which caught on amid the growing unrest of the 1960s and later appeared as the title of Sullivan's 1969 autobiography, helped distinguish Sullivan's approach—what I call Black empowerment politics—from Black Power. Going forward, various politicians and businesspeople worked to demean and mollify Black Power politics, which critics equated with rioting and destruction, while celebrating OIC and other Black empowerment programs as a "constructive" alternative.[69] Doing so required time and deliberate effort. The line between Black Power and Black empowerment was not always clear. Proponents of Black empowerment, including Sullivan, occasionally trafficked in the discourse of Black Power and self-proclaimed Black Power activists, at times, deployed private enterprise as a vehicle for achieving economic power.[70]

Drawing this line and enticing Black people, especially Black youth, away from a militant, radical strand of Black Power politics and toward a more palatable, from their perspective, Black empowerment politics became a preoccupation of US politicians on both sides of the party aisle. In 1967, amid hearings on the War on Poverty, Minnesota Congressman Al Quie, a Republican, foreshadowed Nixon's celebration of OIC when he stated: "I spend a lot of time criticizing poverty programs, and when I run across one that is working well, I like to bring it to the attention of my colleagues," referring to OIC. Among the attributes Quie found praiseworthy were Sullivan's work with local "business leaders," some of whom acted as advisors for the program, and OIC's refusal to provide trainees with a stipend, in contrast to other anti-poverty programs—a sign, in Quie's view, of the program's importance if "the poor in this minority group . . . attend . . . without being paid to learn."[71] Quie's praise found echoes in the testimony of the Democratic senator from Connecticut, Abraham Ribicoff, who similarly hailed OIC as a "huge success."[72]

In addition to the potential cost savings and work partnering with business, members of Congress paid close attention to the ideology undergirding Sullivan's Black empowerment program. Eschewing the anti-capitalist and anti-imperial rhetoric frequently deployed by Black Power activists like Stokely Carmichael and Huey Newton, Sullivan told Congress: "Structures do not make democracies or civilizations. Only attitudes and the spirits and desires of men to promote a change for their own betterment can do this."[73] In other words, Black people needed to help themselves.

Self-help was at the core of OIC's signature Feeder Program, a prevocational program required of all trainees. For too long, Sullivan stated, "[B]lack people had been brainwashed into inferiority." "The feeling had gotten into the crevices of their minds, so that they believed it without saying anything about it."[74] The Feeder Program sought to correct these feelings of insecurity through providing trainees with the self-confidence they needed to thrive in life and in the workplace. Viewed from one angle, the Feeder Program was a continuation of Sullivan's social ministry focused on religious salvation. As Sullivan explained, "the challenge," facing the Feeder Program, which initially took place in an old synagogue several blocks from the refurbished jail, was one of "prov[ing] that we could make a man or woman feel born anew."[75] Yet the Feeder Program, like other Black empowerment programs, combined this emphasis on religious salvation with an emphasis on Black consciousness and "self-confidence" in ways that mirrored the discourse of Black Power.[76] "A race of people is like an individual man; until it uses its own talent, takes pride in its own history, expresses its own culture, affirms its own selfhood, it can never fulfill itself." Thus declared Malcolm X at the founding rally of his Organization of African Unity (OAU) in 1964, sounding quite like Sullivan. Where Malcolm's OAU sought to unify Afro-descended people to "wage an unrelenting struggle against" the "political and economic system of exploitation" plaguing Black communities, Sullivan took a somewhat different tact, harnessing Black history and race pride for the purpose of integrating into an existing US capitalist system.[77] Both Malcolm and Sullivan channeled Black pride into enterprise, broadly construed. Only the latter appealed to those interested in preserving American capitalism. Each week, participants in OIC's Feeder Program took courses on "the Black man and his African heritage," while also learning about good "work habits, [including] punctuality," "company loyalty and responsibility," and good consumer habits.[78] In other words, Black identity was equated with the kind of self-confidence gained from succeeding in the marketplace. Reflecting on their time at OIC, one trainee noted, "Here, they show you what other Negroes have done." Another added, "For the first time, they make you realize that you are somebody."[79]

Often that somebody was male in the minds of OIC's leaders and funders. As part of the Feeder Program, Black male trainees participated in a special "Male Orientation" program designed specifically to socialize young Black men, challenging them to "improve their earning capacities and to assert their masculinity as family breadwinners."[80] This is not to say Black women did not participate in OIC. Indeed, they comprised a significant portion of the organization's student body and teachers. Reflecting and reinforcing the era's broader emphasis on Black masculinity, OIC placed a particular emphasis on helping Black men regain "something . . . that had been taken away by white folk," namely, their "manhood."[81] Testifying before Congress in 1969, Sullivan explained the special efforts OIC undertook to reach this population, while trafficking in a gendered discourse that celebrated Black men's work ethic. In Philadelphia, "you may see many ladies" taking OIC courses, but "that is because the men are working" and can only attend "night . . . programs." In an effort to make it easier for Black men to access job-training, OIC "created . . . a brotherhood program," the success of which could be seen in the Chicago OIC branch, where, Sullivan boasted, "100 percent of the OIC programs are male."[82]

As the mid-1960s gave way to the late 1960s, OIC and other Black empowerment programs doubled down on their work aiding poor and working-class Black urbanites, especially those gendered male, toward a "constructive" path of job-training and Black entrepreneurship, while opposing Black militancy. Echoing Sullivan, Samuel L. Woodward, a Philadelphia Black educator, stated, "If Black Power is the motivational force to cause one to rise above the social, economic, and educational constraints imposed by society, then it is a factor to be lauded rather than degraded."[83] In doing so, proponents of Black empowerment politics likewise distinguished their approach from others promoting social welfare.

"These kids don't have a feeling of belonging. . . . Why should they bother? This is Harlem, they say to themselves, and this is all I'm ever going to do or be. I want to show them what Negroes have done and what we can do," stated Rosalynne Bradham.[84] Bradham's words reflected a common sentiment—one shared by Black Power activists like John Churchville, a Black nationalist who founded the Freedom Library in Philadelphia in an effort to teach Black Philadelphians about Black history. In Bradham's case, cultivating race consciousness was connected to more practical skills as a remedial education instructor at Harlem Youth Opportunities Unlimited, popularly known as HARYOU. Founded in 1962 by Black psychologists Kenneth Clark and Mamie Phipps Clark, and directed by Cyril deGrasse Tyson (father of astrophysicist Neil deGrasse Tyson), HARYOU, like a number of other Black empowerment programs, rejected social welfare, which Clark equated with government "dependence" and "colonial" agents, in favor of education and community development.[85] This rejection of social welfare did not prevent HARYOU and other programs from seeking out and accepting government funding. In 1962, the President's Committee on Juvenile Delinquency awarded HARYOU $230,000 to implement a remedial education and jobs program. This was coupled with $100,000 from the City of New York.[86] Later, mirroring support for OIC, the Johnson Administration expanded this funding, awarding HARYOU $5 million to expand the job-training portion of its project.[87] Known to traffic in the discourse of race consciousness, HARYOU nevertheless agreed to purge itself of people like LeRoi Jones (soon to be Amiri Baraka), closely associated with Black Power, as a condition of government funding.[88] Here was Black empowerment politics in action, trading control for dollars and cents.

During the late 1960s, in response to pushback that the War on Poverty was funding Black radicalism, the Johnson administration expanded its support for Black empowerment programs like OIC and HARYOU, championing job-training, community development, and education, as opposed to social welfare, while simultaneously distancing itself from a more militant strain of Black Power politics. In doing so, the state found an eager partner in US corporations, which joined the growing chorus championing Black empowerment as the solution to the ongoing crisis in US cities.

The Business of Black Empowerment

In October 1964, OIC received one of its biggest endorsements to date when legendary Black baseball player Jackie Robinson visited the center. Recounting his visit for readers of the popular newspaper column "Jackie Robinson Says," Robinson described a "wholesome evening" spent speaking with trainees in this "bold new educational venture."[89] Echoing those like Sullivan, who boasted of the power of job-training and private enterprise in furthering Black advancement, Robinson lauded "the eagerness of these people ... [and] their recognition of the fact that it is one thing to cry out, to picket, to demonstrate for equality and it is equally important to qualify for the 'breaks' when they come to us." Elaborating on his admiration for OIC, Robinson added, "I was [likewise] inspired by the cooperating being given by big business," including General Electric Employee Relations Manager Charles Dates, who spoke alongside Robinson.[90]

Robinson's comments highlight an important development in the rise of Black empowerment politics. While the federal government, via the War on Poverty, provided the majority of funds for programs like OIC, private industry support proved a defining feature of Black empowerment's rise. Business support for Black empowerment was part of a broader shift in corporate America with regard to Black protests. Just several years earlier, amid the selective patronage movement led by Sullivan and other ministers, Philadelphia's white business community found itself under attack by Black activists protesting discrimination. In 1965, speaking with local journalists, Chamber of Commerce executive director W. Thatcher Longstreth boldly proclaimed: "we [can't] afford to let OIC fail."[91] In the span of just a few years, Philadelphia's white business community, mirroring similar developments around the country, moved from vocally criticizing protesters to first quietly and later boldly partnering with Black organizations to promote Black economic empowerment and save US cities from what they perceived as the destruction wreaked by Black Power.

Initially, business and philanthropic support for Black empowerment programs occurred on a relatively small scale. In November 1963, the *Philadelphia Tribune* reported on a series of grants made to OIC from the private sector. Among the contributions was $11,000 from the Philadelphia Foundation; $5,000 from the Smith, Kline, and French Foundation; $2,500 from Scott Paper Company; and nearly $80,000 worth of machinery, equipment, and furnishings from dozens of local businesses, including the Philco Corporation, General Electric, Bell Telephone, the Sharpless Corporation, and International Business Machines.[92] These equipment donations, in particular, significantly cut down on the costs needed to launch the program, while also enabling OIC trainees to practice on the same equipment used by employers.

In time, corporations expanded beyond one-time cash and equipment donations to partner with Black empowerment programs on a deeper, more concrete level. In September 1964, the Western Union Telegraph Company announced it was providing OIC with $10,000 to launch a telecommunications school, with the goal of training students for "immediate absorption into the workforce" in the northeast region.[93] Then, in December 1967, Gulf Oil announced a new partnership with OIC to train gas station attendants and mechanics. The Gulf-OIC partnership revealed a central motivation behind businesses' newfound interest in Black empowerment: access to Black consumer markets. During the 1960s, due in large part to the work of Black marketing firms, a growing number of white-owned companies, including Gulf, launched campaigns to cater to a growing Black consumer market.[94] In 1968, Gulf hired Air Force veteran and Morris Brown College graduate Al Smith to serve as a sales representative for the Black community in Tampa, where he increased Gulf's footprint by recruiting Black dealers "for three stations that had been closed," likely abandoned by their former white dealers during the Tampa riot of 1967. Smith later repeated this process in Atlanta.[95]

The decision to employ Black sales managers and representatives in Black neighborhoods was motivated by more than sales revenue; protecting property likewise mattered amid the ongoing social unrest. The sixties' urban rebellions inspired a number of companies to employ Black managers in their inner-city locations as a means of social insurance. Based on the observation of Black-owned businesses, which placed signs in their windows during the various uprisings, corporate executives reasoned that a store with a Black manager would be less likely to be looted or destroyed during a riot or face boycotts, as in the case of McDonald's decision to partner with Black community organizations in Cleveland and elsewhere.[96]

Similar calculations most certainly informed Gulf's decision to repurpose an old three-bay Gulf Oil station at the corner of 25th Street and Poplar Avenue in North Philadelphia as the site for the new OIC-Gulf Center, transforming an abandoned station into productive property. In addition to the station itself, Gulf donated materials to train OIC trainees in the "fundamentals of service station operation and maintenance," including how to pump gas; change oil and lubricate automobiles; change and repair tires; test, charge, and replace batteries; figure sales tax on purchases; and handle pump island procedures.[97] Under the program, trainees spent six to eight weeks at the training center before being placed at other area service stations, where they continued their on-the-job-training for another sixteen weeks.[98]

Indeed, repurposing "unproductive" industrial space proved a common feature of Black empowerment programs. Long before Clinton's Empowerment Zones, created to attract industry into poor, inner-city neighborhoods, federal and local governments experimented with a similar strategy aimed at attracting US corporations and having them partner with local organizations to promote job-training and economic development in Black neighborhoods in cities across the country. In January 1968, with the blessing of Cleveland's first Black mayor, Carl Stokes, the General Electric Company announced it was donating a 222,598-square-foot plant on Cleveland's predominantly Black east side to support the creation of the Woodland Job Training Center. The building, valued at $5 million, had remained largely unused by GE since 1966.[99] In addition to General Electric, the Center received funding from the Department of Labor. Like OIC, the Woodland Job Training Center combined an emphasis on African American history, with vocational and remedial training, including instruction related to personal hygiene and "good work habits," for Black youth. Under the guidance of James R. Prunty Jr., the center's first director, the Woodland Job Training Center developed partnerships with other companies, including Ford Motor Company.[100]

For corporations, partnerships like these yielded multiple benefits. In exchange for performing a variety of tasks, including assembling thermometers,

Figure 3. Woodland Job Center students Luther Dobbins (left), Michael Colston, and Carlton Banks Jr. with a model of a ranch home they and others built in carpentry classes. Photo by Tim Culek from the Cleveland Press Collections, courtesy of the Michael Schwartz Library Special Collections, Cleveland State University, Cleveland, OH.

salvaging lamps, and welding, Woodlawn trainees received between $2.35 and $2.75 an hour, wages significantly lower than the "prevailing salary levels" trainees hoped to receive once they graduated. These wages were furthermore subsidized and/or reimbursed by grants from the federal government and private foundations like the Martha Jennings Foundation.[101]

They also served to improve corporations' public images, which, during the 1960s, came under increasing fire from civil rights and New Left activists protesting corporations' lack of social responsibility.[102] Speaking on the OIC-Gulf venture, Sullivan hailed the program as "the first partnership of its kind in America," in which "industry and the masses have joined hands for the good of the community." Sullivan's remarks were made at a press conference, where Gulf Vice President E. F. Jacobs described the Gulf-OIC program as evidence of his company's good work "helping to make productive citizens [as part of our] duty and responsibility [as] citizen[s] in Philadelphia."[103] Not long after, in June 1968, Gulf Oil spotlighted their efforts partnering with OIC to train and employ Black salespeople and managers at the *Tribune* Home Service Fair in Chicago. The exhibit featured a replica of the Gulf Oil-OIC service station staffed by a team of Black employees, including Donald A. Young, a dealer development instructor in Washington and Baltimore and a former longtime Philadelphia resident; Paul W. Bennett of the Philadelphia marketing district and Lawrence Edgerson from the Trenton district, both sales representatives and residents of Philadelphia; and Mrs. Olive Richardson, an accounting clerk in Gulf's Eastern Marketing Region office. On display alongside the station was what the *Philadelphia Tribune* described as "an unusual back-lighted panel box showing all of Gulf's 16 Negro dealers in Philadelphia," accompanied by "a small board depicting the grand opening ceremonies of the Gulf-Oil station."[104] The public relations work appears to have paid off. That same week, the *Wall Street Journal* praised Gulf for their "help in the civil rights effort," along with several other major corporations, including General Telephone & Electronics Co., Goodyear, and Ford Motors.[105]

Building on the organization's success partnering with different businesses, in 1969 OIC established the National Industry Advisory Council (NIAC), comprised of representatives from twenty-three major companies and banks and chaired by General Electric chairman Gerald L. Phillippe.[106] In addition to regular contributions of capital and equipment, NIAC members took an active role advising OIC on ways to improve organizational efficiency and cost-effectiveness.[107] Based on the NIAC's recommendation and with their support, OIC adopted a Management Information System (MIS). Widely employed by various kinds of organizations today, management information systems, computer systems used for storing and analyzing large bodies of information in an organization, were relatively uncommon in the late 1960s beyond the US government and large companies with the capacity for a mainframe or minicomputer.[108] In the case of OIC, the organization's acquisition of the MIS system was made possible only with the help of the NIAC, which offered to front the cost. In doing so, the NIAC gave OIC a significant advantage over other community development programs by enabling them to produce large quantities of data desired by funders. At a meeting discussing the implementation of the MIS system, OIC Extension Services Director Elton Jolly boasted about the capabilities of this new managerial tool. "Everything a manager needs to know about his local [including] . . . data such [as] retention rate, number of staff, cost effectiveness, total placement, number of locals" was available with a few clicks of a button.[109] Using MIS, OIC developed immense quantities of statistical data, much of which was compiled into reports sent to the organization's head office and forwarded to OIC's various funders. For example, using MIS, OIC learned that, during 1968, the organization enrolled a total of 36,351 trainees at twenty-six OIC locals across the country. Of those, the organization placed 9,587, or 26 percent, into jobs. Those who found job placements saw their income rise from an average of $2,094 annually to $3,077, on average.[110]

Statistics, as scholars have shown, have long played a crucial role in governing modern society and administering capitalism.[111] Using the information garnered from the MIS, OIC's private and government sponsors expanded their oversight of the organization. Those OIC locals found lacking in "good management," measured by having low numbers of program recruits, job placements, and/or high expenditures, were removed and replaced by those willing to embrace these principles. In April 1968, local anti-poverty officials cited reports of staff disgruntlement and fiscal mismanagement as justification for temporarily shutting down the Los Angeles OIC and suspending its executive director, Oliver Childs, and chief financial officer, Charles Maxey, without pay.[112] Childs was later replaced by Lawrence Aubry. Donning a Masai medallion and sitting in an office featuring the portraits of Malcolm X and Martin Luther King Jr., Aubry exemplified the race consciousness that defined the Black Power era. Aubry also firmly believed in good management. Speaking with reporters about his appointment as the new director of the LA OIC following its run in with auditors, Aubry stated, "There has been a lot of lack of experience here with just taking care of business. . . . This operation simply couldn't continue the way it was. It wasn't sound business."[113] He subsequently worked to get the LA OIC "on a business basis," while emphasizing individual and organizational "accountability," by which he meant a balanced accounting sheet.[114]

Demands for greater accountability permeated the late 1960s. While, rhetorically, OIC touted itself as a community organization, accountable to local residents, structurally, the organization increasingly resembled other nonprofit and for-profit corporations, both of which, by design, privileged the interests of funders.[115] Here was one way of managing Black Power. OIC was one organization. As the Black freedom struggle heated up in the late 1960s, government and business leaders expanded their efforts promoting Black empowerment as a means of stemming the unrest and mollifying Black radicalism. Their efforts were particularly pronounced in cities, where Black Power politics portended to transform the political and economic systems that maintained white supremacy and racial capitalism.

Governing the Black Power City

The late 1960s proved a critical moment for Black Power politics, which, following Malcolm X's advice, began producing gains at the ballot box. In 1967, Carl B. Stokes rode a wave of Black activism to become the first Black mayor of a major US city, where he pursued an ambitious agenda of reforming law enforcement, expanding social welfare, and building Black economic power.[116] One year later, in Philadelphia, local Black Power activists organized the Black Political Forum (BPF) to take on the city's Democratic machine. In 1970, the group invited Richard Hatcher, the recently elected first Black mayor of Gary, Indiana, to keynote the organization's convention, where he told audience members to "get [their] hands on the levers that control power."[117]

Meanwhile, the ongoing rebellion in the streets showed a spotlight on a different, and potentially more volatile, aspect of the Black Power era. According to some estimates, uprisings during 1967 and 1968 alone resulted in 125 deaths, 7,000 injuries, and $127 million in property damage.[118] Those in power were quick to blame the uprisings on Black Power militants. In his July 1967 "Address to the Nation on Civil Disorders," announcing the creation of the Kerner Commission to study the causes of the riots, President Johnson credited "the apostles of violence, with their ugly drumbeat of hatred," for the unrest and vowed "to end disorder" using "every means at [the government's] command."[119] In a memo circulated several days later, the FBI went a step further, claiming Stokely Carmichael and Hubert Gerold Brown (also known as H. Rap Brown), among others, "triggered" the riots that summer with their "exhortations" of "Black Power."[120] Research, including Johnson's own Kerner Commission, revealed deeply entrenched racism and inequality to have played a far greater role in the rebellions.[121] This did not stop the US government from launching an all-out war on radical Black Power activists through expanding the power of law enforcement to go after citizens.[122]

Attempts by Black activists to wield power at the ballot box and in the streets met with staunch resistance from whites. Still, white recalcitrance was not the only strategy employed in response to Black Power politics. Alongside state violence and various other legal and extralegal maneuvering to curtail Black political power, government and business leaders also worked to incorporate would-be Black militants into an American capitalist system. These two responses—government suppression and incorporation—were, moreover, not incompatible. As Sullivan's earlier work combatting juvenile delinquency suggests, Black empowerment politics evolved in conversation with a more punitive politics. Where punitive politics employed violence and intimidation to terrorize Black communities into submission, Black empowerment politics emphasized incorporating would-be Black militants and turning them into "productive" workers and willing capitalists, for whom money-making and liberation were synonymous.

The interplay between state repression and the politics of Black empowerment was on display in an article appearing in the June 1968 issue of *Ebony* magazine, titled "Industry Gives New Hope to the Negro," by *Ebony*'s managing editor Charles L. Sanders. The article began with a reference to the 1967 Detroit uprising and the state's violent suppression of it. "Right after last summer's Black Rebellion, purchasing orders were typed up for $1 million worth of" military equipment—including "100 Stoner machine guns . . . 25 infra-red 'snooper' scopes . . . 5,000 chemical MACE dispensers . . . 9,000 sets of fatigue clothing . . . 500,000 rounds of various kinds of ammunition . . . 8 armored personnel carriers . . . [and] 2 prisoner buses"—all items "the Detroit Common [City] Council thought the city ought to have." "The only item eliminated from the original administration list," according to local activist and head of the Detroit-based People Against Racism, "was the Detroit Air Force, so-called, which was to have consisted of one helicopter and one fixed-wing aircraft."[123] This was one strategy for governing the Black Power city. Sanders quickly shifted gears to highlight another—namely a meeting between local business leaders and Black activists in "that part of Blacktown that had been streaked by fire and now lay in smoldering ruin."[124] The activists were members of the East Side Voice of Independent Detroit (ESVID), run by one-time Black Panther Frank Ditto. Touring the neighborhood with Ditto, "certain things [came] into focus" for the business leaders. "It was just horrible; no wonder people riot," William M. Day, president of Michigan Bell Telephone Company, was later quoted as saying, following the visit.[125] Subsequently, the business leaders joined Governor George Romney and Mayor Jerome P. Cavanagh in forming a thirty-nine-member committee, the New Detroit Committee. Alongside nine Black members, including the head of the NAACP, the majority of the committee members came from the city's white business establishment, including men like Day; Joseph L. Hudson of J. L. Hudson Department Store; William M. Day, president of Michigan Bell Telephone Company; Henry Ford II, chairman of Ford Motor Company; James M. Roche, president of General Motors; and Lynn Townsend, chairman of Chrysler automotive company. In addition to government funds for education and recreational facilities, fair housing, and police reform, New Detroit focused their efforts on "us[ing] business methods and business money to tackle the problems that local politicians and federal programs . . . [had] failed to solve."[126] This was Black empowerment politics, backed by corporate America.

New Detroit's actions paralleled business organizing on a national scale through organizations like the National Alliance of Businessmen, the National Association of Manufacturers, and the Urban Coalition.[127] Co-chaired by Andrew Heiskell, chairman of the board at Time Inc., and civil rights and Black labor organizer A. Philip Randolph, the latter brought together business and civic leaders to address the ongoing urban unrest. Other figures involved in the Coalition included Roy Ash, president of Litton Industries, Henry Ford II, chairman of the Ford Motor Company, James Rouse, president of the Rouse Company, Frederick J. Close, chairman of the board of the Aluminum Company of America, Theodore Schlesinger, president of Allied Stores Corporation, and Asa T. Spaulding, president of the North Carolina Mutual Insurance Company, along with the mayors of Atlanta, Detroit, Chicago, and Philadelphia. At the Coalition's inaugural meeting, held in Washington, DC, in August 1967 and attended by over 1,000 businesspeople and city government leaders, as well as representatives from religious, education, civil rights and labor organizations, the participants outlined a series of objectives, one of which included "a major expansion of the private sector's effort to train and provide jobs for the hardcore unemployed," employing a phrase often used to refer to poor, Black, predominantly male urbanites.[128]

Reaching the "hardcore" was no easy task. Replicating the Ford Foundation's earlier employment of "indigenous leaders," business leaders partnered with various Black organizations. Such partnerships may have given the appearance that business leaders endorsed Black Power. Indeed, some business leaders sought to hide their involvement with such initiatives, fearing such a perception. Expanding on an initial grant of $50,000 to Frank Ditto's ESVID, New Detroit lent its support to an ESVID-initiated community policing program that closely resembled the Black Panther Party, down to its use of all-black uniforms, berets, and combat boots. They also funded an ESVID community cleanup project labeled Project Pride, modeled on a similar program organized by the Young Lords in East Harlem. While the Young Lords' trash cleanup ended in Puerto Rican activists dumping and setting fire to garbage in several intersections to draw attention to governmental neglect of their neighborhood, Project Pride stopped short of embracing such methods, perhaps out of fear they might damage ESVID's relationship with its funders.[129] Even so, ESVID's funders refused to take any chances. In December 1972, New Detroit made future grants conditional on ESVID's willingness to submit to an independent audit and banned the use of New Detroit monies for ESVID's *The Ghetto Speaks* publication, whose endorsement of Ditto for a spot on Detroit's City Council was seen as violating the conditions of ESVID's nonprofit status.[130] Here was a key difference between a radical politics of Black Power—demanding immediate and systematic change to end racism— and Black empowerment, the latter of which increasingly involved working with business executives weary of too much disruption.

Threats of pulled funding and demands to open the books were but two of the many mechanisms through which corporate sponsors worked to dictate the terms of Black empowerment. Business also shaped the post-1960s urban landscape through funding (and thereby elevating) a conservative strain of Black Power politics—one that emphasized self-help, personal responsibility, and, importantly, Black enterprise—over Black militancy and/or other left-wing alternatives. This conservative strain was on full display in the Harlem Commonwealth Council Inc. (HCC), founded in 1967 by Roy Innis and other Black Harlemites. Born in Saint Croix, US Virgin Islands, in 1934, Innis migrated to New York City in 1947, graduating from Stuyvesant High School in 1952. In 1968, Innis was elected national chairman of the Congress of Racial Equality (CORE), overseeing a rightward turn in the organization that saw CORE increasingly embrace Black nationalism and endorse Richard Nixon's candidacy for president, citing the latter's support for "Black economic development" and rejection of social welfare, which Innis decried as "patronizing Band-Aid programs." "Handouts are demeaning. . . . We seek to harness the creative energy of private enterprise . . . to transform the underdeveloped parts of this nation"—liberation through profit.[131]

Similar ideas informed the HCC. Like OIC, HCC owed its founding to the intersection of Black nationalism and the War on Poverty. Initially, HCC's founders proposed to fund the organization with seed money raised from the community in the form of five-dollar voting shares sold to Harlemites. "The [e]ffect would be the creation of a mass-based citizen organization with substantial economic power," they explained. Profits from the HCC would be reinvested in the community, enabling the community to become self-reliant and independent.[132] Instead, contradicting the rhetoric of self-reliance, the initial funding for HCC came in the form of a $50,000 grant from the Office of Economic Opportunity. Later, the organization received support from the Rockefeller Foundation and the Mobil Oil corporation, enabling them to purchase a Mobile gas station.[133] In 1968, HCC partnered with the New York Urban Coalition, in which Innis served, to secure the funds needed to purchase a foundry located at 402 West 126th Street, around the corner from HCC's headquarters at 215 West 125th Street. The Abex Corporation, a manufacturer of control equipment and owner of several other foundries, signed on to provide technical assistance, the Morgan Guaranty Trust Company loaned HCC $50,000, and the Episcopal Diocese of New York lent them another $20,000. Finally, the Coalition itself provided an additional $20,000 through its Venture Corporation, one of two economic development corporations established by the Coalition to aid Black and Puerto Rican businesses in the city.[134] By the mid-1970s, with business's and the government's help, the HCC had grown into a "$32 million corporation," managing a significant portion of "commercial real estate on 125th Street" in Harlem, an indoor shopping mall, an automobile parts manufacturing facility producing parts for General Motors, a company producing supermarket fixtures, and Terrace Sewing Center, selling Singer sewing machines.[135]

A 1977 *New York Times* article captured the political transformation that accompanied the expansion of Black empowerment organizations like HCC and OIC—one sought by the business and government agencies that provided them with the vast majority of their funding. "While the protest leaders of the 1960's often concentrated on dramatic marches, demonstrations and sit-ins," a different "breed of [Black] 'economic-development'" activists are focused on "secur[ing] jobs and establish[ing] income-producing business."[136] While, in this case, the article's author sought to draw a sharp distinction between "Black Power" and "self-help programs" promoting Black empowerment, history proved a bit messier. Alongside HCC's new president, James H. Dowdy, whom, the author stated, "[had] never led a protest march or taken part in a sit-in," the article also spotlighted OIC, whose founder, Leon Sullivan, gained national recognition for protesting racial discrimination in business and some celebrated as "[Philadelphia's] most honored Black Power spokesman."[137]

Messiness—something inherent within every political movement—can be productive. By funding those organizations championing job-training, Black entrepreneurship, and other for-profit ventures over others, businesses and the US government helped mitigate some of the more radical elements of Black Power, including those like the Black Panthers, who sought to take power away from the state and corporations. Such funding, while never enough, likewise proved vital in sustaining Black empowerment programs, enabling them to survive—if not necessarily always thrive—amid a decrease in government anti-poverty spending and the broader economic downturn that occurred during the 1970s and 1980s.

*   *   *

In 1967, President Lyndon B. Johnson—whose War on Poverty provided the fertile soil in which Black empowerment politics began to grow—paid a "surprise" visit to OIC's headquarters in Philadelphia.[138] Led on a tour of OIC by Sullivan, Johnson expressed his unflagging support for the program, noting, "What I have seen this morning has moved me more than I can tell you . . . men and women whose self-respect is beginning to burn inside them like a flame—like a furnace that will fire them all their lives." "[This] movement born of protest has taken the next logical step—to preparation." Invoking a race consciousness frequently associated with Black Power, Johnson continued, OIC "is a place where people find the power that they have always had—power that was always within them." Rather than addressing the very real structural imbalances present in American society, Johnson emphasized individual characteristics, including Black people's "lack of confidence . . . feelings of insecurity . . . [and] self-doubt."[139] Here was Black Power, appropriated by Johnson, stripped of its critique of American liberalism and systemic racism, and remolded into an ideology focused on self-confidence and individual achievement—two key ingredients in the formation of Black empowerment politics.

Another was anti-welfare politics. In 1968, Richard Nixon won a narrow victory over Hubert Humphrey, putting a Republican in the White House for the first time since 1961. Republicans also picked up seats in the House and Senate. Over the next several months, OIC and other Black empowerment programs waited anxiously to see what the new administration would mean for them. As previously mentioned, already by 1966/1967, conservatives in Congress had begun to chip away at the War on Poverty, smearing it as an underwriter of Black radicalism. In late 1969, Congress held hearings on the fate of the Manpower Training Act. During the hearings, Congress heard testimony on several job-training programs that had previously benefited from government funding, including OIC. Testifying on the success of OIC, Pennsylvania congressman Robert N. C. Nix noted that, since its founding in 1964, OIC had trained approximately 50,000 people, 30,000 of whom had been placed in training-related jobs. Many of these trainees, moreover, had previously been on welfare, meaning OIC was saving the US government

Figure 4. Lyndon B. Johnson and Leon Sullivan observe a student working with a machine during the president's visit. June 29, 1967. George D. McDowell Philadelphia Evening Bulletin Photographs, Special Collections Research Center, Temple University Libraries, Philadelphia, PA.

money. "[OIC] has been phenomenally successful [in making] taxpayers out of tax consumers." It had done so, Nix added, at a fraction of the cost of other government-sponsored job-training programs.[140] Nix's testimony found echoes in that of other congresspeople and guests, including Leon Sullivan, who similarly touted OIC as a vehicle for reducing Black Americans' dependence on the government.[141]

The irony was that, by 1969, OIC was receiving approximately $20 million, or 90 percent of its annual operating budget, from the federal government.[142] Rather than social welfare, Sullivan spoke about OIC's budget in market-friendly language, telling Congress:

If OIC is provided the resources to train 100,000 persons for jobs
[in the coming years], it would mean a gain of $66 million annually
to the Government in the form of welfare payment savings; and

> $40 million in additional tax revenue; also, $200 million annually in
> additional income. . . . At the average cost of $1,000 per trainee . . .
> the investment would be returned $3 to $1. . . . Through the medium
> of the OICs, the Nation can turn the corner away from a rising
> "welfare" state for the disadvantaged, to a new "workfare" state of
> self-help for all who are able to work and do a job.[143]

From welfare to workfare, self-help, and return-on-investment, these were
the terms on which OIC and other Black empowerment programs managed
to sustain government and business support amid the mounting backlash
against anti-poverty initiatives.

As OIC and other Black empowerment programs observed, government
and business support frequently came with strings attached, including new
management information systems designed to improve cost-efficiency and
restrictions on how funds could be allocated. Even the threat of pulled funding could act as a deterrent against Black militancy. As the 1960s gave way to
the 1970s, US government and corporate support for Black empowerment
programs continued to aid the process of incorporating Black struggle, align-
ing the interests of Black people and the structure of Black organizations with
American capitalism. This alignment only increased as Black empowerment
made the move from a politics rooted primarily in urban America to one
intertwined with US corporate expansion in Africa.

CHAPTER 4

Empowering Africa

ometime in 1966, Leon Sullivan received an inquiry from a Nigerian physician named Dr. Folorunsho Salawu. Salawu had read of Opportunities Industrialization Center's (OIC) success providing job-training for un- and underemployed Black Americans in the United States and wanted to know about establishing a center in Lagos. With Sullivan's endorsement, Salawu established a steering committee.[1] In August 1968, Sullivan sent OIC director Valo Jordan to Lagos to assess OIC Lagos's prospects.[2] In February 1969, a delegation led by Sullivan and funded, in part, by the US Agency for International Development (USAID) embarked on a multi-week tour of four African countries—Nigeria, Ethiopia, Kenya, and Ghana—to explore the possibility of establishing an OIC program in each country.[3] Not long after, Sullivan addressed his congregation at Zion Baptist regarding his plans.[4] In just a few short years, OIC, which began as a single center in North Philadelphia, had grown into a nationwide program with chapters in over seventy communities across the United States. Even so, the work of empowering the downtrodden was far from over, according to Sullivan. Referencing his recent trip to Africa, Sullivan declared that Africans and Black Americans had been separated for too long, "but we cannot be a people apart or divided at this time or any day to come, for we are brothers," and "[we] . . . must pull together."[5] Henceforth, Sullivan and OIC aimed to empower not just Black Americans, but Black Africans, as well, with the creation of Opportunities Industrialization Centers International (OICI).

First launched in 1969, OICI was just the latest example of Black American engagement with the African continent. This engagement took many forms over the years. Starting in the late eighteenth century and reaching its peak in the mid-nineteenth century, a number of Black Americans, fed up with racism and slavery in the New World, joined the Back to Africa movement, advocating for returning to Africa. In 1815, Paul Cuffe, a wealthy ship captain and philanthropist, led thirty-eight Black American colonists to Sierra Leone, which had recently been designated by the British as a site of relocation for formerly enslaved Africans following Britain's banning of the slave trade. Eclipsing the Sierra Leone colony, an even larger number of Black Americans emigrated to Liberia in a mass movement aided by Black abolitionists like Martin Delany and white supremacists in the American Colonization Society seeking to rid the New World of African-descendant people, particularly free Black people.[6]

While the call for Black Americans to return to Africa never disappeared completely, reappearing in the early twentieth century as a central tenet of Garveyism, the movement increasingly found itself competing with other forms of Black internationalism. The early-to-mid-twentieth century witnessed a flourishing of transnational activity from Black Americans, ranging from W. E. B. Du Bois's involvement with the Pan-African Congress movement, to efforts by Black American women to shape the international women's movement, to the NAACP's campaign for human rights, just to name a few.[7] Following a momentary decline brought on by Cold War anti-communism and a heightened sense of patriotism during and immediately following World War II, Black internationalism came roaring back during the 1960s and 1970s, thanks to the efforts of civil rights and Black Power activists, many of whom drew connections between their own struggle for freedom and the ongoing struggle for decolonization in Africa, Asia, and Latin America.[8] Writing from the Birmingham jail, Martin Luther King Jr. stated: "with his Black brothers of Africa and his brown and yellow brothers of Asia, South America and the Caribbean, the United States Negro is moving with a sense of great urgency toward the promised land of racial justice."[9]

While united in their concern for the wider Black world, Black Americans varied widely in their ideas and approaches to internationalism. Inspired by anti-colonial revolutionaries like Franz Fanon and Che Guevara, groups like the Black Panthers and Malcolm X's Organization of Afro-American Unity expressed solidarity with their Black and Brown brothers and sisters around the world through combating American imperialism in all its manifestations.[10] Making clear their rejection of (white) American culture and politics, many Black Americans adopted African names and/or abandoned the US entirely. This included former Student Nonviolent Coordinating Committee leader and Black Power activist Stokely Carmichael, who, in 1968, changed his name to Kwame Ture and moved to Africa, first settling in Ghana before moving to Guinea in 1969.[11]

Meanwhile, yet another group of Black Americans practiced a kind of Black internationalism that relied on US power and institutions to facilitate racial uplift and Black empowerment. Taking advantage of the US State Department's interest in winning the Cold War in the Third World, Black American jazz musicians like Dizzy Gillespie and lawyers like Thurgood Marshall traveled the world forging connections with African and Asian leaders, all while championing the benefits of American democracy.[12] And then there were people like Sullivan, Johnson & Johnson vice president Harold Sims, and civil rights activist and US ambassador to the United Nations Andrew Young. During the 1970s, building on the ongoing movement in the US, these and other proponents of Black empowerment politics joined the US government and US corporations touting the benefits of American-style free enterprise abroad. In doing so, they were forced to confront Black Africans' own visions of postcolonial development.

One way Black and white Americans worked to reconcile these various visions was through linking Black economic empowerment to a campaign promoting Africa as the "next frontier" of American business. The histories of Black internationalism and US-led economic development programs have frequently been told separately, while the history of post–World War II US corporate expansion into Africa is barely remarked on.[13] The transnational history of Black empowerment politics reveals all three were deeply intertwined. As US government officials and corporate executives worked to promote American-style free enterprise on the continent, they encountered resistance from those promoting socialism and nationalization. In response, both the US Department of Commerce and US corporations frequently relied on Black Americans, including Sullivan, Sims, and Young, to serve as official and unofficial diplomats, smoothing the way for the rise of Black empowerment politics and US corporate imperialism on the continent.[14]

"Not Since . . . Marcus Garvey"—
Africanizing Black Empowerment

Over the years, the story surrounding OICI's origins has shifted. In some versions, Salawu did not approach Sullivan until January 1969, while in the US seeking medical treatment.[15] By that point, OIC's Africa program was well into the planning stages. Indeed, organizational records indicate OIC was in conversation with the US government about developing an Africa program, the initial version of which did not include Nigeria among the list of countries, as early as 1967.[16] Yet Sullivan and others continued to repeat the story of Salawu, turning it into folklore.

Stories, particularly origin stories, connote power. In the case of OICI, Salawu's visit provided a powerful foundational myth that cast the Africa program's beginning as a response to African calls for assistance. Reports on Sullivan's second visit to the continent, in the summer of 1970, reiterated this sense of OICI's African roots. Upon arriving at Ikeja Airport in Lagos, Nigeria, Sullivan encountered "hundreds of Africans [who] waited in the heat of the sun at the airport [holding] a banner welcoming [him]" and his fellow travelers, representing forty OICs in the US. As they walked across the tarmac, one member of the group knelt to kiss the earth, remarking as he did, "Africa, the cradle of my great grandparents, the myth of my fathers and the hope of the Black man."[17] Sullivan reinforced the blood ties linking Black Americans and Black Africans when he told the crowd, "We have come home . . . not as masters or colonialists, not as agents of imperialism, but as your brothers and sisters, as Afro-Americans . . . [as] your soul brothers in deeds."[18] Here and elsewhere, Sullivan appealed to a sense of shared purpose between Black Americans and Black Africans.

Sullivan joined a long list of Black Americans championing Pan-Africanism. Broadly speaking, Pan-Africanism is the belief that African-descended people around the world share not only a common history, but a common destiny.[19] Over the years, Pan-Africanism has evolved to encompass a broad tent, with different flavors and approaches, some, including the Pan-Africanisms of Marcus Garvey and W. E. B. Du Bois, in tension with one another. Educated at some of the most elite universities in the US and Europe, Du Bois spent years appealing to the international community to accept the "Negro race" on equal terms with the other nations of the world. These efforts led Du Bois to organize the 1919 Pan-African Congress, one of several congresses held during the first half of the twentieth century. Over time, Du Bois became more critical of the West, going so far as to embrace socialism and forsake the US for Ghana in the final years of his life. Yet he remained, in many ways, influenced by liberalism and universalist notions of mutual progress and modernity.[20] The early Pan-African Congresses advocated for expanded rights and opportunities for African-descended people within Euro-American society, as opposed to outside it.[21] Garvey, for his part, rejected such universalism, demanding decolonization and independence as preconditions for developing relations of equality.

In the decades following Du Bois's and Garvey's infamous rivalry, Pan-Africanist activists and intellectuals in and beyond the US continued mobilizing in support of global Black liberation. In doing so, many, following Garvey, embraced Black nationalism, a wide-ranging ideology encompassing calls for racial separatism, Black pride, unity, political self-determination, and economic self-sufficiency.[22] Addressing the Organization of African Unity in 1964, having recently departed the Nation of Islam, Malcolm X denounced the "American Government" for failing "to protect the lives and property of your 22 million African-American brothers and sisters. We stand defenseless, at the mercy of American racists who murder us at will for no reason other than we are black and of African descent." Referencing the ongoing Cold War in Africa, Malcolm continued, "we pray that our African brothers have not freed themselves of European colonialism only to be overcome and held in check now by American dollarism. Don't let American racism be 'legalized' by American dollarism."[23] For Malcolm and others, solidarity with Africans meant rejecting US capitalist imperialism, alongside white supremacy.[24]

Those demanding an end to "dollarism" and US imperialism increasingly found themselves competing with another more pro-American, pro-capitalist Black internationalism that celebrated American-style free enterprise as an engine of Black empowerment. Strategically eliding figures like Malcolm X, Stokely Carmichael, and even Martin Luther King Jr., Sullivan laid claim to this more moderate, and more explicitly capitalist, form of internationalism at a rally celebrating the launch of OICI: "Not since the days of Marcus Garvey, one of the great patrons of Africanism, not since the great efforts of W.E.B. Du Bois, has a sensibility been pointed to Africa from [this] country."[25] In place of Malcolm's call for African Americans to help liberate their African brothers and sisters from American capitalist imperialism, Sullivan called on Black Americans to empower Black Africans using American capital and technical know-how. Referencing OICI, Sullivan stated, "the time is not far off when Black [American] technicians, artisans and craftsmen by the thousands and tens of thousands will visit a flourishing Africa, helping to mold that continent into a new greatness glorious to see."[26] Economic development along capitalist lines, not anti-imperialism, took precedence.

In order to begin empowering Africans, Sullivan and OICI needed the support of the US and African governments. In August 1969, OICI signed an agreement with USAID for $5.7 million to help finance the creation of

OICI programs in the four countries visited on Sullivan's initial tour of Africa. This list was later expanded to include Gambia, Sierra Leone, Togo, Liberia, Zambia, and Lesotho.[27] At the same time, Sullivan and other members of OICI's leadership sought approval from various African governments to establish OIC programs in their respective countries. In comparison to the funding received from USAID and other US government departments, OICI requested little in the way of financial support from African governments. OICI's initial request to the Kenyan government, for example, merely asked for their assistance identifying a space, preferably "in or near an industrial complex," for the first OICI center, and for the government to waive customs duties related to the shipment of personal and household effects of OIC staff relocating to Kenya.[28]

Rather than requesting aid, OICI pitched its program to various African governments as helping them meet their economic development and state-building goals. This included some noticeable adjustments. In contrast to OIC America's emphasis on urban areas, OICI touted its role helping stem the wave of rural-to-urban migration through programs geared toward farmers.[29] Elsewhere, including in Nigeria, OICI participated in efforts to reassert "traditional" or chiefly authority over African citizens. Despite the upheavals of the struggles for independence and decolonization, some of which pitted ordinary people against "traditional authorities" vested with power by colonial governments, chiefs retained significant influence in postcolonial Africa, particularly with regard to control and distribution of land and resources.[30] While in Africa, Sullivan did much to ingratiate himself to traditional leaders whom he relied on in promoting OICI. While visiting Lagos, for example, he and other OICI representatives met with local officials at the Oba's Palace on Lagos Island. Converted into an administrative center by Nigeria's first prime minister, Abubaker Tafawa Balewa, the palace had once served as the home to Yoruba chiefs who previously ruled the island.[31] Sullivan put on a similar performance amid festivities celebrating the launch of OIC Ghana. Dressed in kente cloth, he paid homage to Ghana's former Ashanti, Akyem, and Fante royalty, known to have worn this fabric in a toga-like fashion.

Overtime, OICI's networks in Africa expanded to include relationships with a range of different Africans, including military and political leaders. Impressed with what he saw during a visit to OICI-Accra, Ghanaian head of state Colonel I. K. Acheampong declared himself chief patron of the chapter and called for OIC centers to be established in all regions of the country.[32] Sullivan also gained the support of the Organization of African Unity (OAU), an intergovernmental organization founded in 1963 to promote African unity. In February 1969, Sullivan received a signed copy of the OAU Charter from the organization's secretary-general, Diallo Telli, with whom Sullivan struck up regular correspondence.[33] Sullivan's relationship with Telli likely informed his selection of Valfoulaye Diallo to replace Jordan as head of OICI. Diallo was a personal friend of Telli's, and with several other members of the OAU staff. With the OAU's support, Sullivan and Diallo gained introductions to numerous African leaders, as well as an invitation to present to the African representatives to the United Nations, where the minister stressed his desire "to be supportive of the aspirations of Africa," including those for economic development.[34]

Economic development remained a central focus of African and Western governments, including the US, during the 1970s, as it had in the 1960s.[35] Departing from the focus on largescale modernization projects, OICI pitched itself as a community program designed to help individuals and communities address the challenges associated with the demand for skilled labor. "Although the labor pool in most African countries is vastly larger than the existing job market, a great many job vacancies still exist . . . due mainly to the fact that the reservoir of untapped human resource is highly unskilled or unskilled," noted OICI's proposal to USAID for funding.[36] As in the US, OICI likewise emphasized the support it derived from the community in the form of citizens advisory committees and boards of directors comprised of local businesspeople and professionals.[37]

OICI subsequently supplemented local community efforts with financial and technical assistance provided by the home office in Philadelphia. In a call to would-be instructors, OICI encouraged Black Americans from fields like "auto mechanics, building trades, electronics, secretarial science [and/or] management training" to "[do] something constructive to help Black Africa."[38] The call, which evoked centuries-old tradition of Black American missionary work, as well as Pan-Africanism, proved a popular one, attracting Black Power and Black empowerment activists alike. Paralleling Sullivan's efforts developing OICI's Africa program, in 1967, Black Power activist and Student Nonviolent Coordinating Committee (SNCC) executive secretary James Forman traveled to Tanzania as part of a larger SNCC delegation exploring opportunities to collaborate on a similar community economic development program there.[39] SNCC's selection of Tanzania as the base for the organization's Africa program was telling. Earlier that year, Tanzania's governing party, the Tanganyika African National Union, headed by Julius Nyerere, published the Arusha

Declaration, expounding on the party's commitment to African socialism and self-reliance. Subsequently, Tanzania emerged as a major center of Third World radicalism, attracting Black leftists from across the continent and the Americas, including the Caribbean.[40]

Reveling in the chance to see African socialism first hand, Forman remarked: "The freedom with which people talked socialism, armed struggle, the liberation of Africa, was a liberation in itself . . . coming . . . from the repressive atmosphere of the United States."[41] During the visit, Forman met with Nyerere to discuss further collaboration between SNCC and the Tanzanian government, in the form of an Afro-American Skills Bank, later renamed the Pan-African Skills Project (PASP). Launched in 1970, PASP recruited Black Americans—"overseas Africans," in SNCC's terminology—to live and work in Tanzania on temporary government contracts, training Africans. Like OICI, PASP placed a particular emphasis on Black Americans with "industrial skills," including those with experience in engineering and medicine, whose knowledge they perceived as particularly valuable in the context of Africa's postcolonial development.[42]

Skills-training, industrial education—these were strategies that had long permeated Black American outreach efforts, which were variably welcomed and criticized as patronizing by Africans on the continent.[43] Where SNCC and other left-leaning Black Power organizations recruited Black Americans to aid the project of African socialism, OICI found itself drawn toward a different model of economic development, one based on expanding opportunities for private, including corporate, enterprise.

Africa, the Next Frontier for US Business

The expansion of Black-American-led job-training programs into Africa occurred alongside and in conjunction with broader shifts in US approaches to international development. During the 1970s and 1980s, the US moved increasingly away from supporting the kind of large-scale, state-driven international development characteristic of the early Cold War and toward a more small-scale, market-driven approach. This shift was heavily shaped by conservative politicians and economists touting a new ideology celebrating the efficiency of markets over state-driven development.[44]

Subsequently dubbed neoliberalism by scholars and activists, this market-driven approach coincided with the expansion of US business activity on the continent. During the late twentieth century, mirroring Black American empowerment activists, US corporate executives increasingly looked to Africa as the next frontier for American business. In doing so, they benefited from US government assistance, including that provided by USAID and the US Department of Commerce.[45] Starting in the early 1960s, the US Department of Commerce launched a series of trade missions aimed at spurring US investment in Africa. As departmental communications stressed, US corporations had largely been excluded from the continent during colonialism, due to policies that favored European companies. Yet, "[things were] now changing radically." Due to "the substantial removal of dollar import restrictions . . . and the rapid increase in the level of consumption by both private and public sectors [across Africa]," "United States exports have greater prospects for expansion than at any time in the past."[46] The department's optimism was echoed by US Bureau of International Commerce Africa Division director George Dolgin. Playing to Western stereotypes of the continent and its inhabitants, Dolgin described a heightened "tempo of economic activity" with regard to "this overseas frontier for United States businessmen," and encouraged US businesses to act quickly, warning: "those who ignore the drumbeat of Africa's vast marketplace will be missing out on exciting trade and investment opportunities."[47]

Building on the trade missions, the first wave of US investment occurred during the 1960s, including in support of the Volta River Dam in Ghana. First conceived in the early twentieth century, the project subsequently developed as a joint venture between the Ghanaian government, the International Bank for Reconstruction and Development, an Italian consortium known as Impregilo, the US, and the United Kingdom. Meanwhile, the Volta Aluminum Company (VALCO) was created to oversee the accompanying aluminum smelter. While headquartered in Ghana, VALCO operated essentially as a subsidiary of California-based Kaiser Aluminum and Chemical Corporation, which supplied $28.8 million (90 percent) of the initial capital for the company, with the remaining balance covered by another American company, Reynolds Aluminum.[48] Together, Kaiser and Reynolds subsequently used their stake in the plant to negotiate reduced electricity rates, thus guaranteeing a higher return on their investment.

Kaiser Aluminum's and Reynolds Aluminum's involvement in the Volta River Project illustrated a broader trend that saw US corporations profiting from US Cold War investments in Global South development.[49] Speaking on the campaign trail in 1960, John F. Kennedy faulted the Eisenhower administration for neglecting the continent. "We have lost ground in Africa because we have neglected and ignored the needs and aspirations of the African people—because we failed to foresee the emergence of Africa and ally ourselves with the causes of independence."[50] One year later, Kennedy signed the Foreign Assistance Act into law, combining a number of existing economic and technical assistance programs under the newly created US Agency for International Development (USAID).

Any initial hope that USAID might initiate a Marshall Plan for Africa—something called for by many Black Americans and Black Africans—was soon dashed when it came to light that USAID provisioned aid through private organizations.[51] Section 601 of the Foreign Assistance Act (FAA), for example, which outlined the general provisions of the act, called on the US government to "encourage and facilitate participating by private enterprises to the maximum extent practicable."[52] The involvement of private enterprise in development aid was further made possible by various other provisions in the FAA, which enabled the US government to provide loans to American corporations doing business abroad, assistance for surveys, and investment guaranties.[53]

US reliance on private corporations, seen by many as profiting off Africa's misfortunes, quickly turned one-time partners into critics. Feeling betrayed by the US, in 1965, Ghanaian president Kwame Nkrumah famously derided Western aid programs as "neocolonialist traps" intended to "exploit" Africa and forestall its economic development."[54] Elaborating on the concept, which quickly gaining traction across the Third World, Nkrumah wrote: "Old fashioned colonialism is by no means entirely abolished. It still constitutes an African problem, but it is everywhere on the retreat . . . in place of colonialism as the main instrument of imperialism we have today neocolonialism." Neocolonialism, according to Nkrumah, took "various shapes," including military intervention, as seen in the Congo. "More often," he argued, "neocolonialist control is exercised through economic or monetary means."[55]

Following Nkrumah, a growing number of Third World actors criticized an emerging postcolonial political and economic order that enabled the US and other Western nations to prosper from Third World misfortune. In 1974, the United Nations General Assembly adopted the Declaration on the Establishment of a New International Economic Order, articulating a commitment to "equity, sovereign equality, interdependence, common interest and cooperation among all States" and "eliminat[ing] the widening gap between the developed and the developing countries."[56] The declaration coincided with a wave of expropriations of US-owned firms by foreign governments. While, in nearly every case, investors received compensation equal to the value of the property seized, the expropriations served as cause for widespread concern among Western businesspeople and government officials over the "excesses" of decolonization and self-government.[57]

Into this fray stepped Leon Sullivan. Addressing the topic of US investment in Africa in 1973, Sullivan declared that, if US corporations "want to continue their dealings in Africa on a positive basis," they needed to do away with the "colonial concept." Where more radical activists may have meant this as restructuring the international system and/or doing away with the profit-motive altogether, Sullivan asked only that "American businessmen . . . put more [in] than they take out."[58] In other words, US corporations could, in Sullivan's view, avoid neocolonialism and exploitation by supporting Black empowerment.

This included supporting OIC's Africa program. Tapping into his network of corporate executives and financiers, Sullivan contacted former chairman of Chase Manhattan Bank and a longtime OIC supporter George Champion, who joined Sullivan in soliciting US corporate support for OIC's Africa program. In a letter to Henry J. Galbraith, assistant general manager at the Standard Bank, Ltd., in Nairobi, Champion noted: "[Sullivan] has been extremely successful in motivating people . . . here [in the US] and I am sure that the same principle can be just as effective in Nairobi." By way of encouragement, Champion added, "I am sure you will find that any assistance you can give his program will be a very rewarding experience."[59] Champion's comments alluded to the cultural work OICI and other Black empowerment organizations performed smoothing the way for American businesses on the continent.

As fears of nationalization and anti-Western sentiment increased, US corporations turned to Black-American-run empowerment programs like OICI to help them mitigate Third Worldism, a politics promoting solidarity among former African, Asian, and Latin American colonies, anti-imperialism, and self-determination.[60] In 1974, OIC-Ghana announced a new partnership with Texaco Oil to launch a training program for auto mechanics in Ghana. Echoing Champion's white-savior rhetoric, Texaco manager W. K. McNulty exclaimed, "We are convinced that the OICG is doing a good job, providing hope for the otherwise hopeless."[61] McNulty's comments and a picture of the training center were printed in a company bulletin touting Texaco's generosity.

OIC's strategy of partnering with US corporations to empower Africans paralleled that of other Black American organizations, including the African-American Institute (AAI). Founded in 1953 by Lincoln University president

Horace Mann Bond and Howard University president William Leo Hansberry, AAI initially provided scholarships for Africans to study in the US. During the 1950s, the organization received funding from the CIA, which recruited Harold Hochschild, president of the American Metal Company, Dana Creel, head of the Rockefeller Brothers Fund, and Alan Pifer, head of the Carnegie Corporation, to lead the project.[62] In time, however, AAI sought to distance itself from the agency in an effort to bolster its legitimacy. By the late 1960s, AAI had embraced a somewhat new direction focused on economic development.[63]

With AAI's new focus on economic development came an additional role: facilitating ties between corporate America and African leaders. This role was developed under the leadership of William R. Cotter, who, on multiple occasions, stressed the importance of US private investment in Africa.[64] During the 1960s and 1970s, AAI collaborated with US corporations, providing information on conditions in Africa, recruiting local managers to serve in the African operations of US companies, and, crucially, facilitating communication between US companies and African governments.[65] In 1968, AAI launched its annual conference, bringing together government officials, politicians, civil rights activists, philanthropists, and business leaders from Africa and the US to discuss developments on the continent. At AAI's ninth conference, held in Lesotho from November 29 to December 2, 1976, the list of attendees included J. Wayne Fredericks of Ford Motor Company, Melvin J. Hill of Gulf Energy and Minerals Company, Robert M. Hoen of Chase Manhattan Bank, Voter Education Project director and civil rights activist John Lewis, Leteane Modisane of the South African Students Organization, several members of Congress, including Charles Diggs Jr., and future president Joseph Biden.[66] The conferences, combined with private meetings facilitated by AAI, went a long way toward aiding US private investment on the continent. In 1972, for example, AAI facilitated a meeting between US business leaders and representatives of Mozambique's independence movement, including members of FRELIMO, MPLA, and FNLA.[67] Elsewhere, AAI facilitated "private exchanges between executives from Chase Manhattan Bank, Mobil and Exxon Oil, Newsweek, Johnson & Johnson, and Westinghouse Corporation with President Bongo of Gabon, Nigerian Commission for External Affairs Brigadier Joseph Garba, president Khama of Botswana, and Kenyan Foreign Minister Waiyaki."[68] Elaborating on AAI's new role diplomatizing on behalf of corporate America, Cotter noted, "We believe [these communications to be] beneficial not only for AAI and American industry but for Africans as well since it helps them to further their national development goals."[69] Here and elsewhere, Black empowerment politics went hand in hand with US corporate expansion.

In addition to its role mediating between US corporations and African governments, AAI operated a number of education and manpower development programs. Many of these programs served the interests of American businesses through providing training. In a letter to Johnson & Johnson, one of AAI's corporate sponsors, Cotter explained that over 90 percent of the students trained through AAI returned to Africa, where they "provide[d] the new industrial community, including US industries, with the much-needed skills of engineers, economists, business managers and highly-trained technicians."[70]

Through their interactions with organizations like OICI and AAI, US corporations increasingly came to appreciate the utility of Black empowerment politics. Touted as an outgrowth of solidarity between Black Americans and Africans, Black empowerment organizations provided US corporations with an additional tool to contend with Third World challenges to an emerging and dynamic postcolonial global political and economic order. Mirroring the rhetoric of Black empowerment activists like Sullivan and Cotter, these corporations framed private investment as complimentary to Africa's postcolonial economic development. This argument only garnered further traction with the rise of Black American executives as corporate ambassadors in the 1970s and 1980s.

Corporate Diplomacy

In late 1972, Harold R. Sims sat in his office in the executive suite and surveyed the scene at Johnson & Johnson's headquarters in New Brunswick. A decade earlier, this scene, a Black man occupying an executive position at one of the country's leading companies, would have been difficult to imagine. Born July 25, 1935, in Newnan, Georgia, the youngest of four, Sims attended Southern University in Baton Rouge, Louisiana, where he joined the Alpha Phi Alpha fraternity. After college, Sims enlisted in the US Army, which, thanks to A. Philip Randolph and the March on Washington Movement, had begun the process of desegregation. Sims played an important role in furthering desegregation when he was appointed the Army's Black general officer of Promotion and Equal Opportunity Programs, in 1967. Sims subsequently used this experience to launch himself into the world of management, occupying a series of administrative roles, first as executive secretary to Sargent Shriver in the Office of Economic Opportunity, then as acting executive director of the National Urban League, and finally as head of Corporate Affairs at Johnson & Johnson.

Sims's career trajectory mirrored that of other Black professionals who benefited from the transformation wrought by civil rights and Black Power activists. The list included E. Frederic Morrow, a fellow Alpha Phi Alpha and World War II veteran, who, in 1952, became the first Black American to hold an executive position in the White House, serving under Dwight Eisenhower. In 1964, Morrow became the first Black American vice president of Bank of America. Or James S. Avery Sr., a former teacher, who was recruited in 1956 by Esso Standard Oil as a public relations manager tasked with aiding the company on "programs relating to minority groups." Avery subsequently received several promotions and by the early 1970s had become the highest-ranking Black executive in the oil industry.[71] And then there was Sullivan. Following years of working alongside some of the nation's leading businessmen, Sullivan was named to the board of General Motors—then the world's largest corporation—in January 1971. The appointment, the first of a Black American to the board of a major Fortune 500 company, garnered widespread media attention.[72]

As Black Americans increasingly made their way into the executive offices of US multinational corporations, a significant number of them found themselves acting as official and unofficial ambassadors for corporate America. One year following his historic appointment, in January 1972, Sullivan informed reporters that GM had plans to establish "plants . . . in several African countries—*Black* African countries." Emphasizing the opportunity GM's expansion created for Black empowerment, Sullivan continued, "I can't go any further on this, but it will happen. When it does, I will want to see General Motors get more involved in the communities where their plants are located in terms of housing or educational systems and opportunities, even beyond the public educational systems."[73] Subsequently, Sullivan's efforts empowering Africans intertwined with his work diplomatizing for GM and other US corporations on the continent.

Like Black American jazz singers and athletes, who traveled to Africa on behalf of the US State Department, Black American executives functioned as ambassadors for corporate America. Some companies, including Bank of America, made this role more explicit than others. When the Bank appointed Morrow as vice president in 1964, bank executives suggested that they "[were] not interested in [Morrow] becoming an ordinary factotum." Rather, the company sought to take advantage of Morrow's relationship with African leaders and envisioned Morrow in "a role akin to that of a roving international ambassador."[74]

Not all Black American business diplomats were on the payroll of US corporations. Indeed, perhaps one of the most effective corporate ambassadors during the 1970s was someone who initially chose a career in government, as opposed to the private sector: Andrew Young. Having previously served alongside Martin Luther King Jr. as executive director of the Southern Christian Leadership Conference, Young epitomized the shift from protest to politics when he ran and was elected to represent Georgia's 5th district in Congress in 1970.[75] He was subsequently elected three times to the US House of Representatives. In 1977, President Jimmy Carter appointed Young to serve as the US ambassador to the United Nations, where, among other things, he garnered attention for helping negotiate an end to the Zimbabwean War for Independence.[76]

Young's position as US Ambassador to the United Nations gave him frequent opportunities to meet with African leaders, whom he courted on behalf of the US government and American business. In October 1979, on his last formal trip as US ambassador, Young led one of his most important visits to the continent, a trade mission, which included over two dozen US businessmen. Speaking at a press conference on the mission, Young inverted the argument made by Nkrumah and others regarding neocolonialism by drawing attention to the mutual benefit of American investment. "America has the best talent and technology to offer in the whole world. . . . It is about time that we profited from this—that African nations profited from our abilities," stated Young.[77]

Young's words resonated with J. Bruce Llewellyn, who held the distinction of being the first Black American to serve as president and chief executive officer of the Overseas Private Investment Corporation. Llewellyn helped co-organize the trip with Young and Export-Import Bank president John L. Moore, where he made it his mission to promote Black American business in the Third World.[78] Like Llewellyn, Young showed particular interest in helping Black American executives make inroads in Africa. This represented the for-profit side of Black internationalism. His views were shared by those Black American businessmen who accompanied him on the trade mission. "Let's face it," stated Clarence Avant, president of Tabu Productions Inc., a Los Angeles recording and consulting firm, and trade mission participant. "In the United States, most Black businesses are very small and their growth is limited. Africa offers a chance to come into the economic system in a major way."

A. Theodore Adams Jr. of Unified Industries similarly called on Black American businesspeople to use their Blackness to advance their business. "We have a Black connection" rooted in a shared experience of racism. "Let's use it," stated Adams. In total, Black businessmen comprised nearly 30 percent of the twenty-two Americans accompanying Young on his tour of Africa in 1979.[79]

Young and Llewellyn's business diplomacy paid dividends for Black-American-owned business. Thus, for example, Avant returned to the US with an agreement to serve as Tanzania's consultant on motion pictures and recordings. Demonstrating his versatility as a businessperson, Avant also secured a contract to market meerschaum pipes produced by the Tanganyika Meerschaum Corporation.[80] Other Black American businessmen landed similar deals, such as Adams Jr. and Thomas A. Wood, whose TAW International Leasing Inc., secured a $60 million contract to lease transportation equipment in Uganda. Reinforcing this pro-capitalist strain of Black internationalism, Ugandan president Godfrey Lukongwa Binaisa praised Young's skill as a broker, noting, "I have been influenced to a very good extent by Andy Young more than any other Black American I've ever met. . . . I think the potential of relations between Black America and Black Africa is so great

Figure 5. Concluding a $60-million business deal, TAW President Thomas A. Wood (right) and Ugandan President Godfrey Lukongwa Binaisa (left) shake hands. *Jet*, October 18, 1979, 21. Photograph by Moneta Sleet Jr. Credit: Johnson Publishing Company Archive. Courtesy J. Paul Getty Trust and Smithsonian National Museum of African American History and Culture. Made possible by the Ford Foundation, J. Paul Getty Trust, John D. and Catherine T. MacArthur Foundation, the Andrew W. Mellon Foundation, and Smithsonian Institution.

that some people just fail to realize how great and fruitful it could be if they are fully exploited."[81] Ofield Dukes, president of a Black-American-owned public relations firm, similarly praised Young, stating, "Ambassador Young opened new doors of opportunity for American business in general and for minorities in particular."[82]

Dukes's comments may have been a bit overly optimistic. More often, Black American business diplomacy worked for large, predominantly white-owned multinationals. Such was the case for the Houston-based Pullman-Kellogg Company, a subsidiary of Pullman Inc., which by many accounts reaped the biggest deal of the 1979 trade mission, in the form of a $500 million contract to build a chemical fertilizer manufacturing plant in Nigeria. For several years, Pullman-Kellogg had been struggling to secure the contract, faced with strong competition from an Italian firm. It took Andrew Young to seal the deal. "We've got the best salesman in the world working for us," stated company executive vice president E. Newbold Black IV, speaking of Young.[83] Other US multinationals represented on the trip, including Consolidated Petroleum Industries, Excel Mineral Company, International Harvester Company, Motorola Inc., Western Electric Corp., and General Electric. Co. likewise benefited from Young's diplomacy.

Figure 6. Showing appreciation, E. Newbold Black IV, company executive vice president at Pullman-Kellogg (left) thanks US Ambassador Andrew Young (right), who helped him win a $500 million Nigerian fertilizer contract. *Jet*, October 18, 1979, 22. Photograph by Moneta Sleet Jr. Credit: Johnson Publishing Company Archive. Courtesy J. Paul Getty Trust and Smithsonian National Museum of African American History and Culture. Made possible by the Ford Foundation, J. Paul Getty Trust, John D. and Catherine T. MacArthur Foundation, the Andrew W. Mellon Foundation, and Smithsonian Institution.

For Young and other proponents of Black empowerment politics, this was okay, if not favorable. Here and elsewhere, Black empowerment took many forms, including jobs, managerial training, corporate philanthropy, as well as Black enterprise. Speaking about the 1979 trade mission, Young emphasized the potential for US-Africa trade to reduce the trade deficit and produce more jobs for Black people in the US and Africa, regardless of whether it was at a large multinational corporation or Black-owned enterprise.[84]

Many Africans felt differently, arguing that it was not enough for foreign companies to employ Africans. Africans needed to control business. Only then would they be rid of colonialism. As a result, beginning in the 1950s, African nations adopted policies of Africanization, a broad term referring to the promotion of Black Africans to positions of management and ownership. The private sector was slower to embrace Africanization than the public sector; thus, in 1962, in Ghana the civil service was run nearly entirely by Black Africans, while they comprised only 40 percent of management in the United African Company, a subsidiary of Unilever. The percentage was even worse in nearby Nigeria.[85]

Unlike nationalization, Africanization left room for foreign companies to continue investing in Africa, pending their employment of Africans in decision-making positions. One such corporation that experimented with Africanization in the 1970s was Harold Sims's Johnson & Johnson. Founded in 1886 as a medical supply company, Johnson & Johnson subsequently grew into an all-out healthcare company, researching and producing pharmaceuticals, following its acquisition of McNeil Laboratories (the producers of Tylenol), Chemical Industry Laboratory AG (also known as Cilag), and Janssen Pharmaceuticals. The company's initial forays abroad began in 1930, when it established operations in Mexico and South Africa. From the 1930s through the 1960s, with the exception of South Africa, Johnson & Johnson concentrated its international growth elsewhere in the world, including Latin America, which, along with the Caribbean, witnessed a rapid rise in US investment during the first half of the twentieth century.[86] It wasn't until the late 1960s that the corporation set its sights once again on Africa, with the launch of Johnson & Johnson Nigeria (1969), Johnson & Johnson East Africa (1970), and Johnson & Johnson Zambia (1973).[87] Johnson & Johnson's presence later grew to include affiliates in Tanzania, Mozambique, Egypt, and the Ivory Coast.

Like other US companies, Johnson & Johnson turned to Black Americans within the corporation to advise them on navigating the political and economic uncertainties associated with doing business in post-independence

Africa. Initially hired in 1972 to oversee corporate relations with minorities in the US, Sims received a promotion in 1975 to vice president of Corporate Affairs.[88] Along with the new title came new responsibilities, including liaising between the company and various African governments. Sims hired a young Kenyan and Rutgers Business School graduate student, Robert A. Obudho, to help him research conditions on the continent. In November 1975, Obudho completed his initial report. All in all, Obudho conveyed a favorable outlook for Africa and the corporation's plans to expand its outreach to "[Black] African markets." Despite widespread economic instability and "general poverty," Africa was ripe for business, Obudho noted. This was due, in part, to ongoing urbanization and decolonization, both of which contributed to a growing African middle class. Nor, according to Obudho, should company executives ignore the benefits of international development. In his report, Obudho remarked that contributions of Organization for Economic Co-operation and Development countries (including the US), the World Bank, and the International Monetary Fund (IMF) together accounted for a 31 percent increase in development aid, from $586 million in 1967–1968 to $768 million in 1971–1972.[89] This dramatic influx in development aid was bound to enhance Johnson & Johnson's profits, through sales and government contracts related to the expansion of healthcare on the continent.

Still, it was important not to look at Africa with rose-colored glasses. Reflecting a broader weariness within corporate America, Obudho warned Johnson & Johnson officials of ongoing "political and economic uncertainties on the continent," alluding to the ascendant politics of African socialism and African nationalism. Cautioning against a business-as-usual approach, Obudho counseled company executives that Johnson & Johnson must do all it can to "avoid looking foreign." "Under no circumstances should our distribution be a foreign company or a company managed, directed, or owned by non-Black Africans. . . . All distribution of our products MUST be done by Africa-owned and managed local companies." Within ten years, local plants should be "fully manned by able Africans."[90] In other words, Johnson & Johnson must embrace Black empowerment or risk more extreme measures (i.e., government-enacted Africanization or nationalization).

Johnson & Johnson executives, for their part, appear to have largely heeded Obudho's and, by extension, Sims's advice, incorporating Black economic empowerment as part of their business dealings on the continent.[91] One way they did this was through partnering with AAI. In 1976, the company established a special fund to support the nonprofit's education and job-training programs on the continent.[92] In exchange for its financial support, AAI signed a commitment "to assist J&J in its business development, social responsibility efforts in Africa."[93] This relationship proved critical to Johnson & Johnson's success in Africa. In 1977, for example, amid an ongoing civil war in Angola, AAI Vice President Frank Ferrari met with the Angolan permanent representative to the United Nations, Elisio de Figueiredo. Among the issues the two discussed was the reopening of Johnson & Johnson's facility in Angola, for which Figueiredo expressed his support. Ferrari subsequently relayed his conversation to Johnson & Johnson executives in a letter that made explicit the nature of the relationship. Having done his part diplomatizing with the Angolans, Ferrari thanked Johnson & Johnson for their promise of a $5,000 grant and expressed his hope that the funds would reach AAI soon.[94] AAI's work opening the door for corporate America in Africa paid dividends in the form of corporate sponsorship of its programs.

In other instances, Johnson & Johnson relied directly on its most senior Black executive, Sims, to complete the "very sensitive" work, in the words of company president John J. Heldrich, of representing the corporation on the continent.[95] Some of Sims' most effective diplomacy took place in Zambia. Like other African nations, the Zambian government pursued a series of development plans following independence in an effort to improve the standard of living of its citizens. These plans depended heavily on profits derived from the country's copper mines. In 1975, a global decline in copper prices resulted in a massive decline in export earnings, threatening the government's national development plan. In an effort to keep capital flowing into the country, the government agreed to loans from the IMF.[96] At the same time, Zambian President Kenneth Kaunda announced plans to increase private investment. Speaking at the Zambia Trade Fair in July 1978, Kaunda noted "loans on their own cannot induce economic revival." Rather, they must be accompanied by "industries that can generate profit" and solve the country's balance of payments problem.[97]

Not long after Kaunda's speech, Sims met with the president in Zambia to "discuss the present and future potential of J&J as a responsive and responsible multinational in Zambia."[98] During the three-hour meeting, which took place at Kaunda's home, Sims and Kaunda worked to reconcile the interests of Johnson & Johnson and the Zambian government. In an effort to persuade the latter to relax its restrictions on importing raw materials and employing locals, which were necessary, from the company's perspective, to "maximize its various economic functions within Zambia," Sims stressed Johnson &

Johnson's commitment to aiding Zambia's economic development. Countering neocolonial critiques of US multinationals, Sims argued that profit did
not need to come at the expense of Black liberation. Instead, Sims used the
language of "people-centered capitalism" to describe how Johnson & Johnson "maximize[d] its economic performance" while simultaneously serving
"as a productive and constructive social force in the continuing development of the Zambian nation and its people."[99] Sims's argument to Kaunda
echoed an earlier letter to Zambia Minister of Foreign Affairs Siteke Mwale.
In that letter, Sims went to considerable lengths to frame Johnson & Johnson's
actions as responding to the aspirations of the Zambian government, writing,
"I have given long and serious thought to *your* [Mwale's] dream of making
the Republic of Zambia a center for export activity . . . and of *your* desire that
J&J take a leadership role in making this happen" (emphasis added).[100] This
was the work of a Black American business diplomat: convincing Africans
that US corporations were socially responsible by highlighting the ways they
facilitated African development and Black empowerment.

Debating Aid, Contracting US Imperialism

Between July 1, 1975, and June 30, 1976, OIC Lagos trained a total of 171
people, exceeding the chapter's annual goal of 169. A good number of the
trainees, fifty-nine, were placed by the program, excluding those who found
jobs and failed to report them to OIC.[101] The branch's success mirrored that of
OIC's Africa program, more broadly, which, by the mid-1970s had enrolled
several thousand Africans in courses in automobile repair, masonry, carpentry, electricity, etc., across its various programs.[102] Actual job placement rates
varied by country. Some of the most successful OICIs averaged hundreds of
placements per year.[103]

Despite producing results, OICI faced increased scrutiny alongside other
USAID-funded programs. Paralleling the attack on domestic anti-poverty
programs during the 1970s, conservatives led an attack on foreign aid to
the Third World, including Africa, which threatened Black-American-led
empowerment programs like OICI. In an effort to reign in "excessive" spending and improve efficiency, the US government utilized a familiar tool—contracts—to shape Black empowerment projects at home and abroad.

The Senate's 1971 rejection of the Nixon administration's foreign aid
authorization bill proved an early sign of the trouble that would come to

surround USAID and, by extension, the Black empowerment programs that depended on it for funding.[104] It marked the first time that a chamber of Congress had voted down a presidential foreign aid request. Two years later, in 1973, Congress amended the Foreign Assistance Act to require that US foreign aid programs undertake "new directions." These "new directions" included a shift away from long-term operational support to short-term, project-specific grants, the effect of which was to give USAID greater control over grantees and was part of a broader shift in Congress away from supporting large-scale development.[105]

Things came to a head for OICI in 1974. Concerned about the potential of losing funding, OICI turned to long-time friend of the organization and chairman of the African Affairs Subcommittee of the Foreign Relations Committee, Senator Hubert H. Humphrey (Democrat of Minnesota), who directed USAID to grant $3 million for OICI. The directive was subsequently approved by Congress. No sooner had Congress authorized the additional funding for OICI then critics voiced their objections. In February 1975, *The Washington Post* published a front-page article lambasting Humphrey and calling the $3 million "extravagant." One USAID official was quoted saying that the "congressional directive" had placed the agency "in an extraordinarily difficult position" by hampering their ability to deny funding to projects deemed ineffective.[106] Sullivan, for his part, was quick to point out the hypocrisy of these claims. Evoking the antiwar movement, Sullivan charged: "The government will spend billions of dollars in South Vietnam, Cambodia, South Korea and the Far East, but quarrel about a measly $3 million for Africa."[107] Humphrey, too, chimed in, noting that "[OICI had] received praise from African leaders for its efforts. It is the type of private people-to-people program which belongs in an American foreign aid program over burdened by military assistance." "If this organization has management problems, the Agency for International Development . . . should provide it with assistance," he added, throwing responsibility for any inefficiencies back on the US government.[108]

Similar criticism plagued OIC's domestic program. As part of its embrace of New Federalism, the Nixon administration oversaw a number of changes to US government anti-poverty and job-training programs. This included the 1973 Comprehensive Employment and Training Act (CETA), which replaced the Manpower Training Act initiated by the Kennedy administration and supported by Johnson. Under CETA, responsibility for administering job-training shifted from the federal government to the states. This posed a significant challenge to OIC, which previously had received up to 90 percent of its funding from the federal government, including the departments of Labor and Health, Education, and Welfare.[109] In a series of Congressional hearings held between 1973 and 1975, Sullivan and his supporters testified to the decline in government funding for the program as a result of CETA. Without special provisions, "as many as 80 [OIC centers] could be wiped out" as a result of the shift "from national emphasis to local control programming," stated Sullivan. Meanwhile, other OIC programs faced mergers and funding cuts that threatened to destroy the comprehensive nature of OIC, including its unique Feeder Program.[110]

At stake in the debates about domestic and foreign assistance was more than just the level of funding. Control over aid recipients was equally, if not more, important. During the hearings debating government support for job-training, multiple members of Congress questioned whether state governments were not better positioned to determine the efficacy of local OIC programs in their states, implying the OIC national office lacked the ability to adequately assess its various chapters. Sullivan, unsurprisingly, disputed such claims, firing back: "We do not have a monitoring problem." Any problems experienced by local OICs were due to "cutbacks" in funding. In cases where OIC was given adequate "resources . . . [the organization] had fewer problems."[111] Yet skepticism, and close observation of OIC, persisted. In April 1976, Sullivan received notice of an audit of OICI alongside several other USAID grant recipients. The accompanying report confirmed that "OICI program objectives appear[ed] to be in complete agreement with the goals and objectives of the Foreign Assistance Act." Nevertheless, government officials took issue with a number of aspects of the program, including the organization's accounting system, property records, and various expenditures, many of which were detailed in a series of attachments accompanying the report.[112] In essence, the government was accusing OICI of mismanagement.

Accusations of mismanagement coupled with threats to cut funding continued to hound OIC and OICI throughout the 1970s, as they did many Black organizations. While pushing back on some of the accusations, the threats to OIC's funding resulted in the organization doubling down on its association with the US government. This, in turn, increasingly created other problems for OIC, not least of which included activists protesting US foreign policy in southern Africa. For years, the US government had ignored the rise of white supremacist violence in southern Africa, where the Portuguese, Rhodesian, and South African governments fought fiercely to stave off majority

rule. Domestic protests, combined with growing fears of the spread of communism during the 1970s, however, prompted the US government to take
greater notice.[113]

In the spring of 1976, on the eve of President Ford's reelection campaign,
US Secretary of State Henry Kissinger, with Ford's approval, announced a
landmark tour of the continent. The aim: to convince African leaders of US
support for decolonization and democracy in Africa. Kissinger's first stop was
Tanzania, where he met with President Nyerere. During the visit, Kissinger
made the rare gesture of apologizing to Nyerere for the mistakes made by
the US in Vietnam, while also soliciting Nyerere's support in opposing Soviet
and Cuban intervention in southern Africa.[114] The secretary made similar
overtures in Zambia, a country that quickly garnered attention for its support
for anti-colonial movements in the region. Speaking in Lusaka, Kissinger
proclaimed a "new era in American policy" toward Africa. Going forward,
"Black and white people" must work together to bring about a new era of
peace, well-being, and human dignity, declared Kissinger. According to some
reports, Kissinger's remarks prompted an emotional Kenneth Kaunda, leader
of the Zambian African National Congress and Zambia's president, to shed a
tear as he embraced the secretary.[115]

Kissinger's seeming new tone received a warm welcome from OIC, which
honored the secretary by awarding him the keynote address at OIC's twelfth
annual convocation in Philadelphia. The convention, like others before it,
attracted an "impressive list of guest speakers," including representatives of
local and state governments, civil rights groups, businesses, and other organizations. As secretary of state, Kissinger was among the most notable attendees and the highest-ranking US government official to date to deliver the
convocation's keynote.[116] In his speech, Kissinger reiterated previous warnings about the dangers of communism and the need to forestall a race war
in southern Africa through efforts to negotiate a transition to majority rule
in Rhodesia and independence for Namibia, which had been governed ille-
gally by South Africa since 1966. Some of his most poignant words centered
on the economy. "It is economic progress which ultimately will determine
whether Africa can fulfill the aspirations of its peoples," stated Kissinger,
echoing the pronouncements of Black empowerment activists like Sullivan
and Young. In a variation of an analogy often used to bolster calls for Black
economic empowerment, Kissinger stated "it's no good being able to join
the country club if you haven't got the money to buy a drink." Dollars, not
weapons, were the real key to Black progress, and "OIC" with its "vocational

training [program designed] to teach the skills that Africa needs" was the key to helping Africans "realize [their] potential regardless of changing political circumstances."[117]

Not everyone was convinced. Outside of the Philadelphia convention center, where OIC's convocation took place, a group of picketers welcomed attendees with signs proclaiming "Kissinger's Africa Policy is Racist." Many of the activists belonged to the Patrice Lumumba Coalition (PLC). Taking its name from the former Democratic Republic of Congo president, widely suspected of having been murdered with CIA assistance, the PLC was emblematic of a radical, anti-imperialist Black left, which continued to protest neocolonialism and American capitalism well into the 1970s. Rejecting Kissinger's claims to be working on behalf of Africans, Tapson Mawere, a member of the PLC and the Zimbabwe African National Union, declared, "We know Kissinger is connected with the Rockefellers who provide funding for the US corporations who support the minority regimes that have robbed us of our land and resources."[118] The PLC's criticism, moreover, did not stop with Kissinger. Preaching to the crowd gathered outside the Philadelphia convention center, Black nationalist and director of Philadelphia's Black Economic Development Conference Muhammad Kenyatta declared, "Blacks [like Sullivan] who support Kissinger's African policy" were nothing more than sellouts, "repaying debts from white corporate financial support."[119] Similar claims appeared in an earlier manifesto released by the PLC in August 1976, in which the group boldly declared that "there [was] no substitute for revolutionary warfare as the path to genuine independence," including in South Africa, where the government's recent slaughter of high school students protesting apartheid in what came to be known as the Soweto Uprising gave the lie to the US position that the white-minority government represented a legitimate power. The same document likewise derided Black American leaders, including Sullivan, Clarence Mitchell of the NAACP, Vernon Jordan of the National Urban League, former Black Panther Eldridge Cleaver, the Reverend Jesse Jackson, and Bishop H. H. Brookins of the People United to Save Humanity (PUSH), as apologists for US imperialism and white supremacy on the continent.[120]

During the late 1970s, the divisions between different groups of Black internationalists became more pronounced in relation to US policy in southern Africa. Building on the anti-imperialism of Black Power activists, radical Black internationalists like those in the PLC aligned themselves with anticolonial armed resistance and against US capitalist imperialism.[121] Echoing Nkrumah, many of these same activists critiqued US aid as merely giving

cover to white-supremacist rule in southern Africa and demanded reparations and divestment.[122]

This vision, one adopted by left-wing and Third World activists around
the world, increasingly came up against another kind of Black internationalism, which saw US capital as a vehicle for Black empowerment. Speaking
to protesters, Sullivan asserted his commitment to fighting white supremacy and racism, noting, "I used to be on the picket line myself." Times had
changed, he claimed. OIC's "convocation [was] not designed for debate, but
to have people in governmental position express their views and policies to
the community."[123] For Sullivan and other Black American diplomats, now
was not the time for protest. Rather, now was the time for joining hands with
the US government and business to empower Africans.

*   *   *

By 1976, with the help of the US government and American corporations,
OICI was operating in four African countries—Ghana, Nigeria, Ethiopia,
and Kenya—and had established interest groups in over a half-dozen others,
including Togo, Sierra Leone, Gambia, Lesotho, Botswana, and Liberia.[124]
Despite the protestations of conservatives in Congress, OICI continued to
receive funding from USAID, which it supplemented with contributions from
community members and local businesses.[125] In doing so, OICI joined other
Black American empowerment organizations, including AAI, in providing
opportunities for thousands of Africans to gain job-training and business
know-how.[126]

The rise of US-sponsored Black empowerment organizations in Africa
coincided with a concurrent expansion in US-Africa business. In May 1976,
The New York Times used Kissinger's visit to the US as an occasion to publish
a multi-page spread on US private investment in Africa. In just a little over a
decade, US private investment on the continent had grown to over $3.7 bil-
lion.[127] Of particular interest, the article noted the growing rate of investment
and trade with Black Africa—that is, countries governed by Black Africans, as
opposed to white-ruled South Africa and Rhodesia. Despite concerns stemming from the partial nationalization of oil companies in Nigeria, US companies retained more than $2.2 billion or 60 percent of their total assets and
conducted more trade with countries other than South Africa and Rhodesia,
a dramatic change from prior decades.[128]

During the 1970s, these two trends—US-sponsored Black empowerment and US private investment in Africa—reinforced one another. As they had in the US, Black empowerment organizations like OIC relied on donations from business, including US multinational corporations, to supplement the funding they received from the US government. Indeed, business support for OIC and AAI helped them make the case for assistance from the US government, which increasingly embraced private enterprise in its efforts promoting international development. At the same time, the US government and US corporations looked to Black empowerment activists to mediate with African leaders and citizens, launching a new chapter in US corporate diplomacy. This practice of relying on Black American corporate ambassadors only increased during the latter part of the decade, as US corporations faced growing pressure to divest from South Africa.

CHAPTER 5

Black Empowerment in the Boardroom

The morning of March 1, 1971, Leon Sullivan awoke in his hotel room and began to get dressed. A mundane act—one performed every day of his life—and yet, getting dressed that morning took on a particular significance for Sullivan, who was about to attend his first board meeting as a director of General Motors (GM). All eyes would be on him, the first Black person to sit on GM's board and, indeed, the first Black director of any major US company.

Earlier that year, the announcement of Sullivan's appointment garnered widespread coverage in the media. Following a well-rehearsed script that credited corporate enlightenment for Black advancements, *The Wall Street Journal* claimed Sullivan's appointment served as proof of "GM['s] . . . increasing sensitivity to the world in which they do business."[1] But, for the Black press, GM's move to bring Sullivan aboard had little to do with white acceptance; it offered proof of Black Power. Louis Martin, the high-powered Black political advisor, credited Black prowess with any reforms taking place in corporate America. Writing in the *Pittsburgh Courier,* Martin described Sullivan, who stood six feet and five inches tall, as a model of Black masculinity, ready to "tackle" the titans of corporate America through his performance of "raw Black manpower."[2] Similar descriptions appeared in other Black newspapers celebrating Sullivan alongside other Black appointees.[3]

But was this really Black Power, or was it something else? As Sullivan dressed that morning, his choice of outfit signaled a desire to fit in, not unsettle corporate norms. In contrast to the militant uniform donned by the Black Panthers or dashikis worn by Pan-Africanists, Sullivan wore a "new white shirt and Black suit" and a "light gray tie"—nothing too flashy or bold.[4] Sullivan wanted to look the part: a smart, respectable businessman, one deserving of a position on the board of the world's largest corporation.

Merely adding Black directors to the boards of corporate America was a far cry from the structural transformation demanded by many Black Power activists. Rather than Black Power, Sullivan's appointment more aptly reflected Black empowerment, a politics that sought inclusion within American capitalism, including corporate America. Even if their appointment to corporate boards and c-suite positions fell short of the large-scale transformations demanded by activists, Black executives still have much to teach us about Black politics and the modern multinational corporation.

The second half of the twentieth century saw the modern corporation undergo a significant transformation, from the large-scale, centrally organized corporation of the late nineteenth and early twentieth centuries to the more decentralized organization comprised of semiautonomous units we know today.[5] As the world's largest corporation, GM took center stage. Published in 1946, Peter Drucker's *Concept of the Corporation*, pioneering in its analysis of the corporation as a social organization, praised the company for its success, characterizing GM as the quintessential industrial corporation. He also advocated for a new, more decentralized corporate form.[6] Following Drucker, subsequent decades witnessed a noticeable rise in management consultants and other professionals advocating structural changes to promote greater efficiency, entrepreneurship, short-term profits over long-term investments, and the maximization of shareholder value in business and other organizations.[7] For the most part, the history of corporate management during the late twentieth century has remained a colorblind story, linked to the changing nature of global capitalism and the rise of neoliberalism.[8] Yet, managing the multinational corporation, managing GM, during the 1970s and 1980s likewise necessitated new approaches to managing race.[9]

Building on and complicating histories of post–World War II corporate and racial politics, this chapter centers Sullivan and other Black executives in the history of the late twentieth century multinational corporation. In doing so, it sheds light on the racial politics that took place *within*, as well as in contestation with, the corporation, highlighting corporate America's management of the transition from a Jim Crow/apartheid global order to a post–Jim Crow/post-apartheid one. The role of corporate America in domestic politics has garnered significant attention from historians in recent decades.[10] Part of understanding corporate politics necessitates going beyond business-government relations to examine the political battles that occurred inside corporations. This is something long understood by labor historians, who have done much to reveal the power dynamics between workers and management.

Yet, internal company politics is not limited to the contestations that take place on the shop floor or, more appropriate to the late-twentieth-century service economy, behind the counter.[11] Corporate politics also exist at higher levels of the corporation, between directors, executives, and managers.

Following the gains of the 1960s, activists made the corporation, including the corporate board room, an important site in the ongoing Black freedom struggle. Adopting left-wing calls for participatory democracy and "community control," New Left activists, in particular, articulated a vision of the corporation in which diverse workers, consumers, and shareholders all had a say in corporate governance—a people's corporation. This vision was supported by Black politicians and activists, many of whom had roots in the movement for Black Power. In response, corporate executives appropriated the politics of Black empowerment, including appointing Black managers and directors, in an effort to mitigate dissent within and outside the corporation. Over the course of the 1970s, the number of Black men holding executive, administrative, or managerial jobs increased each year at twice the rate of white men.[12]

Black directors and executives, for their part, used these appointments to reinforce their status as "race leaders." Speaking at a press conference shortly after his appointment was announced, Sullivan told the media, "I know General Motors is going to use me as a symbol and sample of how liberal it has become, but I am going to use them. . . . I'll be one voice out of 23 . . . but I'm going to do all I can to help my people—Black people, brown people, underprivileged people."[13] Initially referring to his efforts promoting Black empowerment in the US, Sullivan soon joined other Black American executives, including Harold Sims of Johnson & Johnson, in advocating on behalf of Black and other non-white South Africans living under apartheid.

As the previous chapter noted, South African apartheid emerged during the 1970s as a lightning rod for debates over US foreign policy and the global color line. Building on earlier calls by Black activists, the 1970s witnessed a noticeable rise in anti-apartheid activism demanding sanctions and divestment. Such demands put Black American executives like Sullivan in a tough position, caught between the movement and the corporation. While initially supportive of divestment, Sullivan, building on his earlier work promoting Black empowerment politics in the US and Africa, ultimately broke with sanctions and divestment activists in announcing the Sullivan Principles, a corporate code of conduct. In lieu of divestment, the Principles proffered job-training, affirmative action, Black entrepreneurship, and corporate social responsibility as a means for corporations to oppose divestment and South African apartheid.

Adopted by over 150 US corporations and endorsed, although never codified into law, by the US government, the Principles help highlight the popularity and limitations of corporate-sponsored Black empowerment politics in ending apartheid and uplifting Black Americans and Black Africans.

Black Power and Corporate Responsibility
at General Motors

Pandemonium. That was how *The New York Times*'s reporter described the 1971 General Motors shareholder meeting. "The first public disagreement within memory on the 23-member G.M. board."[14] The chaos derived from Leon Sullivan's bold and unexpected decision to weigh in on the controversial topic of GM's business dealings in South Africa. Rather than sit back quietly observing the proceedings, as colleagues on the board surely hoped, Sullivan used the opportunity of his first shareholder meeting to boldly and publicly take a stand on South African apartheid, calling it "the most ruthless form of dealing with human beings in the world today." "And," added Sullivan, "General Motors, Chrysler, Ford and 300 other U.S. companies underwrite apartheid by being there." "I hold that General Motors should get out of South Africa."[15]

As the world's largest corporation, GM was a central target of shareholder activism in the 1970s. Indeed, one year prior to Sullivan's outburst, GM's shareholder meeting was similarly disrupted by the Project for Corporate Responsibility (PCR). Founded by four Washington-based lawyers, PCR emerged alongside organizations like Public Interest Research Group as a key player in the growing movement for corporate social responsibility in the 1970s. As part of their initial "Campaign GM," PCR organizers took the unconventional step of purchasing GM stock. At the time, for social activists to strategically invest in a corporation was quite new.[16] While a significant number of Americans began purchasing stocks in the 1930s as part of a business-led movement to counter widespread anti-corporate sentiment during the Depression, shareholder involvement focused primarily on the business-side of corporate affairs until the late 1960s.[17] Drawing on this popular view of shareholders' role, GM management rejected PCR's proposition of a shareholder resolution. Management accused PCR of inserting what company officials called "social issues" into the agenda for the corporation's annual shareholder meetings. Here, however, GM faced opposition from the

Securities and Exchange Commission (SEC), which overruled GM's petition to block the PCR resolution. The SEC ruling opened the door to a wave of similar shareholder resolutions by political and religious organizations seeking to transform corporate behavior throughout the 1970s and 1980s.[18]

Having won the initial SEC ruling, PCR introduced a resolution demanding the company restrict operations "detrimental to the health, safety, or welfare of [American] citizens" and alter the corporation's management structure to include greater representation from union members, professors, scientists, and people of color.[19] With a few exceptions, the history of the movement for corporate social responsibility and the Black freedom struggle have been told separately.[20] Yet PCR's inclusion of a Black director in their demands alludes to their interconnectedness. This connection was made clear by the decision of Black elected officials to join PCR's Campaign GM. Having previously voiced criticism of Black empowerment programs that "amounted to subsidizing businessmen so they could hire poor people at low cost . . . and then [lay them] off when [government] subsidies ran out," Brooklyn native and New York Congresswoman Shirley Chisholm joined other Black politicians in pressuring GM on its record of racial discrimination.[21] Speaking at a press conference organized by PCR, Chisholm stated that American companies like GM had failed to respond "to the needs of Black Americans" for too long.[22] Chisholm's comments echoed Congressman Louis Stokes (D-OH, brother of Cleveland's first Black mayor, Carl Stokes), who, evoking Black Power, called for more Black managers and Black directors to wield real "decision-making [power] in American corporations."[23]

Additional evidence of the connection between efforts to transform corporate management and the Black Power movement can be found at one of the era's most important gatherings: the 1969 Black Economic Development Conference (BEDC). Famous for producing the Black Manifesto, which included a demand for $500 million in reparations to be paid by white churches and synagogues for their involvement in slavery and Jim Crow, the BEDC likewise played host to a keynote address by Black economist Robert S. Browne. In his address, Browne stressed the need for more Black managers and Black directors in corporate America, stating "local development projects, small business programs, job training, consumer education, vocational guidance, school improvement, and other community programs" were all well and good. Real power, however, depended on Black people "grasping the levers of control in this society," including corporations.[24] Revealing the shared ideological terrain on which self-identified Black Power and Black empowerment activists operated, Sullivan, echoing Browne, stated, "Black economic development has to be accomplished in terms of integration!" Seeking to draw a contrast between himself and Richard Nixon, whose idea of Black capitalism centered on developing "ghetto enterprises" and not the boardroom, Sullivan declared, in 1972, "There is no such thing as Black capitalism! There is no such thing as Black capital. The economy in this country is tied into everything, everybody, and everything that happens." "Within that system," continued Sullivan, "Black people can develop their own business enterprises, just as the white population and various specific ethnic groups have often done over the years," but "his paramount need is to get inside the door in terms of management, in terms of knowing what the economic structure is, in terms of development and control of capital."[25] Not Black capitalism nor economic justice, Browne, Sullivan, and others demanded Black empowerment, defined in this case as appointing Black managers and executives within the modern corporation.

Efforts to integrate the struggle for Black empowerment and corporate social responsibility reached a fever pitch in the fall of 1970, when PCR activists again confronted GM on its lack of Black representation. The confrontation coincided with one of the largest strikes the company had seen in years, led by the United Auto Workers and an outgrowth, in many ways, of the ongoing struggle for Black Power in and around Detroit.[26] During the action, PCR members accused GM Chairman James Roche of "l[ying] about [the company's] record of progress," declaring: "You have told the shareholders about 100,000 employees, Black employees, of General Motors but you have not said that none of them are in top management positions. You have not told them that none of them are members of GM's Board of Directors. You have not told them that of 13,000 GM dealerships, ten of them, if that many, are Black. Why are there no Blacks on GM's Board of Directors?"[27] To which Roche responded, "Because none have been elected."[28] Roche did not help the situation when he subsequently responded to another question by Campaign GM activists about whether GM was a public corporation by saying: "We are a public corporation owned by free, white . . ." At this point, some people in the audience gasped, while others laughed. Roche stammered, "ummm . . . and . . . and . . . and Black and yellow people all over the world."[29] Reeling from the embarrassment caused by the confrontation with PCR, GM's board rejected Campaign GM's demands to appoint a Black director of the latter's choosing. Instead, the company selected Sullivan, a civil rights leader with a reputation for working with corporate America to promote Black empowerment through OIC, to serve as the company's first Black director, with the official announcement made in January 1971. That same year, GM established Motor Enterprises Incorporated (MEI), a wholly owned subsidiary providing capital, managerial, and technical assistance to minority-owned businesses.[30]

Sullivan's appointment marked the first in a series of similar appointments. Within days of GM's announcement, the New York Federal Reserve Bank and W. T. Grant Company announced they had appointed National Urban League President Whitney Young and former North Carolina Mutual Insurance Company executive Asa Spaulding to their respective boards.[31] Other companies and financial institutions soon followed suit. Whereas in 1969 there had been only one Black American on the board of a *Fortune* 500 company, by mid-1971 there were at least a dozen. By the end of 1972, there were fifty-four Black directors in *Fortune* 500 companies.[32]

Appointment itself was just the first step. Many Black executives found themselves marginalized within their companies, placed in charge of newly created departments somewhat removed from the primary business of the corporation.[33] This did not mean corporations did not value what Black executives did. Quite the opposite. Going by a range of different names, including Urban Affairs, Public Affairs, and Community Relations, these departments shared a common goal: improving corporations' images with regard to race and other related issues and protecting one of each company's most valued assets: its brand.[34] When Johnson & Johnson appointed Harold Sims as vice president for corporate affairs, company executives made this work explicit, noting in an internal memo Sims's role "represent[ing] Johnson & Johnson [to] the minority communities."[35] Johnson & Johnson executives later told Sims that they hoped his actions as a VP, which included recruiting Black and female managers into the company, would reduce chances for "disquiet, company dissension and inflammatory situations" at other companies. These other companies included AT&T, Polaroid, Sears, and MacMillan and Company, all of which had recently experienced heavy criticism from student activists and disgruntled Black employees charging racial discrimination.[36] GM Chairman James Roche similarly referenced Sullivan's "distinguished record of service to his community" as an asset. Sullivan "bring[s] to [the company's] board the benefit of his knowledge and expertise in areas of public concern," stated Roche.[37] Roche's comments are suggestive of the kind of public relations work corporate executives hoped Black executives like Sims and Sullivan would perform.

At the same time, Black American executives likewise had to fit in with the standards of behavior associated with white corporate America. To this point, E. Frederick Morrow, who joined Bank of America in 1964 as the institution's first Black American vice president, told a story of his hiring. After months of discussions with various corporate higher-ups, Morrow was notified of one, final step necessary to approve his appointment: a luncheon with the bank's chief executive officer. "Catherine [Morrow's wife] and I, old hands at this kind of tactic, knew what the luncheon was all about: we were to be exposed to a social situation and our manners and conversation tested to see if they met the standards of 'big business' requirements." These requirements, which included knowing "how to handle the intricacies of a formal meal and participate with ease in the usual social chit-chat" were not race-neutral but rather served as evidence of the careful balancing act Black executives performed, expected to ameliorate Black anger at corporate abuse without upsetting the existing social order.[38]

Black activists-turned-executives, for their part, were not naïve about the expectations surrounding their appointments. Indeed, they often challenged them. Echoing the calls of people like Stokes and Chisholm, Sullivan declared, "I want to see Blacks in executive jobs, and I want to see Blacks on the ladder going up."[39] Rather than elected office, Sullivan demonstrated his commitment to Black empowerment politics, through advocating Black advancement in the private, including in the corporate, sphere.

In this Sullivan was not alone. Many Black executives and directors expressed a faith-like belief in corporate-sponsored Black empowerment, rather than personal financial gain, which they did receive, as justification for accepting c-suite appointments.[40] Harold Sims, for example, noted that he "turned down several offers of equal or greater financial remuneration" to take the position of director of social concerns at Johnson & Johnson. Sims attributed his decision to accept the appointment to the excitement he felt regarding the possibility of assisting one of the world's largest companies "become the corporate leader in multi-racial employment, upgrading and management development at all levels, regardless of sex."[41]

Sims subsequently became outspoken on the links between race and corporate social responsibility. In a 1974 article, entitled "The Quest for Corporate Social Responsibility," published by *Contact* and later read by Congressman Stokes into the Congressional Record, Sims identified "Black America" as "the key catalyst in triggering [the] current movement" for corporate social responsibility through their work showing business the way forward. Black women played a "particularly vital" role in this regard, "as the link between the struggles for racial equity and sex equality." Sims urged business to heed the call from Black Americans and accept the responsibilities associated with their central role in society—if not out of the goodness of their hearts than as necessary for their survival and future prosperity.[42] As chance would have it, newly appointed Black American executives like Sims and Sullivan would soon have the opportunity to evaluate corporate America's response to such demands amid the escalating battle over US corporate investment in South Africa.

Corporate America and Anti-Apartheid

For a moment, following Sullivan's appointment, GM appeared to satisfy its critics or at least persuade the media to turn its gaze elsewhere. This victory proved only temporary. In the spring of 1971, GM was back in the spotlight, facing accusations from protesters of abetting South African apartheid. Located at the southern tip of the African continent, South Africa had long attracted American entrepreneurs, who looked to profit from the country's location at the intersection of Indian and Atlantic Ocean trading networks and its rich mineral resources. Some of the first Americans to do business with South Africa traded in enslaved people.[43] They were followed by American oil and manufacturing companies, in the late nineteenth and early twentieth centuries.[44] Both Ford Motor Company and GM, which established wholly owned subsidiary plants outside Port Elizabeth, played a key role in the development of South Africa's auto-manufacturing industry during the early-to-mid-twentieth century.[45]

Like their European and South African counterparts, US companies profited from the colonial government's program of dispossessing Africans of their land, thereby creating large pools of cheap labor for the country's white-owned agricultural, mining, and manufacturing sectors. This system of generating profits continued after the launch of legal apartheid in 1948. Literally translated to mean separateness in Afrikaans, apartheid's system of racial segregation created the most profitable system in the world, which in turn supported white supremacy in South Africa and other parts of the globe. By one estimate, by the mid-1960s, US investors were averaging a 20.6 percent rate of return, the highest rate in the world. By comparison, the next highest country, Japan, had a 12 percent average return on investment.[46]

Profits wrung through expropriation and exploitation did not go unnoticed. In the US, Black Americans led the charge in condemning apartheid. Throughout the postwar decades, multiple civil rights organizations, including the National Association for the Advancement of Colored People (NAACP), the National Negro Congress, and the American Committee on Africa (ACOA), raised the issue of South African apartheid with the US Congress and the United Nations (UN).[47] In 1962, the UN General Assembly called on member states to break all diplomatic and economic ties with South Africa in response to the Sharpeville massacre, which left no less than sixty-nine people dead and preceded a ramping up of government suppression of anti-apartheid activism, including banning the country's two largest Black political organizations, the Pan-African Congress and the African National Congress.

Sharpeville served as an important turning point in the anti-apartheid struggle. Coinciding with the rise of Black Power, the 1960s and early 1970s witnessed growing demands for sanctions and divestment in the US. In early October 1970, Ken Williams and Caroline Hunter, two Black American Polaroid employees, stumbled on a sample identification badge for the South African Department of Mines at Polaroid's headquarters in Cambridge, Massachusetts. Further investigation revealed that Polaroid was selling its ID-2 system, which could make identification cards nearly instantaneously through its patented photographic technology, to South Africa. These photographs, Williams and Hunter correctly deduced, were used to create passbooks—a tool utilized by the South African government to regulate the movement of non-white South Africans. Subsequently, Williams and Hunter joined several other African American employees and students from nearby Harvard University to found the Polaroid Revolutionary Workers' Movement (PRWM), demanding that Polaroid leave South Africa.[48] Following the PRWM's example, the Boston-based Pan-African Liberation Committee subsequently announced its own boycott of Gulf Oil for its role supporting Portuguese colonialism in Angola, revealing the geographic flexibility and breadth of the divestment and sanctions movement. Not just South African apartheid, but colonial exploitation and white supremacy globally were at stake.[49]

Other companies soon began to feel the heat of the growing sanctions and divestment movement. In early 1971, John Elbridge Hines, president of the Episcopal Church of the United States, sent a letter to GM Chairman Roche condemning apartheid as immoral. Following the strategy pursued by the PCR, the Church, which owned 12,574 shares of GM stock, submitted a shareholder resolution demanding GM proceed with "an orderly winding up of its present manufacturing operations in the Republic of South Africa."[50] To the surprise and disdain of his fellow directors, Sullivan supported the resolution and called for GM to leave South Africa.[51] Later, Sullivan testified on the role of US business in South Africa as part of a series of hearings convened by Congressman Charles Diggs in the latter's role as chair of the House Sub-Committee on Africa. Before Congress, Sullivan reiterated his call for "the US Government [to] support the U. N. . . . and the Organization of African Unity" in enacting an "economic and military embargo" and "break all diplomatic relations with South Africa." There can be no "business as usual," declared Sullivan. Rather, the US government and businesses must come together "to hit apartheid where it hurts most . . . in the pocketbook."[52]

Sounding all too similar to the demands of Campaign GM and the PRWM, Sullivan's declaration in support of divestment was a public relations nightmare for GM executives, who quickly set to work reeling in the newly appointed Black director. Endeavoring to project calm and control, GM Chairman James Roche downplayed the controversy in public. Speaking with *The New York Times*, Roche noted that Sullivan, "always an outspoken man . . . wouldn't be expected to change just by becoming a General Motors director."[53] Behind closed doors, however, company executives struck a noticeably different tone. In a private letter, John A. Mayer, who chaired the GM committee that appointed Sullivan, told the minister, "I am disturbed by some of the rhetoric attributed to you in the press [and] feel that it will eventually damage your ability to be an important influence on the G.M. Board, as indeed it would on any other board that I can think of." The issue, according to Mayer, had less to do with Sullivan's personal views on apartheid, which Mayer noted were "agree[able]," if not to be "admire[d]." Rather, Mayer framed the problem as one of public relations. "As a director you [should] . . . confine your comments to Board meetings where they will be properly considered. *Public* comments elsewhere [were]," otherwise considered "inappropriate" (emphasis added).[54] As Mayer's comments suggest, corporate support for Black empowerment was contingent on Black executives representing themselves and, more importantly, the corporations they served favorably in public. This meant letting the corporation dictate the pace of change, as opposed to Black executives.

Other Black executives recalled similar experiences of surveillance and chastisement for stepping out of line. One Black vice president and company director at a major bank in Chicago recollected that his job was "to promote the visibility and good name" of his bank to the Black community.[55] Another Black director of urban affairs noted that his role was to "make [the company] look good."[56] At times, this hypervisibility could translate into a sense of "paranoia," according to some Black executives, who complained about the pressure put on them by white executives. "You feel as though you're constantly being observed. Your actions are constantly being monitored," noted one Black bank manager.[57] Yet another Black bank manager noted: "Unless a Black comes 360 degrees full circle and bends over backwards to prostitute other Blacks and minorities to their satisfaction, they're not going to feel comfortable with you. In other words, you have to do the things that they would like to see. You have to make them aware that you are in total allegiance to and with them and against other Blacks."[58] To be sure, all employees contend with expectations regarding avoiding statements that might damage a company's image. As hypervisible members of the corporation occupying roles specifically designed to mitigate tensions with the community, however, Black executives bore a particular expectation to uphold a positive corporate image.[59] In his letter to Sullivan, Mayer noted that the latter's appointment had perhaps led to more media attention than any other in the history of corporate boards. Despite these experiences of explicit and implicit racism, many Black executives remained optimistic regarding the possibilities for Black empowerment within corporations. Corporations, moreover, took steps to encourage this enthusiasm. In the same letter reprimanding Sullivan for criticizing GM, Mayer appealed to Sullivan for his cooperation, noting, "I am sure that your service on the Board of this great company can be one of the most rewarding experiences of your life, as well as productive of help to the company." "If you make a success, your people will surely benefit."[60]

The specific benefits of working with, as opposed to against, the company were soon made clear in a series of presentations and reports provided to Sullivan highlighting GM's ongoing efforts "to upgrade [their] Colored and African employees in South Africa," as they had done with "Black employees in the United States." While acknowledging existing racial inequalities—including company statistics that showed white South African wages on average being 643 percent higher than their African counterparts—company executives stressed "positive programs . . . in South Africa," including training programs for Black and other non-white employees, alongside education and housing assistance for Black employees and their families.[61] Such efforts on the part of GM and other US companies reveal corporate America's wielding of Black empowerment politics as an alternative to sanctions and divestment.

Fighting Apartheid "From the Inside"

Sullivan needed more than reports produced by GM officials to convince him that the company was indeed making progress eliminating racial barriers in South Africa. Rather, Sullivan, like many others, desired firsthand verification of conditions in South Africa. Traveling to South Africa as a Black American at this time proved difficult, however. Suspicious that Black Americans, left to their own devices, would promote radical ideas and undermine apartheid, the South African government placed heavy restrictions on Black people traveling within the country. As such, Sullivan required the support of GM and the US State Department, which together agreed to sponsor his 1975 trip to South Africa.[62]

Such conditions ensured that Sullivan's movements within the country, as well as his contact with South Africans, were closely monitored and controlled. During his visit, Sullivan met with various government representatives and South African businessmen, who parroted the claims of American business leaders in their descriptions of the positive changes taking place in the country.[63] South African GM Director Alan de Kock told Sullivan, for example, that just recently "the South African Ambassador to the United Nations, Mr. R. F. Botha . . . announced to the Security Council . . . that 'we shall do everything in our power to move away from discrimination based on race or colour.'"[64] Botha's remarks were part of a broader public relations campaign by the South African government to defend South Africa and apartheid from critics. At its height, during the late 1970s and 1980s, government spending on public relations reached upward of $100 million annually.[65]

These efforts notwithstanding, it was impossible for Sullivan, born and raised in West Virginia, not to recognize the similarities between South Africa and the United States. Recounting his first impression of the trip, Sullivan later wrote "being" in South Africa in 1975 was like "being [in] Mississippi" under Jim Crow. Walking the streets of Johannesburg and Soweto, "every Black person I saw . . . had a large bulge in his or her right pocket," a sign of the hated "passbooks," a physical emblem of apartheid's constrictive logic. In contrast to Botha's pronouncements, Sullivan described a society deeply divided and unequal. Writing of his visit, Sullivan later noted, "[I witnessed] Black workers sweeping and mopping floors, emptying the trash, and carrying things," while white South Africans lived and worked in a state of luxury. "Black [South Africans remained] the have-nots in a land of plenty," Sullivan concluded.[66]

Sullivan's reflections echoed a longstanding refrain among Black Americans and Black South Africans regarding the similarities between their two countries dating back to the nineteenth century. One of the first exchanges between Black Americans and Black South Africans to be recorded took place with members of the Virginia Jubilee Singers, a minstrel troupe that visited South Africa as part of a fin de siècle tour promoting Christianity and good will between the US and the British Empire. While on the tour, troupe leader Orpheus McAdoo and the other members of the troupe met and conversed with Black South Africans regarding their shared experiences of racism.[67] The transatlantic dialogue continued after the Jubilee Singers departed, carried on by Black American missionaries.[68] Throughout the twentieth century, prominent Black Americans, from Paul Robeson to Martin Luther King Jr., continued to draw parallels between the ongoing struggles to end apartheid and Jim Crow in the US and South Africa. For many, solidarity with Black South Africans inspired growing support for sanctions and divestment. Others, including Sullivan, chose to pursue a different path—one that left room for continued US business dealings in South Africa.

Abandoning his earlier calls for divestment, Sullivan returned to the US in June 1975 determined to persuade GM and other US corporations to adopt socially responsible policies promoting Black empowerment—including providing for equal opportunity in employment, hiring and training Black managers, and supporting Black community economic development—in and around their South African operations. What spurred Sullivan to change course is not entirely clear. He later cited discussions with South African union and civic leaders, who "prevailed on [him] to try a new tactic"— namely, "a campaign of corporate responsibility designed to end discrimination" and promote "the rights of black workers" in South Africa. This plan came to be known as the "Principles of Equal Rights for United States Firms in the Republic of South Africa," later renamed the Sullivan Principles.[69]

As with OIC and other previous ventures, Sullivan first shared the Principles with his congregants at Zion Baptist Church. This practice had the effect of bestowing a sense of moral sanctity on the Principles, as if delivered by God themself. In a sermon entitled "The Walls Must Come Down," Sullivan spoke with urgency about the situation in southern Africa to his congregants. "[I] fear that South Africa [will] be thrown into a terrible, bloody, racial war unless something [is] done to end the atrocious racist conditions that [prevail]" in that country.[70] Sullivan's reference to a race war likewise served as a warning against the perils of Black militancy, which, carried too far, in his view, would result in mass casualties for the movement and went against a Christian worldview.

Corporate executives needed no such lesson on the dangers of Black militancy. Yet, many remained reluctant to take measures to oppose apartheid. Not surprisingly, Sullivan began his campaign to persuade corporate America to adopt the Principles at GM. If Sullivan could not get his fellow directors to adopt the Principles, he might as well give up. Thus, one week following his sermon at Zion Baptist, Sullivan met with members of GM's board of directors to discuss the issue. Initially, Sullivan met with strong resistance. Like the vast majority of US business leaders and professionals at the time, GM's white directors avoided the issue, contending that South African apartheid was a domestic issue and outside the purview of American business. Some, such as J. M. Cornely of Firestone Rubber Company, went so far as to argue that any criticism of apartheid undertaken by US corporations was tantamount to "interfering with [South Africa's] sovereign rights" as an independent country.[71]

From these responses, it became clear that further action was needed. Having failed through moral persuasion to convince his fellow board members, Sullivan shifted tactics, threatening to leave the board if they did not support the Principles.[72] This placed GM officials in a tough position. On one hand, they feared that adopting the Principles might provoke retribution, including further restrictions on currency convertibility, a measure used by the South African government to limit corporate profits from leaving the country and promote economic development in South Africa.[73] On the other hand, they also did not want to invite any further negative publicity, which was sure to follow an announcement of Sullivan's resignation. Sullivan, despite his public disagreements, was a valuable asset to the corporation— one not easily replaced. After considerable back and forth, weighing the issue, the board notified Sullivan that it would support the initiative on one condition: Sullivan must secure a critical mass of other corporations willing to join the initiative.

Once again, Sullivan turned to his rolodex of business contacts to stir up support. Indeed, it was in moments like these that the minister revealed the importance of the networks linking corporate America and Black activists. One of the first executives to answer Sullivan's call was International Business Machines (IBM) Chairman Frank Cary. A longtime supporter of OIC, having previously earned the organization's Gold Key Award, given annually to the corporation making the most outstanding contribution to OIC, and a

member of OICI's Industrial Advisory Council, Cary proved an early supporter of the Principles.[74] In the spring of 1976, Cary informed Sullivan of
his willingness to help arrange a meeting with eighteen executives represent-
ing fifteen leading US companies, all with operations in South Africa, where
Sullivan could present his case for the Principles. The companies included
American Cyanamid, Burroughs Corporation, Caltex Petroleum Corporation, Citicorp, Ford Motor Company, GM, IBM Corporation, International
Harvester Company, Minnesota Mining & Manufacturing Company, Mobil
Corporation, Otis Elevator, and Motorola.[75] Reflecting a change in strategy,
Sullivan agreed to keep the conversation private, "out of the way" and "outside
the gaze of public scrutiny."[76] This, among other things, served as an example
of how Black empowerment activists acquiesced to corporate America's way
of doing business: in private.

Meetings conducted in private serve multiple purposes. The meeting's
location, at a remote IBM training facility in Sands Point, Long Island, ensured
that only the invited corporate executives had a seat at the table where one
of the largest corporate social responsibility initiatives of its kind was drafted.
This circumstance may seem obvious to those familiar with contemporary corporate social-responsibility programs, many of which appear as if constructed
as marketing campaigns to bolster corporate America's image. This is, in a
sense, what corporate social responsibility has become. Yet, it is important to
remember that the movement for corporate social responsibility, led by organizations like the PCR, began as an effort to democratize the corporation, to
break down the barriers separating the private corporation from the public. In
a rare, but poignant, observation made following Sullivan's appointment to the
GM board, one PCR representative noted that, while they were "encouraged by
the appointment of a Black man to General Motors' board of directors," PCR
"nevertheless . . . deplore[d] the fact that the process by which GM's directors
are nominated and elected remains an entirely closed affair."[77] By appointing a
Black director, GM, in effect, took credit for the outcome of corporate social
responsibility activism while rejecting the process.

This privatization of corporate social responsibility furthermore had
the benefit of obscuring internal disagreements with regard to the Sullivan
Principles, of which there were many. At the Sands Point meeting, several
executives expressed strong concerns about the Principles. James W. Wilcock, chairman and chief executive of Joy Manufacturing Company, who was
unable to attend the meeting but sent his remarks in a letter to Sullivan, stated,
"I positively refuse to follow the track of too many other Americans by always

Figures 7. Aerial shot of the General Motors board room, including Leon Sullivan (upper left) meeting with executives representing various US corporations. OIC Key News. Leon Howard Sullivan papers, Stuart A. Rose Manuscript, Archives, and Rare Book Library, Emory University. Made possible by the Leon H. Sullivan Charitable Trust.

Figure 8. Leon Sullivan flanked by Thomas Murphy, GM board chairman, and George Champion, Chase Manhattan Bank board chairman, on the left, and Elton Jolly and Frank Cary, IBM board chairman. OIC Key News. Leon Howard Sullivan papers, Stuart A. Rose Manuscript, Archives, and Rare Book Library, Emory University. Made possible by the Leon H. Sullivan Charitable Trust.

sticking my nose into the business of other countries."[78] Meanwhile, supporters of the Principles emphasized the changing political climate—namely, the
rise in calls for sanctions and divestment.

First gaining popularity during the 1958 All Africa Peoples' Conference
in Accra, where it was endorsed by multiple Pan-Africanist and anti-colonial
leaders, the call for divestment and sanctions against South Africa found support among various civil rights groups, religious organizations, student clubs,
and other left-leaning organizations in the US during the 1960s.[79] With the
rise of Black elected officials during the 1970s, the movement entered a new
phase, involving efforts by local and national politicians to pass legislation. At
the 1976 meeting discussing the Principles, Cary reminded his fellow executives that the City of Gary, Indiana, had recently instituted sanctions against
companies with operations in South Africa. In addition to the Gary resolution, Cary noted that members of the newly formed Congressional Black
Caucus had introduced sanctions legislation in Congress.[80] Cary's message
was clear: If US corporations did not do something to confront rising Black
political power, they might be forced out of doing business in South Africa
altogether.

Eventually, most of the executives came around to Cary's position. Even
after agreeing to sign the Principles, however, executives continued to argue
about the exact nature of the program. At stake was corporate executives'
ability to retain decision-making authority over their companies. Thus, signatory company executives rejected a crucial clause proposed by Sullivan that
would have made adherence to the Principles a prerequisite for any future
investment by a signatory company in South Africa.[81] The clause failed to
appear in the final document. Signatory company officials likewise worked
to ensure that the Principles would, in the words of Citibank Vice President Robert E. Terkhorn, "remain [a] private initiative," outside the realm
of public oversight.[82] William Tavoulareas, president of Mobil Corporation,
was particularly adamant on this point, noting that official government support for the Principles effort "[would only] impair our [effort]" by "invit[ing]
government-to-government confrontation" with the South African government, which surely would interpret the Principles as an act of foreign inter-
ference.[83] Despite, or perhaps because of, the private nature of the program,
and with the help of US Secretary of State Cyrus Vance and US Ambassador
to the United Nations Andrew Young, the Principles received the endorsement of the Carter administration, which lauded business involvement as
part of its broader policy of constructive engagement with South Africa.[84]

Here and elsewhere, corporate America welcomed government support, as long as it did not come with state oversight.

The Original Sullivan Principles (published March 2, 1977)

1. Nonsegregation of the races in all eating, comfort, and work facilities.
2. Equal and fair employment practices for all employees.
3. Equal pay for all employees doing equal or comparable work for the same period of time.
4. Initiation and development of training programs that will prepare, in substantial numbers, Blacks and other non-whites for supervisory, administrative, clerical, and technical jobs.
5. Increasing the number of Blacks and other non-whites in management and supervisory positions.
6. Improving the quality of employees' lives outside the work environment in such areas as housing, transportation, schooling, recreation, and health facilities.

Soweto and the "Principled" Response of Corporate America

In contrast to the private nature surrounding their drafting, the official launch of the Principles was a very public affair, with Sullivan taking center stage. The signatory group launched the Principles at a press conference in Washington, DC, in March 1977. At the press conference, Sullivan stood front and center at a podium flanked by GM Chairman Thomas A. Murphy and IBM Chairman Frank Cary. The image of the three corporate executives, dressed in suits, was intended to convey a sense of order and responsiveness amid the ongoing chaos and atrocity in South Africa. Nine months earlier, in June 1976, the world watched in horror as South African police opened fire on Black South African students engaged in their own struggle for freedom and Black Power in Soweto, a Black township located just outside Johannesburg. Footage of the attack on unarmed protesters, including a photograph of a young Mbuyisa Makhubo carrying the lifeless body of Hector Pieterson alongside Hector's visibly distraught sister, Antoinette Sithole, provoked worldwide outrage.

The Soweto Uprising (discussed further in Chapter 6) served as a major turning point in the anti-apartheid movement, igniting a new wave of calls for action around the world. Within South Africa, Soweto preceded a series of labor strikes and urban rebellions unseen since the early 1960s.[85] It also helped fuel the adoption of the Sullivan Principles. Whereas, initially, only twelve companies agreed to sign the Principles, by the end of 1978, under growing pressure from anti-apartheid activists, the number of signatory companies had risen to sixty-one.[86] By 1980, the number of signatories reached well over 150.

Signing the Principles was only the first step. Concerned about the growing public outcry and the prospect of further sanctions, T. J. Barlow, president and chief executive officer of Anderson Clayton & Company, wrote Sullivan, stating, "increased communications . . . [were] necessary" to inform the American public regarding "the [full] scope of the efforts [by American companies] on behalf of their non-white employees in South Africa."[87] What just months prior had been a widely debated program promoting corporate-sponsored Black empowerment in South Africa now took center stage in US businesses' efforts combating divestment/sanctions and apartheid.

Sullivan subsequently undertook a global media campaign to promote the Principles, speaking on radio programs, at private clubs, and in various public forums in the US, Europe, and South Africa over the next decade.[88] Like other Black empowerment initiatives, including OIC, the Principles garnered widespread praise from businesspeople, government officials, church leaders, and some civil rights activists. Immediately following the Principals' launch, *The Washington Post*, for example, hailed the signatory companies for their courage in going beyond the Carter administration's timid response and taking a moral stance on the "[complex] and [volatile] . . . problem" of apartheid.[89] NAACP Executive Director Roy Wilkins expressed similar optimism when he praised the Sullivan Principles as an important step "foreshadow[ing] . . . an end to segregation in South African life."[90] Support for the Principles was not limited to the US, moreover. In 1977, Ivorian politician Dramane Ouattara, writing on behalf of the Organization of African Unity (OAU), wrote Sullivan expressing his "total support" for Sullivan and the Principles. Let me "assure you," Ouattara wrote, "of our readiness to contribute to your effort in whatever way you will find appropriate."[91] These and countless other letters and statements of support attest to the appeal of the Principles, which were perceived by many at the time, including those committed to ending apartheid, as a constructive response.

More so than other Black empowerment initiatives, however, the Principles also elicited criticism from anti-apartheid activists and Black leftists, who charged Sullivan with serving as an apologist for American business. "It seems most questionable that the Rev. Leon Sullivan should spend a year negotiating a 'Statement of Principles' which only seeks to 'curb bias' in a country guilty of some of the most atrocious racial crimes in this age," noted one anonymous reader in a letter to the Baltimore *Afro-American*. "Have we learned nothing from our own struggles for civil rights? How long will those Blacks in positions of influence continue to promote ambiguous or half-way solutions to the intolerable problems of racism and bigotry, not to mention apartheid?"[92] Chicago native and executive associate for the American Committee on Africa (ACOA) Prexy Nesbitt voiced similar skepticism. Addressing a forum on South Africa in Boston, Nesbitt stated, "I have a great deal of trouble as a Black American in this country believing that corporations can help bring about social change [when] these same multinationals have abandoned the United States."[93]

For the moment, Nesbitt's skepticism, which he shared with other members of the ACOA, was drowned out by the chorus of praise for the Principles coming from within and beyond a dynamic anti-apartheid movement in the US. What began as an outgrowth of mid-twentieth-century anti-imperial Black internationalism, the anti-apartheid movement had, by the late 1970s, expanded significantly in size and breadth. Alongside criticism from Black radicals like Nesbitt, a growing number of liberals, including civil rights activists, church leaders, politicians, and businesspeople, voiced their support for the Principles, which some included as part of a broad campaign promoting selective divestment.[94]

As the battle over how best to combat apartheid heated up, Sullivan, for his part, found himself weighing the advantages and limitations of his own program. In a letter to Tim Smith, director of the Interfaith Center on Corporate Responsibility, a corporate responsibility watchdog organization comprised of faith institutions, labor unions, and other socially conscious investors, Sullivan explained that the Principles were only a start. "Much more will come out of the Statement of Principles in the longer run." In the meantime, however, he advised patience and understanding as he worked "to see how far [he] could go" with the signatory companies.[95] Have faith was the message Sullivan sought to convey to Smith and others.

Faith and patience were increasingly in short supply during the late 1970s, however. With the South African government continuing to violently suppress criticism, including the highly publicized murder of Black Consciousness activist Steve Biko in 1977, anti-apartheid activists increasingly demanded immediate and measurable results.

Accounting (for) Success

Two years following their initial launch in 1977, the Carter administration's Assistant Secretary of State for African Affairs Richard Moose gave a speech praising the Sullivan Principles as a model of corporate diplomacy. "I think it fair to say that no single initiative to date has had the impact of that launched by Rev. Sullivan," stated Moose. "The best course of action for the United States [government] is to give our strong support to Rev. Sullivan's efforts, and to urge that others do the same."[96] Moose's endorsement signaled a continuation of the US government's practice of relying on corporations and other private organizations to foster "constructive" change in Africa and other parts of the Global South. Weary of provoking the South Africans, on whom the US depended for a number of important minerals, not to mention their support fighting communism, the US government outsourced part of their efforts to reform apartheid to the private sector.

This divestment of government responsibility did not go unanswered. Rather, as subsequent chapters show, the US government and private institutions met with increasing pressure from anti-apartheid activists to enact legally binding sanctions and divestment against South Africa. One of the primary sites of sanctions and divestment activism during the 1970s and 1980s was college campuses.[97] As Black students gained entrance to previously whites-only institutions across the US, they inspired anticolonial and anti-racist activism on college and university campuses.[98] In his assessment of the Southern Africa Relief Fund and the Pan-African Liberation Committee—two organizations formed at Harvard by Randall Robinson, Brenda Randolph Robinson, and other students, including Christopher Nteta, a South African exile attending Harvard's Divinity School—R. Joseph Parrott reveals how campus activists helped link Black Power politics to "a reenergized anti-apartheid movement, paving the way for national activism of groups like TransAfrica," which emerged in the late 1970s and 1980s at the forefront of the anti-apartheid struggle.[99]

Not unlike his usurping of the student sit-in movement in Philadelphia, Sullivan responded to the uptick in campus anti-apartheid organizing by doubling down on the Principles. Sidestepping calls for sanctions and divestment, Sullivan called on universities and colleges to embrace the program as a constructive alternative—one that proved a far lesser threat to university endowments through offering a way for institutions to pursue selective divestment. The strategy worked. In October 1977, the presidents of the

University of Minnesota, Columbia University, and fifty other leading colleges and universities cosigned a letter to US companies urging them to adopt the Sullivan Principles. Borrowing a page from the playbook of shareholder activists, the presidents of these institutions wielded their power as shareholders to pressure companies to adopt the Principles. "Nearly all American corporations profess abhorrence for the apartheid system, but they seem to be fearful of being caught in the middle of an ideological conflict," stated the letter. In light of such corporate ambivalence, the letter signatories vowed to use their "influence as ethical investors in order to overcome such hesitation quickly."[100] In other words, companies must sign the Principles or risk losing a key institutional investor. The threat proved effective. One year following the launch of the college and university campaign, in December 1978, Sullivan wrote Donald Brown, vice president of finance at the University of Minnesota, noting that since the actions taken by university and college presidents, "we now have 107 American companies that have signed the Principles."[101]

The battle over the Sullivan Principles elucidates the dynamism of corporate politics in the 1970s and 1980s. Business, as historians have shown, took an active role in shaping US politics in the second half of the twentieth century.[102] Corporations were also subject to political pressure from student activists, shareholders, and employees, among others. It was the interaction between activists, the signatory companies, and other institutions, including church groups, universities, and civil rights organizations, that gave meaning to the Principles, turning them into something more than a public relations campaign.

Faced with a rise in campus activism, university administrators, faculty, and students subjected the Principles to rigorous analysis. In December 1978, for example, Sullivan received a letter from Peter Fortune, assistant professor of economics at Tulane University and a member of Tulane's Committee on University Investments. In the letter, Fortune expressed his concern that "the six principles do not incorporate trade union rights for Black workers; and . . . that we know of no mechanism for monitoring the progress of firms and determining whether adherence is real."[103] This omission was later addressed by Sullivan in an amplified version of the Principles that encouraged, but did not require, signatory companies to recognize Black trade unions, a move that coincided with the South African Wiehahn Commission's recommendation recognizing Black Africans as eligible to join registered trade unions in an effort to mitigate ongoing Black labor unrest.[104]

Growing pressure from activists and institutional investors pressured companies to go beyond the simple gesture of signing the Principles and devote resources to monitoring as evidence of the tangible benefits accrued by Black South Africans. To this end, the signatory companies created the Industry Support Unit Inc. (ISU), a suborganization comprised of representatives from several dozen signatory companies. As part of its commitment to improving the monitoring and implementation of the Principles, the ISU agreed to fund a "small administrative" staff to assist Sullivan and hired international consulting firm Arthur D. Little Inc. to oversee a semiannual report on the signatory companies.[105] The ISU furthermore established a series of task forces—sixteen in total—comprised of representatives from the signatory companies. These task forces were active in the US and South Africa in monitoring the signatory companies, including company hiring practices, employee pay, skills-training and management development programs, and employee benefits.[106]

Despite its creation and backing by corporate executives representing the signatory companies, the monitoring process faced significant resistance. Among the complaints received by D. Reid Weedon Jr., the chief accountant from Arthur D. Little Inc. tasked with overseeing the monitoring process, were objections to "the complex and detailed questionnaire[s]" perceived by signatory members as "a distraction from [normal] business." Another signatory took this line of criticism a step further, arguing, counterintuitively, that the monitoring process was not only burdensome, but detrimental to the cause. The questionnaires, complained the anonymous executive, "stand in the way of" the signatory companies' efforts "to improve the conditions for our employees."[107] Better to leave the monitoring to the companies themselves.

These and other complaints highlight some of the limitations of corporate social responsibility and Black empowerment politics, both of which relied on the voluntary efforts of businesses. Generally willing to adopt programs that promoted Black empowerment, including eliminating overt references to race across the company, implementing voluntary affirmative action programs, and investing in education and training opportunities for Black employees, US corporations drew the line at outside supervision. Corporations, in other words, embraced their role as social "do-gooders," while simultaneously rejecting the call for them to become more accountable to society.

These and other limitations notwithstanding, the signatory companies repeatedly touted their success implementing the Principles, revealing the latter's function as a political tool wielded by the signatory corporations to stave off further government regulation. In a letter to Congressman Charles Diggs Jr., for example, Henry Ford II noted that his company had designated $1.1 million for "training and development programs for Blacks and Colored employees" in South Africa. This represented an increase of over 150 percent from 1976 levels.[108] Similar claims appeared in the first official signatory company report released by Arthur D. Little Inc. Published in December 1978, the report highlighted the progress made by the signatory companies with regard to their South African operations. According to the survey results, three-fourths of the reporting companies had integrated facilities (principle 1), while fifty-five out of seventy-eight companies (70.5 percent) reported having common benefit plans in place.[109]

Echoing Ford II, Sullivan stated publicly that he was "encouraged" by the results of the first report, making sure to add, "We are making progress, but much, much more needs to be done to be really effective."[110] Behind closed doors, however, Sullivan showed signs of losing faith. In a letter to Bishop Donald George Ming of the African Methodist Episcopal Church in Cape Town, Sullivan expressed his belief that "[he was indeed] having some success [with the Principles], but [he] really [did not] know for sure." Looking for reassurance, he asked Ming, "If you think the Statement of Principles . . . is having an effect in South Africa please let me know. It would be helpful to know if I am wasting my time."[111] Sensing Sullivan's growing disillusionment, Weedon encouraged Sullivan to see the "the cup [as] half full." It was, according to Weedon, easy to focus on what had yet to be accomplished by the Principles, but the importance was "the [positive] direction of change."[112] Terry Myers, deputy director of the Interfaith Center on Corporate Responsibility offered a similarly rosy-eyed appraisal of the Principles. Having previously voiced skepticism about the Principles, Myers revised his assessment, telling Sullivan, following a recent trip to South Africa, the "companies have made substantial financial commitments to revamping existing eating, toilet or locker facilities to achieve desegregation." Myers juxtaposed this progress with previous resistance on the part of South African subsidiaries, which "told me [in years prior] that desegregation of certain facilities could not be accomplished" due to high costs of "new designs and construction."[113] Some movement was better than none.

Sullivan's doubts were further exacerbated by criticism coming from one of the primary groups targeted by the Principles—namely, Black South African workers. Following their initial release, some Black South African workers embraced the Sullivan Principles as a tool used to contest apartheid in the workplace. A number of Black South African workers wrote Sullivan, who provided an additional outlet for their frustrations beyond their employers and the South African government. Others testified to the relative openness of multinational corporations to desegregation and employee training programs compared to their South African counterparts. Ultimately, however, the vast majority of Black South African workers came to resent the Principles, noting their failure to go beyond the workplace to address the broader apartheid system.[114]

In an effort to put additional pressure on the signatory companies, Sullivan formed the International Council of Equal Opportunity Principles (ICEOP) and set off on yet another fact-finding mission to South Africa in 1979. Comprised of Black ministers, many of whom had worked with Sullivan in OIC, the ICEOP functioned as an independent organization charged with monitoring the signatory companies. Attesting to the need for such a body, the ministers claimed, "companies [will] only do as much as they are forced to do."[115] The fact-finding mission was funded with a thirty-thousand-dollar grant from the Edna McConnell Clark Foundation of New York and led by Sullivan's longtime friends and colleagues Rev. Gus Roman and Daniel Purnell. D. Reid Weedon from Andrew D. Little Inc. also joined the ministers on their visit to South Africa.[116] While in South Africa, ICEOP representatives observed the operations of twenty-four signatory companies. Their observations were subsequently published in an ICEOP report released upon their return to the US.

In contrast to the official signatory company report prepared by Arthur D. Little Inc., the ICEOP report proved highly critical of the signatory companies for "[failing] to fulfill [the] stated purpose" of the Principles. It's conclusions echoed other critical accounts of the Principles, many of which cited evidence carefully omitted from the official signatory reports, such as GM's supplying of the South African military with South-African-made vehicles in defiance of US policy or Ford's firing of 700 Black workers in 1979 following an unofficial strike protesting racism at the company.[117] Critics of the Principles furthermore attacked the self-reported numbers submitted by the signatory companies to Arthur D. Little Inc. as inflated, using a clever deployment of a slippage in racial terminologies. In reporting on the improvements made with regard to hiring and wages, signatory companies used the term non-white. For Americans not well versed in South African racial hierarchies, non-white was assumed to mean Black. In reality, however, non-white was used to obscure company preference for Indians and/or Coloured South

Africans—the latter a broad racial category in South Africa referring to people of mixed race, including the Cape Coloureds, a heterogenous group of people comprised of descendants of indigenous Khoi- and Bantu-speaking Africans, Europeans, and Malay, the latter of whom were enslaved and brought to the Cape by the Dutch in the seventeenth and eighteenth centuries—over Black Africans, mirroring the racial hierarchy undergirding South African apartheid.[118] In an audit conducted by the South African Institute of Race Relations (SAIRR) at Ford Motors, for example, researchers discovered that the company's claim to have increased the percentage of non-white salaried staff by 187 percent in three years was largely due to the hiring of Coloured workers viewed by company officials as more dependable and hard-working than Black Africans. Of the 165 new employees hired by Ford, 108 were Coloured, compared to only fifty-seven new Black employees.[119]

At stake in the ICEOP, SAIRR, and other reports was the signatory companies' failure to measure up to the commitments embedded in the Principles program. Critical of the signatory companies' implementation of the Principles, these and other liberal organizations nevertheless remained supportive of the Principles themselves, choosing to believe in their efficacy. The Sullivan Principles would be effective if only the signatory companies would implement them fully.

Others were less forgiving in their assessment. As the 1970s came to a close, left-wing activists became more vocal in their criticism of the Principles. One report, written by anti-apartheid activist and scholar Elizabeth Schmidt proved particularly impactful. In the report, Schmidt observed that of 135 companies that had signed the Principles as of October 1979, "only two companies, Ford and Kellogg, had recognized Black trade unions, and only Kellogg had actually signed a contract." Even this should be treated with suspicion, Schmidt elaborated, due to policies in South Africa that made it fairly easy for companies to get around union contracts. Absent protections for Black workers, the Sullivan Principles, Schmidt concluded, stood little chance of affecting real and meaningful change toward the dismantling of apartheid.[120]

*   *   *

By the early 1980s, over 150 corporations had signed on to the Sullivan Principles, making them one of the biggest coordinated corporate social responsibility campaigns of the twentieth century. In addition to turning Sullivan into a household name across the US and South Africa, the Principles played a crucial role linking US Black empowerment politics with the anti-apartheid struggle. Not just US corporate executives, but countless US politicians, civil rights and African leaders, university presidents, and religious figures championed the Principles as a valuable weapon in the battle to end apartheid, and even as part of a broader campaign calling for selective divestment.

Still, the Principles were not without their critics. Addressing the limits of boardroom activism in 1978, Thomas N. Todd, a Chicago-based civil rights lawyer, declared: "corporations will always put profit before people . . . and, given this . . . it is better for Blacks not to go into board rooms rather than be used to create an optical illusion . . . of progress and change."[121] Todd's comments resonated with testimony by Randall Robinson, executive director of TransAfrica, before the US Subcommittees on Africa and International Economic Policy and Trade. Emerging out of the 1976 Black Leadership Conference on Africa, and officially incorporated on July 1, 1977, TransAfrica represented the growing efforts of Black Americans to wield power in Washington with regard to US foreign policy. It soon emerged as the most important lobby organization for Africa and the Caribbean.[122] Speaking before Congress on the Sullivan Principles, Robinson reminded his audience that business support for apartheid was not just an issue in South Africa:

> As the Civil Rights bill was being debated on the floor of Congress
> in 1964, the business community was busy in its attempts to gut
> the Equal Employment Opportunity Commission on the eve of its
> birth. . . . If American business has been less than zealous in observ-
> ing fair employment principles in the United States with our govern-
> ment prodding it along, how can we reasonably expect the same
> business community to be more progressive in South Africa with the
> ruling regime diametrically opposed to meaningful change?[123]

Responding to this and other criticism of the Principles, Sullivan resorted to a familiar strategy—namely, threatening the signatory companies. In a speech delivered in Johannesburg in 1980, Sullivan boasted he was "going to turn the screws on [the signatory companies]. . . . I will reach into corporation board rooms and take the cover off your companies. . . . You American businessmen in South Africa and other parts of Africa had better get yourselves together."[124] Elsewhere, Sullivan stated he "was not wedded to the six principles" and suggested his willingness to leave the program if it was discovered that "[the] program [was] being used as a copout for firms which don't have the guts to do what is right."[125] Here again, Sullivan sought to demonstrate his power over corporate America. This was Black empowerment, a politics that put its faith in the ability of the individual to create change.

To some extent, it worked. Facing growing pressure in the US and South Africa, many US corporations doubled down on corporate social responsibility and Black empowerment politics in an effort to stave off divestment and sanctions (see Chapter 7). That commitment was accompanied by growing evidence testifying to the Principles' ineffectiveness in bringing down apartheid. Rather than dramatically altering the conditions of millions of Black workers in South Africa, the Principles had perhaps their greatest impact on the fortunes of a group of Black South African entrepreneurs, who, like other African businesspeople across the continent, capitalized on US investment in Black empowerment politics to pursue their own political and economic interests.

PART III

Returns

CHAPTER 6

Apartheid's Entrepreneurs

Leon Sullivan and the signatory companies may have believed they were bringing Black empowerment to a destitute, disenfranchised population of Black South Africans via the Sullivan Principles. Yet, many of the ingredients for the emergence of Black empowerment politics were already present in South Africa by the 1970s, including among a small but tenacious group of Black entrepreneurs. Starting in the 1950s and 1960s, while Sullivan and others were advocating for job-training, Black entrepreneurship, and corporate-community partnership in the US, Black South African entrepreneurs were busy creating their own engine of Black empowerment: the National African Federated Chamber of Commerce (hereafter the African Chamber).

Led by the charismatic Tswana businessman Samuel Motsuenyane, the African Chamber initially focused on the economic empowerment of its members through channeling the collective consumer power of African traders. South Africa's apartheid regime, which placed significant restrictions on Black entrepreneurs and, at times, attempted to curtail the Chamber's efforts, pulled the organization into the realm of anti-apartheid politics. Addressing American and European business leaders in 1974 at the International Chamber of Commerce meeting in Europe, Motsuenyane declared: "The future of the white man would certainly be in jeopardy if he would not share his power; his comfort; his wealth and his know-how on more equitable terms with the rest of the people of [South Africa]. . . . Africans are becoming proud of being Black. Blackness [can] no more be accepted as a tag of inferiority."[1] At the time of Motsuenyane's address, South Africa was witnessing a surge in Black pride associated with the Black Consciousness movement. Drawing inspiration from the Black Power movement in the US and elsewhere, South Africa's Black Consciousness movement helped reignite mass protest, which had been largely absent from South Africa since the banning of the African

National Congress (ANC) and Pan-African Congress (PAC), in 1960. In doing so, Black Consciousness activists combined aspects of Black nationalism, Pan-Africanism, and Black theology to construct a movement based on the values of self-reliance and self-enlightenment.[2] As part of a broader effort to construct an independent Black movement, free from the influence of white liberals and Bantu authorities, the latter of whom were viewed by many as complicit in apartheid, Black Consciousness activists founded a number of community development programs, including a healthcare clinic and leatherwork factory.[3] Others, expanding on a distinct South African theory of racial capitalism, which probed the particular and context-specific ways racism and capitalism combined to give rise to apartheid, embraced socialism, advocating for revolution led by the Black working class.[4]

In this context, Motsuenyane and the African Chamber offered international business leaders a means of reconciling Black Consciousness, anti-apartheid politics, and global capitalism. Elaborating on his earlier remarks regarding the rise of Black Consciousness, Motsuenyane declared that Black Africans must be "encouraged to become creative and contributors to the overall development of [South Africa]."[5] They must have opportunities to become successful businesspeople. In other words, they must be empowered to act in the private sector.

At the time, Motsuenyane and Sullivan represented related but distinct strands of the transnational politics of Black empowerment being forged around and across the Atlantic. Over the course of the 1970s and 1980s, growing resistance to apartheid from both within and beyond the borders of South Africa helped to ensure that these two strands intersected and ultimately became intertwined, as US corporations and financial institutions looked to Black empowerment activists to help them renegotiate their relationship to South Africa. In the process, all three—Black Americans, Black South Africans, and US corporations—worked to construct Black empowerment politics—including support for vocational training, Black entrepreneurship, and free enterprise, more broadly—as central to ending apartheid and constructing a post-apartheid global order.

Sowing Seeds—The Life of Samuel Motsuenyane

As in the United States, Black empowerment's roots in South Africa lay entangled in the long history of racism and anti-racist movements. Born

February 11, 1927, in Potchefstroom, South Africa, some five years and 8,000 miles apart from Leon Sullivan, Motsuenyane encountered a country still reeling from war and struggling to make a name for itself in a world dominated by Euro-American capital. Following the defeat of the Afrikaners in the Anglo-Boer wars, the British set about consolidating what had been four separate colonies, including the Cape Colony, the Colony of Natal, the Transvaal Colony, and the formerly independent Afrikaner Orange Free State, renamed the Orange River Colony, to form single country, the Union of South Africa, which gained the status of a self-governing dominion of the British Empire in 1910.

Like earlier waves, this most recent extension of European power had a dramatic effect on Africans in the region. During the Second Boer War (also known as the South African War), an estimated 13,000 to 20,000 Black Africans died in concentration camps, while countless others had their lands seized and/or lost employment. Conditions hardly improved with independence. Some of the first pieces of legislation passed by the new government included a series of laws to limit the rights of native people and reinforce white supremacy. In 1913, the newly empowered South African government passed the Natives' Land Act, which, among other things, lent support to the ongoing project of native dispossession by constricting Africans' ability to own land to an area equivalent to 7 percent of the overall territory of South Africa.[6] The act also included anti-squatter provisions aimed at restricting Black South Africans' ability to enter into sharecropping agreements with white farmers. This was done to pressure said farmers to rent land to poor whites instead, pushing Africans like Motsuenyane, whose family worked as sharecroppers for a brief period, even farther down the chain of agricultural labor. Other legislation, including the Urban Areas Act of 1923, the Colour Bar Act of 1926, and the Native Administration Act of 1936, designed to make Black Africans second-class citizens in their homeland, followed.

Such restrictions did not go uncontested. Rather, joining their brothers and sisters in the diaspora, Black South Africans participated in various transnational movements, including Ethiopianism and Garveyism, promoting race consciousness and self-determination during the early twentieth century. Black mobilization reached a fever pitch following the World War II period, in response to rising white Afrikaner nationalism. The year 1948 served as a turning point in South Africa's history, when the Herenigde Nasionale Party (HNP), allied with the Afrikaner Party, defeated the liberal United Party and its leader, incumbent Prime Minister Jan Smuts. Due to existing franchise restrictions, few Coloured people and Asians voted in the election. Africans had been largely banned from voting since the late 1930s.

During the election, the HNP appealed to white-nationalist sentiment with promises to implement a policy of strict racial segregation. This system was later termed apartheid. Despite its literal meaning, translating to apartness in Afrikaans, apartheid was as much about maintaining white supremacy and suppressing Black and other non-white mobility as it was about keeping the races separate, a fact made clear by the government's wielding control over African affairs. Thereafter, the South African government, led by white nationalists, implemented a new wave of segregationist legislation, including the Prohibition of Mixed Marriages Act (1949) and the Group Areas Act (1950), the latter of which paved the way for the large-scale removal of Africans, Indians, and Coloureds from newly created whites-only urban areas.

Opposition to South African apartheid was widespread and came from multiple directions. Indeed, the decade-and-a-half following the end of World War II represented one of the greatest challenges to white supremacy and racial capitalism in South Africa prior to the Soweto Uprising. On August 9, 1956, an estimated 20,000 women of various ethnic and racial backgrounds converged on the Union Buildings in Pretoria, which housed the administrative government of South Africa, to protest the reimplementation of the pass system for African women, following a period of loosened restrictions. Pass laws were a system of internal passports aimed at restricting Black mobility and were frequently tied to employment. The pass system had long applied to African men, as Motsuenyane experienced when he was arrested for violating the pass laws in the Hillbrow neighborhood of Johannesburg. As he recalled, "At that time I carried a work-seeking special pass which I considered to be still valid. They [the police], however, arrested me, took my bicycle and kept it at the police station." Motsuenyane spent fourteen days in jail awaiting trial. Thereafter, Motsuenyane was brought as part of a group before the local magistrate. "The magistrate addressed us as a group without putting any questions to individual detainees," recalled Motsuenyane. The magistrate emphasized that "Johannesburg was a place of labour, 'You are allowed to look for employment within a period of fourteen days, failing which you are not allowed to be living as vagrants in the city.'"[7]

Such repression met with increased resistance from anti-apartheid organizations. In 1952, the ANC—founded in 1912 and South Africa's oldest and largest anti-apartheid organization—called on people to purposefully defy apartheid in a mass campaign aimed at overwhelming the prison system.

Spearheaded by Nelson Mandela, Oliver Tambo, and Walter Sisulu, who together led the push to establish the ANC Youth League, in partnership with the South African Indian Congress, the defiance campaign marked a new militancy within South Africa's anti-apartheid movement, resulting in an estimated 8,000 arrests. The demonstrations caught the attention of the United Nations, where thirteen Asian and African member states requested the UN General Assembly consider "the question of race conflict in South Africa resulting from the policies of apartheid."[8]

This militancy was furthermore reflected in the growing alliance between the ANC and the Communist Party of South Africa (CPSA). Having previously shunned communism, the ANC began working more closely with the CPSA (later renamed the South African Communist Party) in the 1940s and 1950s, signaling the former's embrace of leftist politics. During the 1940s, the CPSA and ANC were involved in a number of strikes, including the 1946 South African mine workers' strike. In response to their growing influence, in 1950, the South African government passed the Suppression of Communism Act, officially banning the CPSA. The act's broad phrasing made for a potent weapon, as seen in the state's use of it to prosecute a broad swath of people perceived as threatening to the government. Among them was ANC leader Nelson Mandela, charged on December 2, 1952, along with nineteen others, for violating the act and sentenced to nine months of hard labor.

Still, the question of how to respond to the expansion of racial capitalism and apartheid was far from settled. While many Black, Indian, Coloured, and some white South Africans drew inspiration in the new militancy of the ANC and CPSA, others, including Motsuenyane, found themselves charting a different course—one that would ultimately help give rise to a South African version of Black empowerment politics.

As in the United States, Black empowerment politics in South Africa found its feet in a set of organizations dedicated to moral uplift, starting with the Moral Re-Armament Movement (MRA). Founded in 1938 by American minister Frank Buchman in response to the escalating crisis in Europe, the MRA made its way to South Africa, where its proponents preached nonviolence, racial uplift, and cooperation between Blacks and whites in response to apartheid. During the 1950s, the organization attracted a number of Christian-educated Black South Africans, who, while opposed to apartheid, felt alienated by the rise of Black militancy and Black nationalism within the anti-apartheid movement. Among those who joined the MRA were several former ANC leaders, including Victor Selope Thelma and Phillip Qipu

Vundla. In 1955, Vundla participated in an MRA-led effort to negotiate an end to school and bus boycotts organized by more militant ANC members. He was later attacked by members of the local ANC Youth League and hospitalized.[9] Speaking to the turn to African nationalism within the anti-apartheid movement—made manifest with the formation of the Pan-African Congress in April 1959—Thelma told attendees at an MRA conference in Johannesburg, "We must . . . today accept the reality that the old slogan 'Africa for the Africans' can no longer serve as an appropriate vision for the future. We must now all seek and strive to build a new vision of an Africa for all—an Africa that transcends our present narrow ethnic and racial differences."[10]

Among those attracted to the MRA was a small yet growing cohort of urban Black businessmen, including J. C. P. Mavimbela, S. J. J. Lesolang, J. M. Mohlala, and Bigvai Masekela, the latter of whom served as a business partner to Motsuenyane in the formation of the Bampa Syndicate, a short-lived cartage company that operated in Soweto during the mid-1950s. In 1955, these and other Black businessmen, many of whom were based in the Johannesburg area, came together to form the African Chamber of Commerce (ACOC), a predecessor organization to the National African Federated Chamber of Commerce. Unlike Thelma, many of them embraced the turn to African nationalism, as evidenced by the group's invitation to Black nationalist and PAC President Robert M. Sobukwe to address the organization in 1959.[11] Sobukwe's speech before ACOC occurred not long before his arrest.

Sobukwe's arrest was part of a nationwide government crackdown targeting anti-apartheid activists. In 1960, facing widespread rebellion, the South African government instituted a state of emergency. During this period, large numbers of anti-apartheid activists were imprisoned and/or killed, including a group of PAC supporters protesting the pass system in the Black township of Sharpeville. The incident, which started when police opened fire on the protesters, killing sixty-nine and injuring some 250 more, garnered international attention, laying bare the violence of the apartheid regime. Immediately following that, the South African government added the PAC and ANC to the list of banned organizations, joining the CPSA. Those who managed to escape arrest or death were forced into exile.

Motsuenyane's position within the MRA and the African National Soil Conservation Association, a government-backed program focused on rural development, meant he and many of his fellow Christian-educated Black businessmen remained relatively isolated from these developments. Indeed, in 1960, as the state of emergency was being put into effect, Motsuenyane was busy on an adventure of his own, living in the US, having been selected to serve as the first Black South African to participate in the United States-South Africa Leadership Exchange Program (USSALEP). When he returned, he did so to a country where public defiance of the kind witnessed during the late 1940s and 1950s had been all but quashed, leaving private initiatives as one of the few avenues by which to pursue Black empowerment.

An American (Ad)Venture

Founded in 1955, USSALEP represented an attempt to preserve the "special relationship" between the US and South Africa. For decades, this bond had existed as a result of the two nations' intertwined histories as imperial white settler societies founded in the expropriation and exploitation of native and Black lands and labor.[12] Going back to the nineteenth century, white Americans played a central role in the construction of a racial capitalist system in South Africa, providing much-needed capital, technical expertise, and experience managing race across North America and the US's growing overseas empire.[13] US support for South Africa remained strong through the early Cold War, despite the latter's apartheid policies.[14] By the 1950s, however, that special relationship had begun to strain due to the somewhat divergent responses of each country to the "race problem." To be sure, the United States was and continues to be a haven for white supremacists.[15] Racism, moreover, as an institutional practice, remained deeply embedded in late twentieth century American society, ensuring that the profits of racial capitalism and democracy accrued disproportionately to white Americans. At the same time, coinciding with the US's mid-twentieth-century rise as a global superpower, a growing number of white Americans in business and government began to distance themselves from the kind of crude racist discourse associated with Jim Crow and embrace racial liberalism, prompting tensions with South Africa and its apartheid policies.[16]

From its founding as an outgrowth of the American Friends Service Committee and the African American Institute, USSALEP dedicated itself to fostering racial liberalism through its work facilitating exchanges between "like-minded" South Africans and Americans, with the ultimate goal of ensuring South Africa remained in the "mainstream contemporary" world with regard to technology, industry, culture, and social relations.[17] As part of this mission, in 1959, USSALEP selected Motsuenyane as the program's first

African exchange to the US. The program proved an equal boon for USSA-
LEP, whose program served a useful purpose, persuading Black South Africans like Motsuenyane of the benefits of American-style free enterprise.

Following an arduous journey by ship, Motsuenyane arrived in the US
in January 1960, amid "the worst snow storm the country had seen in eleven
years."[18] Motsuenyane was accompanied by his wife, Jocelyn née Mashini,
whom he met six years earlier, at the Alexandra Methodist Church, where the
two taught Sunday school.[19] Following a short stay in New York City, where
Sam Motsuenyane was detained by immigration officials on suspicion that
he might have tuberculosis, the Motsuenyanes settled into their new home in
Durham, North Carolina, where Sam Motsuenyane was to study agricultural
development at North Carolina State College.[20]

Motsuenyane's placement was a fortuitous one. On one level, Motsuenyane noted living in the US South in the early 1960s was like living in South
Africa. Years later, Motsuenyane recalled an incident while traveling in Kentucky wherein he was denied a seat in a restaurant and forced to "sit on soap
boxes and to have [the] meal that way." The moment proved formative for his
understanding of the US. "[I] realized that what we were seeing and experiencing was no different from what we experienced back home in spite of
the enlightened, non-racial constitution of the American people."[21] In both
places, Motsuenyane noted, "The problem [was] essentially not a Negro or
Native problem as is often alleged, but one of human selfishness on the part
of those people who desire to keep out and dominate the Negro for all time
and in all spheres of life."[22]

Despite these circumstances, or perhaps because of them, Motsuenyane
came away astounded by the state of Black business in the US. By 1960,
Durham's "Black Wall Street" was long past its peak in the early 1900s. Even
so, the continued presence of Black businesses like the North Carolina Mutual
Insurance Company were enough to impress Motsuenyane, who described
Durham's Black enterprises as unlike anything he had seen in his home country.[23] While there, Motsuenyane befriended several of the city's Black business
elite, including John Wheeler and Berkley Burrel, president of the National
Negro Business League, who impressed Motsuenyane with their "sophisti-
cat[ion]" and, as he later recalled, helped to spark his interest in establishing
an African financial institution along the lines of Durham's renowned North
Carolina Mutual Insurance Company.[24] Other Black South African businesspeople traveled to the US during this time, as well. As part of a broader effort
to help "solv[e] the urban problems in both nations," USSALEP launched the

Figure 9. Several South African participants in USSALEP's Small Business Project exchange program pose for a photograph in Durham, North Carolina. USSALEP, "The First Decade (1959–1968)," pg. 10. Courtesy of the Historical Papers Research Archive, University of the Witwatersrand, South Africa.

Small Business Project, which, among other things, helped to bring a number of African entrepreneurs to the US to gain American business acumen.[25] Among those who participated in the program were current and future African Chamber leaders S. Z. Conco, S. P. Kutumela, and F. S. M. Mncube.[26]

More than an opportunity to travel overseas, a luxury for Black South Africans living under apartheid, USSALEP's Small Business Project reveals the circumstances in which Black Americans and Black South Africans constructed diaspora during the second half of the twentieth century. For all the ways people of African descent imagined themselves as belonging to a broader community, maintaining a diasporic consciousness frequently required some physical contact.[27] This was especially true for the connections forged between Black Americans and Black Africans, whose physical contact with one another for much of the twentieth century paled in comparison to the flow of Black migrants from the Caribbean. For a period, particularly during the late nineteenth and early twentieth centuries, Black American missionaries did a lot of the work of facilitating a cross-Atlantic exchange. These crucial engines of diaspora did not go away in the latter half of the twentieth century. In the case of South Africa, however, their work was made significantly more difficult by the apartheid state, which came to see Black American missionaries as unwanted agitators deserving of close scrutiny.[28]

Apartheid, which relied on restricting Black mobility, created a situation whereby diasporic connections, including those formed through face-to-face contact, often required some kind of official approval. This is not to say that Black Americans did not maintain relationships with those involved in the anti-apartheid struggle. In May 1975, for example, while representing Georgia's 5th district in Congress, civil rights leader and former aide to Martin Luther King Jr. Andrew Young welcomed Miliswa and Dinilesizwe Sobukwe to his home in Atlanta. Miliswa and Dinilesizwe were the daughter and son of PAC leader Robert Sobukwe, who had been imprisoned and banned by the South African government from speaking publicly since the 1960s. Even this arrangement required the approval of the US and South African governments.[29]

By heavily restricting some forms of Black internationalism—namely, those rooted in Black militancy, leftist politics, and/or Black nationalism—apartheid opened the door for other institutions, including USSALEP, with close ties to American business, to take a greater role facilitating diasporic politics and connections. In this regard, Black American business came to play a particular role fusing Black internationalism and capitalist enterprise.[30]

Like Motsuenyane, Collins Ramusi, who spent time during the 1960s as a student at Northwestern University in Illinois, found much to admire in American private enterprise, including Black American business. Addressing Black South African businessmen gathered at the inaugural meeting of the African Chamber, Ramusi encouraged fellow Black African entrepreneurs to follow the example set by "American Negroes who," in Ramusi's telling, "had risen from a position of dire economic poverty to a position of strength."[31] "It is one of the exciting phenomena that coming from the House of Bondage the Negroes [in the United States had] got[ten] ahead so well in trade and industry," explained Ramusi. "Let us go forward in the hope that we can also follow in their footsteps."[32] Ramusi's veneration of Black American business was shared by Hudson Ntsanwisi, who traveled to the US as part of a delegation representing the Gazankula Bantustan, and expounded on the "particular importance" of "America . . . to Black businessmen" in South Africa. "In America," Ntsanwisi explained, "one comes into contact with hard-nosed businessmen schooled and nurtured in good business management." More than any particular skill or industry, Ntsanwisi lauded the spirit of entrepreneurship that seemed to permeate American society. "The Black businessmen of the future must travel, learn, think, imagine and dream and then make their dreams a reality."[33]

As Ntsanwisi's comments suggest, it was not just Black business but, in many ways, American business more broadly that proved "a real eye opener," in the words of fellow African Chamber member S. Nyamakazi.[34] Traveling around the US South, Motsuenyane observed the efforts of Black students engaged in the sit-in movement in Greensboro, North Carolina. He also visited a Cherokee Indian reservation, where he later recalled being inspired by their stories of resistance against "a sort of apartheid state" that had tried to exterminate them.[35] It was the "New South" capital of Atlanta, Georgia, that made a particularly lasting impression on the Tswana man from South Africa, however. There, Motsuenyane met with members of the Southern Regional Council (SRC). Formed out of the Commission on Interracial Cooperation, the SRC functioned as a private organization, the goal of which was to promote economic growth and "racial harmony"—in other words, keep whites and Blacks from rioting—through small concessions intended to tweak, but not dismantle, the boundaries of Jim Crow.[36] Among its founding members, the organization counted a number of prominent white and Black southern elite, including Atlanta journalist and publisher Ralph McGill, Fisk University President Charles Johnson, Atlanta University President Rufus Clement, and, to Motsuenyane's amazement, "several Negro business executives."[37]

Seeing all those Black men dressed in suits and sitting at the same table conversing with the region's white elite may have reminded Motsuenyane of the MRA, which similarly tried to foster a sense, albeit limited, of racial liberalism. It certainly left him with something to aspire to. In a report to USSALEP, Motsuenyane noted, "in the United States segregation and colour discrimination are on their way out." This change was due, in no small part, to the work of "interracial" organizations like the SRC. "One wishes [the Council's] work could be multiplied a thousand-fold."[38] Returning to South Africa in 1962, Motsuenyane soon embarked on a mission to do just that, forging partnerships between the African Chamber and white executives representing the international business community.

Negotiating Apartheid

Both within and from outside the borders of the country, Black South Africans boldly and defiantly protested the racist regime that cast them as second-class citizens.[39] Even so, significant aspects of Black life under apartheid took place outside the frame of overt resistance.[40] For Motsuenyane and other members of the African Chamber, the 1960s and 1970s constituted a period of experimentation on the way to forging a South African version of Black empowerment politics, which, while opposed to racial discrimination and segregation, valorized other aspects of South Africa's political economy, including for-profit enterprise, as a vehicle for Black advancement.

Motsuenyane's return to South Africa in 1962 coincided with a flourishing of Black business activity. Despite the government's attempts to police Black mobility and keep Black Africans rooted primarily in the rural "native areas," Black migration to urban areas continued to grow during apartheid. By 1951, the number of Africans living in urban areas had increased to 2.3 million from 1.1 million in 1936.[41] Black migration to the city only expanded in subsequent decades, picking up steam in the late 1960s and reaching record heights in the late 1970s and 1980s.[42] In the process, Black migrants created a thriving consumer market.

Postwar material culture played an important role in shaping Black life in South Africa's segregated urban areas, engendering a kind of Black modernity routed through consumption based in the market.[43] Among those who benefitted from this rise in postwar Black consumerism were Black businesses, which saw their fortunes grow alongside the rise of the Black metropolis. Starting in the 1930s and 1940s, African traders located in the Black townships around Johannesburg formed a number of cooperatives in an effort to increase their market power and compete with white-owned businesses. This included the Orlando Cartage Association, of which Motsuenyane was a member.[44] These efforts eventually led to the formation of the African Chamber of Commerce, later, reorganized as the National African Chamber of Commerce (NACOC), a predecessor to the National African Federated Chamber of Commerce.

Despite statements made to the contrary, NACOC, from the beginning, was politically engaged. Addressing members in 1964, Bigvai Masekela, who preceded Motsuenyane as president of the organization, prophesized, "In this country[,] there is a case for bloodless revolution. . . . If we go the right way about it[,] traders can play an important part in making life meaningful."[45] In other words, Black entrepreneurship could serve as the basis for Black liberation. Such a vision, reiterated by Motsuenyane and others, put NACOC in an interesting position vis-à-vis the South African government. On one hand, NACOC appealed to the South African government for material and other forms of assistance. In meetings with the South African government, including the Bantu Administration and Development ministry, charged with overseeing policy toward Black Africans, NACOC members emphasized the compatibility between their organization and apartheid policies. Africans, they insisted, wanted to develop economically in ways similar to other groups, including Afrikaners.[46] This was in keeping with apartheid's emphasis of separate development.

On the other hand, NACOC resisted the government's policy of Bantuization, which sought to restrict African political and economic development through isolating Black Africans in so-called "native homelands" located on the periphery of the country. This conflict came to a head in 1969, when the South African government mandated NACOC reorganize itself along ethnic lines. Fearing retaliation if they refused, NACOC, which by this point was headed by Motsuenyane, obliged with the government's request, reorganizing into a federated structure that required members to belong to one of several regional divisions in accordance with the ethnic identities ascribed to them by the apartheid regime. Still, they did not miss an opportunity to make known their protest to the South African government. In response to a notice sent by Deputy Minister of Bantu Administration and Development P. J. Koornhof, Motsuenyane decried the request to reorganize NACOC along tribal lines as "outmoded" and in conflict with the principles of a free-market economy. "Commerce was indivisible; it was strange that Africans were expected to run their Chamber of Commerce on tribal lines," while "white businessmen in the country were attempting to club themselves into one group to improve the industrial and commercial life of the country."[47] Here, and elsewhere, the African Chamber relied on the language of free enterprise to oppose apartheid.

Complying with the government's order to reorganize NACOC along regional lines proved a blessing in disguise. In particular, it forced the organization's leadership, which heretofore had been concentrated largely in the Johannesburg area, to seek out and cultivate new leaders to aid with the African Chamber's growth at the regional and local level. In doing so, the African Chamber relied on a number of key vehicles to promote itself, including the organization's annual conference. Like OIC's annual conventions, African Chamber conferences were spectacles to behold. When they began, in the 1960s, entering the conference was like stepping into another world—one

Figure 10. Sam Motsuenyane delivers the presidential addresses at the 21st NAFCOC conference. *African Business*, August 1985, pg. 18.

in which Black executives, as opposed to white, functioned as decision-makers. Years later, when the African Chamber opened up the organization to include an associational membership for multinational corporations, the African Chamber's conferences took on a somewhat lighter shade. Still, photographs from the organization's 1984 meeting show a sea of Black businessmen dressed in grey and black suits with matching ties and pocket squares. To complete the look, the organization sold badges, cuff links, and ties.[48]

Alongside the racial dynamics on display, Chamber conventions were highly gendered affairs. Indeed, this was part of the organization's appeal. Among the consequences of colonialism and apartheid was the disturbance of traditional patrilineal patronage networks. Absent these networks, many African men struggled to acquire the resources, including land and cattle, necessary to pay bride wealth and ascend into their place atop African society.[49] By the mid-twentieth century, these developments helped give rise to a perceived crisis in Black masculinity in South Africa, paralleling the "crisis" in Black masculinity in the US. Unable to meet the expectations of "traditional society," a growing number of African male youth turned to bootlegging, gambling, and other kinds of illicit behavior in an effort to assert their masculinity.[50]

As members of a Christian urban elite, the African Chamber's leaders observed the proliferation of youth gangs comprised of young African males with trepidation. In comments remarking on the 1976 Soweto Uprising, Motsuenyane emphasized the damage caused to Black business at the hands of African youth. Ignoring the violence deployed by South African police against protesters, many of whom were children and young adults, Motsuenyane boldly declared: "At times of unrest the Black businessman was the most vulnerable . . . least protected from all forms of criminal onslaught, exploitation and victimization."[51] In doing so, he positioned the African Chamber, like OIC, as offering an alternative vehicle for disciplining Black male youth and (re)asserting patriarchal authority.

Central to this process was a reorientation of Black male frustration from protest toward market participation via formal, as opposed to informal and illicit, private enterprise. At the Chamber's annual conference, Black businessmen competed for the title of "Black Businessman of the Year." Established in 1976 with the help of Gilbey Distillers, the contest proved productive in moderating ethnic tensions by channeling them into friendly competition. Remarking on the competition, Selby Ngcobo, who served as director of the KwaZulu Development Corporation, noted the "clever and shrewd" business skills of "the Xhosa people of the Transkei," whose region had produced five winners of the African Chamber's annual Black Businessman of the Year contest. In what was clearly meant as a nudge to other Chamber members, Ngcobo added, "I am sure, however, that Black businessmen from other parts of this country will seek to challenge and dethrone businessmen from the Transkei."[52]

Ngcobo's choice of words, particularly "dethrone," was telling of how the African Chamber fused free-market ideology together with references to "African tradition."[53] Besides Ngcobo's reference to African monarchies, Chamber members demonstrated their allegiance to the ancestors with traditional warrior dances. These performances, historically associated with the transition to manhood, further drove home the message that entrepreneurship was a means for African men to regain the rights and privileges denied them by colonialism and apartheid.

A similar message, one emphasizing patriarchal authority, accompanied what quickly became one of the highlights of the African Chamber's annual conference: the beauty pageant. Selected by the local and regional chapters to represent them at the national conference, woman beauty contestants had to abide by a series of strict rules and meet "the highest international standards," in the words of one Chamber member.[54] In an effort to promote obedience, the organization warned contestants that the organization reserved the right to take "disciplining measures . . . against those [women] who displayed unbecoming behavior."[55] Used by the African Chamber's all-male leaders to assert their authority and police Black femininity, the contest served a somewhat different purpose for the beauty contestants, whose experiments wearing make-up, donning sleek and colorful bathing suits, and, of course, the latest hairdos exhibited by Black American women on the covers of magazines signaled their efforts to embody a transnational, modern Black female identity, which emerged alongside, and sometimes in tension with, the image of the modern Black business*man*.

In 1974, the African Chamber reported that ticket sales from the beauty contest had generated a total of 367 rand—equivalent to approximately R24,000 or $1,242 in 2025—in revenue, far exceeding the money earned from the sale of the organization's magazine, *African Business*, which brought in a meager R29 that year.[56] As time went on, the organization increasingly looked to take advantage of the demand for beauty contestants, who were featured in advertising campaigns and an annual calendar used to raise funds for the organization.[57] In 1979, international cosmetic and beauty care company Elida Gibbs took over as primary sponsor for the Chamber's beauty contest in an effort to increase the company's market share among Black women in South Africa. Elida Gibbs's sponsorship brought the African Chamber into the world of global fashion, providing access to experts and beauty industry professionals from Paris, Milan, and the United States.[58] In doing so, Elida Gibbs joined a wave of multinational corporations, including many from the US, in partnering with the African Chamber on a range of new ventures promoting Black enterprise and free-market politics.

These new partnerships, which flourished amid the push for corporate accountability that followed the 1976 Soweto Uprising and looked to take advantage of a growing Black consumer class in southern Africa, signaled a turning point in the history of the African Chamber and Black empowerment politics in South Africa. Having spent the first decade of its existence struggling to build a national constituency—one that challenged the government's Bantuization policy—the Chamber increasingly looked to multinational capital, and US corporations in particular, to raise the organization's profile and provide material and technical support needed for Black empowerment.

Figure 11. Contestants in the 1985 NAFCOC Beauty Competition. *African Business,* June 1985, cover.

Capitalizing (on) Diaspora

"Never before has a NAFCOC conference witnessed such solidarity of opinion from business leaders of all race groups," stated *African Business* in a report on the organization's 13th Annual Conference in Cape Town.[59] The conference drew, for the first time, a large number of white executives representing domestic and international concerns. Their presence portended a literal change in the Chamber's fortunes. Between February 1976 and February 1977, the African Chamber witnessed a 13.5 percent increase in income from R56,870 to R64,511 with the majority of new revenue coming from large, white-owned multinational corporations.[60] In 1977, Chamber leaders decided to formalize their relationship with international business by creating the category of associate membership.[61] In exchange for official recognition from the African Chamber, associate members were required to pay annual fees one-third higher than regular members. Justifying this policy, Chamber leaders cited the significantly greater access to capital that these multinational companies had compared to African entrepreneurs.[62] By the end of 1978, the African Chamber boasted over eighty associate members, including industry leaders like Coca-Cola, Mobil Oil, and the Anglo-American Corporation.[63]

Like the Sullivan Principles, the sudden outpouring of multinational corporate support for the African Chamber was inextricable from the surge in anti-apartheid activism occurring within and outside the country. As Motsuenyane alluded to in his comments to the International Chamber of Commerce meeting, South Africa, during the 1970s, witnessed a growing wave of Black consciousness. Inspired, in part, by the global Black Power movement, a new generation of Africans championed self-determination and Black pride. The Soweto Uprising was but one example of the effects of the Black Consciousness movement. In the weeks following the uprising, the Transvaal appeared as if a war zone, as demonstrators clashed with police in Black townships across the region, including in Tokoza, Mabapone, Mamelodi, Lowveld, and Lekozi.[64] Subsequent demonstrations emerged in the areas surrounding Cape Town and Port Elizabeth in the south and southeastern parts of the country. For many, including those in the ANC and PAC in exile, Black Consciousness signaled renewed hope of defeating apartheid.[65]

Still, not everyone was keen on the rebellion unfolding within South Africa. Many Black businessmen, in particular, drew a line between what they saw as legitimate and illegitimate forms of resistance. In a Presidential Policy Statement issued by the African Chamber in the wake of the unrest, Motsuenyane stated, while sympathetic to the students protesting the continued "deni[al of] basic and fundamental civil rights," he lamented the damage done to Black businesses.[66] While the unrest included a number of physical attacks on Black businessmen, the chief concern voiced by Chamber members had to do with assaults on property. Echoing Motsuenyane, Don A. S. Mmesi, who owned a small supermarket in Roodepoort, just north of Soweto, decried the "township unrest [which] cost [him] over R100,000 in stock losses" and temporarily forced him to close his business. Similar complaints permeated the pages of *African Business*. Overall, the African Chamber estimated the total cost of property damages accrued during the Soweto Uprising, referred to by the Chamber as a "riot . . . [at] a staggering figure of . . . R1,043,000," or $8,163,050 in 2025 dollars.[67]

Like the organization's earlier dispute with the South African government over its structure, the dramatic wave of social unrest ultimately benefited the African Chamber, while reinforcing the link between Black rebellion as a catalyst in the transnational rise of Black empowerment politics. In the months and years following the Soweto Uprising, a growing number of corporations, including a number of Sullivan signatory companies, declared their support for the African Chamber, including through advertisements like one by GM declaring, "We're all for NAFCOC," which appeared in *African Business*. Such advertisements were about more than selling a product. Rather, they spoke to US corporations' interest in forging political alliances with African business around the protection of private property, private enterprise, and the profit motive.

As in other parts of Africa, Black empowerment in South Africa also profited from the kind of private negotiation that had increasingly come to define US international relations on the continent. One of the first examples of this kind of business diplomacy took place in relation to the African Bank. The origins of the African Bank are somewhat difficult to discern. Some accounts cite Collins Ramusi as having first introduced the idea of a bank back in 1964, inspired by the example of Black Americans during his recent visit to the US. Indeed, Black Americans played a direct role in the bank's early history. In 1974, Motsuenyane returned to the US to meet with representatives from the North Carolina Mutual Bank and the Farmers and Mechanics Bank, as well as a number of Black business organizations, including the National Negro Business League and the National Bankers Association, whose president, Edward Irons, later addressed the Chamber at the organization's eleventh annual conference in Phuthaditiaba.[68] The African Bank likewise built on examples of

Black finance closer to home, many of which took the form of cooperative savings clubs similar to those established by Africans elsewhere.[69]

Like their counterparts in the US, many of these African financial institutions struggled to survive, compelled by apartheid to rely on a capital-poor population for deposits. In the absence of hard currency, one African Chamber chapter, the Inyanda chapter, turned to faith to supply the needed boost to help get the African Bank off the ground and running. The chapter president, P. G. Gumede, noted how the chapter had instituted a "holy month" during August to assist with the Bank initiative. "We closed our businesses for an hour every Thursday and joined the various women confraternities in prayer for the success of the Black Bank venture."[70] Later, another Chamber member, N. H. Motlana, cited the example of Leon Sullivan and his 10–36 program implemented in Philadelphia to inspire Black South African churchgoers in "establish[ing] real business empires that could give employment to hundreds of thousands of Blacks from accountants to sweepers."[71] Such proclamations underline the significance of Christianity, and Black churches in particular, in paving the way for Black empowerment politics in South Africa, as they did in the US.

Religious conviction, while not the best provider of wealth on its own, provided an important foundation for the partnerships forged by the African Chamber with corporate America. As the previous chapter showed, the latter was, at this very moment, becoming increasingly invested in a moral mission to redeem corporate America's image. This was particularly relevant for those companies doing business in South Africa, where growing public outrage over corporate complicity in apartheid led some 150 US corporations to sign the Sullivan Principles, a corporate code of conduct promoting desegregation and Black economic empowerment. As part of this effort, Leon Sullivan wrote to the Principles signatory companies encouraging them to "deposit R50,000 to R100,000 in the African Bank" in addition to contributing to the "NAFCOC student bursary programme," the latter of which enabled Black South Africans to study business at colleges and universities in South Africa and the US.[72] Then, in 1979, Chase Manhattan Bank, home of Sullivan's long-time friend George Champion, invited Motsuenyane to visit the bank in New York, where he received training to assist him in his role as director of the African Bank.

Similar offers of assistance further help to illuminate the conjoining of the movements for Black empowerment in the US and South Africa. A year before his visit with Chase Manhattan, Motsuenyane visited the US, where he met with Sullivan and fellow Black executive Harold R. Sims, who, like Sullivan, had spent the last several years negotiating partnerships between his company, Johnson & Johnson, and various African leaders with the aim of promoting Black empowerment. During their meeting, the trio discussed plans to establish a South African Small Business Development Center to provide financial support and training to Black business outside of the "native reserves."[73] The pair responded to the proposal with enthusiasm. Sims, in particular, encouraged Motsuenyane to look at a similar program developed by Johnson & Johnson in conjunction with the Rutgers University School of Business Administration in the aftermath of the 1967 unrest in Newark as a model.[74]

Subsequently, Motsuenyane and Sims travelled back and forth between the US and South Africa, generating support for the program, whose stated aim was "to develop and expand African entrepreneurial activities and improve the success rate of African small business." Speaking to his colleagues and superiors at Johnson & Johnson, Sims emphasized the moral, as well as material, benefits to be had by the company if it agreed to help fund the program. "Africa," as stated in the program proposal, "[was] a vast, complex continent with enormous potentials for human and natural development." In order to realize its full potential, however, Africa required "all the assistance it can get from the world's multinational corporations," like Johnson & Johnson, which, in turn, stood to benefit from the "recognition at home and abroad for their contributions to" the program.[75] As the Soweto Uprising made clear, "the fragile winds of certain change" were blowing in South Africa, much as they were across the rest of the continent. Rather than wait and let history take its course, Sims encouraged his superiors to consider the "long-term impact" of Johnson & Johnson's continued investment in South Africa, including in training and hiring more Black South Africans in high-paying, managerial positions. Such continued investments, Sims argued, "may be just as revolutionary [as the ongoing political transformation] but without drastic loss of South African skills and capital."[76] Other US companies followed suit. During the late 1970s, Coca-Cola partnered with the African Chamber to sponsor one person from each region to attend management classes. Meanwhile, IBM and Mobil Oil lent company representatives to serve as volunteers in a Chamber training center located in Sebokeng.[77]

It was not just US corporations that stood to benefit from assisting Black business in South Africa. Rather, in his conversations with the South African government, Sims emphasized the important work such a program could have for helping improve the country's international image, which had suffered significantly in the wake of the Soweto massacre. Writing to South African Secretary of Health J. DeBeer in follow-up to a recent visit to the country, Sims emphasized: "There is no other country of potentially greater value to South Africa, whatever direction it takes ultimately or now, than the U.S. Because no other country in the world has had to pass through its own apartheid and achieve miracles in overcoming its limitations a mere generation ago" (underlining in original). Here and elsewhere, Black empowerment activists, like Sims, deployed US history to their advantage. Eliding the ongoing white counterrevolution in the US, Sims positioned the US as a leader in overcoming racial conflict. Crucial to the US's success in this regard, according to Sims, was "develop[ing] a [Black] commercial constituency and a leadership—able, experienced and committed to freedom as we aspire for it."[78]

Freedom, commerce, racial uplift: These were ideas the apartheid government could get behind, at least in theory. Government approval for the South African Small Business Development Center came in 1978, a year after the government introduced a number of changes expanding the categories of business in which Africans could legally engage, including dentistry, bookselling, catering, accounting, and electrical equipment dealing. Subsequently, Motsuenyane, Sims, and Sullivan set about soliciting financial contributions from US corporations and financial institutions to help with the center, including a number of Principles signatory companies.[79] In what may have appeared as a snub to the African Chamber, Johnson & Johnson selected Constance Ntshona to oversee the center.[80] Having previously managed a department store in a shopping plaza in Soweto, Ntshona served on the boards of several community organizations and local government institutions, including the South African Institute of Race Relations, the Black Sash, the Soweto Urban Bantu Council, and the Soweto Traders Association, giving her access to a range of government and business leaders.[81] In correspondence between Sims and Johnson & Johnson's local distributors in South Africa, Sims expressed optimism concerning Ntshona's ability to "help [Johnson & Johnson] explore in depth . . . our business opportunities with the Black community of South Africa [including the company's] marketing strategy towards the Black woman" in the "health care [and] pharmaceutical business."[82]

The late 1970s and early 1980s witnessed dozens of similar partnerships between US multinational corporations and Black entrepreneurs in and around South Africa. With Polaroid's departure from South Africa in 1977—the result of a multiyear struggle with activists involved in the Polaroid Revolutionary Workers Movement—Kodak looked to take advantage of the moment to increase its share of the South African market by employing Black managers and salespeople.[83] Late in 1978, Kodak hired Ishmael Maumakwe and Arthur Mbambo, two sales representatives charged with training Black shopkeepers in photographic sales and development, as part of the company's new Black Market Development program. Praising the program in the pages of *African Business*, Ramsay Ramushu, one of thirty-seven participants, noted that the program had exceeded his expectations. "This type of diversification can only help the Black businessman," he stated.[84] Ramushu's comments speak to the ways the engagement between US corporations and Black South African entrepreneurs facilitated more than a material exchange. It also engendered an exchange of ideas—ideas about business and its role in the broader struggle for Black liberation.

Debating Free Enterprise

In March 1977, the Chamber's premier magazine, *African Business*, ran an article on Tom Molete, manager of Barclay's Soweto branch. Molete had recently visited the US on a trip funded by the US Department of Information. The trip provided Molete with an opportunity to study the US financial system with a "particular emphasis on the development of small businesses and education in money management techniques."[85] Reporting on his time there, Molete impressed upon his fellow Chamber members the importance of Black enterprise as the basis for the advancement of Black South Africans. South Africa, Molete emphasized, must avoid the "dismal failure of the rest of Africa[,] who have gained their political freedom [and yet remain] depend[ent] on foreign aid." This dependence, according to Molete, was a direct result of other African states' embrace of large-scale government-led development projects. Instead, it was on South Africans to build an economy based on private enterprise, including Black business. Here, the US, with its programs targeting Black business development, offered "a suitable model," in Molete's opinion.[86]

As more and more opportunities emerged for African Chamber members to travel and dialogue with Americans, the conditions emerged for a series of debates about American-style free enterprise and its relationship to Black empowerment. Pointing to the US as an example, white corporate executives and business professionals encouraged the Chamber to take on a greater role in shaping South African politics in order to "demonstrate that private enterprise is not synonymous with exploitation" and that "individual as well as public welfare and freedom are better served by a responsible free enterprise system," in the words of the Africa Institute's Gerhard Max Erich Leistner.[87] Addressing the African Chamber in June 1979, Motsuenyane predicted that the organization and Black businessmen more broadly would come to play "a very important role . . . as bridge builders" ensuring the stability needed for economic development. To do so, however, the organization needed to avoid involving itself in "party politics," including the Bantustans, where close ties between the African Chamber and the homeland governments had only bred conflict and distrust.[88] Private enterprise, not government-sponsored development, was, in Motsuenyane's view, the way forward for Black South Africans.

Motsuenyane's comments found a welcome audience among Chamber members and their white supporters, both of whom increasingly adopted the language of free enterprise to describe the post-apartheid political economy they hoped to build. "Free enterprise . . . [is] the only system in which initiative, efficiency, drive, ability, dedication received their maximum rewards . . . irrespective of race, colour or creed," stated J. J. Fouché, whose company Gilbey Distillers cosponsored the Businessman of the Year competition.[89] Fouché's words resonated with the members of African Chamber, who used the organization's 1977 meeting to declare "the strengthening of the free enterprising system [as] one of Nafcoc's major principles."[90]

That white and Black businesspeople in South Africa embraced free enterprise amid the Cold War is, in and of itself, unsurprising. Across the Global North, and increasingly in the Global South, social scientists, businesspeople, and politicians adopted the discourse of free markets in direct response to progressive movements promoting social welfare, government regulation, and wealth redistribution.[91] Many of the conversations about free enterprise at the African Chamber were similar to those occurring elsewhere at the time. In words familiar to those used by Sullivan to rally corporate support for the Sullivan Principles, South African professor of business George Marais warned that the free enterprise system was under attack. Alluding to people like Julius Nyerere, whose ujamaa program promised to bring African socialism to Tanzania, Marais warned the Chamber that "an elite group of very nationalistic orientated politicians" across the "Third World" had led their countries astray economically, contributing to "a decline in industrialization." Only by "follow[ing] an independent road away from the attraction of the homeland government" could the African Chamber avoid a similar fate.[92]

Many Chamber members agreed. Yet, for them, free enterprise meant more than a reduction in government regulation and an opposition to socialism. Rather, free enterprise entailed ensuring Black South Africans had the resources to compete with whites. In order to "demonstrate to young people the advantages and incentives of a free enterprise system . . . the free enterprise system in South Africa would need to become free for all race groups."[93] This was the argument made by Chamber members in their protestations to the South African government. Black empowerment, not free enterprise, remained the Chamber's ultimate goal. For this to occur, Africans also needed training, capital, and other kinds of material support.

To this end, the African Chamber passed a series of resolutions at the organization's 1979 annual convention. The resolutions help to clarify the Chamber's stance on the relationship between Black and white businesses. "True partnership can only exist and thrive in a climate of equality and mutuality of trust," emphasized members. In addition to eliminating barriers to doing business, including "all discriminatory policies affecting Blacks," Chamber members demanded "that Black businessmen trading in the Black areas for the time be protected . . . from the more affluent and privileged white businessmen." Furthermore, they demanded that any and all partnerships between Black and white business be pursued with "the primary objective . . . [of] ensur[ing] that Blacks derive maximum benefit and are fully protected from diverse forms of exploitation." And, last, but not least, they demanded that support should be extended to Black businessmen in the form of "access to capital" and training.[94] Free enterprise, according to Black South African businessmen, must be accompanied by Black empowerment.

* * *

As the 1970s neared their conclusion, Black businesspeople in South Africa, a growing number of whom had joined the African Chamber, began the process of formulating and articulating their own vision for a post-apartheid South Africa. In doing so, they, like their white multinational corporate supporters, embraced the discourse of free enterprise to challenge apartheid regulations on Black business. At the same time, they made clear that free enterprise would not truly be free for everyone unless it was accompanied by Black empowerment, a condition not always met by the Chamber's international partners, who preferred to focus their attention on eliminating government red tape.

Despite clear and obvious tensions, Black entrepreneurs and multinational corporations continued to partner together in promoting private enterprise as a "productive" alternative to the growing Black labor movement and revolutionary, left-wing Black internationalism. In doing so, the former helped pave the way for the transnational politics of Black empowerment to take hold within South Africa. As South Africa moved increasingly toward ungovernability in the 1980s—the outcome of continued anti-apartheid organizing and state efforts to suppress it—the African Chamber and their corporate partners doubled down on their efforts promoting private enterprise, including deregulation, corporate welfare, and joint for-profit ventures, as central tools in the broader effort to eliminate apartheid. As they did, they found new allies in predictable and unexpected places.

CHAPTER 7

(Di)vesting

n November 1980, the *Philadelphia Bulletin*—once Philadelphia's largest newspaper, now on its last legs—published a multipart exposé lambasting Leon Sullivan's Opportunities Industrialization Centers Inc. (OIC).[1] Touting a popular refrain, the article described OIC as a drain on (white) American "tax dollars," which, in the author's estimation, were being used to produce "questionable results." Elsewhere, the exposé trafficked in racial stereotypes, describing OIC leaders as inept and corrupt.[2] What at first seemed a momentary bump in the road quickly snowballed into something much bigger and consequential for the seventeen-year-old Black empowerment program. Within several months, OIC found itself the focus of at least eight different audits, including one by Arthur D. Little—the accounting firm involved in monitoring the Sullivan Principles—and the US Government Accountability Office.[3] Making matters worse, President Ronald Reagan implemented a federal hiring freeze, which OIC executives bemoaned threatened OIC's contract with the government to place youth job candidates.[4] OIC and Black empowerment politics had come face-to-face with the politics of austerity.

OIC was far from unique in the challenges it faced during the 1980s. In the previous two decades, the US government had pumped millions of dollars into Black empowerment programs like OIC in an effort to ameliorate and mollify Black militancy in US cities (see Chapter 3) and postcolonial Africa (Chapter 4). These programs, in turn, provided job-training and economic opportunity to countless Americans and Africans. By the 1980s, US-based Black empowerment programs found themselves increasingly grouped with other social welfare programs, smeared as wasteful by conservatives eager to push forward with a counterrevolution against the Black freedom struggle. This was somewhat ironic, given the history of Black empowerment, which supporters frequently portrayed as a pro-market alternative to Black dependency on government welfare. In an effort to stave off the attacks, proponents of Black empowerment doubled down on their anti-welfare rhetoric. Responding to Ronald Reagan's proposed cuts to education and job-training programs in 1981, Sullivan noted that the cuts would only increase the number of people on government welfare "beyond today's crisis." Repeating a well-worn argument about the link between government welfare and public frustration, Sullivan equated the failure to provide job opportunities for Black and other marginalized Americans to earn a living with pouring fuel on "social dynamite threatening to explode."[5]

In a way, Sullivan was right. Far from passive victims, Black Americans in the 1980s contested government divestment of its responsibility for Black citizens alongside the reassertion of white supremacy, in what one historian has described as a Black Power resurgence.[6] This resurgence took multiple forms, including the National Black Independent Political Party (NBIPP), the founding conference of which took place on November 21, 1980, at Ben Franklin High School in North Philadelphia, located a mile south of Sullivan's Progress Plaza. Positioning itself as an independent political organization modeled on the African National Congress (ANC) and the Mississippi Freedom Democratic Party, the NBIPP served as proof of the vitality of radical Black (inter)nationalism during the Reagan era.[7]

Meanwhile, other instances of 1980s-era Black organizing assumed a decidedly more liberal veneer. Building on his earlier work aiding Martin Luther King Jr. and heading Operation People United to Save Humanity (Operation PUSH), Reverend Jesse Jackson became the second Black person, after Shirley Chisholm, to mount a national campaign for president of the United States. In an early speech delivered to a joint session of the Alabama state legislature—the first Black man since Reconstruction to address the body—Jackson avoided mentioning some of the more controversial tenets of his campaign platform, such as cutting defense spending and reparations for the descendants of enslaved Black Americans, in favor of racial reconciliation through supporting American industry and economic opportunity. "We put too much focus on the schoolyard and not enough on the shipyard," said Jackson. "It's about time we forget about Black and white and started talking about employed and unemployed."[8] Elsewhere, Jackson joined Sullivan in rejecting social welfare as the solution to the country's, and Black people's, in particular, economic woes, declaring in August of 1982, "We want trade, not social aid."[9] Jackson's words echoed those of his former Southern Christian Leadership Conference (SCLC) colleague Andrew Young. In a campaign speech, part of his successful 1981 bid to become Atlanta's second Black mayor, Young outlined his vision for Atlanta—one centered on cooperation with the private sector. "The decade of the 40's was the development phase . . . the 50's . . . the legal phase where we fought against segregation laws. The 60's was the mass implementation phase with sit-ins, marches and demonstrations. The 70's . . . the political phase . . . [and] the 80's will be the economic phase . . . with a fully integrated work force and a strong group of black entrepreneurs."[10] Black economic empowerment—not reparations nor government welfare—took center stage in the administrations of Andrew Young, Coleman Young, Tom Bradley, and other Black mayors during the 1980s.[11]

And then there was Leon Sullivan. Having spent the 1960s and 1970s promoting Black empowerment through bringing OIC to cities and towns across the US and Africa—a task aided by his appointment to the board of General Motors (GM)—Sullivan joined others in giving his attention to the ongoing crisis in South Africa. During the 1980s, the international anti-apartheid movement emerged as a central plane on which battles over racial inequality and white supremacy were fought. Inserting themselves between activists demanding sanctions and divestment and conservatives calling for "constructive engagement," proponents of Black empowerment championed the power of private enterprise as a vehicle for Black advancement.

Such investment was by no means guaranteed. Facing pressure from anti-apartheid activists and a deteriorating situation in South Africa, a growing number of US corporations made the decision to sell plants and close up shop in South Africa during the 1980s in a move hailed by the media as a victory for the sanctions and divestment movement. Divestment itself was not a simple thing. At the same time that they agreed to divest themselves of their equity assets, US corporations launched a new set of joint ventures under the guise of empowering Black South Africans. In doing so, they relied on and helped to further solidify networks connecting Black American and Black South African entrepreneurs, while also paving the way for corporate America to play a prominent role in constructing a post-apartheid new world order.

Black Empowerment and Its Discontents
in Reagan's America

Ronald Reagan's nomination as the Republican presidential nominee in 1980 met with widespread disappointment and anger on the part of Black

Americans, many of whom correctly predicted the devastation it would bring. During his campaign, Reagan repeatedly allied himself with a resurgent white nationalism, including holding a rally in Neshoba County, Mississippi, the site of the brutal murders of Student Nonviolent Coordinating Committee (SNCC) activists James Chaney, Michael Schwerner, and Andrew Goodman. Elsewhere, the Hollywood actor turned New Right warrior alienated Black voters by rejecting an invitation to speak to the National Association for the Advancement of Colored People (NAACP)—the only one of four major presidential contenders to do so. The refusal prompted NAACP executive director Benjamin Hooks to speculate "that [Reagan] has written off the black vote."[12]

Tensions only increased following Reagan's inauguration as the 40th president of the United States of America. Early in his presidency, Reagan oversaw one of the largest tax cuts in US history, in the form of the Economic Recovery Tax Act. Speaking in November 1981, less than a year after Reagan took office, Jesse Jackson made plain the racist overtones of the "Reagan revolution," stating: "President Reagan cut the public economy, which affected blacks disproportionately. Then, with his emphasis on deregulation, he told the Congress and the private sector that they didn't have to provide affirmative-action help to take up the slack." Henceforth, Jackson continued, "we have concluded that we have to become our own Equal Employment Opportunity Commission."[13] Where government enforcement of civil rights proved inadequate, Jackson and other Black Americans turned to the private sector to secure Black empowerment.

It was, in many ways, an old story.[14] Frequently denied the protections of citizenship, Black Americans had long resorted to private means to claim rights and freedom. Jackson's actions in 1981 were directly out of the 1960s', if not the 1930s', civil rights playbook, utilizing direct action to pressure corporations to open their doors to more Black Americans. The specific vehicle Jackson utilized, Operation PUSH, had been formed in 1971 as a successor to Operation Breadbasket—itself modeled on Leon Sullivan's selective patronage movement. Like its predecessor organizations, Operation PUSH utilized boycotts and other methods to pressure corporations into supporting Black economic empowerment, including employing Black managers and contracting with Black-owned businesses.

One of PUSH's most publicized campaigns during the early 1980s targeted Coca-Cola. On July 11, 1981, following eight months of negotiations without a resolution, Jackson and Operation PUSH called for a "withdrawal of enthusiasm" for Coca-Cola products.[15] Not long after, Coca-Cola products were removed from the shelves of four Black-owned 7-Eleven franchises in Washington, DC, and one hundred Chicago-area stores. Meanwhile, the mayor of Gary, Indiana, Richard Hatcher, launched an initiative to remove Coke machines from 194 city halls, highlighting the symbiotic relationship between Black political power and Black empowerment politics.[16]

It did not take long for Coke executives to respond. On August 10, just under a month after Jackson's announcement, Coke executives announced their willingness to "accelerat[e] and [enlarge] . . . programs already in place" giving Black Americans "a well-deserved piece of the action."[17] The so-called "moral covenant" included a commitment by Coca-Cola to invest in Black businesses, including $2 million in advertising dollars to Black-owned newspapers and magazines, appointing thirty-two Black-owned distributorships, and increasing its deposits with and loans to Black financial institutions. Coke also pledged to up its charitable giving to Black organizations.[18] Altogether, Coke agreed to invest $34 million in Black America.[19] Following the victory against Coke, Operation PUSH went on to stage successful boycotts of Anheuser Busch, CBS, Nike, and other US corporations.

Joining the chorus lauding corporate-sponsored Black empowerment, Black journalist William Raspberry dubiously hailed the agreement as, perhaps, "as important to black America as the [Montgomery bus] boycott."[20] This was surely an overstatement. Where the Montgomery bus boycott and other direct-action campaigns targeted spaces and amenities utilized by large numbers of working-class Black Americans, the agreement between PUSH and Coca-Cola benefited a much smaller group of Black entrepreneurs and corporate professionals. Corporate professionals like Carl Ware, who, in March 1982, following the PUSH boycott, became the company's first Black vice president.[21] Having previously served on the Atlanta City Council, including as its president from 1976 to 1979, Ware explained his decision to join corporate America in terms similar to those used by other Black executives. "My decision to leave city government was one of the toughest I've ever made in life," stated Ware in an interview with the *Atlanta Journal/Constitution*. "However, the difficulty of the decision was lessened when I came to grips with the fact that Public Service is not confined to electoral politics. Many of the same issues and community needs that are addressed by elected officials are also addressed by Corporate America [sic]."[22] The private sector, in Ware's estimation, was an equally, if not even more important, site through which to pursue Black empowerment.

Doing so required leverage. In 1982 and 1983, Ware set about proving his value to Coca-Cola. Despite his official title as vice president of urban affairs, a newly created position within the corporation, Ware's role within the Coca-Cola corporation, like Sullivan and Harold Sims before him, went well beyond US cities, handling a wide range of issues in and around the Black world. Ware acknowledged as much in a 1984 memo to Coke executive Earl Leonard, in which he noted that, despite his title, "[his] responsibilities [were] more international," including "monitoring and working with entrepreneurs in Third World and Caribbean countries to help open up and expand those markets."[23] Unsurprisingly, Ware also became the corporation's go-to man in one of the decade's biggest racial conflicts: the struggle to end South African apartheid.

The 1980s proved an auspicious decade for the anti-apartheid movement. Following years of recalcitrance on the part of white politicians and government officials, who publicly condemned apartheid and yet resisted undertaking meaningful action against the South African government, anti-apartheid activists scored an important victory with the election of Black officials to local and state governments. During the early 1980s, these local and state governments began passing divestment policies targeting South Africa. Indeed, the American Committee on Africa (ACOA) declared: "1982 . . . a year of major victories for the movement to withdraw public funds from companies whose investment in South Africa subsidizes the apartheid system. Massachusetts, Michigan, Connecticut and the cities of Philadelphia, Wilmington and Grand Rapid all enacted legislation that will force the divestment of up to $300 million."[24] Such actions were a direct result of decades of activism. One might argue they were an indication of Black Power in action in Reagan's America. They also served as evidence of the anti-apartheid movement's growing acceptance among a broader swath of the American public, including among liberals.

Nicknamed the "city too busy to hate," for its seeming relative racial liberalism, Atlanta, Georgia—Coca-Cola's hometown—emerged as an important site of anti-apartheid activism. In April 1982, in response to previous calls by the (South) African National Congress (ANC) and the Southwest Africa People's Organization, the Atlanta branch of the Southern Africa Support Committee staged an anti-apartheid protest in Gordon Park, on the border of the city's historic Old Fourth Ward. Speaking to the press, Thandi Gcabashe, the daughter of former ANC leader Albert Luthuli, who resided in Atlanta at the time, stated that the organization "hope[s] the rally will expose the work we are doing to freedom-loving people in Atlanta and inform them of policy decisions their government is making without their input."[25] Later that summer, former SNCC chairman turned politician John Lewis led the charge in Atlanta's City Council to pass a nonbinding resolution requesting the removal of all city pension funds from banks making loans to the South African government and corporations doing business in the country.[26] The movement for divestment had come to Georgia.

Investing $34 million in Black entrepreneurs—an amount equal to approximately 33 percent of Coke's first quarter earnings in 1982—was one thing.[27] Divesting from South Africa, a country that accounted for 5 percent of the company's worldwide sales and where Coca-Cola claimed 90 percent of the soft-drink market, was another.[28] In May 1983, Coca-Cola Senior Vice President Earl T. Leonard Jr. sent Ware to meet with Georgia State Representative Tyrone Brooks to see what could be done on the issue. Brooks had recently announced plans to introduce divestment legislation into the Georgia General Assembly.[29] Ware, however, endeavored to persuade Brooks of Coca-Cola's positive work in South Africa, including multiple initiatives aimed at improving labor conditions and expanding educational opportunities for Black South Africans. In a follow-up memo to Leonard Jr., Ware promised to continue meeting with Brooks to ensure he and other state legislators were "fully informed [regarding] the Company's activities so as to minimize or negate any general or negative references."[30]

Nor did Coca-Cola's meddling in anti-apartheid politics stop there. At the same time that Black elected officials—many of them veterans of the civil rights and Black Power movements—were waging a battle in local, state, and national legislatures, a new generation of student activists were leading their own revolt on campuses across the US.[31] High on the list of priorities, alongside student demands for greater Black representation, curriculum reform, and increased attention to institutional-community partnerships, was divestment from South African apartheid. For many, these issues were closely related. At the Atlanta University Center—representing a consortium of Black colleges, including Clark College, Morehouse College, Spelman College, and Atlanta University—student activists linked their anti-apartheid activism to ongoing efforts to reorient the university to better serve poor and working-class Black communities in southwest Atlanta. Commenting on the group's decision to boycott the grocery chain Winn Dixie, Clark College student president Kevin Houston linked the struggles against racism in Atlanta and South Africa, stating, "Winn Dixie has been very blatant in their racism. . . . In addition to having South African products in their stores, Winn Dixie has fewer than

100 black managers in approximately 1,200 stores."[32] Others took advantage of the opportunity created by the anti-apartheid movement to raise questions about their institutions' close ties to large US corporations, including Coca-Cola. On April 26, 1986, Spelman's board of trustees responded by voting to divest from companies doing business in South Africa, making the college the first Black college to do so.[33]

Having lost the battle at Spelman, Coca-Cola had better luck across town at the predominately white Emory University, whose links to the soft-drink behemoth—including what, at the time, amounted to the single largest donation to any institution, in the form of $105 million in Coca-Cola stock donated to Emory in 1979—earned the school the nickname Coca-Cola University.[34] The gift, which coincided with Emory University president James T. Laney's appointment to Coca-Cola's board, was pivotal in elevating the school's reputation from regional to national prominence.[35] During the 1980s, amid ongoing debates over both institutions' ties to South Africa, Coca-Cola played an important role in expanding Emory's role on the international stage. When students at Emory's Candler School of Theology began protesting South African apartheid, Laney, unlike some other university presidents, appeared sympathetic. Writing Candler professor and fellow Yale Divinity School alum Jon Gunnemann, Laney lambasted "the poisonous harvest reaped from policies of racial intolerance [currently unfolding] in the Union of South Africa." Connecting apartheid to the history of Jim Crow in the United States, Laney continued: "Many at Emory feel compelled to do something—not because we aren't also concerned with flagrant abuses of human rights and liberties in other parts of the world, but because as Americans we carry in ourselves a deep sensitivity to the kind of starkly racial injustice so clearly evident in South Africa today."[36] Here Laney echoed anti-apartheid activists by highlighting the countries' shared history.

Where activists called for US institutions to divest from South Africa, however, Laney deployed this shared history for alternative means. Alluding to Emory's history as an institution founded by Methodist missionaries, Laney advocated for Emory to become *more* invested, as opposed to less, in South Africa. "Part of our claim to being a university must lie in our being able to address an issue of this magnitude with great reason and imagination. Emory has a long tradition of preparing men and women for lives dedicated to relieving suffering and bringing greater justice and light into the world." Like the Sullivan Principles, which advocated corporate social responsibility and corporate-sponsored Black empowerment as an alternative to divestment, Laney touted the moral leadership of private institutions, stating: "we at Emory are equipped to engage difficult issues in ways that the federal government in Washington cannot" through "exchanging students and faculty with universities there, and by strengthening our connections with the prominent and largely black South African Methodist Church and with other organizations in South Africa."[37] Constructive engagement, not divestment, was private America's response to apartheid.

While Emory administrators increasingly expressed their support for empowering Black South Africans, some on the president's advisory committee on South Africa, including African historian Kristen Mann, questioned the university's response. In a letter to Gunnemann, who chaired the committee, Mann stated: "You and the President can count on me to cooperate fully in any effort to strengthen African studies on this campus." This focus, Mann continued, however, should not distract from ongoing efforts "addressing the problems of blacks at home."[38] Her comments were echoed by religious studies professor Jacqueline Irvine, who held the distinction of being the only Black committee member. "As an Afro-American and a tenured member of this faculty, I know that commitments go unfulfilled and interests waiver and disappear as the majority culture gets bored with old causes," stated Irvine. She then cited a lack of notable progress on "increas[ing] the presence of Afro-Americans on [Emory's] campus" and support for "Afro-America[n]" Studies as "a valued and respected field of studies," as justification for full and complete divestment as the only ethical response with regard to South Africa.[39] If Emory could not fulfill its commitment to empowering Black Americans on its own campus, it stood little chance of exerting true moral leadership in the case of South African apartheid.

Contradicting Mann and Irvine, other committee members argued that Emory could make a greater impact by continuing to invest in companies doing business in South Africa and encouraging—or pressuring, depending on one's perspective—them to engage in ethical and/or "social investment."[40] Supporters of this strategy gained an influential ally in Ware, who kept close tabs on the conversation unfolding around divestment at Emory. Addressing the committee, Ware touted Coca-Cola's affirmative action policies and support for Black franchisees in South Africa as evidence of the company's role empowering Black South Africans.[41] In the end, the committee sided with Coca-Cola and against Mann and Irvine, voting in favor of maintaining the university's $222 million investment in companies doing business in South Africa, pending they remain signatories to the Sullivan Principles.[42] For the time being, Coca-Cola, with Ware's help, had succeeded in forestalling divestment at Emory. Black empowerment politics, in the form of the Sullivan Principles and other corporate programs promoting Black entrepreneurship and integration into corporate America, remained alive and well.

Reckoning with Apartheid

At the same time Coca-Cola was facing pressure from anti-apartheid activists regarding its business dealings with South Africa, Leon Sullivan was in the midst of his own reckoning. In September 1980, while in South Africa promoting the Sullivan Principles, the civil rights minister and GM director faced some of the harshest criticism he had received to date. As of 1980, 137 US corporations overseeing 78,572 South African workers had signed onto the Principles. Yet, resistance on the part of the signatory companies to the reporting measures undertaken by Arthur D. Little Inc. and the International Council of Equal Opportunity Principles (ICEOP) had only increased. Whereas in 1979, 94.2 percent of the signatory companies submitted reports attesting to their compliance with the Principles, only 87 percent did so in 1980.[43] At a speech at the University of Witwatersrand in Johannesburg on September 5, Sullivan warned US companies that if things did not change soon, he would be compelled to "turn the screws" on them at home, including "re-examining [his] position on disinvestment" and, possibly, calling on the US government to impose sanctions and penalties for those firms which failed to comply.[44] Elsewhere, Sullivan spoke more cautiously, telling *The Philadelphia Inquirer*, for example, "I'm tightening the screws *slowly*" (emphasis added). Sullivan's faith in the Principles appeared shaken. Still, he maintained, "progress [was] being made."[45]

Others were not so sure. While initially the Sullivan Principles—and corporate-sponsored Black empowerment more broadly—garnered widespread praise, including from the SCLC and the Organization of African Unity, public criticism of the Principles increased significantly during the 1980s, including in Sullivan's hometown of Philadelphia. There, mirroring events in Atlanta, the City Council spent 1981–1982 debating legislation requiring the city's municipal pension fund to divest from South Africa. Among the key proponents behind the legislation was Republican councilwoman Joan Specter. Initially, Specter introduced legislation that would have only required the pension board to divest itself of bonds and securities in companies that failed to comply with the Principles. This reflected a broader trend whereby states, municipalities, and other institutions exempted the Principles' signatory companies from divestment. Yet, Specter subsequently revised her views, stating: "While the 'Sullivan Principles' themselves are a sincere effort at bettering the lives of black workers [in South Africa], they miss the crux of the issue which is apartheid as a national policy." Repeating a common criticism of the Principles, Specter noted, "American companies employ a tiny fraction (less than 1 percent) of the black labor force and [thus] it [was] highly unlikely that treating those workers any differently [would] have the landslide effect of dismantling apartheid."[46] In the end, the City Council voted to require the pension fund fully divest itself of $85 million it had invested in companies in South Africa, regardless of their Principles' signatory status. Other cities and states soon followed suit, leading to a decline in the Principles' signatory membership.[47]

Meanwhile, similar legislative debates were unfolding in Congress, led by the Congressional Black Caucus (CBC). Established in 1971 by thirteen Black representatives elected to Congress on a tide of Black political power, the CBC emerged as a powerful voice on issues concerning Black Americans, including South African apartheid. Starting in 1969, Rep. Charles Diggs, who served as the CBC's first chairman, used his position as chair of the House Subcommittee on Africa to bring attention to South African apartheid through hearings on the issue. Building on those hearings, Rep. Ronald Dellums (D-CA) introduced the first anti-apartheid bill in Congress in 1972. Dellums's actions were followed by other CBC members, including Rep. Julian Dixon (D-CA), who, in 1983, introduced a motion demanding the US executive director of the International Monetary Fund (IMF) reject loans to any country that practiced apartheid.[48] The motion followed the IMF's approval of a $1.1 billion loan to South Africa to aid the country's war in Angola and Namibia. That year, Rep. William H. Gray III (D-PA), who made history in 1978 as the first Black American to chair the House Budget Committee, introduced H.R. 1392 as an amendment to the Export Administration Act of 1979, calling for an immediate prohibition on all new investment in South Africa. A week later, Rep. Stephen J. Solarz (D-NY), who had supported the Gray amendment, introduced H.R. 1693, requiring US companies adhere to a code of conduct, which closely mirrored the Sullivan Principles. The bill received Gray's and other CBC members' endorsement.[49]

A key turning point came in October 1983, when the US House of Representatives passed the Export Administration Act with the Gray and Solarz amendments included. Occurring during the lead-up to the 1984 presidential election, Democrats in particular viewed the bill as an opportunity to challenge Reagan on his foreign policy toward South Africa and gain points with Black voters. Taking aim at the president, Solarz stated, "constructive engagement has failed and is flawed."[50] Still, others criticized the Gray and Solarz amendments for not going far enough.[51] Echoing others, William R. Cotter, president of the African-American Institute, for example, described the Solarz amendment as moderate, noting its similarity to the Sullivan Principles. Such codes "will not bring about political powersharing, which is the real issue in South Africa; 80,000 black employees of American firms, even if their lives are enormously improved, will have no effect upon the 19 million other blacks in this society who do not share in those direct benefits," stated Cotter in testimony before Congress.[52] In this context, political support for the Principles and similar codes increasingly gave way to support for divestment and sanctions.

Criticism of the Principles reached a fever pitch in 1985 following a scathing report by the ACOA criticizing the Principles. The report cited testimony from Black workers at Ford Motor Company's plant outside Pretoria who described the Principles as a "toothless package," "[a] piece-meal reform that allows this cruel system of apartheid to survive" through helping to "modernize" it.[53] Under pressure, Sullivan again felt compelled to go on the offensive, releasing a statement in which he promised that "if in 24 months statutory apartheid had not been abolished, and there was not a clear commitment of the vote for Blacks, he would call for the [signatory] companies' withdrawal, and an Embargo against South Africa."[54] This was the strongest criticism of the Principles by Sullivan to date. Yet, it was quickly followed by another statement in which Sullivan reiterated his faith in the program. In May 1985, Sullivan told *The Washington Post* "the Sullivan Principles are working" and, indeed, had "started a revolution in industrial race relations across South Africa . . . become[ing] a platform for many in South Africa arguing for equal rights in government and other places."[55] Despite mounting evidence to the contrary, Sullivan continued to champion the potential of corporate-sponsored Black empowerment.

By the mid-1980s, faith and potential were no longer enough. On July 20, 1985, in response to growing civil unrest, the South African government declared a state of emergency. Initially confined to the Eastern Cape and the Pretoria-Witwatersrand-Vaal area, which included Johannesburg, the order was eventually expanded to cover the entire country. For many, the state of emergency proved the last straw. By January 1986, at least thirty-nine major US firms had sold their operations in South Africa, up from only seven the previous year.[56] The state of emergency likewise proved decisive in moving the needle in Congress, which, building on earlier attempts to curb US investment in South Africa, passed H.R. 4868, otherwise known as the Comprehensive Anti-Apartheid Act, in September 1986. Among the regulations included in the act was a new ban on bank loans to South Africa, along with a list of prohibitions on steel, iron, coal, uranium, agricultural products, and food products.[57] Ten days following Congress's initial passage of the bill, President Reagan announced his decision to veto the bill, claiming it amounted to "economic warfare" and threatened ongoing "efforts to peacefully end apartheid."[58] In a rare display of bipartisan action, Congress subsequently overrode Reagan's veto of the bill, marking the first time since the Vietnam War that Congress had overridden a presidential veto on foreign policy.

With the passage of the Comprehensive Anti-Apartheid Act, Sullivan was all but compelled to concede the Principles' failure. Making good on his earlier promise, he released a statement calling for the complete and immediate withdrawal of all US corporations from South Africa until "statutory apartheid" had been eliminated and Black South Africans given "a clear commitment for equal political rights."[59] The statement, delivered at a press conference outside the Dupont Plaza Hotel in Washington, DC, mirrored the Principles' launch, with one notable exception: the white executives who had stood proudly by Sullivan's side in 1977 were absent. Instead, in a move that proved revealing of US corporations' appropriation of Black empowerment politics to serve their own interests, a twelve-member steering committee representing the 104 remaining signatory companies held their own press conference, during which they reasserted their commitment to the vision first introduced by Sullivan a decade earlier. It is with "profound regret," Colgate Palmolive CEO Reuben Mark, W. Michael Blumenthal of Unisys, and Mobil CEO William Tavoulareas told reporters, that the group received the news of Sullivan's departure from the Principles program. "We owe a great debt to Leon Sullivan . . . but we will now have to carry out the Sullivan Principles without Sullivan." Doubling down amid growing attacks on the Principles and record-high support for divestment, the signatory companies reiterated their commitment to the "tried and true" approach of corporate-sponsored Black empowerment, encouraging all "signatory companies . . . [to] *renew* and *increase* their efforts to end the apartheid system" (emphasis added). Appropriating the rhetoric of anti-apartheid activists, Tavoulareas noted, "[we, the signatory companies,

Table 1. Comparison of the Sullivan Principles and Code of Conduct in Title II of
the Comprehensive Anti-Apartheid Act of 1986 (H.R. 4868)

Original Sullivan Principles	H.R. 4868—Code of Conduct
1. Nonsegregation of the races in all eating, comfort, and work facilities;	1. Desegregating employment facilities;
2. Equal and fair employment practices for all employees;	2. Providing equal employment opportunity for all employees;
3. Equal pay for all employees doing equal or comparable work for the same period of time;	3. Assuring that the pay system is applied to all employees;
4. Initiation and development of training programs that will prepare, in substantial numbers, Blacks and other non-whites for supervisory, administrative, clerical, and technical jobs;	4. Establishing a minimum wage and salary structure;
5. Increasing the number of Blacks and other non-whites in management and supervisory positions;	5. Increasing the number of persons in managerial, supervisory, administrative, clerical, and technical jobs who are disadvantaged by apartheid;
6. Improving the quality of employees' lives outside the work environment in such areas as housing, transportation, schooling, recreation, and health facilities.	6. Taking reasonable steps to improve the quality of employees' lives outside the work environment; and
	7. Implementing fair labor practices by recognizing the right of all employees to unionize.

believe] the decisive arena of this historic struggle is inside South Africa
itself." Where anti-apartheid activists made such claims as part of a broader
argument about the rights of Black and other non-white South Africans to
self-determination and in support of divestment, Tavoulareas encouraged
US corporations to remain active within the country, where their "resources
[could] be most effectively brought to bear" on bringing about change.[60]

Frequently portrayed in the press and in subsequent histories of the anti-
apartheid struggle as contradictory, the signatory companies' continued support for the Sullivan Principles were actually in line with the letter, if not the

spirit, of the Comprehensive Anti-Apartheid Act. Taking a page from the Sullivan Principles' playbook, Title II of the Act included multiple incentives for US corporations and other entities to continue promoting Black empowerment in South Africa, including earmarked funds for education and training programs, preferential status for Black and other non-white organizations—a nod to minority business programs in the US—and a requirement that all US nationals employing more than twenty-five persons in South Africa implement a Code of Conduct emulating the Sullivan Principles. Similar efforts to *increase* investment in Black empowerment programs in South Africa appeared as part of local and state-level public and private policies related to divestment.[61] By transferring ownership of South African subsidiaries to Black South Africans, contracting with Black retailers to continue selling American consumer products, and other kinds of contractual relationships, US corporations found ways to continue profiting from South Africa after "divestment," while accumulating evidence of American private enterprise as a vehicle for Black empowerment—evidence subsequently deployed by US corporations in positioning themselves as partners in building a new post-apartheid South Africa.

Corporate Diplomacy Revisited

Apartheid was largely absent from the conversations surrounding Coca-Cola's centennial celebrations in Atlanta in May 1986, or so corporate executives hoped. The festivities took place at the Omni hotel downtown, where guests, including 14,000 bottlers from around the world, were treated to a $23 million spectacle featuring miniature Coke trucks zipping up and down the aisles while scantily clad dancers twirled to loud music. Company executives' hopes of a conflict-free celebration were dashed, however, when anti-apartheid activists showed up outside the hotel with signs and chants of "Coca-Cola Sweetens Apartheid."[62] Protesters even managed to snag the attention of media at a parade rounding up the celebration. As photographers snapped pictures of the barrage of Disney characters, baby elephants, and celebrities that made up the parade, they also captured signs reading "Get Coke Out of South Africa," creating the perfect advertisement for protesters.[63]

Despite garnering national headlines, the protest initially appeared to have little effect. Responding to protesters, Coca-Cola chairman Roberto Goizueta argued, "[Coca-Cola] cannot ban Coke because pulling out of South Africa is

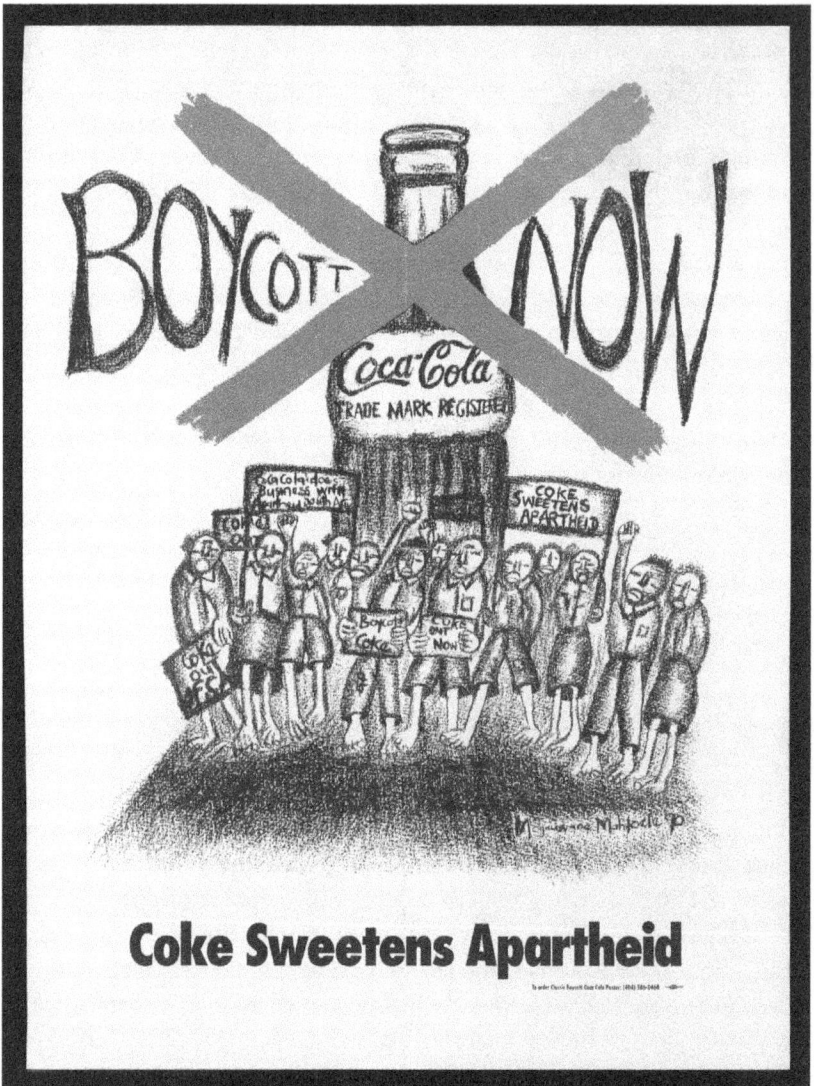

Figure 12. "Boycott Coca-Cola Now; Coke Sweetens Apartheid" Poster, American Friends Service Committee, Africana Posters Collection, Michigan State University Libraries Special Collections. Courtesy of the African Activist Archive. Used by permission of the American Friends Service Committee.

like moving out of Atlanta."[64] The comment was intended to highlight Coca-Cola's commitment to serving the world's diverse population. Having gotten its start selling to local soda fountains, Coca-Cola joined other southern companies in making the transition to a global corporation, pursuing Robert Woodruff's dream of putting Coke into the hands of people around the globe.[65] In time, this mission was reflected in the company's executives, including the Cuban-born Goizueta, who, in 1980, became Coca-Cola's first chief officer born outside the US, and the first Hispanic CEO of a Fortune 500 company. Goizueta's appointment may have succeeded in boosting Coca-Cola's brand in the Spanish-speaking world. In this case, his comparison of South Africa and Atlanta had the opposite effect. Flipping Goizueta's argument on its head, anti-apartheid activists acknowledged the similarities between South Africa and Atlanta, while highlighting Coke's role maintaining a system of apartheid in both.[66] Under pressure from activists and facing the potential passage of the Comprehensive Anti-Apartheid Act in Congress, Coke announced it was joining other corporations and divesting from South Africa.[67]

Divestment is a finicky thing. Where anti-apartheid activists defined divestment as severing all business ties with South Africa, many US corporations lobbied politicians and institutional investors to define divestment more narrowly to minimize its effects on their bottom line. Specifically, corporate executives advocated for a definition of divestment meaning no longer holding equity assets (i.e., property) or having employees in South Africa. This helps explain Coca-Cola Vice President Carlton Curtis's careful word choice in announcing Coke's divestment. Speaking to reporters, Curtis noted that when divestment was completed in 1987, Coca-Cola would have "no assets, no employe[e]s and pay no taxes in South Africa."[68] To do this, Coca-Cola relocated the company-owned syrup manufacturing facility from Durban to the neighboring Kingdom of Swaziland.[69] At the same time, a new company, National Beverages Services Ltd., was created to buy Coca-Cola's assets, monitor quality and use of the Coca-Cola trademark, and ensure continued adherence to the Sullivan Principles in South Africa.[70]

It was the final piece of Coca-Cola's divestment that sparked the most conversation, however. Seeking to usurp the moral high ground from anti-apartheid activists, Coca-Cola's president and chief operating officer, Donald Keough, noted Coke's divestment "[was] a statement of our opposition to apartheid *and* of our support for the economic aspirations of black South Africans" (emphasis added).[71] As part of its "divestment," Coca-Cola agreed to sell its remaining 30 percent share in the South African bottling company Amalgamated Beverages Industries (ABI) to a multiracial group of investors and create a new $10 million Equal Opportunity Fund (EOF) to fund opportunities for Black South Africans in business, housing, and education. Solidifying the fund's reputation as a vehicle for Black empowerment, Coke appointed prominent South African anti-apartheid leaders, Bishop Desmond Tutu and Rev. Allan Boesak, to oversee it. Divestment, at least in Coca-Cola's case, was linked with the company's renewed commitment to supporting Black empowerment in South Africa.

News of Coca-Cola's divestment, combined with the launch of the EOF, garnered significant support from Atlanta's Black elite, many of whom had long championed Black empowerment politics in Atlanta. Speaking on behalf of the company, Carl Ware touted the fund as "putting our money where our mouth is."[72] His comments were echoed by the SCLC president, Rev. Joseph Lowery. Just months after threatening a boycott of Coca-Cola if they did not divest, Lowery lavished praise on Coca-Cola for showing that "strong moral[s]" and "sound . . . business" could go hand in hand.[73] Here and elsewhere, proponents of Black empowerment equated racial progress with support for Black enterprise, including Black enterprise in South Africa. "People forget there is a small but significant black middle class in South Africa," stated Atlanta mayor Andrew Young, defending Coca-Cola's manner of divesting.[74] This small but "significant," according to Young, Black middle class in South Africa included members of the National African Federated Chamber of Commerce (African Chamber), some of whom, building on the organization's history of partnering with US corporations, greeted divestment as an opportunity to expand their share of the South African economy.

Not long after Coca-Cola announced its plans to sell its remaining 30-percent stake in ABI, prominent South African Black businessman and former president of the African Chamber Richard Maponya announced his plans to bid for the shares, establishing a new entity, Black Equity Participation, as a vehicle to "buy out companies and shares in companies divesting from South Africa."[75] Maponya likely believed his chances of winning the contract were good, having previously served as one of several Black distributors for Coca-Cola.[76] Instead, Coca-Cola opted to sell its shares to several thousand Black traders, in an effort to foster local buy-in among those who continued to sell the product in Black townships and rural areas.[77] That same year, a Soweto-based group of Black businessmen, organized into the Soweto Investment Company Ltd., purchased what was the last remaining Pepsi plant in South Africa.[78] In doing so, these Black South African businessmen took advantage of what the African Chamber hailed as "a golden opportunity" given to Black entrepreneurs by divestment—one in which they had the chance "to give meaning to the concept of Black economic empowerment."[79]

Not everyone agreed. Solidifying her reputation as a leading critic of Coca-Cola and Black empowerment politics more broadly, Tandi Gcabashe pressed for a boycott of the company, noting that, while Coca-Cola might no longer own any assets in South Africa, it continued to fund apartheid through the sales of its products. In her criticism, Gcabashe pointed out that for every eighty-cent bottle of Coke sold in South Africa, the South African government collected ten cents in taxes, which it used to oppress Black and other non-white South Africans. In this context, Coca-Cola's Equal Opportunity Fund was "an insult," a mere "drop in the bucket."[80] Gcabashe's criticism found support among other anti-apartheid activists, who maintained boycotts against Coke and other US corporations profiting from continued sales in South Africa throughout the late 1980s and early 1990s.[81] Black youth and labor activists in South Africa likewise proved critical of the manner by which US corporations divested, including attempts by Black entrepreneurs to profit from it. In doing so, they provided an early glimpse of the kind of criticism of Black empowerment politics that would emerge as a prominent feature of a post-apartheid South Africa.

During the mid-to-late 1980s, these critics had a hard time convincing the American public, many of whom were all too happy to put the issue of apartheid behind them. US corporations, moreover, had a powerful weapon in their pocket—namely, the alliances they had forged with Black American and Black South African proponents of Black empowerment. In response to criticism of the company by Gcabashe and others, Coca-Cola executives enlisted the support of the company's newest Black ambassador: Desmond Tutu. In a letter to Carl Ware, Tutu expressed sympathy for the trouble the company faced, "accused of aiding and abetting the apartheid regime. Nothing could be further from the truth." He went on to describe Coke's Equal Opportunity Fund as "a potent weapon in our struggle to establish a new nonracial and democratic South Africa" and thanked Coca-Cola for their "important work in [the] struggle." "You have sought by your manner of disinvesting to empower blacks economically and to help us prepare manpower for the post-apartheid South Africa" and, for that, "I am grateful." Tutu concluded the letter with a statement encouraging Ware to use the letter as he saw fit, including to counter criticism of Coca-Cola.[82]

Figure 13. Coca-Cola President Donald Keough, Archbishop Desmond Tutu, Executive Vice President of Coca-Cola Carl Ware, and Coca-Cola CEO Roberto Goizueta, 1986, Carl Ware Papers, Atlanta University Center Robert W. Woodruff Library.

With Tutu's help, Coca-Cola executives soon gained an introduction to another potential partner—one with even greater potential to help the company change the narrative surrounding Coke and other US corporations. In his letter to Ware, Tutu noted that he had met repeatedly with "top ANC leadership." "At no time was my involvement with the EOF called in question by the ANC nor by the mass democratic movement."[83] Subsequently, Tutu helped facilitate a series of meetings between Coca-Cola executives and top ANC officials, including, eventually, Nelson Mandela. In time, these connections came to play a crucial role in Coca-Cola's efforts to rebrand itself a vehicle of Black empowerment and a partner in building a new, post-apartheid South Africa.

Returns (from Exile)

As an ANC leader, Mandela was an unlikely ambassador for Coca-Cola. During the 1940s and 1950s, as cofounder of the party's Youth League, Mandela had been at the forefront of the ANC's embrace of direct action, helping transform it from a mouthpiece for the country's Christian-educated

African elite into a revolutionary party representing the disenfranchised and oppressed Black African majority. Like other African revolutionaries of his generation, Mandela was heavily influenced by Marxism. In the late 1950s, Mandela secretly joining the South African Communist Party (SACP)—an association he later denied—collaborating with the party in launching the ANC's military wing, uMkhonto weSizwe ("Spear of the Nation," also known as MK), in 1961.[84] Mandela's bold defiance subsequently served as evidence against him in the Rivonia Trial. During the trial, Mandela and seven of his colleagues, including Walter Sisulu and Govan Mbeki, were charged with and convicted of sabotage and given a life sentence by the South African government. Mandela subsequently served twenty-seven years in prison, eighteen of which were spent on Robben Island.

By the time of his release in 1990, much had changed, including Mandela's relationship with communism. During his years imprisoned on Robben Island, Mandela reasserted his belief that the ANC and SACP, while strategically aligned, must remain separate.[85] Even so, the perception that Mandela and the ANC were communist pawns continued to hold sway in many parts of the world, including among some Black Americans. Recalling an encounter he had with a Black American cab driver in New York City in 1974, ANC ambassador to the UN Johnny Makatini noted, "the cabby realized his passenger wasn't from the US, and asked where he was from." An elated Makatini, who believed Black Americans "constitute[d] a natural ally" for the ANC began exclaiming about the ANC's recent victory to suspend South Africa from the UN. The cabby, however, interrupted him, saying, "No, I don't agree with the communists," referring to the ANC.[86]

Anti-communism infused Black struggles during the Cold War.[87] Targeted by government and liberal civil rights organizations during the 1940s and 1950s, a growing number of Black Americans turned away from communism and toward Black nationalism. Let down by white leftists' failure to internalize an anti-racist critique of capitalism, many Black Americans, according to Makatini, remained perplexed, if not hostile, toward the ANC's "position that whites should also participate in the liberation struggle," preferring to throw their support behind the ANC's rival, the Pan-African Congress (PAC), whose Black nationalist politics resonated with an American audience raised on Black Power.[88] The irony of the situation, whereby Black nationalists in the US rejected the ANC in favor of the PAC, was that, in some ways, it created the space for Black American liberals and entrepreneurs to serve as the ANC's primary intermediaries in the US during the 1980s.

Meanwhile, developments within the ANC itself help explain the party's embrace of Black American entrepreneurs as partners and of Black empowerment politics more generally. Having long relied on the Soviet Union for political and material support, the ANC, like other anti-colonial organizations, faced growing challenges in the late 1980s with the USSR's decision to pull back from its global commitments in order to focus on internal reforms.[89] This gave those within the ANC who were more oriented toward the West leverage for advocating for stronger ties with the US: ANC members like Thabo Mbeki, the son of Govan Mbeki, imprisoned on Robben Island with Mandela.

For years, the South African government funded a propaganda campaign in the US that demonized the ANC and other liberation organizations, while portraying apartheid as a benign policy meant to foster racial autonomy.[90] Taking on the role of the organization's chief public relations advisor, as deputy to Duma Nokwe in the Department of Information and Propaganda, later renamed the Department of Information and Publicity, Thabo Mbeki helped lead a counter public relations campaign on behalf of the ANC using the organization's contacts in Hollywood. Having previously collaborated with American television network CBS on a documentary called *The Battle for South Africa* in 1978, Mbeki helped greenlight a series of films and shows on the ANC's struggle and the organization's chief martyr, Nelson Mandela.[91] Nelson and Winnie Mandela, in turn, became responsible for launching the careers of a number of Black American entertainers in a mutually beneficial relationship promoting their respective celebrity statuses.[92] The first actor to play Nelson Mandela was Danny Glover, whose portrayal of Mandela in the 1987 film bearing the former's name played a key role in shifting American public perception of Mandela from a dangerous militant to a known and sympathetic hero.[93]

Hollywood stardom, in turn, translated into direct earnings for the ANC and its leaders. In 1987, for example, Camille Cosby paid Winnie Mandela an undisclosed sum for the rights to produce a movie about her life.[94] Meanwhile, Camille's husband, Bill Cosby, used his fame to raise thousands for the "Unlock Apartheid's Jail" campaign organized by the Africa Fund. Dramatizing the South African state's "unlimited [police] powers," including the ability of police "to seize whomever they chose and to hold them indefinitely, without trial, without charge and without any rights of access to lawyers, family or friends," the campaign collected thousands of keys from churches, synagogues, and other community institutions, which were then delivered to the South African consulate in Washington. Within weeks of Cosby's endorsement, over

2,000 churches, synagogues and civil rights and community organizations had joined the campaign."[95] Months later, when ANC President Oliver Tambo required hospitalization in London following a severe stroke, Cosby again came to the ANC's aid, helping to pay for Tambo's medical expenses.[96] Black investment paid twofold in this regard. Whereas Black Americans traded fundraising and media networks for privileged access to the ANC, often bolstering their own careers in the process, the ANC profited from its investment in Black America in the form of much needed capital and sympathetic publicity. This was Black empowerment as Leon Sullivan, Harold Sims, and others had envisioned, with Black Americans and Black Africans profiting together.

Then came the big day. On February 2, 1990, following years of pressure from anti-apartheid activists within and beyond South Africa, South African president F. W. de Klerk announced his plans to release Nelson Mandela from prison and unban the ANC and other political organizations. A little over a week later, on February 11, Mandela walked out of Victor Verster Prison in Paarl, a suburb of Cape Town, a free man. Later that day, Mandela, accompanied by his then-wife, Winnie, gave his first public address to a crowd of some 100,000 Black and white South Africans who had gathered outside Cape Town's City Hall.

The weeks and months following Mandela's release proved a whirlwind, as the seventy-two-year-old Mandela prepared to assume the ANC presidency. Immediately following his speech in Cape Town, Mandela was whisked away to Desmond Tutu's house in the whites-only suburb of Bishopscourt, where Tutu's status as Archbishop allowed him an exemption from apartheid's otherwise strict residential segregation. Perhaps it was there that Mandela first became aware of Ware, who had been working closely with Tutu through Coke's EOF. Not long after, according to multiple sources, Ware became the first American businessman to meet Mandela following the latter's release from prison in 1990.[97]

Business, including US business, was on Mandela's mind as he and others worked to negotiate South Africa's transition to a post-apartheid democracy. This is clear from the press conference delivered by Mandela at the archbishop's residence the day following his release. Responding to comments made by Mandela in his City Hall speech regarding the need to nationalize South African mines, foreign investors reacted predictably, wiping out the equivalent of $1 billion from the Johannesburg Stock Exchange. Subsequently, Mandela worked to reassure the international community, and whites in particular, telling reporters that the ANC was committed to a post-apartheid South

Africa that would suit all South Africans, "Blacks and whites."[98] Mandela's comments coincided with the ANC's broader embrace of a "mixed economy," combining government intervention with private-sector-led development.

As part of his efforts to assuage foreign capital, Mandela met with Ware and other Coke executives several times in South Africa, during which the company tried to convince him of its commitment to Black empowerment. In addition to Tutu, Coca-Cola also relied on Yusuf Surtee to facilitate these meetings.[99] Having previously served as a tailor for Mandela and Coca-Cola Senior Vice President Neville Isdell in Johannesburg, Surtee subsequently rose to prominence in the ANC and international business. In 1986, Surtee became a trustee of the Coca-Cola Foundation.[100]

The bonds between Mandela and Coca-Cola, in many ways, mirrored Sullivan's earlier dance with General Motors. In public, Mandela remained defiant, supportive of the continued boycott organized by anti-apartheid activists against the soft drink behemoth. In June 1990, four months after his release from prison, Mandela embarked on a whirlwind twelve-day tour of the US with stops in New York; Boston; Washington, DC; Atlanta; Miami; Detroit; Los Angeles; and Oakland. Leading up to Mandela's arrival, numerous reports circulated that the ANC had rejected an offer by Coca-Cola to finance the tour.[101] Speaking to reporters at the stadium in Atlanta, where anti-apartheid activists unsuccessfully attempted to have Coke products banned during Mandela's speech, one attendee, Deborah Marshall, told reporters, "We refuse to buy Coke products" in protest of Coke's continued presence in South Africa, "so we came with our own snacks."[102] Her comments echoed Sifio Makhathini, chairman of the Atlanta chapter of the ANC, who claimed, "It would offend Mr. Mandela to sell Coke during the rally," reflecting widespread anti-corporate sentiment held by many within the anti-apartheid movement.[103] Still others, singing a now well-rehearsed refrain, stood by the company, touting its record of Black empowerment. Responding to news of the ANC's rejection of Coke's offer of assistance, the civil rights leader Congressman John Lewis (D-GA), whose district included significant parts of Atlanta, said, "I think that's unfortunate. In Atlanta, you don't do much without Coca-Cola. And Coca-Cola has been a very responsible corporate citizen."[104] Engaging corporate America made sense/cents, in Lewis's estimation.

Some within the ANC agreed. While publicly shunning Coca-Cola, Mandela and the ANC engaged other US businesses during their initial tour of the US. Some of these interactions came about as a matter of necessity. With weeks before the scheduled start of the tour, the ANC, in its rush to capitalize on the outpouring of interest in Mandela, had yet to secure a plane to transport the ANC leader and his entourage around the country. After several failed requests to the US State Department and several other private charter operations—the former agreeing only to provide Mandela with an armored limousine for parts of the tour—Mandela's team negotiated a deal that, in retrospect, appears absurd. In June 1990, the ANC paid $130,000 to rent a 727 jet from Donald Trump, who was, at the time, under pressure from creditors and struggling to hold onto the airline he had purchased for $365 million in 1989.[105] The ANC's choice of business partners surprised many, particularly considering the Trump family's reputation for exploiting Black and other people of color in New York City.[106] Yet, Christine Dolan, who handled the arrangements, told the *Los Angeles Times* only that "the Mandela Welcoming Committee is very thankful to Donald Trump."[107] Pragmatism had its part to play in ending apartheid.

Trump was not the only American businessman to strike a deal with the ANC. While declining Coca-Cola's offer to sponsor the tour, the ANC accepted contributions from a number of other American businesspeople, including Reebok International chairman Paul Freeman and Joseph Lavante of the Vantage Group, who co-chaired a series of events as part of the tour in an effort to raise $1 million for the resettlement of South Africans living in exile. That effort was overseen by Themba Vilakazi, who was among those in the ANC who proved more willing to work with American capital. Born in South Africa, Vilakazi, like many young Africans drawn into the struggle, fled South Africa in the 1960s and ultimately made his way to the US and attended Boston University.[108] During the 1980s, Vilakazi was active in the Boston Coalition for the Liberation of Southern Africa (BCLSA), making numerous speeches in favor of divestment.[109] Vilakazi increasingly spent his time and energy amassing much-needed resources for the ANC and South Africans suffering amid deteriorating conditions associated with the state of emergency. Thus, in 1985, he joined other exiled South Africans in forming the Fund for a Free South Africa (later renamed the South Africa Development Fund) to fundraise for progressive organizations in South Africa. Many of the initiatives supported by the Fund echoed earlier self-help programs like those initiated by the Black Panthers and Leon Sullivan, including Solomon Mahlangu Freedom College—an ANC school providing education, including adult education classes, to South African refugees in Tanzania—a health clinic focused on training youth to serve as "barefoot doctors" in the ongoing war being fought with police and "vigilantes" in South Africa, and a silk-screening business run by the ANC's Women's Section in Zimbabwe.[110] In 1988 alone, the organization raised enough to award fifteen grants totaling $77,000. Its efforts were supported by prominent figures within the anti-apartheid movement in the US and South Africa, including Winnie Mandela; Albertina Sisulu, wife of ANC leader Walter Sisulu and cofounder of the United Democratic Front; actor Danny Glover; California State Representative Maxine Waters; and US Congressman Ronald V. Dellums.[111]

The growing willingness of those overseeing the Fund to partner with, as opposed to protest, American capital was reflected in a series of advertisements that appeared in a souvenir booklet created on the occasion of Mandela's June 1990 visit to Boston. Alongside messages of support from local businesses, law firms, and political organizations, one advertisement stood out as marking an important shift in the anti-apartheid movement: an ad placed by The First National Bank of Boston (FNBB). For years, the bank had faced pressure from local anti-apartheid activists for its role loaning money to the government and private institutions in South Africa. During the late 1970s, the BCLSA urged Bostonians to take their money out of the bank with slogans like "TAKE YOUR MONEY OUT OF FNBB" and "FIRST NATIONAL BANK OF BOSTON means SUPPORT FOR APARTHEID and CUTBACKS FOR BOSTON."[112] Subsequently, in 1985, FNBB announced it was discontinuing loans to South African banks.[113]

Divestment, as we have seen, did not end US business engagement with South Africa but rather marked a turning point. Several years later, FNBB took its rebranding efforts a step further with the advertisement appearing in the Fund for a Free South Africa souvenir booklet. The advertisement, like those previously featured in NAFCOC's *African Business*, was devoid of any mention of financial products or services offered by the bank. Instead, the ad focused entirely on highlighting the bank's compatibility with the anti-apartheid struggle. It did this through juxtaposing a carefully selected quote by Nelson Mandela—"I have cherished the ideal of a democratic and free society in which all persons live together in harmony and with equal opportunities"—emphasizing his commitment to liberal ideas of freedom, democracy, and equal opportunity with the bank's logo, under which appeared the words "Putting our strength to work." Above, a photograph of a bald eagle with the word "soar" rounded out the message about the power of US finance to aid Mandela's vision for a post-apartheid society.[114]

This seemingly rapid realignment, whereby Black activists and (white-owned) American corporations and financial institutions on opposite sides of the picket line reemerged as business partners was typical of the turn to Black empowerment politics. It furthermore underscores the faith among a growing number of Black activists, entrepreneurs, and politicians across the diaspora in the possibility of American capital to serve as an engine of Black liberation, as opposed to a bulwark. I say possibility because that outcome was far from a foregone conclusion in the minds of many anti-apartheid leaders, including those in the ANC. In one of his first speeches directed at the business community, in May 1990, Mandela spoke at length about the mistrust that existed between the ANC and the business community, along with the need to address the serious power imbalances that existed in South Africa. "If we are genuinely interested in ending the old social order and bringing in a new one, characterized by the notions of justice and equity, it is quite obvious that the economic power relations represented by the reality of the excessive concentration of power in a few white hands have to change."[115] At the same time, he also conveyed an openness to working together, assuming business could demonstrate they were on board with the ANC's agenda of equitable economic growth.[116]

That agenda was, as others have noted, very much in flux. Long associated with socialism in the minds of Western leaders, the ANC, as Mandela stressed to business leaders, contained a multitude of economic visions beyond "nationalization and redistribution." Indeed, as the ANC made the transition from a revolutionary party to a government-in-waiting, a move that coincided with the collapse of the Soviet Union, a powerful contingent within the organization made the case that the West, including the US, while not a perfect ally by any means, could serve as a guide in "deracializing," to use the ANC's own language, the economy. In a speech to South African and foreign business leaders at the Options for Building an Economic Future Conference in May 1990, Mandela cited US antitrust laws and "the work of the Monopolies Commission in Great Britain" as potential models for a post-apartheid South Africa.[117] Elsewhere, Mandela added his support for affirmative action and job-training programs, which he framed as part of the movement's broader "commit[ment] to the empowerment of the most disadvantaged sections of our people."[118] Echoing Sullivan, Mandela emphasized that business must embrace their "obligation to engage in [the] process" of transformation.[119] This message was conveyed in even more forceful terms a month later in an address by Mandela to American business leaders, whereby the former outlined a list of requests for US corporations, including supplying material resources to aid the ANC and in the training of Black South

Africans, while simultaneously welcoming US capital as partners in building a post-apartheid South Africa. "We look forward to the time when you will join hands with our people to form a partnership of freedom and prosperity for the peoples of South Africa and the United States."[120]

Many US corporations were more than happy to heed Mandela's call to partner with the ANC in building a "New South Africa." That included Coca-Cola, which continued to make efforts to demonstrate its support for Black empowerment even after the company's "divestment." During the late 1980s and early 1990s, Coca-Cola continued to support several programs promoting education, Black entrepreneurship, and economic development in South Africa. A number of these programs were headed by Black South African businesspeople, including Nthato Motlana. In 1983, Motlana led a protest against Coca-Cola for its treatment of Black South Africans. A supporter of the Sullivan Principles, Motlana called on Coca-Cola to appoint more Black people to managerial positions. Subsequently, Motlana met with Ware, who helped to convince the former of Coca-Cola's commitment to Black empowerment and later recommended Motlana co-lead the EOF.[121] Coca-Cola also continued to make overtures to the ANC, including meeting with Thabo Mbeki in Atlanta.[122]

It helped Coca-Cola that these two groups—Black South African businesspeople and ANC leaders—had overlap. Motlana, Mandela's physician and a member of the ANC Youth League, had previously been tried alongside Mandela during the 1952 Defiance Campaign. He later played a prominent role during the Soweto Uprising as a member of the Black Parents' Association and Soweto Committee of Ten. Like others, Motlana increasingly came to see business as a central site of struggle, and launched several enterprises of his own, including Africhem, the first Black-owned chemicals company in South Africa, and Phaphama Africa Commercial Enterprises. Speaking on the connection between business and the anti-apartheid struggle, Motlana later reflected that he initially got into business as a means of providing support for his family during his numerous stints in prison as a result of his activism.[123] During the 1980s, he joined Tutu in launching the Get Ahead Foundation, which, among other things, focused on matching Black South African entrepreneurs with large corporations.

Nor was he alone. Overtime, Coca-Cola's multiple overtures succeeded in gaining support within the ANC. Then, in late 1994, Mandela agreed to sit down with company executives at Coke's headquarters in Atlanta. The meeting occurred during the newly elected president's first official state, and

Figure 14. Nelson Mandela tours The Coca-Cola Company headquarters in Atlanta, Georgia, accompanied by Coca-Cola Senior Vice President E. Neville Isdell and Executive Vice President Carl Ware.

second ever, visit to the US. Unlike the first visit, this visit carried a much more welcoming message from Mandela, who encouraged US corporations to invest in South Africa and aid Black empowerment there.[124]

* * *

Historians of the anti-apartheid struggle have, understandably, tended to focus on the movement for sanctions and divestment. Divestment played a crucial role in pressuring the South African government to release Mandela and enter into the negotiations that culminated in the end of apartheid. Divestment was only part of the story. While anti-apartheid activists were pressuring public and private institutions to implement tighter restrictions on US capital in South Africa, corporate America was forging connections with Black South Africans in an effort to shape the country's post-apartheid development.

A key partner in this mission was Leon Sullivan. In 1994, on the brink of South Africa's first democratic elections, Sullivan formed what he called the Post-Apartheid Corporate Social Responsibility Leadership Council, with the goal of encouraging US companies to invest in South Africa, aiding Black empowerment, and avoiding a situation whereby "political apartheid [became] economic apartheid." "We must do all that's possible to encourage American businesses and multinationals from around the world to return to South Africa with vigor and new business ideals to help create jobs and to support the new South African government." "But we want the companies to help the people [of South Africa] . . . with education, job training, housing, and other needs."[125] Similar themes permeated a speech Sullivan gave before the South African parliament several months later, where, greeted by a standing ovation, he promised to continue holding US corporations accountable and bring OIC to South Africa.[126]

Echoing Sullivan, corporate America likewise promoted a vision of itself as partners in building a "New South Africa" and promoting Black empowerment. On June 17, 1994—less than two months following the election of Nelson Mandela—Coca-Cola announced its plans to resume business operations with a "commit[ment] to creating a Coca-Cola system which fully embraces the spirit of the new South Africa," including affirmative-action policies aimed at recruiting more Black and women managers, alongside programs supporting Black-owned bottling franchisees and retailers.[127] In reality, Coca-Cola had never really left, having continued licensing its product to the Coke-created

Figure 15. South African President Nelson Mandela, right, welcomes Coca-Cola Africa Group president Carl Ware, left, to his office, where the latter briefed Mandela on The Coca Cola Company's return to South Africa. Photograph Michael Pugh/Atlanta Journal-Constitution. Courtesy of the Associated Press.

National Beverages Services Ltd. Still, the company's "return," like that of other US corporations, was noteworthy—all the more so because of the welcome the company received from the new ANC-led government.

Coke's announcement came following a meeting between Ware and Mandela, who, by this point, greeted each other like old friends. More than a personal fondness for one another, Ware and Mandela shared a vision of US corporations as partners, rather than foes, in the struggle against apartheid. This belief was captured in a letter Mandela wrote to Ware one year earlier. In the letter, Mandela told his friend: "When the history of our struggle is properly reviewed in the near future, only then will the world be privy to fully understand your catalytic role in that struggle. We in the ANC know of your countless contributions . . . in your capacity as one of the decision-makers within Coca Cola . . . [and] in your own right as a conscientious human being of African descent."[128] Like Sullivan, Sims, and countless other Black American executives, Ware's diplomacy helped pave the way for a new relationship between Coca-Cola and South Africa—one in which the former was viewed as a harbinger of Black empowerment.

That image, one of US-supported Black empowerment, proved a powerful one, capable of creating partners out of one-time foes. Yet, it also sparked frustration and anger when the vision failed to live up to reality.

CHAPTER 8

The Black Empowerment Decade

On the evening of April 29, 1992, Americans received the first news of social unrest in Los Angeles, where a nearly all-white jury had just acquitted four Los Angeles Police Department officers charged with using excessive force in the arrest and beating of Rodney King. By the next morning, the front page of newspapers across the country had declared Los Angeles a city "under siege," with reports of nine dead and widespread looting and arson.[1] It was the largest Black rebellion in the United States in decades.[2]

The uprising occurred amid the 1992 presidential election. In the days following, Democratic presidential candidate Bill Clinton visited South Central Los Angeles, where the majority of the unrest occurred. He used the moment to criticize the Republican Party for contributing to the riot through years of neglecting the country's cities. At the same time, Clinton distanced himself from the New Deal and Great Society programs of past Democratic administrations. According to Clinton and other "New Democrats," the problem with those approaches was their overreliance on the government. The government's role was not to provide social welfare but, rather, to "stimulate redevelopment of businesses" in inner cities—"businesses that could be owned by all ethnic groups."[3] Walking through the neighborhood, Clinton met with community leaders like Margaret Bush-Ware. Bush-Ware's position as executive director of Youth Opportunities Unlimited, a job-training and job-placement program, highlights the important role Black women played in local Black empowerment programs, despite often being overlooked for leadership positions at the national level. Not long after meeting Clinton, Bush-Ware partnered with Shell Oil to found the Shell Oil Youth Services Academy, providing job-training and business education to "at risk" youth in Los Angeles.[4] Remarking on his conversation with Bush-Ware, Clinton stated, "[she] didn't ask for a grant or a handout." Rather, she and other community organization heads "asked for investment in small businesses, for help in creating a free enterprise system in the inner city." "The key to . . . long-term progress" in US cities was not government welfare but, rather, "the economic and political empowerment of the people who are most disadvantaged," stated Clinton.[5]

Clinton's 1992 visit to Los Angeles, during which he touted private investment and minority business as the solution to the problems of US cities, subsequently laid the basis for his signature urban policy: Empowerment Zones and Enterprise Communities (EZ/EC), enacted during the first year of his presidency. Much like the War on Poverty programs Clinton criticized, EZs/ECs used a combination of grants and tax-incentives to encourage private investment and promote entrepreneurship in "depressed areas." It was but one example of Black empowerment politics embraced by political and business leaders during the 1990s. Meanwhile, another example was taking place across the Atlantic in South Africa. There, the African National Congress (ANC), which had recently made the transition from revolutionary freedom fighters to governing party, touted similar rhetoric and policy solutions, including programs promoting the transfer of private and state-owned companies to Black South Africans, diversifying corporate boards, job-training, and affirmative action. The party's signature Black Economic Empowerment (BEE) policy appeared to be a means of reconciling the ANC's stated commitment to large-scale economic transformation with the demands of international investors to respect private property and, importantly, repay South Africa's sovereign debt. Post-apartheid South Africa would, according to the ANC, be a place where private enterprise played a central role in empowering Black people.[6]

The Clinton administration's Empowerment Zones and the ANC's BEE programs formed part of a broader process of institutionalization, whereby various state and private actors translated Black empowerment politics into new policies and programs adopted by local, national, and international governments and non-governmental organizations over the course of 1990s and early 2000s. As this process unfolded, it relied on a transnational network of politicians, corporate executives, entrepreneurs, and religious and civic leaders, some of whom, like Leon Sullivan and members of the National African Federated Chamber of Commerce (African Chamber) were long-time veterans of the movement for Black empowerment. Together, they led the way in codifying corporate social responsibility and Black entrepreneurship as central vehicles for addressing racial inequality.[7] The decade of Black empowerment produced its share of victors, not least of which were a number of ANC members who benefited from a wave of Black empowerment deals pursued by the South African government with the private sector. These individual successes notwithstanding, Black empowerment policies often failed to produce the large-scale transformation needed to undo the racial wealth gap that was decades in the making.

The Return of Leon Sullivan

On a chilly day in early January 1988, Leon Sullivan, the great Lion of Zion, shocked his congregation by announcing his retirement as pastor of Zion Baptist Church in North Philadelphia.[8] The news came at a time of renewed racial tensions in the city. Sullivan's retirement followed not long after Philadelphia police bombed the headquarters of revolutionary Black nationalist group MOVE—destroying sixty-one homes in the process—and was announced within days of the second inaugural address of Wilson Goode, Philadelphia's first Black mayor, who had just barely defeated former mayor and notoriously racist police chief Frank Rizzo in a contentious election. Taken together, these events left many residents on edge and feeling a sense of frustration at the lack of racial progress. Still, news of Sullivan's retirement prompted only expressions of gratitude, with Black and white Philadelphians joining together in their praise of all the minister and his organizations had accomplished. Speaking to reporters following the service, Ruth Harper, a state representative and member of Sullivan's congregation, with tears of gratitude in her eyes, expressed what many in North Philadelphia and beyond felt about Sullivan, noting, "He has given so much of himself to the church and to the world."[9] It was a fitting end to nearly a half-century-long career.

Except it wasn't the end. Responding to questions about his retirement from Zion, Sullivan stated, "Time to move on. . . . God wants me to help train and feed the poor people of Africa."[10] Several years later, Sullivan was back on the continent championing Black empowerment via a new initiative: the African-African American Summit. The summit was organized with the help of the International Foundation for Education and Self-Help, initially founded to help oversee and administer the Sullivan Principles. The first summit took place in Abidjan, Ivory Coast, in April 1991, and was attended by over 1,000 people, representing twenty-three African nations, including five heads of state and nine cabinet ministers.[11] Speaking at a subsequent summit in Dakar about the motivation behind the gatherings, Sullivan declared:

Many in America—in the world—have for centuries exploited, dominated, and subjugated Africa and its people, and have attempted to
keep us divided. . . . But today . . . we have defied what others have
said should or could not be done and we're here together, united
and indivisible as one, and we want the world to know that as black
people we shall NEVER be separated again. NEVER! NEVER!
NEVER! NEVER! NEVER![12]

Sullivan's speech was noticeably similar to one he had given over two decades
prior at the launch of Opportunities Industrialization Centers International.
While the rhetoric around uniting Black Americans and Black Africans
remained largely unchanged, a sign of Pan-Africanism's enduring appeal, the
circumstances facing the continent had changed significantly since the late
1960s and early 1970s.

One of those changes emerged as a prominent topic of discussion during
the first several summits—namely, Africa's debt crisis. Following the initial
optimism and economic growth stemming from independence, the continent entered a period of economic recession, the result of a combination of
the 1970s oil shocks, declining commodity prices, drought, unfavorable trade
policies adopted by the West, and political instability. As a result, many African nations were forced to accept onerous loans under structural adjustment
programs.[13] In 1988, the World Bank, one of the central institutions, alongside the International Monetary Fund, responsible for structural adjustment,
designated twenty-two sub-Saharan African states as "debt distressed" due
to their debt service ratio—the amount of income (i.e., taxes) divided by the
nation's total debt, including interest—having exceeded 30 percent.[14] Sullivan
used much brasher language to describe the situation. Evoking the history of
slavery, colonialism, and lynching, Sullivan equated Africa's debt to having
"a 'millstone' round the neck of African countries." Echoing a popular call
across the continent, he demanded the immediate cancellation of more than
$100 billion in debt held by African countries.[15]

At the summit, participants also debated the ramifications of the end of
the Cold War. In a prescient remark on the collapse of the Iron Curtain and
its role in sparking renewed calls for Euro-American (i.e., white) unity, Sullivan observed how "the end of the Cold War" had left "[white] people feel[ing]
freer to send aid to Eastern Europe." Rather than critique the racial logic
undergirding such capital flows, Sullivan embraced it, encouraging a similar
"kinship" on the part of "black Americans . . . for the nations of sub-Saharan

Africa."[16] With the Cold War order rapidly disintegrating, the time was ripe to construct new alliances and networks based on appeals to racial solidarity.[17]

Distinguishing this moment, the early 1990s witnessed few calls for left-leaning Black internationalism. Instead, both the debt crisis and the end of the Cold War, in the views of summit participants, engendered renewed calls for capitalist development. Indeed, the collapse of the Soviet Union and Africa's ballooning debt crisis acted as a death knell for African socialism, which was already on the decline due, in large part, to punitive international aid/loan/ trade policies and military interventions. At the same time, the West's appetite for large-scale aid packages, used during the Cold War as a weapon against the spread of communism, decreased significantly. This left African leaders, many of whom attended the summits, looking to foreign, private investment to help ease their countries' economic woes. In the same speech denouncing Africa's debt, Sullivan repeated a familiar call describing the continent as a "New Frontier" for US corporations. "Africa," proclaimed Sullivan, is a land "full of opportunity and an abundance of natural resources; and a continent full of people eager to work toward meeting their full potential."[18] Sullivan's message was reinforced by the Declaration of Principles and Actions adopted by the first summit's participants. Among the resolutions included in the declaration, participants called for "Africans, African Americans, and other friends of Africa [to] collaborate in the creation of a climate that shall encourage investment, trade, and industrialization," including "the removal of bureaucracy and red tape;" "more African and African-American business partnerships;" and "joint-ventures by American corporations and . . . African entrepreneurs."[19]

That a gathering of African leaders would call for US corporations to invest shows just how far things had shifted politically since the days of Kwame Nkrumah, Julius Nyerere, and Patrice Lumumba, who, together, championed a left-leaning, anti-colonial, Pan-Africanist vision for the continent. Instead, summit participants reached for corporate codes to hold US corporations accountable.[20] In words reminiscent of the selective patronage movement and the Sullivan Principles, Sullivan told the press, "We will keep a list of those companies who support Africa, and we will encourage Black America to support those companies with their purchasing power."[21] Corporate codes and Black consumer power, as opposed to government regulation, were the tools promoted by the summit to ensure foreign capital became an engine of Black empowerment, as opposed to neocolonialism.

Meanwhile, US corporations needed little persuasion to lend their support to the summits. By the 1990s, many executives had come to see Sullivan and other proponents of Black empowerment as valuable, if not indispensable, allies in their business dealings on the continent. In June 1992, in between the first and second summits, a group of US corporate executives representing a familiar list of companies met with Sullivan in a meeting hosted by the Colgate-Palmolive Company in New York.[22] There they formed the Business Support Committee to provide support—material and otherwise—to the summits. In an invitation to 140 US companies to join the newly formed committee, Sullivan, repeating a now well-worn argument, touted the African-African American Summit as an opportunity to "improve the business climate in Sub-Saharan Africa and, in particular, expanded involvement by US companies" and "African-American companies."[23] Together, white and Black American capital could empower Africans, while also delivering a profit.

Such partnerships, bringing multinational corporations and Black Africans together to promote corporate social responsibility and Black enterprise, received endorsements from some of Africa's leading politicians, further aiding Black empowerment politics' institutionalization. Addressing attendees of the fourth African-African American Summit, which met in Harare, Zimbabwe, in July 1997, Nelson Mandela praised Sullivan for his service to the continent. As "a freedom fighter," one must never "forget those who were with him when you were all alone," stated Mandela. "This is the importance of the [work] that the Rev. Sullivan is [doing]. It brings together those men and women in the United States of America, who, in spite of their own freedom, decided that the world is the battleground for their endeavors. . . . They gave us support. They gave us their loyalty. They gave us their love. . . . And we have won, not only because of the sacrifices we ourselves made in our own country, but because of the support of the international community in general, and in particular, the people of the United States of America." Returning the compliment, Sullivan called Mandela an "icon." It was later noted that the experience of addressing an audience that included Mandela "was one of the three proudest moments in [Sullivan's] life, second only [to] when he met his wife Grace . . . and when he was called to pastor Zion Baptist Church."[24]

Two years later, Sullivan announced the Global Sullivan Principles, giving a second life to the corporate code once championed as a means of fighting South African apartheid. Sounding noticeably more optimistic about the original Sullivan Principles than the minister had a decade prior, during the height of the sanctions and divestment movement, Sullivan stated, "There were two great forces in South Africa: the government and the businesses. I couldn't move the government, but I believed I could move the companies.

And then I felt the companies could move the government."[25] Here was Sullivan's theory of social change—one rooted in a particular reading of history. Like the original Principles, the Global Sullivan Principles were "hammered out in cooperation with executives from . . . multinational companies," some of whom—including Alan Detheridge of Shell Oil, Reuben Mark of Colgate-Palmolive, and John F. Smith Jr. of General Motors—read statements of support at the program's launch.[26]

Launched at a special meeting of the United Nations on November 2, 1999, and endorsed by UN Secretary General Kofi Annan, the Global Sullivan Principles marked the culmination of Sullivan's career and an endorsement of his approach of working with multinational corporations to empower Black people coming from one of the most important international organizations of the twentieth century.[27] Less than a month later, the world watched as over 40,000 protesters converged on the World Trade Organization meeting in Seattle.[28] As activists risked pepper spray and stun guns to shine a light on the inequalities and various forms of exploitation engendered by the new world order and its embrace of "free markets," the Global Sullivan Principles, by definition, lent credence to the proponents of unregulated global capital as a voluntary code. Even more, the code and its supporters, which, by 2001, included a hundred multinational corporations, celebrated private capital as harbingers of social change—even justice. Writing in the preamble to the new Global Principles, Sullivan described them as "support[ing] economic, social and political justice by companies where they do business," including through encouraging them to "support human rights . . . equal opportunity at all levels of employment, including racial and gender diversity on decision making committees and boards . . . [and] train[ing] and advanc[ing] disadvantaged workers for technical, supervisory and management opportunities."[29] Alongside the African-African American Summits and OIC—both of which continued to operate through the early 2000s and the latter still in operation in 2025—the Global Sullivan Principles institutionalized Sullivan's vision of Black empowerment, ensuring its continuation for years to come.

Empowering US Cities

Back on Sullivan's home turf in the United States, Black empowerment politics found further substantiation, transformed into policy amid the urban renaissance of the 1990s. For years, US cities had been in crisis.[30] Years of declining revenue streams combined with expanding municipal debt contributed to a situation whereby city governments were overburdened with high loan repayments and unable to deliver many of the basic services that residents relied on.[31] The rise of austerity occurred alongside an expansion of racialized punitive and carceral logics undergirding the War on Drugs, mass incarceration, and (anti-)welfare politics during the 1960s, 1970s, and 1980s, devastating poor and working-class communities of color, while also reasserting white innocence.[32] Together, these real and man-made crises functioned as kindling for a spate of urban uprisings during the 1980s and 1990s—reminders to the rest of the country, and the world, that the US still had work to do in coming to terms with racism and apartheid within its borders.

That coming to terms took a familiar shape in the case of the 1992 Los Angeles uprising. Early on during the unrest, the city's first Black mayor, Tom Bradley, appeared in public visibly frustrated at the injustice meted out by the jury in the arrest and police beating of Rodney King. On April 29, at a press conference in which he also criticized the city's police chief, Daryl F. Gates, Bradley told the public, "I [am] outraged . . . today that [the] jury asked us to accept the senseless and brutal beating of a helpless man."[33] Several days later, with the unrest mostly under control, due, in large part, to federal troops and the National Guard still occupying the city, Bradley had changed his tune somewhat. Addressing the media again, the mayor called for a program of "economic empowerment" to aid Black residents, especially Black men between the ages of 16 and 25.[34] The decision to single out Black males between 16 and 25 reflected popular perceptions about who was responsible for the riots. Such assumptions informed the Black empowerment programs that emerged in the uprising's wake, many of which focused on young Black men as the targets of reform and racial uplift.

Bradley's call soon garnered a response in the form of the Clinton Administration's Empowerment Zones and Enterprise Communities program. Launched in 1994, the initiative built on earlier proposals put forward by congressmen Robert Garcia (D-NY) and Jack Kemp (R-NY). They, in turn, were inspired by a similar program implemented in the United Kingdom. During the late 1970s, British geographer and urban planner Peter Hall proposed creating special areas where various government regulations and taxes would be suspended and/or relaxed, in an effort to stimulate private investment. Hall initially termed them "freeports," in reference to the use of free ports employed by the British empire. They were later renamed enterprise zones and enacted by Margaret Thatcher.[35]

Building on the earlier bill introduced by Garcia and Kemp, on March 23, 1982, President Ronald Reagan submitted his own proposal for enterprise zones, called the Enterprise Zone Tax Act. In his address to Congress, Reagan touted the zones as "an experimental, free market-oriented program for dealing with the severe problems of our Nation's economically-depressed areas," while simultaneously gutting various programs designed to redress the historic exclusion of Black and other marginalized people, including an executive order that had previously forced corporate recipients of federal contracts to file affirmative action programs. Under the new rules, the minimum for submitting such plans was raised from $50,000 to $1 million contracts.[36] Ultimately, neither the Kemp-Garcia bill nor the Reagan Administration's enterprise legislation made it out of committee. Lacking federal support for other kinds of economic development and facing an increasingly competitive capital market, many states experimented with their own form of enterprise zones. By 1985, over forty states had passed some kind of enterprise zone legislation.[37]

It was the Clinton Administration, searching for a response to the LA uprising, that gave the program a new life at the national level with its Empowerment Zones and Enterprise Communities (EZ/EC) program. In doing so, Clinton took what had been a clarion call of conservatives—namely for special economic zones where capital could operate with limited government, and, notably democratic, oversight—and married it to the discourse of empowerment.[38] By the early 1990s, the phrase "empowerment" had become quite popular, used by liberals and conservatives alike in conjunction with a range of initiatives targeting marginalized communities. In some instances, the discourse of empowerment came to be associated with Black militancy. Such was the case in several articles describing the controversial Black nationalist and leader of the revived Nation of Islam, Louis Farrakhan.[39] More often, however, empowerment functioned as a means of tempering and/or even countering the politics of Black Power. Where once Black Power activists demanded accountability, equity, and justice, Black empowerment emphasized individual responsibility and private enterprise.

"I'd like for us to not only have welfare reform, but to re-examine the whole focus of all our programs that help people to shift them from entitlement programs to empowerment programs. In the end, we want people not to need us anymore." These were President Clinton's words in his first speech outlining his economic agenda to Congress in early 1993.[40] Later that year, Clinton authorized the EZ/EC program when he signed the 1993 Omnibus Budget Reconciliation Act.[41] Like existing enterprise zones, the program used tax incentives and various forms of government-enabled finance to stimulate private investment in "depressed areas"—the racially neutral term used by the Clinton administration to characterize the communities targeted by the program.[42] Under the legislation, businesses in designated zones were eligible for a 20 percent tax credit on the first $15,000 of wages and training expenses per employee who lived and worked in the zone. Businesses were also eligible for tax write-offs related to the purchase of new equipment, as well as tax-exempt financing, including bonds, for certain kind of economic development.[43] At the time of its launch in December 1994, the estimated total in new tax incentives created by the EZ/EC program amounted to $2.5 billion.[44] In a notable divergence from enterprise zones, the EZ/EC program also included $1 billion in social service block grants to support job-training, education, housing, and/or social services for residents of the designated areas.[45] Rather than an expansion of public welfare, these grants followed an increasingly common trend in government grantmaking, restricted to activities aimed at "promot[ing] economic self-sufficiency and reduc[ing government] dependency."[46] In other words, empowerment functioned as an anecdote to an older model of combating poverty through expanding the welfare state and buttressed Clinton's broader promise to "end welfare as we know it."

These limitations notwithstanding, including the government's announcement that only nine localities—six urban and three rural—would receive empowerment zone designation under the initial legislation, the program proved quite popular. Conditions facing US cities translated into fierce competition for the program. During the spring and summer of 1994, some 295 cities and 230 rural areas prepared applications, with 77 cities applying for designation as an EZ, as opposed to the smaller EC award.[47] Adding to the competitiveness of the program, the government further stipulated that one of the six urban EZs would be awarded to a joint application submitted by two cities from neighboring states, while another was reserved for a city with a population of less than 500,000. One city that chose to submit a joint application, thereby increasing its chances, was Philadelphia, which combined forces with Camden, New Jersey, in applying for EZ status.[48]

The sizeable crowd—over 400 people—packed into the auditorium at William Penn High School represented one of the largest public hearings on the city's EZ plan, and attested to local interest in the program among North Philadelphia residents.[49] The area, extending between Montgomery Avenue and Poplar Street, from 6th to 23rd, as well as Germantown Avenue to 6th Street, and Susquehanna Avenue to the Reading railroad tracks, was one of four areas included in the joint Philadelphia/Camden empowerment zones, designated the North Philadelphia/American Street area. Contemporary descriptions were not dissimilar to Sullivan's earlier characterization of the neighborhood. "Never" had he "seen so many dilapidated houses, row upon row," claimed Sullivan following a tour of North Philadelphia in 1950.[50] Four decades later, those championing North Philadelphia's inclusion in the city's EZ plan revealed little had changed, noting that close to 8,000 people, or 56 percent of the area's residents, lived below the federal poverty level, while the area had a 25 percent unemployment rate. Meanwhile, 40 percent of area homes sat vacant—many left uninhabitable by multiple arson waves that had burned through Black and Brown neighborhoods in recent years.[51] Reminiscing, Floyd Alston, who grew up at 19th Street and Susquehanna Avenue and now served as president of the Philadelphia Board of Education and headed a local nonprofit, Beech Corp., recalled the days when the neighborhood had been "a mecca" of Black economic and cultural life, with restaurants and clubs like Zanzibar on the Avenue, Vogue, and The Pheasant Restaurant, and "mom-and-pop" stores and boutiques selling everything from candy to women's clothes" dotting Columbia Avenue (later renamed Cecil B. Moore after the civil rights activist and city council member). By the 1990s, however, "most of the street [had become] a wasteland of empty lots, abandoned houses, graffiti and trash . . . a dramatic example of urban decay [and] blight that the empowerment zone hopes to remedy."[52]

While showing noticeable interest in the EZ program, local residents also expressed a healthy dose of skepticism, reflecting their disappointment with past initiatives aimed at ending poverty and improving the neighborhood. "There has to be money put in the neighborhood, but the problem is, does it get to the neighborhood people?" asked Lawrence Needle, a seventy-year-old resident of North Philadelphia and owner of Needle and Boonin Pharmacy. His comments were echoed by Wayne Staton, president of the Cecil B. Moore Business Association. "For the record, I'm not going to sell my people on empowerment zones," said Staton. "We've seen other types of programs launched by different administrations, but they just couldn't see their way through the maze of democracy."[53]

Some of these programs had come as recently as the mid-1980s. In 1986, W. Wilson Goode—notable as Philadelphia's first Black mayor—launched an initiative, known as the "North Philadelphia Plan," to revitalize parts of the neighborhood. Proposing "to focus attention on North Philadelphia as an investment area . . . to turn around the trend of disinvestment that had taken place over a 25-year time frame," in Goode's words, the plan ultimately left many disappointed, taking months to get underway and falling short of its stated goal to transform the neighborhood.[54]

The North Philadelphia Plan fell victim to the same problems facing similar city initiatives in the 1980s, namely a lack of federal support. Despite dedicating half of Philadelphia's Community Development Block Grant to the neighborhood in 1989, the money proved only enough to make a small dent in addressing deeply entrenched problems of poverty and urban decline. In response to decaying infrastructure, the city managed to find funding to fix-up the facades of empty storefronts lining Cecil B. Moore Avenue.[55] Reporting on the progress made by the plan in 1993, seven years after its initial launch, local media noted: "Fresh coats of paint cover once-fire-scarred buildings on Cecil B. Moore Avenue," yet few new businesses had moved into the empty storefronts. In an abandoned lot once slotted to become a community park, "dried yellow weeds, crumpled potato chip bags and empty crack vials" called into question the sign above, which read: "North Philadelphia Plan. Keeping Promises."[56]

Despite the lackluster results produced by the North Philadelphia Plan, some area residents remained hopeful that the new EZ program, with backing from the federal government, could help turn the neighborhood around.[57] Some of the most vocal proponents were local Black entrepreneurs, who saw the program as an opportunity to generate wealth, while also engendering a sense of "pride" among the residents of North Philadelphia.[58] One way they did this was through embracing tourism. The growth of initiatives promoting Black tourism represented a subtle yet important shift in the history of Black empowerment. Where earlier Black empowerment programs tended to focus on manufacturing—reflected by the industrialization in OIC's name—and, to a lesser extent, retail, by the early 1990s, a growing number of Black entrepreneurs had joined the chorus of business leaders embracing the post-industrial economy as representing the future of US cities. In 1993, the Cecil B. Moore Avenue Business Association, aided by a $26 million grant from the William Penn Foundation, spearheaded an effort to revitalize the neighborhood's historic Black business district. The program, which mirrored similar initiatives in cities like Atlanta, Chicago, and New Orleans, followed a report citing Philadelphia as the number one destination for Black tourists.[59] These efforts were later incorporated into the city's EZ proposal, alongside a $450,000 jazz and blues center located within Temple University's new $80 million Apollo entertainment complex.[60] Other plans included a proposal for a new

50,000-square-foot supermarket and a youth mini-mall, the latter operated as "a youth entrepreneur training center."[61]

Helping to anchor the EZ was the North Philadelphia branch of OIC, situated at 1231 Broad Street, in the middle of the zone. "There needs to be a glue . . . that sort of ties it all together," stated OIC president Robert Nelson. Who better to perform this role than an organization well-known for championing Black empowerment in North Philadelphia, and beyond, for three decades. Using a combination of empowerment zone money and private donations, OIC promised to invest $800,000 into job-training and other kinds of community programs for residents.[62] Reflecting the broader shift to focus on tourism and hospitality, media coverage of North Philadelphia's EZ showcased trainees William Moses and Stephanie Jones practicing waiting on tables as part of OIC's "culinary arts" program.[63] Meanwhile, other OIC students enrolled in classes operated out of Opportunities Inn, a mock hotel designed to help trainees gain work in the city's hospitality sector.[64] Initially paid for by the state, the bulk of the funding for the project came via a provision in the lease and service agreement between the city and the new Pennsylvania Convention Center Authority, which was responsible for overseeing the management of Philadelphia's new convention center. The provision obliged the authority to devote 5 percent of the total hotel tax it collected toward a training fund split between the Opportunities Inn and the Philadelphia High School Academies, a non-profit organization partnering with business to reform education in Philadelphia.[65] Within seven months of the program's launch, Opportunities Inn had trained seventy-two students, sixty of which had found jobs in the industry. It is a tremendously popular program, with "a waiting list for the next class," said an OIC representative.[66] Intended as an endorsement of the program, the demand was also likely an indicator of local unemployment, which reached between 25 and 30 percent in parts of North Philadelphia. Here, and elsewhere, Black empowerment programs served as indices of the market's failure to eradicate Black poverty.

The limitations of a program that relied heavily on private enterprise to fill the gap left by a decreased welfare state were made clear by the mixed assessments offered by observers of the EZ/EC program, several years into its existence. In Philadelphia, whose joint application with Camden proved successful, selected as one of the six initial urban EZs, several examples attested to the program's success in aiding business and keeping jobs in the neighborhood.[67] This included the Philadelphia Coca-Cola Bottling Company, locally known as Philly Coke, owned by Black American businessman and lawyer

J. Bruce Llewellyn. Llewellyn's path toward Coca-Cola bottler franchisee status was a direct result of Black activism. In July 1983, in partial fulfillment of the company's agreement with Operation PUSH, Coca-Cola announced the sale of part of its New York bottling company to Llewellyn, whose experience included turning a "tattered chain of supermarkets" in Harlem and the Bronx into a company with $100 million in annual sales, alongside a number of leadership positions in government. At the time, Llewellyn was named a member of the board of directors of Coca-Cola's New York bottling company and chairman of the board of the Philadelphia Coca-Cola Bottling Co.[68] Then, in December 1985, Llewellyn partnered with basketball star Julius "Dr. J" Erving to purchase a 52 percent share of Coca-Cola's Philadelphia bottling plant, making Llewellyn and Erving the first Black Coke bottling franchise owners in history.[69] Coca-Cola, meanwhile, retained a 48 percent stake in the company, mirroring a pattern in corporate transfers to Black ownership across the diaspora.[70]

Black ownership paid dividends, or so it seemed. In the mid-1980s, Pepsi dominated the Philadelphia soda market. Within five years of the company changing hands, Philly Coke made $210 million in sales, up 42 percent from 1984, making it the third-largest Black-owned business in the US.[71] That number eventually increased to $400 million in annual sales, making Philly Coke the fourth-largest Coca-Cola bottling operation in the country.[72] Central to Erving and Llewellyn's business strategy was increasing the company's share of the Black consumer market, something they achieved through popular commercials featuring the beloved "Dr. J" (Erving) showing off his basketball skills—in this case a crumpled piece of paper shot into a metal trash can in Philly Coke's offices—and an agreement to distribute Barq's root beer, "popular along the Mississippi Gulf Coast." Following a pattern employed by other franchises, including McDonalds, Philly Coke positioned itself as a vehicle of Black and women's empowerment through "sponsoring scholarships and other programs for youth" and affirmative action programs focused on expanding "female and minority hiring."[73]

Even so, Philly Coke's relationship with the city's Black community had its challenges. In January 1997, amid hard times, Llewellyn considered moving the company out of the city. One of the main reasons the company stayed was its inclusion in the North Philadelphia/American Street Empowerment Zone. In 1998, Philly Coke acknowledged receiving $500,000 in state tax credits related to the program. The company subsequently used the money to complete a renovation of its North Philadelphia facility at 725 East Erie Avenue, including "spruc[ing]-up [its] buildings and install[ing] neat landscaping."[74] Remarking on the decision, Philly Coke President and Chief Operating Officer Ronald Wilson spoke to the community investment goals embodied by the EZ/EC program, noting, "A lot of people believe you've got to go to the 'burbs to be successful. [We] showed that that's not true."[75] Undermining the program's assumption that private investment would necessarily empower local residents, however, a mere 22 percent of Philly Coke's employees were minorities.[76]

A substantially more negative picture emerged from a 1999 article assessing Philadelphia's Empowerment Zone's progress. In North Philadelphia, an area with 39,000 residents, the article noted, only about 125 new jobs could be attributed to the zone's economic-development efforts. Meanwhile, some of the Black businesses that had benefited from tax breaks and government loans made available through the EZ program came under fire for misusing funds. Once championed as a "national model" by Clinton's "empowerment czar," Andrew Cuomo, by the late 1990s, Philadelphia's Empowerment Zone found itself facing multiple federal and local investigations. One of which found the North Philadelphia Financial Partnership, an eleven-member board comprised of community leaders appointed by the city to help oversee the dispersal of EZ funds, had approved $2 million in loans for projects in which two of its members had a financial stake and exaggerated the program's accomplishments.[77] Similar charges of misuse of funds and corruption plagued other EZs, including in Atlanta and Detroit.[78]

In the end, the issues facing the EZ/EC program went well beyond a few instances of misspent funds—some of which were later found to be baseless. While benefiting numerous individual businesses and job-seekers, the EZ/EC program ultimately failed to solve the structural issues facing the communities they sought to empower. In 2005, a Harvard University study found nearly half of the country's eighty-two largest municipalities lost jobs between 1995 and 2003, compared to surrounding metropolitan areas, only one of which lost jobs during the same period. Noteworthy was the fact that the vast majority of the best-performing cities hadn't participated in the EZ program, while a majority of cities with EZ designations were on the list of cities that lost jobs, suggesting the program had little to no effect on overall job creation.[79] Capital, while responsive to government incentives, including tax breaks and write-offs, continued to do what it had always done in prioritizing profits over people. It was a familiar story—one that accompanied Black empowerment's rise in the US, as well as in southern Africa.

A New South Africa?

In July of 1993, as the EZ/EC program was being debated in Congress, US President Bill Clinton found himself in Philadelphia for a different kind of event. Earlier that year, it was announced that Clinton would bestow the Liberty Medal on Nelson Mandela and South African President F. W. de Klerk for their roles in bringing about a peaceful end to apartheid. The award ceremony itself took place at Independence Hall and served as the keynote for the grand opening of the new Philadelphia Convention Center—staffed, partially, with workers trained via OIC—and kicked off an eleven-day celebration, "Welcome to America," aimed at attracting business and investment to the city. At the ceremony, just behind the two world leaders, stood Leon Sullivan, invited to deliver the invocation.[80]

The presence of these three men—Clinton, Mandela, and Sullivan—on the stage together in Philadelphia was more than a photo op. Rather, it symbolized

Figure 16. President William J. Clinton with Nelson Mandela, participating in the Philadelphia Liberty Medal Awards Ceremony and Festival outside Independence Hall in Philadelphia, Pennsylvania. Standing just behind Mandela is the Reverend Leon H. Sullivan. Photograph by Robert McNeely. Courtesy of the William J. Clinton Presidential Library.

a coming together of a vision. At another event, held at the White House in October 1994, announcing a new $600 million trade and investment package for South Africa, Clinton stated, "Americans have always invested, and will invest more, in private capital in South Africa to help that country's economy grow," particularly "small [and] medium sized business enterprises . . . [and] heal the legacies of apartheid."[81] Clinton's words were echoed by those of Mandela, who toured the US that fall encouraging US investment in a post-apartheid South Africa.[82] Both, moreover, echoed the calls of Sullivan, who, in a series of speeches delivered around South Africa's democratic transition, repeated a familiar call for corporate social responsibility and Black empowerment. Addressing the first democratically elected South African parliament, where he was greeted with a thunderous round of applause, Sullivan announced his plans to form a Post-Apartheid Corporate Social Responsibility Leadership Council, stating, "We must do all that's possible to encourage American businesses and multinationals from around the world to return to South Africa with vigor and new business ideals to help create jobs and to support the new South African government . . . with [providing] education, job training, housing, and other needs." Otherwise, there was a risk that "political apartheid [would] become economic apartheid."[83] Political freedom alone was not enough. South Africa, like the US and other parts of Africa, required Black economic empowerment.

This message subsequently became a central rallying cry of US corporations and Black American entrepreneurs, who together embarked on a spate of new business ventures in the "New South Africa." One of those companies was Pepsi, which made headlines in 1994 with its announcement of a new partnership involving Black Americans and Black South Africans known as New Age Beverages Ltd. Following Pepsi's departure in 1985, a group of Black South African businessmen, organized in the Soweto Investment Company Ltd., purchased the old Pepsi plant with the intention of reviving it.[84] The venture lasted only a few years, however, before it was shuttered, citing poor performance.[85] The experiment revealed the difficulty of trying to operate a large facility in South Africa while lacking the material and managerial expertise of the parent company.

This history, and the lessons it held with regard to the limitations of corporate transfers of assets between US corporations and Black entrepreneurs, remained largely absent from discussions of New Age Beverages, which was celebrated as a symbol of Black empowerment. Announcing the new venture, Christopher A. Sinclair, president and chief executive of PepsiCo Foods and

Beverages, described New Age Beverages Ltd. as a sign of "[Pepsi's] commitment . . . to create the most dynamic and most admired black-managed and
black-owned company in South Africa."[86] His comments were bolstered by the
fact that Pepsi itself remained a minority partner in the venture, responsible
only for $5 million out of a $20 million initial capital investment. Meanwhile,
the remaining $15 million came from Egoli Beverages, founded by white
South African Ian Wilson and backed by a star-studded list of Black American investors, including Motown Record Co. Chairman Clarence Avant, Los
Angeles attorney Johnnie L. Cochran Jr., actor Danny Glover, and basketball
star Shaquille O'Neal.[87] Meanwhile, heading up operations in South Africa was
forty-year-old self-proclaimed "former revolutionary" Khehla S. Mthembu.
Having previously served as president of the Azanian People's Organization
(AZAPO) during the 1970s, Mthembu turned to business in the mid-1980s.
He began by selling insurance to the growing trade union movement, as well
as to taxi drivers and football players. As apartheid was beginning to fall in the
early 1990s, Mthembu joined the Black-owned Business and Personal Insurance Company Ltd, later renamed the African General Insurance Company,
as the company's managing director. Echoing the rhetoric coming from the
US, Mthembu described Pepsi's actions as representing "a process of empowerment" through involving "black people in . . . ownership and management
to community support programs."[88]

For Mthembu and other Black businesspeople involved in the venture,
New Age Beverages defined Black empowerment in the New South Africa.
This understanding was not shared by all, however. On December 19, 1994,
media reported that, for months, following the company's reentry in September, Pepsi executives "arriving for work in their fancy new cars" had been
greeted by protesters demanding jobs. At the time, Black unemployment in
parts of South Africa reached approximately 50 percent. As a result, the number of hopeful employees far outstripped the 150 jobs New Age Beverages
had available.[89] In an early criticism of the ANC's strategy of appealing to
international investment, Machipu Mathlejoane, one of the leaders of the self-
proclaimed Gauteng Job Seekers Committee, told reporters, "We appeal to foreign investors to come here . . . but if Pepsi can't benefit all South Africans then
it shouldn't come at all."[90] The protests gave rise to rumors that the demonstrations were orchestrated by Pepsi's chief rival, Coca-Cola, based on the com-
plaint that Pepsi's New Age Beverages acquired the majority of its employees
through "poaching" them from Coca-Cola, as opposed to hiring unemployed
workers. "The company [is] not creating jobs for the unemployed," charged

Norman Nxasano, another Job-Seekers Committee representative. Rather, "it [is] a relocation of workers from one place to another place."[91] Pepsi fired back, arguing they needed experienced bottlers in order to compete with Coca-Cola, which, despite "divesting" in the mid-1980s, continued to claim an estimated 70 to 75 percent of the South African soft drink market.[92] Speaking to reporters, Monwabsi P. Fondeso, another Black South African Pepsi executive, noted that, as a Black-owned company, New Age was "more humane, understanding," than the average business. "We are also, first and foremost, a business," however.[93] Profit, not people, remained the driving force behind Pepsi and other companies doing business in the New South Africa.

These and other criticisms of US companies reentering South Africa notwithstanding, the ANC-led government championed private foreign investment as a necessary and, in some instances, desired part of the country's democratic transition. In his first State of the Nation Address, delivered two weeks following his historic election as South Africa's first Black and democratically elected president, Mandela spoke of the need to create "an attractive investment climate for both domestic and foreign investors" in order to prevent the country from falling into further economic depression.[94] Rather than profit-seeking, exploiters of South Africa's human and natural resources, Mandela touted the private sector as a potential contributor to "black economic empowerment," including through their support for community banks, Black business development, and "creating the jobs which our people need." Subsequently, the ANC lent its support to a number of Black economic empowerment initiatives aimed at "deracializing and democratizing the economy" through promoting Black ownership and management of corporations, as well as affirmative action, job-training, and other kinds of private action.[95]

Moving forward, Black economic empowerment emerged as one of the core economic policies of the ANC-led government. In one of the first Black empowerment deals negotiated with the help of the government, the state-owned Industrial Development Corporation provided financing that enabled the newly established New Africa Investments Ltd., a consortium of Black South African investors led by African Chamber member and anti-apartheid activist Nthato Motlana, to purchase 10 percent of South African insurance company Metropolitan Life from Sanlam.[96] The deal utilized creative financing, in which eighty-three million common voting shares previously held by Sanlam were transferred to a trust, which held them on behalf of Motlana;

parliament member and son of former ANC stalwart Walter Sisulu Zwelakhe Sisulu; lawyer and former Robben Island inmate Dikgang Moseneke; and Jonty Sandler until the group could finish paying Sanlam for them. Another two billion non-voting shares were sold to outside investors.[97] Similar deals subsequently became a regular feature of post-apartheid South Africa. Many of these deals involved prominent Black business executives and ANC leaders—a distinction that became increasingly blurry over the course of the 1990s and into the 2000s as the ANC deployed a number of party members to the business sector to manage newly privatized companies.[98] This list included people like Saki Macozoma, a former member of the ANC's National Executive Committee, who was appointed Deputy Managing Director of Transnet; Sizwe Nxasana, who became CEO of Telkom in 1998; and, perhaps most notably, Cyril Ramaphosa, who became director of New Africa Investment Ltd. These deals were facilitated by a range of ANC initiatives, including the National Empowerment Fund, which utilized public funds to purchase shares of large (white-owned) corporations for transfer to Black investors, and, later, the Broad-based Black Economic Empowerment Act of 2003.[99]

The ANC's Black Economic Empowerment policies gave public backing, including the use of taxpayer dollars, to programs and practices already underway in South Africa. Building on its past work with the Sullivan Principles' signatory companies and other corporations, in 1990, the National African Federated Chamber of Commerce (African Chamber) announced what it called the "3-4-5-6" program. The program took its name from a series of targets aimed at improving Black ownership and control of the economy by the year 2000, including:

Black people holding 30 percent of the seats of boards of companies registered with the Johannesburg Stock Exchange (JSE);
Black people holding 40 percent of the equity of companies registered with the JSE;
Black enterprises sourcing 50 percent of the country's inputs; and
Black people occupying 60 percent of managerial posts.[100]

The African Chamber's plan was followed by similar calls from other Black South African business organizations, the number of which exploded with the end of apartheid. Alongside the African Chamber, groups like the Black Management Forum, the Federation of African Business and Consumer

Services, the Black Enterprise Trust, and the Black Enterprise Network (BEN), all lent momentum to the idea that Black business was to play a central role in the New South Africa. Speaking to *Black Enterprise* (South Africa) magazine—modeled after the US version—Joe Manchu, a founder of the BEN, noted "[the] Black will to empower ourselves economically cannot be overestimated. This drive manifests itself from the classroom, through the factory to the hawker into the university commerce departments. It is not just a mood: it is an intention to become economically powerful."[101] For these and other Black South African entrepreneurs, the reward for having overthrown apartheid was owning and profiting from the nation's industries.

The dream was one that likewise inspired a number of Black Americans. In July 1994, *The Crisis* magazine published an article remarking on the large number of "African-American Settlers Flock[ing] to South Africa."[102] The situation mirrored other moments in which decolonization and the commencement of Black rule in Africa had engendered a rush of Black American emigration.[103] This latest wave took on a particular entrepreneurial flare.[104] Following in the footsteps of the international Black American beauty industry, in January 1991, Elise Cooper, who had previously taught cosmetology in Los Angeles, made the decision to move to South Africa to establish a beauty salon, Salon Excellence, in downtown Johannesburg. She was soon joined by her family, including husband Buzz Cooper, son Andre, daughters Channel and Eboni, and nephew D'Juan Tyler. The salon catered to other Black Americans, along with the city's growing Black elite, including TV performers, entertainers, and Nelson Mandela's daughter, Zinzi. Others, like Leyland R. Hazlewood, found a place consulting for US corporations seeking reentry and/or to expand their foothold in a post-apartheid South Africa. Head of the Maryland-based Black consultancy Dimpex Associates Inc., Hazlewood moved to South Africa in 1992, where he played a central role in the deal that brought Nike to South Africa in 1994.[105]

For the most part, Black American entrepreneurs and executives were welcomed into the New South Africa. Following in the footsteps of Kwame Nkrumah and Julius Nyerere, Mandela extended what amounted to an open invitation to Black Americans to "come home" and "help [South Africa] rebuild." His comments were echoed by Walter Sisulu and other high-ranking members of the ANC.[106] At times, however, some Black American businesspeople reported experiencing a sense of alienation and even resentment from Black South Africans, some of whom viewed these migrants as competition.[107] In 1992, competition between Black American and Black South African entrepreneurs resulted in legal action, when Luster Products, a Chicago-based, Black-American hair products company, filed suit against a South African company, Magic Style Sales CC, for trademark infringement related to the latter's use of the former's "S-Curl" brand. In 1996, the South African courts ruled in favor of Luster Products, compelling Magic Style to give up its use of the "S-Curl." The suit revealed another truth about capitalism. As Black business historian Juliet E. K. Walker observed, quoting political economist Lester Thurow: "Driving others out of the market and forcing their incomes to zero—conquering their earning opportunities—is what competition is all about."[108] Competition and Black empowerment, as Hazlewood observed, were not always compatible. In an interview with *Black Enterprise* magazine, he advised fellow Black American emigres that they should not come to South Africa "to compete with South Africans," but rather "to help them." "This is the day of the black South African," said Hazlewood. Black Americans should be agents of empowerment, not competition.[109] Herein lay one of the problems with the transnational politics of Black empowerment, which touted Black liberation through a capitalist system that incentivized competition and individualism, as opposed to solidarity. Meanwhile, the bulk of the profits and power derived from Black empowerment ventures continued to flow to white capitalists at home and abroad.[110]

*   *   *

The 1990s and early 2000s witnessed Black empowerment politics flourish at multiple scales, from the local to the global. Building on the earlier support by the Johnson and Nixon administrations for private programs promoting job-training, Black entrepreneurship, and corporate social responsibility, multiple politicians and government officials led the way in further institutionalizing Black empowerment politics through policies and programs designed to encourage private investment in Black areas and businesses. Headlining the sixth African-African American Summit in Abuja, Nigeria, President George W. Bush Jr. delivered a speech testifying to Black empowerment's centrality to US foreign policy toward Africa. Alongside references to the dangers of terrorism and the need to bolster security on the continent—an increasing theme in post–September 11, 2001, US policy—Bush touted Africa as a place of opportunity and prosperity, themes echoed in the recently adopted African Growth and Opportunity Act, which sought to bolster African entrepreneurship and trade through providing eligible countries with duty-free access to the US market for approved goods. Echoing Sullivan, Bush touted his support for "greater trade" between the US and Africa, "corporate responsibility," and "partnerships among . . . businessmen and doctors and bankers and teachers and clergy" as a means of creating "new opportunities for farmers and workers and entrepreneurs all across Africa."[111]

Bush's comments foreshadowed similar remarks made by President Barack Obama over a decade later, highlighting the longevity of and bipartisan support for Black empowerment politics. Speaking at the Global Entrepreneurship Summit, in Nairobi, Kenya, in July 2015, Obama championed entrepreneurship for "offer[ing] a positive alternative to the ideologies of violence and division that . . . too often fill the void when young people don't see a future for themselves." Obama continued, boasting to those gathered in Nairobi about his administration's efforts suffusing US foreign policy with the "spirit of entrepreneurship" and "empower[ing] hundreds of thousands of entrepreneurs" and business and government leaders through the Young African Leaders Initiative.[112]

Bush's and Obama's remarks found a welcoming audience on the continent, where many Africans embraced calls for new (private) investment following decades of disinvestment and failed state-led economic development programs. This included the ANC, which championed Black economic empowerment, including government programs incentivizing Black ownership and management of private corporations, as a central tool in addressing the legacy of apartheid.[113] Addressing the annual national conference of the Black Management Forum, Thabo Mbeki, who succeeded Mandela and served as South Africa's president between 1999 and 2008, declared Black economic empowerment "an important part of the process of the deracialisation of the ownership of productive property in our country." "As part of the realization of the aim to eradicate racism in our country, we must strive to create and strengthen a black capitalist class," stated the president.[114]

Across the Black world, success stories stemming from the implementation of Black empowerment policies and programs abounded: the local bottling plant now owned and operated by a Black American, the $225 million in federal assistance—much of it doled out in the form of tax breaks—to capital-starved inner-city neighborhoods in an effort to attract business and development.[115] Media accolades were particularly common in relation to South Africa, where Black empowerment promised to help mend the wounds created by apartheid.[116] Black empowerment likewise garnered criticism. Over time, that criticism grew louder, as the limitations of programs designed to redress decades, if not centuries, of racial inequality via pro-market solutions became clear.[117] Widely hailed as offering Black people hope and opportunity, Black empowerment politics' reliance on private enterprise proved, time and again, incapable of engendering the kind of structural transformation necessary to create an economy wherein capitalism's profits were distributed equally. Instead, in the US, South Africa, and elsewhere, wealth remained largely in the hands of white capitalists.[118]

Afterlives of Black Empowerment

Reverend Leon Howard Sullivan died of leukemia on April 24, 2001, at the age of seventy-eight. At the time, he and his wife, Grace, were living in Scottsdale, Arizona, where Sullivan retired following four decades pastoring Zion Baptist Church in North Philadelphia. The days following Sullivan's death witnessed an outpouring of accolades for the "Lion of Zion." The *Arizona Daily Star* minced no words, declaring Sullivan's life "one of the most productive and principled lives of the 20th century."[1] Meanwhile, *The Washington Post* hailed Sullivan as a "civil rights leader whose relentless crusade . . . helped put an end to . . . apartheid" in South Africa.[2]

Sullivan's funeral, held at the First Institutional Baptist Church in Phoenix, was no less revelatory. Lasting over three hours, the ceremony featured a guest list that included prominent civil rights leaders, local and national politicians, as well as representatives from the United Nations, twenty African nations, and multiple corporations. In between hymns, attendees heard speeches by renowned civil rights leader Rev. Jesse Jackson, who compared Sullivan to Martin Luther King Jr.—"same symphony, different instruments"—and former US Department of Housing and Urban Development Secretary Jack Kemp, among others.[3] It was a fitting tribute to a man who dedicated his life to working with government, business, and civic leaders to uplift Black and other marginalized people, locally and globally.

At the time of his death, Sullivan had been preparing for the sixth African-African American Summit in Nigeria.[4] Joining the chorus of accolades coming from around the US, multiple African leaders praised Sullivan's work empowering Black Africans. Swazi ambassador to the United States Mary Kanya, for example, noted that "Sullivan was a man who saw injustice and worked to change it. . . . Africa is mourning a hero."[5] United Nations Secretary-General Kofi Annan, who worked with Sullivan on the Global

Sullivan Principles, expressed "great sadness" at the news of Sullivan's passing, describing the minister as someone "known and respected throughout
the world for the bold and innovative role he played in the global campaign
to dismantle the system of apartheid in South Africa."[6]

While death brought an end to Sullivan's sixty-plus-year career, his vision
of empowering Black Americans and Black Africans to achieve freedom and
prosperity through the private sector lived on with the help of friends, family,
and supporters. In May 2003, two years following Sullivan's death, news
spread that former UN ambassador and fellow civil rights leader and Black
empowerment proponent Andrew Young and Hope Sullivan, the youngest of
Sullivan's three children, had formed the Leon H. Sullivan Foundation to continue the minister's work, including the African-African American Summits,
renamed the Leon H. Sullivan Summits.[7] Meanwhile, the two largest Black
empowerment organizations founded by Sullivan, Opportunities Industrialization Centers of America (OIC) and Opportunities Industrialization Centers International (OICI), likewise persisted in carrying out Sullivan's vision
of providing job-training and community economic development programs
in the US and Africa, and continue to do so to this day.[8] In 2023, McKen-
zie Scott, former wife of Jeff Bezos and one of the world's wealthiest women,
announced a $5 million grant to OIC to launch the Sullivan Training Net-
work, providing "employer-designed" training in high-demand fields, including cyber security, health care, office work, and logistics.[9]

Others, who may not have known the minister personally, but later
learned of his work, likewise helped carry on Sullivan's legacy of promoting Black empowerment politics. During his 2008 presidential campaign,
Senator Barack Obama held a campaign rally at Progress Plaza, the Black-
owned shopping center in Philadelphia founded by Sullivan in 1968. At the
rally, a charismatic and energetic Obama spoke to the crowd, some of whom
had camped out overnight to see the senator, about the ongoing economic
crisis. "I know these are difficult times," said Obama. "But I also know now
is not the time for fear, now is not the time for panic. Now is the time for
resolve and steady leadership. Because I know we can steer ourselves out of
this crisis."[10] A little over a year later, in December 2009, still dealing with
the effects of an economic recession, the Congressional Black Caucus (CBC)
lobbied the Obama administration to invest in job-training and job-creation
programs combating Black unemployment, which had risen from 8.9 percent to 15.6 percent in two years.[11] At the same time, the Leon H. Sullivan
Foundation requested $22 million from the Department of Labor to train

12,000 people at OICs.[12] In response, Obama stated, "I cannot pass laws that say I'm just helping black folks," reflecting a broader reluctance on the part of the president to appear as if he was favoring Black people.[13]

Obama's unwillingness to claim the mantle of race-consciousness speaks to the limits placed on Black elected officials in the era of colorblind politics—limits soon thereafter tested by a new generation of Black activists organizing under the banner Black Lives Matter.[14] When it came to partnering with business, however, Obama's approach more closely aligned with Sullivan and other Black empowerment activists. This included tax breaks to small businesses, as well as to companies that "increase their payroll by adding new workers or increasing the wages of current worker[s]," and federal grants promoting job-training programs developed in partnership with industry.[15] Reviving a common logic popular during the Kennedy and Johnson administrations, Obama placed a particular emphasis on low-income youth. Following the failure of the American Jobs Act, which met with strong resistance from Republicans and some Democrats in Congress, Obama announced the Summer Jobs+ program with the goal of creating 250,000 employment opportunities for low-income youth. "America's young people face record unemployment," stated Obama in a press release announcing the program. "We need to do everything we can to make sure they've got the opportunity to earn the skills and a work ethic that comes with a job." Developed in partnership with business, including industry leaders like AT&T and Bank of America, the jobs program focused on reaching school drop-outs and other "disconnected" youth, who the Obama administration branded "Opportunity Youth," echoing the language used by Sullivan and others during the 1960s.[16]

Obama's championing of Black empowerment politics was likewise on display in Nairobi, Kenya, in July 2015. Speaking at the Global Entrepreneurship Summit, Obama hailed entrepreneurship for "offer[ing] a positive alternative to the ideologies of violence and division that . . . too often fill the void when young people don't see a future for themselves." Underlining the shift in liberalism since the mid-twentieth century toward a greater reliance on the market to combat poverty and inequality, Obama credited private enterprise with the ability "to lift up people's lives and shape their own destinies . . . creat[e] new jobs . . . new ways to deliver basic services . . . [and] hel[p] citizens stand up for their rights." "Encouraging . . . [the] spirit of entrepreneurship" was, Obama argued, "particularly relevant to Africa," where he vowed to "empower hundreds of thousands of entrepreneurs" via the Young African Leaders Initiative.[17]

Obama's championing of job-training, entrepreneurship, and business partnerships should come as no surprise. By the early 2000s, empowerment politics, which had by that point broadened to focus on women and other marginalized populations, alongside Black people, had come to play a crucial role in shaping US urban and international policy. Moving into the 2010s, Black Americans continued to witness government and business leaders tout the benefits of private enterprise, including job-training, Black entrepreneurship, and corporate-community partnerships, in response to a series of political and economic crises. Thus, for example, in Baltimore in 2016, in response to the Freddie Gray uprising, twenty-five local businesses and other organizations, led by Johns Hopkins University, came together to form BLocal. Standing in front of the Zion Baptist Church in East Baltimore, the group pledged to invest over $69 million toward contracting "with local, minority-owned and women-owned companies, expand [hiring] from distressed neighborhoods, purchase more from Baltimore-based vendors and generate direct investments in [the] community."[18] Similar pledges on the part of corporate America proved popular in response to a wave of protests against police brutality and racism. Critics of such programs observed that, in addition to being voluntary, the vast majority—90 percent, according to one estimate—of private sector commitments to addressing racial inequality came in the form of loans and investments in which businesses stood to profit.[19] In other words, Black lives mattered only in so much as they aided businesses' bottom lines.

Criticism of Black empowerment politics, especially those aspects that gave credence to corporations as agents of social change, appeared even more forcefully in South Africa. Speaking on the occasion of Sullivan's death, Tom Manthata, the former general secretary of the Azanian People's Organisation and aide to Archbishop Desmond Tutu, praised the Sullivan Principles, the corporate code championed by Sullivan and business leaders in response to apartheid, as "the right thing at the right time." Manthata's comments were echoed by Black South African activist and head of South Africa's Independent Electoral Commission Brigalia Ntombemhlope Bam, who stated: "[Sullivan] understood that democracy had no meaning without economic empowerment, a lesson we're still learning. . . . We as South Africans owe a lot to him." His own admiration for Sullivan and the Principles notwithstanding, Manthata admitted that, for many members of "a younger generation, [the Principles are] just another wishy-washy liberal approach."[20]

Adding to the skepticism regarding the market's ability to function as a catalyst for Black advancement, recent decades have witnessed a barrage of criticism lambasting the efficacy of the ANC's program of Black Economic Empowerment (BEE). First appearing in ANC policy documents in the early 1990s, BEE has come to encompass a wide array of government programs aimed at facilitating broader participation in the economy by Black people through various incentives promoting Black ownership and management, skills training, and access to capital. In 2003, the government codified this approach in the Broad-based Black Economic Empowerment Act. The act defined Black people as Africans, Coloureds, and Indians.[21] Subsequent versions of the act further specified that beneficiaries of the program must be South African citizens by birth or descent, or naturalized prior to April 27, 1994.[22] This definition intentionally excluded other Black Africans and Black people from beyond the continent.

The 2003 legislation, with its emphasis on "broad-based" Black economic empowerment, was intended to address criticism that earlier Black empowerment programs had only benefited a small Black elite.[23] In response, South African President Thabo Mbeki and the ANC vowed to make BEE work for a greater number of Black South Africans, including Black women.[24] A key component of the 2003 act included the creation of a BEE scorecard used in the process of securing certain incentives and/or government contracts and designed to measure business compliance with the goals of Black economic empowerment.

Despite these and other efforts, criticism of BEE continued to grow during the 2000s as more and more South Africans grew frustrated at the ANC's failure to deliver on its promise of a more equitable and inclusive South Africa. In 2004, anti-apartheid activist and one-time cochair of Coca-Cola's Equal Opportunity Fund Archbishop Desmond Tutu attacked BEE as a program that only further enriched a wealthy Black elite. "What is Black empowerment when it seems to benefit not the vast majority but an elite that tends to be recycled?" questioned Tutu. Left unchanged, South Africa was "sitting on a powder keg," predicted Tutu. Rather than rely on the private sector, the South African government needed to do more to assist the millions of South Africans suffering "gruelling, demeaning, dehumanizing poverty," including implementing a guaranteed income of $16 a month.[25]

Tutu's assessment of BEE found echoes in the 2015 annual Nelson Mandela lecture delivered by famed economist Thomas Piketty. Speaking to a packed crowd in the historic Black township of Soweto, located outside Johannesburg, Piketty stated: "I think it's fair to say that black economic empowerment strategies, which were mostly based on voluntary market transactions [. . .] were not that successful in spreading wealth." Instead, Piketty called for "increased transparency about wealth and about who owns what in South Africa," as well as progressive taxation and reform to address deepening inequality, which, he noted, had only increased since the end of apartheid.[26] Indeed, two reports from the World Bank and International Center for Transitional Justice, released in 2002, cited South Africa as the most unequal country in the world, with "race [remaining] a key driver of high inequality."[27] In South Africa and other locales, Black empowerment programs and policies failed to solve the problem of racial inequality, which endured and remains a defining feature of American and South African society to this day.

*   *   *

In order to understand the successes and limitations of present-day programs promoting Black economic empowerment, we must look to the past. Building on and combining aspects of racial uplift politics, self-help, Pan-Africanism, Victorian morality, and Protestant theology, Black empowerment politics took root in the post-WWII Black metropolis, where it intersected with a number of movements, including, most notably, the movement for Black Power. During the 1960s and early 1970s, Black Power's capaciousness enabled Black empowerment activists, at times, to claim the mantle of this radical movement. This slippage was productive, creating space for proponents of Black empowerment to proffer job-training, Black entrepreneurship, and even corporate-community partnerships as vehicles for racial pride, self-determination, and community control. Still, even in these formative years, important differences between Black Power and Black empowerment politics were evident. Where Black Power activists frequently demanded greater accountability from the US government, including an expansion of the New Deal welfare state, and an end to US imperialism and racial capitalism, Black empowerment politics eschewed such demands. For Black empowerment activists like Leon Sullivan, the opportunity to participate as employees, managers, and capitalists in an expanding American free-enterprise system took priority over government welfare and socialist revolution, locally and globally.

During the 1960s and 1970s, Black empowerment programs promoting job-training, Black entrepreneurship, and corporate social responsibility found willing, if not enthusiastic, partners in the US government and corporate America, which appropriated Black empowerment politics in response to various challenges posed by Black Americans and Black Africans frustrated with the lack of progress. In the US and Africa, Black American corporate ambassadors like Harold Sims and Andrew Young performed critical cultural and political labor countering the claims of Black nationalists and socialists, and incorporating—sometimes quite literally—the aspirations of Black people for economic development and prosperity into something compatible with the expansionary visions of US capitalists.

US capitalists did their best to curtail the most radical elements of the global Black freedom struggle through appropriating Black empowerment politics, but Black politics shaped American capitalism, as well, as evidenced by the contest over South African apartheid. For much of the first half of the twentieth century, American capitalism evolved with and profited from global apartheid.[28] By the 1970s, that order appeared to be crumbling in many parts of the world, not least the United States, and yet remained firmly in place in South Africa. In this context, South Africa emerged as a barometer for American liberalism and capitalism, both of which faced significant criticism from activists for their failure to deliver on the promise of racial equality and Black freedom.[29] For critics, South Africa—whose apartheid system offered investors the highest rate of return in the world—proved capitalism and white supremacy went hand in hand. Such an argument inspired a growing number of anti-apartheid activists to declare divestment—cutting off capital—from South Africa as the only ethical and practical policy.[30]

Here again, Black empowerment politics proved critical. Adopting a playbook previously used to counter Black unrest in US cities and other parts of postcolonial Africa during the 1960s and 1970s, Black empowerment activists, corporate executives, politicians, university presidents, and African entrepreneurs promoted Black entrepreneurship and corporate social responsibility to oppose divestment and apartheid. In doing so, they married anti-apartheid politics to free-market politics. Echoing Sullivan's declaration—"We believed in free enterprise!"—during the selective patronage movement, Black South African entrepreneurs in the African Chamber made clear their belief that "free enterprise" was not only compatible with but necessary to bringing an end to apartheid and facilitating Black empowerment.

What began as a movement for Black economic empowerment, frequently existing at the margins of 1960s Black politics, by the 1990s had become mainstream. During the 1990s and early 2000s, numerous politicians and private organizations, including the Clinton administration and the African

National Congress, embraced Black empowerment politics to combat long-standing racial inequalities at the local, national, and international level. In many cases, including in the US, these policies reinforced long-standing trends of using a variety of government tools, including tax breaks, grants, and preferential contracts, to incentivize private investment and entrepreneurship in Black communities.

One need only browse the annual reports of Black empowerment organizations like Opportunities Industrialization Centers or the renamed Africa-America Institute to get a taste of the impact of these programs, which, over the years, have transformed lives through providing opportunity, training, and community to countless Black and other marginalized people at home and abroad. Speaking at a block party celebrating OIC's sixtieth anniversary in 2023, Darlene Jones, who was arrested as a teen for fighting, praised OIC for helping her become an entrepreneur, opening her own restaurant, Star Fusion Express, in West Philadelphia. According to Jones, OIC helped teach her that "anything is possible."[31] Meanwhile, in South Africa, the National African Federated Chamber of Commerce and other organizations continue to support Black South African entrepreneurs, a number of whom have witnessed tremendous success in post-apartheid South Africa.[32] Black empowerment politics has likewise made a noticeable impact on corporate America, where, until recently, it was common to see corporations partnering with Black community organizations on a range of programs promoting equal opportunity, diversity, and empowerment.[33] These accomplishments deserve to be celebrated—all the more so in a period of political and economic uncertainty and while DEI and affirmative action are under attack. At the same time, it is important to account for the limitations of Black empowerment politics, including its failure to undo the racial wealth gap, despite promises to the contrary.

Long hailed as a solution to the challenges faced by Black people in the US and Africa, Black empowerment programs and policies have frequently resulted in an expansion, as opposed to a reduction, in inequality.[34] This is, in many ways, a predictable outcome. Corporations, while capable of being incentivized or pressured into embracing certain measures, including job-training and affirmative action programs, resolutions promoting diversity and equal opportunity, and partnerships with Black community organizations, ultimately are in the business of making money. In this context, business will always prioritize profits over freedom, equality, and social justice. Corporate America's appropriation of Black empowerment politics to rebrand itself as a partner in ending Jim Crow/apartheid and colonialism, while continuing to profit off both, only serves as evidence of this point. Rather than looking to the private sector to empower individuals, we should instead look to the proven methods of expanding social welfare and providing direct assistance, including in the form of reparations, to address the legacies of apartheid and colonialism and enable all people to live prosperous and dignified lives.[35] This would be in keeping with what Sullivan and other Black empowerment activists desired, but lacked the right tools and vision to achieve.

NOTES

Introduction

1. Rose DeWolf, "7000 Negroes Cheer at Rites for New Job Study Center," *Philadelphia Inquirer*, May 3, 1965.

2. Johnson and Sullivan quoted in DeWolf, "7000 Negroes."

3. Sullivan quoted in Audrey Weaver, "The Self-Help Story: Chicagoans See Progress in OIC's," *Chicago Daily Defender*, August 22, 1970.

4. *Elements of HEW and Labor Dept. FY75 Budget Requests: Hearings on H.R. 15580, July 16, 1974, Before the Subcomm. on Departments of Labor & Health, Education, and Welfare and Related Agencies*, 93rd Cong. (1974) (statement of Dr. Leon Sullivan, Chairman of the Board, OIC).

5. "African-American Empowerment Network," Obama Foundation, https://www.obama.org/my-brothers-keeper-alliance/about/communities-were-serving/african-american-empowerment-network/; "Black Empowerment Works," United Way Greater Cincinnati, https://www.uwgc.org/your-impact/programs-initiatives/Black-led-social-change/Black-empowerment-works; National Black Empowerment Council, https://www.thenbec.org/.

6. Maegan Vazquez, "Trump Unveils 'Platinum Plan' for Black Americans," CNN, October 7, 2020, https://www.cnn.com/2020/09/25/politics/donald-trump-Black-empowerment-platinum-plan/index.html. Trump revived his use of Black empowerment during a "Black Empowerment Financial Literacy" event in Charlotte, North Carolina in September 2024. See Donald Trump for President, "Media Advisory: Black Empowerment Financial Literacy Event," September 26, 2024, https://www.donaldjtrump.com/news/45c252d7-e486-4234-955b-5e8387653de5. While not apt to employ the term itself, 2024 Democratic presidential candidate Kamala Harris made a similar appeal to Black people, particularly Black men, with her Opportunity Agenda for Black Men, which promised to "help entrepreneurs access the capital and resources they need to launch and grow their businesses . . . especially Black male entrepreneurs," and "championing education, training, and mentorship programs that help Black men get good-paying jobs in high-demand industries." As of October 29, 2024, the aforementioned quotation appeared on Kamala Harris's website under the title "Kamala Harris Will Deliver for Black Men," https://kamalaharris.com/agenda/. The page has since been taken down along with other pages detailing Harris's agenda.

7. Black Economic Development Conference, "Black Manifesto," April 26, 1969, The Archives of the Episcopal Church, https://www.episcopalarchives.org/church-awakens /exhibits/show/specialgc/black-manifesto.

8. "Methodist Grant Disappointing," *Bay State Banner*, October 30, 1969.

9. *Elements of HEW and Labor Dept. FY75 Budget Requests: Hearings on H.R. 15580, July 16, 1974, Before the Subcomm. on Departments of Labor & Health, Education, and Welfare and Related Agencies*, 93rd Cong. (1974) (statement of Dr. Leon Sullivan, Chairman of the Board, OIC).

10. Stokely Carmichael and Charles V. Hamilton, *Black Power: The Politics of Liberation in America* (Penguin, 1969); Malcolm X and Alex Haley, *The Autobiography of Malcolm X* (Grove Press, 1965).

11. Stokely Carmichael, "Black Power," 1966, BlackPast.org, published online July 13, 2010, https://www.blackpast.org/african-american-history/speeches-african-american -history/1966-stokely-carmichael-black-power/.

12. "What We Want Now! What We Believe," *The Black Panther* 1, no. 2 (May 15, 1967): 3, https://www.marxists.org/history/usa/pubs/black-panther/01n02-May%2015 %201967.pdf. Other versions of what came to be known as the ten-point program substituted the words white man with capitalists. See "The Black Panther Party Ten-Point Program" in Huey P. Newton, *War Against the Panthers: A Study of Repression in America* (University of California, Santa Cruz, 1980). On anti-imperialism as a component of Black Power politics, see Joshua Bloom and Waldo E. Martin, Jr., *Black Against Empire: The History and Politics of the Black Panther Party* (University of California Press, 2016); Nikhil Pal Singh, *Black Is a Country: Race and the Unfinished Struggle for Democracy* (Harvard University Press, 2005); Timothy B. Tyson, *Radio Free Dixie: Robert F. Williams and the Roots of Black Power* (University of North Carolina Press, 1999); Komazi Woodward, *A Nation within a Nation: Amiri Baraka (LeRoi Jones) & Black Power Politics* (University of North Carolina Press, 1999).

13. Huey P. Newton, "Intercommunalism," (1974), reprinted in *Viewpoint Magazine*, June 11, 2018, https://viewpointmag.com/2018/06/11/intercommunalism-1974/. On Black Power and socialism, see Peniel Joseph, *Waiting 'Til the Midnight Hour: A Narrative History of Black Power in America* (Henry Holt and Company, 2006), 7, 21–24, 34–42, 56–60, 219; Robin D.G. Kelley and Betsy Esch, "Black Like Mao: Red China and Black Revolution," *Souls: A Critical Journal of Black Politics, Culture, and Society* 1, no. 4 (Fall 1999): 6–41.

14. This point is emphasized by Matthew J. Countryman in his study of Black Power in Philadelphia. Outside of national leaders like Carmichael and Newton, Countryman notes that most "Black Power activists could not afford" to adhere to "a sharp bifurcation" between revolution or reform. Rather, in Philadelphia and elsewhere, they embraced both, depending on the particular circumstances. See *Up South: Civil Rights and Black Power in Philadelphia* (University of Pennsylvania Press, 2006), 256.

15. Annelise Orleck and Lisa Gayle Hazirjian, eds., *The War on Poverty: A New Grassroots History, 1964–1980* (University of Georgia Press, 2011); Guian A. McKee, *The*

Problem of Jobs: Liberalism, Race, and Deindustrialization in Philadelphia (University of Chicago Press, 2008); Annelise Orleck, *Storming Caesars Palace: How Black Mothers Fought Their Own War on Poverty* (Beacon Press, 2005); Rhonda Y. Williams, *The Politics of Public Housing: Black Women's Struggles against Urban Inequality* (Oxford University Press, 2004).

16. On the Black Panther Party's engagement with electoral politics, see Jakobi Williams, *From the Bullet to the Ballot: The Illinois Chapter of the Black Panther Party and Racial Coalition Politics in Chicago* (University of North Carolina Press, 2013); Donna Jean Murch, *Living for the City: Migration, Education, and the Rise of the Black Panther Party in Oakland, California* (University of North Carolina Press, 2010), 226–28.

17. Angela Y. Davis, speech delivered at the Embassy Auditorium, Los Angeles, California, June 9, 1972, American Radio Works, https://americanradioworks.publicradio .org/features/blackspeech/adavis.html. The relationship between Black Power and American liberalism has been the topic of significant discussion. Countering an older narrative that blamed the Black Power movement for the decline of American liberalism, recent scholarship by people like Devin Fergus and Karen Ferguson has revealed a productive engagement between the two. See Devin Fergus, *Liberalism, Black Power, and the Making of American Politics, 1965–1980* (University of Georgia Press, 2009); Karen Ferguson, *Top Down: The Ford Foundation, Black Power, and the Reinvention of Racial Liberalism* (University of Pennsylvania Press, 2013). On Black Power activists engaged in efforts to wield and reform American capitalism, see Laura Warren Hill and Julia Rabig, eds., *The Business of Black Power: Community Development, Capitalism, and Corporate Responsibility in Postwar America* (University of Rochester Press, 2012); Laura Warren Hill, *Strike the Hammer: The Black Freedom Struggle in Rochester, New York, 1940-1970* (Cornell University Press, 2021).

18. On the neoliberal turn in Black politics, see Lester K. Spence, *Knocking the Hustle: Against the Neoliberal Turn in Black Politics* (Punctum Books, 2015).

19. On Black business's integral role within the Black freedom struggle, see Juliet E. K. Walker, *The History of Black Business in America* (Macmillan, 1998); Adam Green, *Selling the Race: Culture, Community, and Black Chicago, 1940–1955* (University of Chicago Press, 2006); Tiffany Gill, *Beauty Shop Politics: African American Women's Activism in the Beauty Industry* (University of Illinois Press, 2010); Shennette Garrett-Scott, *Banking on Freedom: Black Women in U.S. Finance Before the New Deal* (Columbia University Press, 2019); Brandon K. Winfred, *John Hervey Wheeler, Black Banking, and the Economic Struggle for Civil Rights* (University Press of Kentucky, 2020); Carmichael and Hamilton, *Black Power*, 334.

20. The literature on the Black Power movement is replete with references to efforts to establish cooperative alternatives to capitalism. See, for example, Orleck, *Storming Caesars*, 263; Hill and Rabig, *The Business of Black Power*, 30; Ashley D. Farmer, *Remaking Black Power: How Black Women Transformed an Era* (University of North Carolina Press, 2017), 97, 102. Efforts to wield collective Black economic power are also evident in the era's Black-led consumer and labor movements. See Traci Parker, *Department*

Stores and the Black Freedom Movement: Workers, Consumers, and Civil Rights from the 1930s to the 1980s (University of North Carolina Press, 2019); David Goldberg and Trevor Griffey, eds., *Black Power at Work: Community Control, Affirmative Action, and the Construction Industry* (Cornell University Press, 2010).

21. Damon Freeman, "Kenneth B. Clark and the Problem of Power," *Patterns of Prejudice* 42, no. 4–5 (2008): 423.

22. On the government's reliance on the—for-profit and non-profit—private sector to administer anti-poverty programs, see Brent Cebul, *Illusions of Progress: Business, Poverty, and Liberalism in the American Century* (University of Pennsylvania Press, 2023); Claire Dunning, *Nonprofit Neighborhoods: An Urban History of Inequality and the American State* (University of Chicago Press, 2022).

23. Leon H. Sullivan, *Build, Brother, Build: From Poverty to Economic Power* (Macrae Smith, 1969), 78.

24. Robert E. Weems, *Desegregating the Dollar: African American Consumerism in the Twentieth Century* (New York University Press, 1998); Brenna Wynn Greer, *Represented: The Black Imagemakers Who Reimagined African American Citizenship* (University of Pennsylvania Press, 2019); Keith Wailoo, *Pushing Cool: Big Tobacco, Racial Marketing, and the Untold Story of the Menthol Cigarette* (University of Chicago Press, 2021).

25. Jennifer Delton, *Racial Integration in Corporate America, 1940–1990* (Cambridge University Press, 2009).

26. Marcia Chatelain, *Franchise: The Golden Arches in Black America* (W. W. Norton, 2020); Hill and Rabig, *Business of Black Power.*

27. Declaration on the Establishment of a New International Economic Order, United Nations General Assembly, 6th special sess., resolution no. 3201–3202, May 1, 1974, United Nations Digital Library, https://digitallibrary.un.org/record/218450?ln=en&v=pdf.

28. Ryan M. Irwin, *Gordian Knot: Apartheid and the Unmaking of the Liberal World Order* (Oxford University Press, 2012). On the global context, including decolonization, informing the Black Power movement, see Nico Slate, ed., *Black Power beyond Borders: The Global Dimensions of the Black Power Movement* (Palgrave Macmillan, 2013); and Anne-Marie Angelo, *Black Power on the Move: Migration, Internationalism, and the British and Israeli Black Panthers* (University of North Carolina Press, 2023). Black Power had particular resonance in South Africa, where it helped to inspire the Black Consciousness movement. See Gail M. Gerhart, *Black Power in South Africa: The Evolution of an Ideology* (University of California Press, 1978); Daniel Magaziner, *The Law and the Prophets: Black Consciousness in Southern Africa, 1968–1977* (Ohio University Press, 2010).

29. Richard W. Hull, *American Enterprise in South Africa: Historical Dimensions of Engagement and Disengagement* (New York University Press, 1990), 250.

30. On racial capitalism, see Cedric Robinson, *Black Marxism: The Making of the Black Radical Tradition* (Zed Books, 1983). Robinson first encountered the term while in

England, where he met intellectuals who used the phrase to refer to South Africa's political economy under apartheid. He later expanded on the concept to articulate a general theory of modern capitalism. See Robin D. G. Kelley, "What Did Cedric Robinson Mean by Racial Capitalism," *Boston Review*, January 12, 2017, https://www.bostonreview.net/articles/robin-d-g-kelley-introduction-race-capitalism-justice/.

31. On the sanctions and divestment movement, see Francis Njubi Nesbitt, *Race for Sanctions: African Americans against Apartheid, 1946-1994* (Indiana University Press, 2004); Donald R. Culverson, *Contesting Apartheid: U.S. Activism, 1960-1987* (Westview Press, 1999); Eric J. Morgan, "Into the Struggle: Confronting Apartheid in the United States and South Africa" (PhD diss., University of Colorado, 2009); Robert Kinloch Massie, *Loosing the Bonds: The United States and South Africa in the Apartheid Years* (Nan A. Talese, 1997); Les de Villiers, *In Sight of Surrender: The U.S. Sanctions Campaign against South Africa, 1946-1993* (Prager, 1995); Nicholas Grant, *Winning Our Freedoms Together: African Americans and Apartheid, 1945-1960* (University of North Carolina Press, 2017).

32. These autobiographical works include Sullivan, *Build, Brother, Build*; Leon H. Sullivan, *Alternatives to Despair: The Founder of OIC States the Case for Black Economic Development* (Judson Press, 1972); Leon H. Sullivan, *Moving Mountains: The Principles and Purposes of Leon Sullivan* (Judson Press, 1998). Sullivan likewise appears in numerous histories of the civil rights and anti-apartheid movements, including S. Prakash Sethi and Oliver F. Williams, *Economic Imperatives and Ethical Values in Global Business: The South African Experience and International Codes Today* (Springer, 2000); Countryman, *Up South*; McKee, *The Problem of Jobs*; James B. Stewart, "Amandla! The Sullivan Principles and the Battle to End Apartheid in South Africa, 1975-1987," *Journal of African American History* 96, no. 1 (2011): 62-89; V. P. Franklin, "'The Lion of Zion': Leon H. Sullivan and the Pursuit of Social and Economic Justice," *Journal of African American History* 96, no. 1 (Winter 2011): 39-43; V. P. Franklin, "Pan-African Connections, Transnational Education, Collective Cultural Capital, and Opportunities Industrialization Centers International," *Journal of African American History* 96, no. 1 (Winter 2011): 44-61; Stephanie Dyer, "Progress Plaza: Leon Sullivan, Zion Investment Associates, and Black Power in a Philadelphia Shopping Center," in *The Economic Civil Rights Movement*, ed. Michael Ezra (Routledge, 2013): 137-53; Mattie C. Webb, "People Before Profit?: Ford, General Motors & the Spirit of the Sullivan Principles in Apartheid South Africa (1976-84)," *Ethnic Studies Review* 44, no. 3 (2021): 64-87.

33. Harold R. Sims to John Heldrich, Corporate Vice President for Administration, Johnson & Johnson, January 8, 1972, Harold R. Sims Papers, box 11, Special Collections and University Archives, Rutgers University Libraries, (hereafter cited as Sims Papers).

34. This gendering of empowerment politics is reflected in the broader discourse on empowerment. A Google Ngrams search illustrates how it is only more recently, since the 1990s, that the term women's empowerment emerged following Black empowerment's earlier appearance in the late 1960s and 1970s. See "Black empowerment" + "women's

empowerment," Google Books Ngrams Viewer, search performed on October 30, 2024, https://books.google.com/ngrams/graph?content=Black+empowerment%2C+women +empowerment&year_start=1960&year_end=2020&corpus=en&smoothing=3&case _insensitive=true. Similar results can be found through conducting a ProQuest search for these terms.

35. The punitive politics undergirding state violence during the late twentieth century is a central topic in recent scholarship on policing and incarceration. See, for example, Heather Ann Thompson, "Why Mass Incarceration Matters: Rethinking Crisis, Decline, and Transformation in Postwar American History," *Journal of American History* 97, no. 3 (2010): 703–34; Elizabeth Hinton, *From the War on Poverty to the War on Crime: The Making of Mass Incarceration in America* (Harvard University Press, 2017); Simon Balto, *Occupied Territory: Policing Black Chicago from Red Summer to Black Power* (University of North Carolina Press, 2019); Stuart Schrader, *Badges Without Borders: How Global Counterinsurgency Transformed American Policing* (University of California Press); Carl Suddler, *Presumed Criminal: Black Youth and the Justice System in Postwar New York* (New York University Press, 2019); Melanie Newport, *This Is My Jail: Local Politics and the Rise of Mass Incarceration* (University of Pennsylvania Press, 2022). It is no coincidence that this history coincides with the rise of Black empowerment politics, which, in its own way, served a disciplining function for Black Americans on the outside.

36. Elizabeth Schmidt, *Decoding Corporate Camouflage: U.S. Business Support for Apartheid* (Institute for Policy Studies, 1980), 40–41. Several recent articles likewise emphasize the limitations of the Sullivan Principles as a tool for improving working and living conditions for Black workers and challenging apartheid. See Jessica Ann Levy, "Black Power in the Boardroom: Corporate America, the Sullivan Principles, and the Anti-Apartheid Struggle," *Enterprise & Society* 21, no 1 (2020): 170–209; Zeb Larson, "The Sullivan Principles: South Africa, Apartheid, and Globalization," *Diplomatic History* 44, no. 3 (2020): 479–503; Webb, "People Before Profit," 64–87; Amanda Joyce Hall, "Black Students and the U.S. Anti-Apartheid Movements on Campus, 1976–1985," *Zanj: The Journal of Critical Global South Studies* 6, no. 1 (2022): 8–28. In South Africa, the term Coloured functions as an official racial category, alongside Black and Indian. It refers to people of mixed ancestry, including descendants of indigenous Khoi- and Bantu-speaking Africans, Europeans, and Malay, the latter of whom were enslaved and brought to the Cape by the Dutch in the seventeenth and eighteenth centuries. I have opted to capitalize Coloured for the same reasons I have capitalized Black and Brown, in acknowledgment of their historical constructedness, as racial (and legal) categories, and in recognition of the ways these terms function as assertions of identity and reclamation for many marginalized people. At the same time, I have opted to use a lowercase "w" when referring to white people due to the association between White (capitalized) and white supremacy. For a view that mirrors my own, see Mike Laws, "Why We Capitalize 'Black' (and Not 'White')," *Columbia Journalism Review*, June 16, 2020, https://www.cjr .org/analysis/capital-b-black-styleguide.php.

Chapter 1

1. Famously derided by W. E. B. Du Bois as "represent[ing] . . . the old attitude of adjustment and submission," Washington's legacy has undergone a transformation in recent decades, reclaimed by historians as a revered figure, renowned across the Black world as a symbol of self-determination and Black excellence. Historians have also contextualized, while not apologizing for, his tendency toward accommodationism, situating Washington alongside other Black intellectuals from the Jim Crow South. See, for example, Raymond Smock, ed., *Booker T. Washington in Perspective: Essays of Louis R. Harlan* (University Press of Mississippi, 2006); W. Fitzhugh Brundage, ed., *Booker T. Washington and Black Progress: Up From Slavery 100 Years Later* (University Press of Florida, 2003); Louis R. Harlan, *Booker T. Washington: The Wizard of Tuskegee, 1901–1915, Volume 2* (Oxford University Press, 1983); and Louis R. Harlan, *Booker T. Washington: The Making of a Black Leader, 1856–1901* (Oxford University Press, 1972).

2. Indeed, *Up From Slavery* was the most popular Black American autobiography until Malcolm X's.

3. Booker T. Washington, *Up from Slavery* (1901; repr., Doubleday, Page & Company, 2006), 74. Citations refer to the 2006 edition. Underlying its significance, variations of this idiom appear twice more in Washington's autobiography, on pages 66 and 229. The reference on page 74 is the only one that includes usefulness alongside happiness as a goal.

4. Washington, *Up From Slavery*, 74.

5. On racial uplift, see Michele Mitchell, *Righteous Propagation: African Americans and the Politics of Racial Destiny after Reconstruction* (University of North Carolina Press, 2004); Kevin Gaines, *Uplifting the Race: Black Leadership, Politics, and Culture in the Twentieth Century* (University of North Carolina Press, 1996). Distinguishing himself from Du Bois, Washington emphasized economic independence, in particular, as a prerequisite for achieving political power. See Jacqueline M. Moore, *Booker T. Washington, W.E.B. Du Bois, and the Struggle for Racial Uplift* (Rowman & Littlefield, 2003).

6. On Washington's influence on Black education around the world, see Frank Andre Guridy, *Forging Diaspora: Afro-Cubans and African Americans in a World of Empire and Jim Crow* (University of North Carolina Press, 2010), especially chapter 1; Brandon Byrd, *The Black Republic: African Americans and the Fate of Haiti* (University of Pennsylvania Press, 2020), especially chapter 4; Angela Zimmerman, *From Alabama to Africa: Booker T. Washington, the German Empire, and the Globalization of the New South* (Princeton University Press, 2010); Michael O. West, "The Tuskegee Model of Development in Africa: Another Dimension of the African/African-American Connection," *Diplomatic History* 16, no. 3 (1992): 371–87; W. Manning Marable, "A Black School in South Africa," *Negro History Bulletin* 37 (June/July, 1974): 258–61.

7. Lara Putnam, *Radical Moves: Caribbean Migrants and the Politics of Race in the Jazz Age* (University of North Carolina Press, 2013).

8. Vivian Bickford-Smith, *The Emergence of the South African Metropolis: Cities and Identities in the Twentieth Century* (Cambridge University Press, 2016).

9. David Corbin, *Life, Work, and Rebellion in the Coal Fields: The Southern West Virginia Miners, 1880–1922* (University of Illinois Press, 1981), 5.

10. Joe William Trotter, *Coal, Class, and Color: Blacks in Southern West Virginia, 1915–1932* (University of Illinois Press, 1990), 9.

11. *Polk's Greater Charleston Directory* (R. L. Polk & Co., 1922), 14:676. Two years later, the 1924 directory listed Charles and Helen Sullivan's address as 1333 Washington Ct. See *Polk's Greater Charleston Directory* (R. L. Polk & Co., 1924), 14:646. These directories are viewable via Ancestry.com's US City Directories, 1822–1995.

12. References to Sullivan as a modern-day Booker T. Washington appear in both Nathanial Wright Jr., "Black Empowerment; Leon Sullivan: Ultimate Humanitarian," *Washington Informer*, July 1980, 14; and Rotan Edward Lee, "Growing up at the Lion of Zion's Knee, I Learned About True Greatness," *Philadelphia Tribune*, April 27, 2001, 3B.

13. On fossil fuels and the rise of global capitalism, see Thomas G. Andrews, *Killing for Coal: America's Deadliest Labor War* (Harvard University Press, 2010).

14. On racialized labor and the mineral revolution, see Mae Ngai, *The Chinese Question: The Gold Rushes, Chinese Migration, and Global Politics* (W. W. Norton, 2021); Dunbar T. Moodie, *Going for Gold: Men, Mines, and Migration* (University of California Press, 1994); Francis Wilson, *Labour in the South African Gold Mines, 1911–1969* (Cambridge University Press, 1972). There is a substantial scholarly literature on corporations' role in constructing the global color line. For some recent accounts of this process, see Chelsea Shields, *Offshore Attachments: Oil and Intimacy in the Caribbean* (University of California Press, 2023); Gregg Mitman, *Empire of Rubber: Firestone's Scramble for Land and Power in Liberia* (New Press, 2021); Nan Enstad, *Cigarettes, Inc.: An Intimate History of Corporate Imperialism* (University of Chicago Press, 2018); Elizabeth Esch, *The Color Line and the Assembly Line: Managing Race in the Ford Empire* (University of California Press, 2018).

15. Price Fishback, "Segregation in Job Hierarchies: West Virginia Coal Mining, 1906–1932," *Journal of Economic History* 44, no. 3 (1984): 755–74.

16. Chuck Kinder, *Last Mountain Dancer: Hard-Earned Lessons in Love, Loss, and Honky-Tonk* (Da Capo Press, 2005), 149. See also Robert Shogan, *The Battle of Blair Mountain: The Story of America's Largest Labor Uprising* (Westview Press, 2004).

17. Robin D. G. Kelley, "'We Are Not What We Seem': Rethinking Black Working-Class Opposition in the Jim Crow South," *Journal of American History* 80, no. 1 (1993): 95. See also Trotter, *Coal, Class, and Color*, 65, 108, 264–65.

18. On the conditions of Black women's domestic labor, see Danielle L. McGuire, *At the Dark End of the Street: Black Women, Rape, and Resistance—a New History of the Civil Rights Movement from Rosa Parks to the Rise of Black Power* (Penguin Random House, 2011), 12, 71; Kali N. Gross, *Colored Amazons: Crime, Violence, and Black Women in the City of Brotherly Love, 1880–1910* (Duke University Press, 2006), 41–49; Victoria W. Wolcott, *Remaking Respectability: African American Women in Interwar Detroit* (University of North Carolina Press, 2001), 27–31; Darlene Clark Hine, "Rape and the Inner Lives of Black Women in the Middle West," *Signs* 14, no. 4 (1989): 912–20.

19. Washington, *Up from Slavery*, 44.

20. Washington, *Up from Slavery*, 53.

21. Leon H. Sullivan, *Build, Brother, Build: From Poverty to Economic Power* (Macrae Smith, 1969), 31.

22. On Black woman laundresses, see Tera W. Hunter, *To 'Joy My Freedom: Southern Black Women's Lives and Labors after the Civil War* (Harvard University Press, 1998), especially chapter 4.

23. Unknown, interview with Rev. Leon Sullivan in Philadelphia, Pennsylvania, May 1996, http://fliphtml5.com/fdsu/wksp/basic.

24. Washington, *Up from Slavery*, 47–49, 53.

25. Guridy, *Forging Diaspora*, especially chapter 1; Zimmerman, *Alabama in Africa*.

26. Second Morrill Act of 1890, Pub. L. No. 51–841, 26 Stat. 417.

27. "Booker T. Washington Institute," West Virginia State University, https://www.wvstateu.edu/about/history-and-traditions/booker-t-washington-institute.aspx.

28. Jacqueline Anne Goggin, *Carter G. Woodson: A Life in Black History* (Louisiana State University Press, 1993), 53–54; James Haskins, *Carter G. Woodson* (Millbrook Press, 2000), 33.

29. Gene Anderson, "Dr. John Warren Davis, Adviser to Five Presidents," *The Record* (Hackensack, NJ), July 13, 1980.

30. Unknown, Sullivan interview in Philadelphia.

31. Leon H. Sullivan, *America Is Theirs and Other Poems* (Sayle & Wimmer, 1948).

32. Unknown, Sullivan interview in Philadelphia.

33. Michelle R. Boyd, *Jim Crow Nostalgia: Reconstructing Race in Bronzeville* (University of Minnesota Press, 2008). Sullivan's recounting of the Black community in Charleston echoes Earl Lewis's chronicling of Black people's striving to turn segregation into "congregation" in nearby Norfolk, Virginia. See *In Their Own Interests: Race, Class, and Power in Twentieth Century Norfolk, Virginia* (University of California Press, 1991), 10.

34. Hazel P. Wooster, "Garnet High School," in *e-WV: The West Virginia Encyclopedia*, published January 28, 2013; last modified July 13, 2023, https://www.wvencyclopedia.org/articles/2081; The destruction of "The Block District" included the running of interstates 64 and 77 through the middle of the neighborhood. See Anthony Kinzer Sr., "The Block District was Socially Rich," *Daily Mail WV*, July 12, 2018, https://www.wvgazettemail.com/dailymailwv/anthony-kinzer-sr-the-block-district-was-socially-rich-daily-mail-opinion/article_acd477c7-9b50-52f0-af6b-110f1032683e.html.

35. Unknown, Sullivan interview in Philadelphia.

36. E. Franklin Frazier, *The Negro Family in the United States* (University of Chicago Press, 1939); Gaines, *Uplifting the Race*, xviii, 12, 34–35, 78, 93, 142; Kenneth Marvin Hamilton, *Black Towns and Profit: Promotion and Development in the Trans-Appalachian West, 1877–1915* (University of Illinois Press, 1991), 55, 104. Such adherence to Victorian mores did not go uncontested, as evidenced by Black middle-class women's challenges to patriarchal theology and traversing of the public/private divide. See Elsa Barkley Brown, "Womanist Consciousness: Maggie Lena Walker and the Independent Order of Saint

Luke," in *The Black Studies Reader*, ed. Jacqueline Bobo, Cynthia Hudley, and Claudine Michel (Routledge, 2004); Shirley J. Carlson, "Black Ideals of Womanhood in the Late Victorian Era, *Journal of Negro History* 77, no. 2 (1992): 61–73; Evelyn Brooks Higginbotham, *Righteous Discontent: The Women's Movement in the Black Baptist Church, 1880-1920* (Harvard University Press, 1994). Elsewhere, Black leftists rejected Victorian morality altogether. See Erik S. McDuffie, *Sojourning for Freedom: Black Women, American Communism, and the Making of Black Left Feminism* (Duke University Press, 2011).

37. Leon H. Sullivan, *Alternatives to Despair* (Judson Press, 1972), 48.

38. Tera W. Hunter, *Bound in Wedlock: Slave and Free Black Marriage in the Nineteenth Century* (Harvard University Press, 2017); Deborah Gray White, *Ar'n't I a Woman?: Female Slaves in the Plantation South* (W. W. Norton, 1985).

39. Register of Marriages, Staunton, 1932, Virginia Marriages, 1853-1935, viewable on Ancestry.com.

40. Sullivan, *Build, Brother, Build*, 43.

41. Unknown, Sullivan interview in Philadelphia.

42. Sullivan, *Build, Brother, Build*, 43–44.

43. Sullivan, *Build, Brother, Build*, 50; Leon H. Sullivan, *Moving Mountains: The Principles and Purposes of Leon Sullivan* (Judson Press, 1998), 2–3.

44. Zimmerman, *Alabama in Africa*; Sven Beckert, "From Tuskegee to Togo: The Problem of Freedom in the Empire of Cotton," *Journal of American History* 92, no. 2 (2005): 498–526.

45. Mitman, *Empire of Rubber*, 143–45; West, "The Tuskegee Model of Development in Africa," 375.

46. Dube quoted in Robert Trent Vinson, *The Americans Are Coming!: Dreams of African American Liberation in Segregationist South Africa* (Ohio University Press, 2012), 45. See also R. Hunt Davis Jr., "John L. Dube: A South African Exponent of Booker T. Washington," *Journal of African Studies* 2, no. 4 (1975): 497–528.

47. Christopher Kuria Githiora, *African Immigrants' Attitudes Toward African American Language/English* (Phd diss., Michigan State University, 2008), 10–11; Vinson, *The Americans Are Coming*, 40–41. While financing racial uplift, white philanthropy frequently functioned to reinforce white supremacy. See Maribel Morey, *White Philanthropy: Carnegie Corporation's An American Dilemma and the Making of a White World Order* (University of North Carolina Press, 2021).

48. Vinson, *The Americans Are Coming*, 40–41. On Washington's influence in South Africa, see Andrew Barnes, *Global Christianity and the Black Atlantic: Tuskegee, Colonialism, and the Shaping of African Industrial Education* (Baylor University Press, 2017); West, "The Tuskegee Model of Development in Africa;" Marable, "A Black School in South Africa."

49. William Beinart, Peter Delius, and Stanley Trapido, eds., *Putting a Plough to the Ground: Accumulation and Dispossession in Rural South Africa 1850-1930* (Raven Press, 1986); Colin Bundy, *The Rise and Fall of the South African Peasantry* (James Currey,

1988); Charles H. Feinstein, *An Economic History of South Africa: Conquest, Discrimination, and Development* (Cambridge University Press, 2005); John Higginson, *Collective Violence and the Agrarian Origins of South African Apartheid, 1900–1948* (Cambridge University Press, 2014).

50. Samuel Motsuenyane, *A Testament of Hope: The Autobiography of Dr. Sam Motsuenyane* (KMM Review Publishing, 2011), 1–2; Andre Wedepohl, "Kgosi Kgaswane and the Bakwena ba Modimosana ba Mmatau of the Tswana People," *The Heritage Portal Newsletter*, March 3, 2021, http://www.theheritageportal.co.za/article/kgosi-kgaswane-and-bakwena-ba-modimosana-ba-mmatau-tswana-people; Vincent Carruthers, *The Magaliesberg: Biosphere Edition* (Protea Book House, 2014), 215.

51. Vusumuzi Rodney Kumalo, "The African Struggle for Independent Education: A History of Wilberforce Institute, 1905 to 1950s," (PhD diss., University of the Witwatersrand, 2018), 123; Higginson, *Collective Violence and the Agrarian Origins of South African Apartheid*, 285–87; Timothy J. Keegan, *Facing the Storm: Portrait of Black Lives in Rural South Africa* (David Philip, 1988); Charles van Onselen, *The Seed is Mine: The Life of Kas Maine, A South African Sharecropper, 1894–1985* (David Philip, 1996).

52. Kumalo, "The African Struggle for Independent Education," 124. In the neighboring Transvaal, African land ownership gained further legitimacy thanks to the efforts of Edward Tsewu, who successfully petitioned the courts to allow Africans to buy and register land in their own names. See Vusumuzi Rodney Kumalo, *From Plough to Entrepreneurship: A History of African Entrepreneurs in Evaton, 1905–1960s* (University of Witwatersrand, 2014), 34.

53. Motsuenyane, *A Testament of Hope*, 6.

54. The 1908 Rights of Coloured Persons in Respect of Fixed Property Act 42 required tenants, including sharecroppers, to sign contracts. In doing so, the act transformed what had been a relatively advantageous situation, whereby Africans maintained a degree of autonomy over the land, into one of labor tenancy. See Kumalo, "The African Struggle for Independent Education," 131; John Boje and Fransjohan Pretorius, "Black Resistance in the Orange Free State during the Anglo-Boer War," *Historia* 58, no. 1 (2013): 43.

55. Motsuenyane, *A Testament of Hope*, 6.

56. Motsuenyane, *A Testament of Hope*, 7–8.

57. Samuel M. Motsuenyane, "A Tswana Growing Up with Afrikaners," *Munger Africana Library Notes*, 47 (February 1979): 5–7.

58. Veit Erlmann, "'A Feeling of Prejudice': Orepheus M. McAdoo and the Virginia Jubilee Singers in South Africa, 1890–1898," *Journal of Southern African Studies* 14, no. 3 (1988): 331–50.

59. James Campbell, *Songs of Zion: The African Methodist Episcopal Church in the United States and South Africa* (Oxford University Press, 1995); Vinson, *The Americans Are Coming*, 20–22.

60. Kumalo, "The African Struggle for Independent Education," 133, 138–139, 179, 195.

61. Kumalo, 250–251.

62. Union of South Africa, Natives (Urban Areas) Act, Act No. 21 of 1923.

63. Kumalo, "The African Struggle for Independent Education," 126–129; Kumalo, *From Plough to Entrepreneurship*.

64. Wilberforce Institute (Transvaal, South Africa), Leaflet for Wilberforce Institute, ca. 1925. W. E. B. Du Bois Papers (MS 312), Special Collections and University Archives, University of Massachusetts Amherst Libraries.

65. Kumalo, "The African Struggle for Independent Education," 246. See also Campbell, *Songs of Zion*; J. Mutero Chirenje, *Ethiopianism and Afro-Americans in Southern Africa, 1883–1916* (Louisiana State University Press, 1987).

66. Vinson, *The Americans Are Coming*.

67. Kumalo, "The African Struggle for Independent Education," 208.

68. Kumalo, *From Plough to Entrepreneurship*, especially chapter 7.

69. Motsuenyane, *A Testament of Hope*, 14–15.

70. Helen Bradford, "Mass Movements and the Petty Bourgeoisie: The Social Origins of the ICU Leadership, 1924–1929," *Journal of African History* 25, no. 3 (1984): 298.

71. Kumalo, "The African Struggle for Independent Education," 149, 250.

72. For more on Charlotte Maxeke's life and contributions, see Athambile Masola, "The Politics of the 1920s Black Press: Charlotte and Nontsizi Mgqetho's Critique of Congress," *International Journal of African Renaissance Studies—Multi-, Inter- and Transdisciplinarity* 13, no. 2 (2018): 59–76; April Thozama, "Theorising Women: The Intellectual Contributions of Charlotte Maxeke to the Struggle for Liberation in South Africa," (PhD diss., University of the Western Cape, 2012).

73. Campbell, *Songs of Zion*, 178.

74. Sullivan, *Build, Brother, Build*, 34.

75. Notwithstanding local particularities, apartheid's global scale was, perhaps, best captured by W. E. B. Du Bois, who famously noted that Jim Crow was but a local articulation of a global problem. Building on Du Bois's insight, historians have subsequently pushed back on popular associations of Jim Crow as exclusive to the American South through detailing the emergence of apartheid in the North. See, for example, Matthew J. Countryman, *Up South: Civil Rights and Black Power in Philadelphia* (University of Pennsylvania Press, 2006); Thomas J. Sugrue, *Sweet Land of Liberty: The Forgotten Struggle for Civil Rights in the North* (Random House, 2008); Jeanne F. Theoharis and Komozi Woodard, eds., *Freedom North: Black Freedom Struggles Outside the South, 1940–1980* (Palgrave Macmillan, 2003).

76. Motsuenyane, *A Testament of Hope*, 17–24.

77. Sullivan, *Build, Brother, Build*, 45.

78. On Black Marxists in mid-twentieth-century Harlem, see Minkah Makalani, "An Apparatus for Negro Women: Black Women's Organizing, Communism, and the Institutional Spaces of Radical Pan-African Thought," *Women, Gender, and Families of Color* 4, no. 2 (2016): 250–73; Charisse Burden-Stelly and Jodi Dean, eds., *Organize, Fight, Win: Black Communist Women's Political Writing* (Verso, 2002), 16, 45, 86, 91–92;

Charisse Burden-Stelly, *Black Scare/Red Scare: Theorizing Capitalist Racism in the United States* (University of Chicago Press, 2023), 58–59.

79. Martha Biondi, *To Stand and Fight: The Struggle for Civil Rights in Postwar New York City* (Harvard University Press, 2003), 3. On urban America as fertile ground for the rise of Black Power, see Donna Jean Murch, *Living for the City: Migration, Education, and the Rise of the Black Panther Party in Oakland* (University of North Carolina Press, 2010).

80. Adam Ewing, *The Age of Garvey: How a Jamaican Activist Created a Mass Movement and Changed Global Black Politics* (Princeton University Press, 2014); Keisha N. Blain, *Set the World on Fire: Black Nationalist Women and the Global Struggle for Freedom* (University of Pennsylvania Press, 2018).

81. Cheryl Lynn Greenberg, "Don't Buy Where You Can't Work," in *Consumer Society in American History: A Reader*, ed. Lawrence B. Glickman (Cornell University Press, 1999), 248. See also Cheryl Lynn Greenberg, "Citizens' League for Fair Play," in *Organizing Black America: An Encyclopedia of African American Associations*, ed. Nina Mjagkij (Garland Publishing, Inc., 2001).

82. Charles V. Hamilton, *Adam Clayton Powell, Jr.: The Political Biography of an American Dilemma* (Macmillan, 1991), 95.

83. Memorandum of Agreement Between the Uptown Chamber of Commerce and the Greater New York Coordinating Committee for Employment in Relations to the Employment of Negroes in Harlem Stores, July 20, 1938, New York Historical Society, New York, NY.

84. Sullivan, *Build, Brother, Build*, 44–45.

85. Sullivan, 46.

86. "Ray Tucker's Letter from Washington," *Brooklyn Daily Eagle*, June 28, 1941, 6.

87. Sullivan, *Build, Brother, Build*, 48.

88. Far from an anomaly, Black elites proved frequent, if junior, partners in governing the Jim Crow city. See N. D. B. Connolly, *A World More Concrete: Real Estate and the Remaking of Jim Crow South Florida* (University of Chicago Press, 2014).

89. Cheryl Lynn Greenberg, *Or Does it Explode? Black Harlem in the Great Depression* (Oxford University Press, 1991), 211–214; Carl Suddler, *Presumed Criminal: Black Youth and the Justice System in Postwar New York* (New York University Press, 2019), 39.

90. White residents' claims about the association between Black and Brown migrants and crime are undermined by statistics revealing a decrease in violent crime rates between 1925 and 1940. See Jeffrey S. Adler, "Less Crime, More Punishment: Violence, Race, and Criminal Justice in Early Twentieth-Century America," *Journal of American History* 102, no. 1 (2015): 34–46.

91. Emily M. Brooks, *Gotham's War within a War: Policing and the Birth of Law-and-Order Liberalism in World War II–Era New York City* (University of North Carolina Press, 2023).

92. Luis Alvarez, *The Power of the Zoot: Youth Culture and Resistance during World War II* (University of California Press, 2008), 56–65. The World War II–era crackdown

was but one episode in a long history of racialized policing targeting Black New Yorkers. See Shannon King, *Whose Harlem Is This, Anyway?: Community Politics and Grassroots Activism During the New Negro Era* (New York University Press, 2015), especially chapter 4.

93. Shane White, Stephen Garton, Stephen Robertson, and Graham White, *Playing the Numbers: Gambling in Harlem between the Wars* (Harvard University Press, 2010), especially chapter 8; Will Cooley, "Jim Crow Organized Crime: Black Chicago's Underground Economy in the Twentieth Century," in *Building the Black Metropolis: African American Entrepreneurship in Chicago*, ed. Robert E. Weems and Jason P. Chambers (University of Illinois Press, 2017).

94. Minutes of Confidential Meeting with Mayor LaGuardia, June 30, 1944, Rectory of Monsignor McCann, reproduced from the Collection of the Manuscript Division, Library of Congress, *History Vault*; Sullivan, *Build, Brother, Build*, 48–49. On Black professional gains as an intended result of negotiated desegregation, see Tomiko Brown-Nagin, *Courage to Dissent: Atlanta and the Long History of the Civil Rights Movement* (Oxford University Press, 2011).

95. Sullivan, *Build, Brother, Build*, 48.

96. Sullivan, *Build, Brother, Build*, 48.

97. On Black calls for community policing, see Connolly, *A World More Concrete*, 124–128; Khalil Gibran Muhammad, *Condemnation of Blackness: Race, Crime, and the Making of Modern Urban America* (Harvard University Press, 2010), 187.

98. Minutes of Confidential Meeting with Mayor LaGuardia, June 30, 1944.

99. Sullivan, *Build, Brother, Build*, 59.

100. Sullivan, 48–49.

101. On the intersections between Black athletics, youth development, and racial uplift, see Amira Rose Davis, "Watch What We Do: The Politics and Possibilities of Black Women's Athletics, 1910–1970," (PhD diss., Johns Hopkins University, 2016).

102. Minutes of Confidential Meeting with Mayor LaGuardia, June 30, 1944.

103. Program, "What the Negro Wants in the Post War World," Post War Planning Conference, October 21–22, 1944, Abyssinian Baptist Church, New York, reproduced from The Claude A. Barnett Papers: The Associated Negro Press, 1918–1967, Part 2: Associated Negro Press Organizational Files, 1920–1966, *History Vault*; "Youth Group Will Fight Delinquency," *New York Amsterdam News*, May 20, 1944.

104. Minutes of Confidential Meeting with Mayor LaGuardia, June 30, 1944.

105. Jean Comaroff and John L. Comaroff, *Theory from The South: Or, How Euro-America Is Evolving Toward Africa* (Routledge, 2011).

106. Putnam, *Radical Moves*.

107. Adam Ewing and Ronald J. Stephens, eds., *Global Garveyism* (University Press of Florida, 2019); Vinson, *The Americans Are Coming*.

108. Robin D. G. Kelley, *Freedom Dreams: The Black Radical Imagination* (Beacon Press, 2002); Burden-Stelly and Dean, eds., *Organize, Fight, Win*.

Chapter 2

1. W. E. B. Du Bois, *The Philadelphia Negro: A Social Study*, Publications of the University of Pennsylvania Series in Political Economy and Public Law, No. 14 (Ginn & Co., 1899), 97.

2. Du Bois, *The Philadelphia Negro,* 390–91. Elsewhere, Du Bois noted that a "special effort" would need to be made "to train Negro boys for industrial life" (97).

3. Mark Bricklin, "8,000 Jam N. Phila. Training Center Opening Sunday: Speakers Cite Benefits of New Jobs Approach: All Segments of Community Will Profit They Say," *Philadelphia Tribune,* January 28, 1964.

4. McKissick quoted in Steven Knowlton, "Soul City: Black Will Have 'Culture' Control," *Charlotte Observer,* January 19, 1969.

5. McKissick quoted in Warne King, "Soul City, N.C., Is Moving From Dream Stage to Reality," *New York Times,* January 4, 1974.

6. Laura Warren Hill and Julia Rabig, eds., *The Business of Black Power: Community Development, Capitalism, and Corporate Responsibility in Postwar America* (University of Rochester Press, 2012); Marcia Chatelain, *Franchise: The Golden Arches in Black America* (W.W. Norton, 2020); Joshua Clark Davis, *From Head Shops to Whole Foods: The Rise and Fall of Activist Entrepreneurship* (Columbia University Press, 2020); Laura Warren Hill, *Strike the Hammer: The Black Freedom Struggle in Rochester, New York, 1940-1970* (Cornell University Press, 2021) .

7. I am indebted to N. D. B. Connolly for my understanding of civil rights capitalism. Connolly uses the term, albeit in passing, to describe investments made by white real estate developers in Black housing in south Florida. See *A World More Concrete: Real Estate and the Remaking of Jim Crow South Florida* (University of Chicago Press, 2014), 150. In this chapter, I expand on this concept in relation to the ideas and actions of civil rights activists like Leon Sullivan and SCLC.

8. "Leon Sullivan," *Sunday Gazette-Mail* (Charleston, WV), December 26, 1965.

9. 1930 US Census, viewable on Ancestry.com; Philadelphia, Pennsylvania, Marriage Index, 1885–1951, Ancestry.com. Meanwhile, the US Census confirms that Grace's parents, Julia and Carter Banks remained in Baltimore, where they resided at 903 North Stricker St. with Grace's siblings, Reginia, George, Junius, and Susie. See 1930 US Census, Ancestry.com.

10. 1940 US Census, Ancestry.com.

11. Philadelphia, Pennsylvania, Marriage Index, 1885-1951, Ancestry.com; "Woman Behind the Scene: The Minister's Lady Mrs. Grace Sullivan," *Philadelphia Tribune,* October 9, 1965.

12. Leon H. Sullivan, *Alternatives to Despair* (Judson Press, 1972), 48.

13. In his autobiography, Sullivan claims to have taken courses at the Union Theological Seminary and "completed [a] master's degree in religion at Columbia University." See Leon H. Sullivan, *Build, Brother, Build: From Poverty to Economic Power* (Macrae Smith Company, 1969), 52. I have only been able to verify his attendance and graduation

from the Teacher's College Columbia Commencement Files, 1947–1949, Series I: Commencement Box 15, Columbia University Archives, Columbia University, New York, NY.

14. Sullivan, *Build, Brother, Build*, 52.

15. Helen Terrell Parsons, West Virginia, US, Deaths Index, 1853–1973, Ancestry .com.

16. James Wolfinger, *Philadelphia Divided: Race and Politics in the City of Brotherly Love* (University of North Carolina Press, 2007), 179.

17. "Lone Woman Holds a Mob of 500 White Brutes at Bay: Adella Bond Shoots into Mob Attempting Violence," *Philadelphia Tribune*, August 3, 1918. See also "Mrs. Bond Determined to Occupy Her House," *Philadelphia Inquirer*, July 31, 1918; "Man Shot in Race Riot Over Negro Resident," *Philadelphia Inquirer*, July 28, 1918.

18. Matthew J. Countryman, *Up South: Civil Rights and Black Power in Philadelphia* (University of Pennsylvania Press, 2006), 69, 73; Kevin Boyle, *Arc of Justice: A Saga of Race, Civil Rights, and Murder in the Jazz Age* (Henry Holt and Co., 2005); Kevin Kruse, *White Flight: Atlanta and the Making of Modern Conservatism* (Princeton University Press, 2005).

19. On white flight in Philadelphia see Thomas J. Sugrue, *Sweet Land of Liberty: The Forgotten Struggle for Civil Rights in the North* (Random House, 2008), 205; Countryman, *Up South*, 69, 72–73; and James Wolfinger, *Philadelphia Divided: Race and Politics in the City of Brotherly Love* (University of North Carolina Press, 2007), 178. Bucking the broader trend, some Philadelphia-area communities, including West Mount Airy, rallied to promote racial integration. While successful in resisting resegregation, these efforts were, as Abigal Perkiss shows, not without problems. See *Making Good Neighbors: Civil Rights, Liberalism and Integration in Postwar Philadelphia* (Cornell University Press, 2014).

20. Sullivan, *Build, Brother, Build*, 57–58.

21. "Mapping Inequality: Redlining in New Deal America," Digital Scholarship Lab, University of Richmond, https://dsl.richmond.edu/panorama/redlining/#loc=10 /40.015/-75.456&city=philadelphia-pa; David M. P. Freund, *Colored Property: State Policy and White Racial Politics In Suburban America* (University of Chicago Press, 2007), 113–16; Sugrue *Sweet Land of Liberty*, 204–5.

22. Sullivan, *Build, Brother, Build*, 56–57.

23. Marcus Anthony Hunter, *Black Citymakers: How the Philadelphia Negro Changed Urban America* (Oxford University Press, 2013), 133–35.

24. On state-financed infrastructural racism, see Rhonda Y. Williams, *The Politics of Public Housing: Black Women's Struggles against Urban Inequality* (Oxford University Press, 2004); Connolly, *A World More Concrete*.

25. "Church History," Zion Baptist Church of Philadelphia, https://www.zionbapt philly.org/church-history/.

26. "Good Templars Will Discuss Order Work," *Philadelphia Inquirer*, June 27, 1914.

27. "Broad St. Church Buys in Suburbs," *Philadelphia Tribune*, February 20, 1955.

28. "Many New Churches Rising: Different Types of Architecture Are Represented," *Philadelphia Inquirer*, September 25, 1956; Mark Muddler, *Shades of White Flight: Evangelical Congregations and Urban Departure* (Rutgers University Press, 2015).

29. Conflicting accounts put the amount that Zion Baptist Church paid for the building between $220,000 and $250,000. See "Profile: In the Battle for Rights," *Philadelphia Inquirer*, July 30, 1963;

30. Sullivan, *Build, Brother, Build*, 58.

31. Sullivan, *Build, Brother, Build*, 63. Sullivan's recounting of the origins of CCJAD in *Build, Brother, Build* conflicts with a letter to the editor he wrote in late July 1953, in which he dated the organization launch seven months prior, in December 1952/January 1953. See Leon H. Sullivan, "All Out For Youth: To the Editor of The Inquirer," *Philadelphia Inquirer*, July 30, 1953.

32. "New Group Maps Fight on Crime," *Philadelphia Inquirer*, March 7, 1953.

33. "Fight Goes On: Enthusiastic Meeting Vows No Let-Up in Fight Against New Area Taprooms," *Philadelphia Tribune*, February 2, 1954. See also Alice O'Connor, *Poverty Knowledge: Social Science, Social Policy, and the Poor in Twentieth-Century U.S. History* (Princeton University Press, 2001), 28–40, 64.

34. "Practical Program to Fight Youth Crime Planned Here," *Philadelphia Tribune*, March 24, 1953.

35. Sullivan quoted in "Police Captains to Help Group Fight Child Crime," *Philadelphia Inquirer*, April 7, 1953.

36. Sullivan, *Build, Brother, Build*, 63–64.

37. Sullivan quoted in "City Groups Aid Drive on Gangs," *Philadelphia Inquirer*, November 16, 1954.

38. Khalil Gibran Muhammad, *The Condemnation of Blackness: Race, Crime, and the Making of Modern Urban America* (Harvard University Press, 2010), 10.

39. "Rev. Leon Sullivan to Address Lion Gridmen Tonight," *The Gazette and Daily* (York, PA), November 20, 1957; "Sullivan To Be Speaker at Preaching Mission," *Johnson City Press* (Johnson City, TN), January 27, 1957.

40. The Annual Report of the Philadelphia Branch of the National Association for the Advancement of Colored People, 1953, 16, reproduced from the Collections of the Manuscript Division, Library of Congress, ProQuest History Vault. On the transformation of Philadelphia's NAACP, see Countryman, *Up South*, 35–47, 90–92. While giving airtime to Sullivan and the CCAJD, Countryman notes that, at other times, the Philadelphia NAACP failed to give attention to many of the issues, including juvenile delinquency, that drove Black community activism in Philadelphia in the 1950s, prioritizing working with the city's liberal establishment on legislative and judicial gains instead.

41. On the history of Black radio, including its relative paucity until after World War II, see Gilbert A. Williams, *Legendary Pioneers of Black Radio* (Praeger, 1998).

42. "Young Man of 1955 Award to Rev. Leon H. Sullivan," *Philadelphia Tribune*, June 10, 1956; "Rev. Sullivan Presented 'Outstanding' Award," *Atlanta Daily World*, February 8, 1956.

43. Sullivan quoted in "Young Man of 1955 Award to Rev. Leon H. Sullivan," *Philadelphia Tribune*, June 10, 1956.

44. Muhammad, *The Condemnation of Blackness*, 10.

45. Elizabeth Hinton, *From the War on Poverty to the War on Crime: The Making of Mass Incarceration in America* (Harvard University Press, 2017).

46. Marc Lamont Hill, *Nobody: Casualties of America's War on the Vulnerable, from Ferguson to Flint and Beyond* (Simon and Schuster, 2016). See also Bench Ansfield, "The Broken Windows of the Bronx: Putting the Theory in Its Place," *American Quarterly* 72, no. 1 (2020): 103–27.

47. Muhammad, *Condemnation of Blackness*, 10–11.

48. On Philadelphia's policing of Black and Brown neighborhoods, see "Numbers Suspect Feels Law's Fist," *Philadelphia Tribune*, October 27, 1953.

49. Sullivan, *Build, Brother, Build*, 65.

50. "Church to Open Its New Home," *Philadelphia Inquirer*, September 10, 1955; Sullivan, *Build, Brother, Build*, 65–66.

51. Thomas J. Sugrue, "Affirmative Action from Below: Civil Rights, the Building Trades, and the Politics of Racial Equality in the Urban North, 1945–1969," *Journal of American History* 91, no. 1 (2004): 149–50; Countryman, *Up South*, 66–67, 92.

52. Countryman, *Up South*, 158.

53. Sullivan quoted in "Hundreds of Teeners Swamp New Agency in Search for Jobs," *Philadelphia Inquirer*, February 2, 1960.

54. "Ministers' Idea Pays Off for Youngsters: $250,000," *Afro-American* (Baltimore, MD), November 5, 1960.

55. 86 Cong. Rec A5265 (1960) (statement of Sen. Scott).

56. "Ministers' Idea Pays Off for Youngsters: $250,000.".

57. "Our History," Second Macedonia Baptist Church, http://www.smbapt.org /about-us/our-history.html.

58. Ayana Jones, "Obituary: Frederick Miller, 82, community leader," *Philadelphia Tribune*, January 26, 2014, https://www.phillytrib.com/obituaries/frederick-miller-82 -community-leader/article_7da11256-efd3-587e-8aee-85d7c0117f4f.html; "Our History," Second Macedonia Baptist Church, http://www.smbapt.org/about-us/our-history .html.

59. On the failures of racial liberalism and traditional civil rights strategies, including those that relied on the courts, see Countryman, *Up South*; Lani Guinier, "From Racial Liberalism to Racial Literacy: *Brown v. Board of Education* and the Interest-Divergence Dilemma," *Journal of American History* 91, no. 1 (2004): 92–118.

60. Michael C. Dawson, *Black Visions: The Roots of Contemporary African-American Political Ideologies* (University of Chicago Press, 2003).

61. W. Manning Marable, *Malcolm X: A Life of Reinvention* (Penguin Books, 2011), 86–93.

62. Malcolm X and Alex Haley, *The Autobiography of Malcolm X* (Random House, 1973). Marable contests this narrative, implying that Malcolm and/or Haley likely

embellished details related to Malcolm's illicit behavior for the sake of the biography. See Marable, *Malcolm X*, 60–69.

63. Malcolm X quoted in Marable, *Malcolm X*, 105.

64. Anonymous FBI informant quoted in Countryman, *Up South*, 88.

65. Joseph quoted in Marable, *Malcolm X*, 106.

66. Countryman, *Up South*, 88–89.

67. Dennis Carlisle, "Peeling Back the Layers on Malcolm X's Mosque #12," *Hidden City: Exploring Philadelphia's Urban Landscape*, January 24, 2017, https://hiddencityphila .org/2017/01/peeling-back-the-layers-on-malcolm-xs-mosque-12/.

68. Judith Weisenfeld, *New World A-Coming: Black Religion and Racial Identity during the Great Migration* (New York University Press, 2017); Arthur Huff Fauset, *Black Gods of the Metropolis: Negro Religious Cults of the Urban North* (University of Pennsylvania Press, 2001).

69. J. T. Roane, *Dark Agoras: Insurgent Black Social Life and the Politics of Place* (New York University Press, 2023).

70. Building on the pioneering scholarship by historians like Deborah Gray White, Nell Irvin Painter, and others, recent years have witnessed an explosion of new work on Black women's activism. See, for example, Peter J. Ling and Sharon Monteith, eds., *Gender and the Civil Rights Movement* (Rutgers University Press, 2004); Danielle L. McGuire, *At the Dark End of the Street: Black Women, Rape, and Resistance—A New History of the Civil Rights Movement from Rosa Parks to the Rise of Black Power* (Knopf, 2010); Martha S. Jones, *Vanguard: How Black Women Broke Barriers, Won the Vote, and Insisted on Equality for All* (Basic Books, 2020); Jeanne F. Theoharis, *The Rebellious Life of Mrs. Rosa Parks* (Beacon Press, 2013). On the life and work of Black queer activist Bayard Rustin, see John D'Emilio, *Lost Prophet: The Life and Times of Bayard Rustin* (University of Chicago Press, 2004).

71. Jacquelyn Dowd Hall, "The Long Civil Rights Movement and the Political Uses of the Past," *Journal of American History* 91, no. 4 (2005): 1233–63; Jeanne F. Theoharis and Komozi Woodard, eds., *Freedom North: Black Freedom Struggles Outside the South, 1940–1980* (Palgrave Macmillan, 2003); Kevin Boyle, "Labour, the Left and the Long Civil Rights Movement," *Social History* 30, no. 3 (2005): 366–72. For a critique of the "long movement" frame, see Sundiata Keita Cha-Jua and Clarence Lang, "The 'Long Movement' as Vampire: Temporal and Spatial Fallacies in Recent Black Freedom Studies," *Journal of African American History* 92, no. 2 (2007): 265–88.

72. Scholarship in this vein includes Tiffany M. Gill, *Beauty Shop Politics: African American Women's Activism in the Beauty Industry* (University of Illinois Press, 2010); Quincy T. Mills, *Cutting Along the Color Line: Black Barbers and Barber Shops in America* (University of Pennsylvania Press, 2013); Connolly, *A World More Concrete*; Brenna Wynn Greer, *Represented: The Black Imagemakers Who Reimagined African American Citizenship* (University of Pennsylvania Press, 2019); Chatelain, *Franchise*; and Hill, *Strike the Hammer*.

73. Sullivan, *Build, Brother, Build*, 78.

74. Countryman, *Up South*; Sugrue, *Sweet Land of Liberty*, 126–29.

75. Sugrue, "Affirmative Action from Below," 152.

76. Countryman, *Up South*, 50–51.

77. US Bureau of the Census, *U.S. Census of Population: 1960. Vol. 1, Characteristics of the Population. Part 40, Pennsylvania* (Washington, DC: US Government Printing Office, 1963), 40–372, 431; Guian A. McKee, *The Problem of Jobs: Liberalism, Race, and Deindustrialization in Philadelphia* (University of Chicago Press, 2008), 115.

78. Clayborne Carson, *In Struggle: SNCC and the Black Awakening of the 1960s* (Harvard University Press, 1981); Iwan Morgan and Philip Davies, *From Sit-Ins to SNCC: The Student Civil Rights Movement in the 1960s* (University Press of Florida, 2012); Martha Biondi, *The Black Revolution on Campus* (University of California Press, 2012).

79. "Student Sit-Down Strike Spreads to Segregation Demonstrations Go Into Second Week," *Philadelphia Tribune*, February 13, 1960; "Anti-Bias Group Pickets Store Here," *Philadelphia Inquirer*, February 21, 1960; "Boycott Spreads Here: Movement Gains Supporters: Pickets Empty Stores at 52nd and Market, 40th and Lancaster," *Philadelphia Tribune*, March 1, 1960.

80. Countryman, *Up South*, 98–99.

81. Adam Fairclough, *To Redeem the Soul of America: The Southern Christian Leadership Conference and Martin Luther King, Jr.* (University of Georgia Press, 1987), 17.

82. Countryman, *Up South*, 98–110; Hannah Lees, "The Not-Buying Power of Philadelphia Negroes," *Reporter* (Lansdale, PA), May 11, 1961.

83. Barney Seibert, "Report on Scope and Success of Selective Patronage Campaigns," *Record-American* (Mahonoy City, PA), February 18, 1963.

84. Sullivan, *Build, Brother, Build*, 79.

85. Walter Weare, *Black Business in the New South: A Social History of the North Carolina Mutual Life Insurance Company* (Duke University Press, 1993), 87, 188–189; Juliet E .K. Walker, *The History of Black Business in America: Capitalism, Race, Entrepreneurship* (Macmillan, 1998), xxi, 112.

86. Scholarship on the intersections between American religion, particularly Christianity, and capitalism has grown significantly in recent decades. See, for example, Bethany Moreton, *To Serve God and Wal-Mart: The Making of Christian Free Enterprise* (Harvard University Press, 2009); David Walker, *Railroading Religion: Mormons, Tourists, and the Corporate Spirit of the West* (University of North Carolina Press, 2019); Kevin Kruse, *One Nation Under God: How Corporate America Invented Christian America* (Basic Books, 2015). For an excellent analysis of the ways religion, business, and Black activism intersected in the early nineteenth century, see Timothy Rainey II, "Capitalism in Color: Religion, Companies, and Black Economic Activism in the Age of Paul Cuffee, 1807–1817" (PhD diss., Emory University, 2021).

87. "Interracial Service Sunday," *Lancaster (PA) New Era*, January 8, 1960.

88. Bob Queen, "Pulpit Boycott Rocks Empire of 'Liquid Gold'" *Pittsburgh Courier*, January 5, 1963; Edward F. Woods, "Eastern Negro Clergymen Press Boycotts Against Hiring Bias," *St. Louis Post-Dispatch*, December 16, 1962.

89. Countryman, *Up South*, 104–5.

90. Claudia Jones, "An End to the Neglect of the Problems of the Negro Woman!" *PRISM: Political & Rights Issues & Social Movements* 467 (Jan. 1949), https://stars.library .ucf.edu/prism/467.

91. Display Ad 18—Tasty Baking Company Outlines Fair Employment Program, *Philadelphia Tribune*, July 2, 1960.

92. Enrico Beltramini, "SCLC Operation Breadbasket: From Economic Civil Rights to Black Economic Power," *Fire!!!* 2, no. 2 (2013): 18–19.

93. Sullivan, *Build, Brother, Build*, 83.

94. McKee, *The Problem of Jobs*, 121; Countryman, *Up South*, 101–10, 117–19.

95. Muhammad Ahmad, "History of RAM—Revolutionary Action Movement" (1979), Freedom Archives, https://freedomarchives.org/Documents/Finder/DOC513 _scans/RAM/513.RAM.History.of.RAM.pdf.

96. Sullivan, *Build, Brother, Build*, 78.

97. Bob Queen, "Ministers Found Breyer Ice Cream Co. Tough Bias Obstacle to 'Melt,'" *New Pittsburgh Courier*, January 12, 1963.

98. Steve Estes, *I am a Man!: Race, Manhood, and the Civil Rights Movement* (University of North Carolina Press, 2006).

99. McKee, *The Problem of Jobs*, 122–23.

100. Sullivan, *Build, Brother, Build*, 78–79.

101. "Ministers Win Drive Against Gulf Oil. Co.," *New York Amsterdam News*, February 4, 1961.

102. Countryman, *Up South*, 108.

103. "Gulf Oil Plans to Boost Capital Expenditures in 1961 to $400 Million," *Wall Street Journal*, February 13, 1961.

104. Bob Queen, "Pulpit Boycott Rocks Empire of 'Liquid Gold,'" *Pittsburgh Courier*, January 5, 1963.

105. Edward F. Woods, "Eastern Negro Clergymen Press Boycotts Against Hiring Bias," *St. Louis Post-Dispatch*, December 16, 1962.

106. Sullivan quoted in Edward F. Woods, "Eastern Negro Clergymen Press Boycotts Against Hiring Bias," *St. Louis Post-Dispatch*, December 16, 1962.

107. In his broader examination of the shift from civil rights to property rights, Richard L. Schur argues for understanding Martin Luther King Jr., who would later come to question capitalism, as initially advocating for Black inclusion in an expanded capitalist marketplace. See *Parodies of Ownership: Hip-Hop Aesthetics and Intellectual Property Law* (University of Michigan Press, 2009), 15–16.

108. "Dr. Sullivan to Address Mass Meet," *Atlanta Daily World*, October 28, 1962.

109. Negro Ministers of Atlanta, press release, n.d. (circa Spring 1963), Box 172.2, SCLC Records, Martin Luther King Center, Atlanta, GA.

110. Mark Bricklin, "8,000 Jam N. Phila. Training Center Opening Sunday: Speakers Cite Benefits of New Jobs Approach: All Segments of Community Will Profit They Say," *Philadelphia Tribune*, January 28, 1964.

111. *Hearings on the H.R. 10908, the Comprehensive Manpower Act of 1969, H.R. 11620, the Manpower Act of 1969, and H.R. 13472, the Administration Manpower Training Act (MTA) of 1968, First and Second Sessions, Before the Select Subcomm. on Labor-Management Relations, Committee on Education and Labor.* 91st Cong. (statement of Rev. Leon Sullivan, Founder of the Opportunities Industrialization Center).

112. Sullivan, *Build, Brother, Build*, 86.

113. Sullivan quoted in Paul J. Levine, "Pastor Forms Negro Training, Industry Center," *Philadelphia Inquirer*, July 30, 1963.

114. Sullivan quoted in Levine, "Pastor Forms Negro Training, Industry Center."

115. Levine, "Pastor Forms Negro Training, Industry Center."

116. "Negro Training Center Is Given $50,000 by Anonymous Donor," *Philadelphia Inquirer*, September 25, 1963.

117. Interview with Kenneth Salaam by Diane Turner, Charles L. Blockson Afro-American Collection, Temple University, Philadelphia, Pennsylvania, May 9, 2011. See also "Numbers Suspect Feels Law's Fist," *Philadelphia Tribune*, October 27, 1953; "Accuse Policeman of Beating Man Without Cause," *Philadelphia Tribune*, April 7, 1953.

118. Capt. Joseph Bonner, "North Philly Beat," *Philadelphia Tribune*, August 15, 1959; "Clearing Site of 2-District Police Station," *Philadelphia Tribune*, October 10, 1959.

119. Sullivan, *Build, Brother, Build*, 87–88.

120. Lou Potter, "Old 19th & Oxford Police Station Sought for School," *Philadelphia Tribune*, August 24, 1963; Sullivan, *Build, Brother, Build*, 88.

121. Paul Friggens, "Toward Self-Help in Philadelphia," *Christian Science Monitor*, September 15, 1965.

122. Bob Queen, "The 'Miracle' of OIC—Reclaims Lives, Trains," *Afro-American* (Baltimore, MD), May 7, 1966.

123. Sullivan quoted in Paul Friggens, "Toward Self-Help in Philadelphia," *Christian Science Monitor*, September 15, 1965.

124. "Rev. Sullivan Given $19,000 More for Training Program," *Philadelphia Tribune*, November 23, 1963.

125. Sullivan, *Build, Brother, Build*, 90.

126. Bob Queen, "The 'Miracle' of OIC—Reclaims Lives, Trains," *Afro-American* (Baltimore, MD), May 7, 1966.

127. "Rev. Sullivan Given $19,000 More for Training Program," *Philadelphia Tribune*, November 23, 1963.

128. Jefferson Cowie, *Capital Moves: RCA's Seventy-Year Quest for Cheap Labor* (New Press, 2001), 88–91.

129. Elizabeth M. Nix and Deborah R. Weiner, "Pivot in Perception: The Impact of the 1968 Riots on Three Baltimore Districts," in *Baltimore '68: Riots and Rebirth in an American City*, ed. Jessica Elfenbein, Thomas Hollowak, and Elizabeth Nix (Temple University Press, 2011).

130. McKee, *The Problem of Jobs*, especially chapter 2.

131. Keith Wailoo, *Pushing Cool: Big Tobacco, Racial Marketing, and the Untold Story of the Menthol Cigarette* (University of Chicago Press, 2021); Chatelain, *Franchise*.

132. Greer, *Represented*; Hill and Rabig, *Business of Black Power*.

133. Andrew W. Kahrl, *The Black Tax: 150 Years of Theft, Exploitation, and Dispossession in America* (University of Chicago Press, 2024); Destin Jenkins, *The Bonds of Inequality: Debt and the Making of the American City* (University of Chicago Press, 2021).

134. Thomas J. Sugrue, *The Origins of the Urban Crisis: Race and Inequality in Postwar Detroit* (Princeton University Press, 1996); Kruse, *White Flight*; Robert O. Self, *American Babylon: Race and the Struggle for Postwar Oakland* (Princeton University Press, 2005).

135. Williams, *The Politics of Public Housing*; Annelise Orleck, *Storming Caesars Palace: How Black Mothers Fought Their Own War on Poverty* (Beacon Press, 2005).

136. McKee, *The Problem of Jobs*, 115.

137. Sugrue, *Sweet Land of Liberty*, 277–79.

Chapter 3

1. Peniel E. Joseph, *Waiting 'Til the Midnight Hour: A Narrative History of Black Power in America* (Henry Holt, 2006); Nikhil Pal Singh, *Black Is a Country: Race and the Unfinished Struggle for Democracy* (Harvard University Press, 2005); Donna Jean Murch, *Living for the City: Migration, Education, and the Rise of the Black Panther Party in Oakland, California* (University of North Carolina Press, 2010); Matthew J. Countryman, *Up South: Civil Rights and Black Power in Philadelphia* (University of Pennsylvania Press, 2006); Robert O. Self, *American Babylon: Race and the Struggle for Postwar Oakland* (Princeton University Press, 2005); Rhonda Y. Williams, *The Politics of Public Housing: Black Women's Struggles against Urban Inequality* (Oxford University Press, 2004); Nico Slate, ed., *Black Power beyond Borders: The Global Dimensions of the Black Power Movement* (Palgrave Macmillan, 2013).

2. Stokely Carmichael, "Speech at University of California, Berkeley," October 29, 1966, American Radio Works, *American Public Media*, https://americanradioworks .publicradio.org/features/blackspeech/scarmichael.html.

3. Nikhil Pal Singh, "The Black Panthers and the 'Undeveloped Country' of the Left," in *The Black Panther Party Reconsidered*, ed. Charles E. Jones (Black Classic Press, 1998): 57–90.

4. Bobby Seale, *Seize the Time: The Story of the Black Panther Party and Huey P. Newton* (Random House, 1970), 30. See also Murch, *Living for the City*, especially chapter 5.

5. On the 1960s uprisings, see Elizabeth Hinton, *America on Fire: The Untold History of Police Violence and Black Rebellion since the 1960s* (Liveright, 2022); Malcolm McLaughlin, *The Long, Hot Summer of 1967: Urban Rebellion in America* (Palgrave Macmillan, 2014); Gerald C. Horne, *Fire This Time: The Watts Uprising and the 1960s* (DeCapo Press, 1995). Correctly or incorrectly, many of the rebellions became associated with Black Power. See Joseph, *Waiting 'Til the Midnight Hour*, 174.

6. Henry T. Benjamin, "Philyaw Slaying Stirred Furor: Rioting, Vandalism Erupted Along Susquehanna Ave. After Slaying," *Philadelphia Tribune*, December 31, 1963; Countryman, *Up South*, 154.

7. Louis Hyman, "Ending Discrimination, Legitimating Debt: The Political Economy of Race, Gender, and Credit Access in the 1960s and 1970s," *Enterprise & Society* 12, no. 1 (2011): 203–13.

8. Peter B. Levy, *The Great Uprising: Race Riots in Urban America during the 1960s* (Cambridge University Press, 2018).

9. Laura Warren Hill and Julia Rabig, eds., *The Business of Black Power: Community Development, Capitalism, and Corporate Responsibility in Postwar America* (University of Rochester Press, 2012); Marcia Chatelain, *Franchise: The Golden Arches in Black America* (W.W. Norton, 2020), 103, 232; Laura Warren Hill, *Strike the Hammer: The Black Freedom Struggle in Rochester, New York, 1940–1970* (Cornell University Press, 2021).

10. "Dr. Leon Sullivan Hits 'Front Man' Charge in Progress Plaza Speech: Fronts for No One But God, Minister Says," *Philadelphia Tribune*, October 29, 1968; "Dedication of Phillip's Progress Plaza Shopping Attracts 10,000," *Pittsburgh Courier*, November 16, 1968.

11. Leon H. Sullivan, *Build, Brother, Build: From Poverty to Economic Power* (Macrae Smith, 1969), 95, 111.

12. On Black Power activists' embrace of electoral politics, see Jakobi Williams, *From the Bullet to the Ballot: The Illinois Chapter of the Black Panther Party and Racial Coalition Politics in Chicago* (University of North Carolina Press, 2013); Matthew J. Countryman, "'From Protest to Politics': Community Control and Black Independent Politics in Philadelphia, 1965–1984," *Journal of Urban History* 32, no. 6 (2006): 813–61; Murch, *Living for the City*, 226–28.

13. Journalist John Chamberlain, for example, characterized Sullivan's approach as "productive Black power" through "put[ing] Black people into businesses." See "Rev. Leon Sullivan Seed for Growing Black Power," *Bryan (TX) Daily Eagle*, April 28, 1969.

14. Black Panther Party Boycott of Bill's Liquor Store, 1971–1972, FBI Files on Black Extremist Organizations, Part 2: Huey Newton and Eldridge Cleaver of the Black Panther Party, Jan 01, 1971–Dec 31, 1972, Folder 101788-008-0612, *HistoryVault*.

15. Karen Ferguson, *Top Down: The Ford Foundation, Black Power, and the Reinvention of Racial Liberalism* (University of Pennsylvania Press, 2013); Devin Fergus, *Liberalism, Black Power, and the Making of American Politics, 1965–1980* (University of Georgia Press, 2009).

16. Richard Nixon, "Address Accepting the Presidential Nomination at the Republican National Convention in Miami Beach," Florida, August 8, 1968, online at The American Presidency Project, https://www.presidency.ucsb.edu/node/256650.

17. *Oxford English Dictionary*, s.v. "incorporation (*n.*)," https://doi.org/10.1093/OED /9460539274.

18. Hill and Rabig, *Business of Black Power*; Kimberley Johnson, "Community Development Corporations, Participation, and Accountability: The Harlem Urban

Development Corporation and the Bedford-Stuyvesant Restoration Corporation," *The ANNALS of the American Academy of Political and Social Science* 594, no. 1 (2004): 109–24; Michael Brower, "The Emergence of Community Development Corporations in Urban Neighborhoods," *American Journal of Orthopsychiatry* 41, no. 4 (1971): 646–58; Harry Edward Berndt, *New Rulers in the Ghetto: The Community Development Corporation and Urban Poverty* (Greenwood Press, 1977).

19. Claire Dunning, *Nonprofit Neighborhoods: An Urban History of Inequality and the American State* (University of Chicago Press, 2022).

20. Mark Bricklin, "Testing of 2500 Applicants Now in Full Swing: 1500 Have Applied in Past 2 Weeks," *Philadelphia Tribune*, February 15, 1964.

21. "Job Training Gets Big Grant," *Washington Post*, March 19, 1964.

22. "$19,000 Boost Is Given to Opportunities Center," *New Journal and Guide* (Norfolk, VA), December 7, 1963.

23. Sullivan, *Build, Brother, Build*, 90.

24. Sullivan, 95.

25. On the prosperity gospel, see Lester K. Spence, *Knocking the Hustle: Against the Neoliberal Turn in Black Politics* (Punctum Books, 2015), 61–72, 115–116.

26. "Job Training Gets Big Grant"; Guian A. McKee, *The Problem of Jobs: Liberalism, Race, and Deindustrialization in Philadelphia* (University of Chicago Press, 2008), 135.

27. On the culture of poverty, see Alice O'Connor, *Poverty Knowledge: Social Science, Social Policy, and the Poor in Twentieth-Century U.S. History* (Princeton University Press, 2001).

28. Ferguson, *Top Down*, 9.

29. Ylvisaker quoted in Ferguson, *Top Down*, 53–54, 58. On the Global South as a fertile testing ground for midcentury liberalism, see Amy Offner, *Sorting Out the Mixed Economy: The Rise and Fall of Welfare and Developmental States in the Americas* (Princeton University Press, 2019); Daniel Immerwahr, *Thinking Small: The United States and the Lure of Community Development* (Harvard University Press, 2015), 135.

30. Ferguson, *Top Down*, 63.

31. Countryman, *Up South*, especially chapter 4.

32. McKee, *The Problem of Jobs*, 96, 135; Countryman, *Up South*, 126–29; Sam Klug, "Paul Ylvisaker, 'Indigenous Leadership,' and the Origins of Community Action," *Rockefeller Archive Center Research Report*, July 21, 2021, https://rockarch.issuelab.org/resource/paul-ylvisaker-indigenous-leadership-and-the-origins-of-community-action.html.

33. Exchange between Ford II and Sullivan quoted in Ferguson, *Top Down*, 63.

34. Thomas J. Sugrue, *Sweet Land of Liberty: The Forgotten Struggle for Civil Rights in the North* (Random House, 2008), 277–79. See also McKee, *The Problem of Jobs*; Gordon Lafer, *The Job Training Charade* (Cornell University Press, 2002).

35. Sullivan, *Build, Brother, Build*, 166–68; Vincent Thompson, "Sullivan Celebrates 'a Dream Fulfilled,'" *Philadelphia Tribune*, August 24, 1993.

36. On the post-WWII rise in charitable trusts, see Wallace Howland, "The History of the Supervision of Charitable Trusts and Corporations in California," *UCLA Law*

Review 13, no. 4 (1966): 1029–40; Thomas A. Troyer, "The 1969 Private Foundation Law: Historical Perspective on Its Origin and Underpinnings," *The Exempt Organization Tax Review* 27, no. 1 (January 2000): 52–65.

37. "Phila. Baptist church awarded $1,300,000 for housing project," *Afro-American* (Baltimore, MD), May 30, 1964, 15.

38. Thomas J. Sugrue, *The Origins of the Urban Crisis: Race and Inequality in Postwar Detroit* (Princeton University Press, 1996); Arnold R. Hirsch, *Making the Second Ghetto: Race and Housing in Chicago, 1940–1960* (University of Chicago Press, 1998); Self, *American Babylon*; David M. P. Freund, *Colored Property: State Policy and White Racial Politics in Suburban America* (University of Chicago Press, 2010), 186–87, 358; Beryl Satter, *Family Properties: Race, Real Estate, and the Exploitation of Black Urban America* (Henry Hold and Company, 2010).

39. Guian A. McKee, "A Utopian, a Utopianist, or Whatever the Heck It Is: Edmund Bacon and the Complexity of the City," in *Imagining Philadelphia: Edmund Bacon and the Future of the City*, ed. Scott Gabriel Knowles (University of Pennsylvania Press, 2009), 59; Nathan Glazer, "The Renewal of Cities," *Scientific American*, September 1965, 195.

40. Keeanga-Yamahtta Taylor, *Race for Profit: How Banks and the Real Estate Industry Undermined Black Homeownership* (University of North Carolina Press, 2019), 42.

41. Such a perspective mirrors Lizabeth Cohen's chronicling of Ed Logue's efforts to wield urban renewal as a tool of social integration, as well as physical reconstruction. See *Saving America's Cities: Ed Logue and the Struggle to Renew Urban America in the Suburban Age* (Farrar, Straus & Giroux, 2019).

42. On Black elites' support for urban renewal, see N. D. B. Connolly, *A World More Concrete: Real Estate and the Remaking of Jim Crow South Florida* (University of Chicago Press, 2014), 282–83. On the FHA loan, see McKee, "A Utopian, a Utopianist, or Whatever the Heck It Is," 64; "Housing Chief Hails Philadelphia Plan," *New York Times*, July 19, 1965. On the shift within the FHA toward investing in cities and its shortcomings, see Taylor, *Race for Profit*; Rebecca K. Marchiel, *After Redlining: The Urban Reinvestment Movement in the Era of Financial Deregulation* (University of Chicago Press, 2020).

43. "Housing Chief Hails Philadelphia Plan"; "Weaver lauds churches for role in housing," *Afro-American* (Baltimore, MD), July 31, 1965.

44. "Dr. Leon Sullivan Hits 'Front Man' Charge"; "Dedication of Phillip's Progress Plaza Shopping Attracts 10,000."

45. Jesse L. Jackson memo to staff and fellow ministers, September 1968, in *Chicago 1966: Open Housing Marches, Summit Negotiations, and Operation Breadbasket*, ed. Garrow (Carlson Publisher, 1989), 306.

46. Gordon K. Mantler, *Power to the Poor: Black-Brown Coalition and the Fight for Economic Justice, 1960–1974* (University of North Carolina Press, 2013), 224; Nishani Frazier, "A McDonald's That Reflects the Soul of a People: Hough Area Development Corporation and Community Development in Cleveland," in *The Business of Black Power*, ed. Hill and Rabig, 68–92.

47. Richard Nixon, "Bridges to Human Dignity, the Programs," remarks on the NBC Radio Network, May 2, 1968, online at The American Presidency Project, https://www.presidency.ucsb.edu/node/326764.

48. On the War on Poverty's reliance on private enterprise to combat poverty, see Brent Cebul, *Illusions of Progress: Business, Poverty, and Liberalism in the American Century* (University of Pennsylvania Press, 2023). Marcia Chatelain has likewise observed that the Democratic Party's support for Black capitalism preceded Nixon's popularization of the term, including as an important component of the War on Poverty. See *Franchise*, 72–77.

49. Lyndon B. Johnson, "Annual Message to the Congress on the State of the Union," January 8, 1964, online at The American Presidency Project, https://www.presidency.ucsb.edu/node/242292; Lyndon B. Johnson, "Special Message to the Congress Proposing a Nationwide War on the Sources of Poverty," March 16, 1964, online at The American Presidency Project, https://www.presidency.ucsb.edu/node/239636.

50. US Department of Commerce, Area Redevelopment Administration, "ARA Project Activity," *Redevelopment*, November 1964, 8; McKee, *The Problem of Jobs*, 137.

51. Gregory S. Wilson, *Communities Left Behind: The Area Redevelopment Administration, 1945–1965* (University of Tennessee Press, 2009), xviii.

52. Wilson, 125–27.

53. On the Ford Foundation's, especially the Gray Areas project's, impact on the War on Poverty, see Ferguson, *Top Down*, 63–64.

54. "Dr. Herbert E. Striner," W. E. Upjohn Institute for Employment Research, http://www.upjohn.org/dr-herbert-e-striner-0; Megan McDonough, "Obituary: Herbert E. Striner," *Washington Post*, August 20, 2015, https://www.washingtonpost.com/local/obituaries/herbert-striner-a-business-school-dean-at-american-university-dies-at-92/2015/08/20/77382864-450b-11e5-846d-02792f854297_story.html.

55. Sullivan, *Build, Brother, Build*, 108–10.

56. John D. Pomfret, "U.S. Gives $458,000 to Train Negroes," *New York Times*, December 19, 1964; *Amendments to the Manpower Development and Training Act of 1962, Hearings on H.R. 4257 and H.R. 4271, 1st session, Before the Select Subcomm. on Labor of the Comm. on Education and Labor*, 89th Cong. (1965) (statement of Rev. Leon H. Sullivan, Opportunities Industrialization Center).

57. McKee, *The Problem of Jobs*, 137.

58. Economic Opportunity Act of 1964, Pub. L. No. 88–452, 78 Stat. 2642 (1964).

59. Sonia Song-Ha Lee, *Building a Latino Civil Rights Movement: Puerto Ricans, African Americans, and the Pursuit of Racial Justice in New York City* (University of North Carolina Press, 2014); Annelise Orleck and Lisa Gayle Hazirjian, eds., *The War on Poverty: A New Grassroots History, 1964–1980* (University of Georgia Press, 2011).

60. Annelise Orleck, *Storming Caesars Palace: How Black Mothers Fought Their Own War on Poverty* (Beacon Press, 2004); Williams, *The Politics of Public Housing*.

61. McKee, *The Problem of Jobs*, 98–108, 138; Hunter, *Black Citymakers*, 176–78.

62. In addition to serving as a mentor to Bowser, Gray officiated Bowser's wedding to Barbara Gertrude Potts. In 1963, the two welcomed Martin Luther King Jr. to North Philadelphia together. See "Remembering Charlie: Charles W. Bowser, 1930–2010," *Philadelphia Sun*, August 29, 2010, https://philasun.com/local/remembering-charlie-charles-w-bowser-1930-2010/; Richard Jones, "In N. Phila., a day for Dr. King and many others," *Philadelphia Inquirer*, January 17, 1995.

63. "Pastor Installed at Canaan Church," *Philadelphia Tribune*, June 17, 1967.

64. "The Men of Kappa Alpha Psi Plan Mammouth 44th Anniv. Observance," *Philadelphia Tribune*, February 15, 1966.

65. Herman quoted in Destin Jenkins, *The Bonds of Inequality: Debt and the Making of the American City* (University of Chicago Press, 2021), 107. For further detail, see pages 104–9.

66. Herman quoted in Nicholas von Hoffman, "Programs' Stifle a Lofty Ghetto," *Washington Post*, August 28, 1966. Herman's statement, along with the article, were later read into the Congressional record: 89 Cong. Rec. H26933–4 (1966).

67. 89 Cong. Rec. H26929 (1966) (statement of Rep. Fino).

68. Sullivan quoted in "'Build, Brother, Build,' Rev. Sullivan Pleads," *Philadelphia Daily News*, December 13, 1966; Sullivan, *Build, Brother, Build*, 179.

69. This notion of Black empowerment as a "constructive" alternative to a radical politics of Black Power was reiterated in Rev. L. V. Booth's remarks on the establishment of OIC-Cincinnati. According to Booth, "the driving force behind its development came from local clergy, many of whom "were particularly concerned about the growing patterns of racial tension in Cincinnati beginning in 1965," including tensions resulting from "rent strikes and demonstrations" against "the discriminatory practices of the labor unions." Later, "individually directed incidents of violence" emerged. "In an effort to make a positive response to the existing conditions," the ministers reached out to Sullivan to inquire about setting up an OIC chapter, which launched in July 1967. See *Comprehensive Manpower Act of 1969, the Manpower Act of 1969, and the Administrative Manpower Training Act of 1968, Hearings on H.R. 10908, H.R. 11620, H.R. 13472, December 10, 1969, Before the Select Subcomm. on Labor-Management Relations, Comm. on Education and Labor*, 91st Cong. 1–2 (1969) (statement of Rev. L. V. Booth, Chairman of the Board, Opportunities Industrialization Center, Cincinnati, Ohio).

70. Stokely Carmichael and Charles V. Hamilton, *Black Power: The Politics of Liberation in America* (Penguin, 1969), 334.

71. 89 Cong. Rec. 12207 (1966) (statement of Rep. Quie).

72. 90 Cong. Rec. 1247 (1967) (statement of Sen. Ribicoff).

73. 90 Cong. Rec. 1247 (1967) (statement of Rev. Leon H. Sullivan).

74. Sullivan, *Build, Brother, Build*, 98.

75. Sullivan, 99.

76. Brochure, "Building America—Together: OIC & Industry," undated, Box 24, Opportunities Industrialization Centers of America Records, Special Collections

Research Center, Temple University Library, Philadelphia, Pennsylvania (hereafter cited as OICA Records).

77. Malcolm X, "Malcolm X's Speech at the Founding Rally of the Organization of Afro-American Unity," in *By Any Means Necessary: Speeches, Interviews, and a Letter by Malcolm X* (Pathfinder Press, 1970), 35–67.

78. Sullivan, *Build, Brother, Build*, 101–2. Another OIC brochure, entitled "Building America—Together OIC & Industry," listed "loyalty to an employer," "personal appearance," and "ability to communicate" among the skills taught by the Feeder Program. See brochure, "Building America—Together: OIC & Industry," Box 24, OICA Records.

79. OIC trainees quoted in Paul Friggens, "Toward self-help in Philadelphia: Opportunity to learn," *Christian Science Monitor*, September 15, 1965.

80. Eric Augenbraun, "'Stand on Your feet, Black Boy!': Leon Sullivan, Black Power, Job Training, and the War on Poverty," *2009–2010 Penn Humanities Forum on Connection* (University of Pennsylvania, 2010), 45–46.

81. Letter from Herb Boyer to Fred Miller, September 6, 1972, Box 4, Folder 15, OICA Records.

82. *Comprehensive Manpower Act of 1969, the Manpower Act of 1969, and the Administrative Manpower Training Act of 1968, Hearings on H.R. 10908, H.R. 11620, H.R. 13472, December 10, 1969, Before the Select Subcomm. on Labor-Management Relations, Comm. on Education and Labor*, 91st Cong. 1–2 (1969) (statement of Rev. Leon Sullivan, Founder of the Opportunities Industrialization Center, Philadelphia, PA).

83. Samuel L. Woodward, "Black Power and Achievement Motivation," *The Clearing House*, October 1969.

84. Bradham quoted in R. W. Apple Jr., "Domestic Peace Corps Lending a Hand to Children of Harlem," *New York Times*, July 7, 1964.

85. Kenneth B. Clark, *Youth in the Ghetto: A Study of the Consequences of Powerlessness and a Blueprint for Change* (HARYOU, 1964), 388, 64–80; Damon Freeman, "Kenneth B. Clark and the Problem of Power," *Patterns of Prejudice* 42, nos. 4–5 (2008): 413–37.

86. Arnold H. Lubasch, "City Plans to Aid Harlem's Youth," *New York Times*, June 13, 1962; Freeman, "Kenneth B. Clark," 414.

87. Freeman, "Kenneth B. Clark," 423.

88. Allen J. Matusow, *The Unraveling of America: A History of Liberalism in the 1960s* (University of Georgia Press, 1984, repr. 2009), 259.

89. Jackie Robinson "Jackie Robinson says: 'A Bold New Educational Venture' in Philadelphia," *New Journal and Guide* (Norfolk, VA), October 31, 1964.

90. Robinson, "Jackie Robinson Says."

91. Longstreth quoted in Friggens, "Toward Self-Help in Philadelphia."

92. "Rev. Sullivan Given $19,000 More for Training Program," *Philadelphia Tribune*, November 23, 1963.

93. Western Union Telegraph Company, untitled advertisement, *New York Amsterdam News*, September 12, 1964.

94. Jason Chambers, *Madison Avenue and the Color Line: African Americans in the Advertising Industry* (University of Pennsylvania Press, 2009); Brenna Wynn Greer, *Represented: The Black Imagemakers Who Reimagined African American Citizenship* (University of Pennsylvania Press, 2019); Robert E. Weems, *Desegregating the Dollar: African American Consumerism in the Twentieth Century* (New York University Press, 1998).

95. "Gulf Oil Chief Knows Education Pays Off," *Chicago Daily Defender*, March 22, 1969.

96. Chatelain, *Franchise*.

97. "OIC, Gulf Form New Partnership," *Philadelphia Tribune*, December 12, 1967.

98. "Skill Training Center to Pave Road for Work," *Afro-American* (Baltimore, MD), December 30, 1967.

99. "GE Will Donate Plant to Cleveland Schools for Job-Training Plan," *Wall Street Journal*, January 11, 1968; "Training Plan for Dropouts in Cleveland," *Chicago Daily Defender*, January 13, 1968.

100. "Job Trainees Go to Work," *Chicago Daily Defender*, June 5, 1969; Christopher Morris, "Woodland Job Training Center," *Cleveland Historical*, December 12, 2016, https://clevelandhistorical.org/items/show/778.

101. "Job Trainees Go to Work." See also McKee, *The Problem of Jobs*; Ferguson, *Top Down*; Fergus, *Liberalism, Black Power, and the Making of American Politics*.

102. Terry H. Anderson, "The New American Revolution: The Movement and Business," in *The Sixties: From Memory to History*, ed. David Farber (University of North Carolina Press, 1994).

103. Sullivan and Jacobs quoted in "OIC, Gulf Oil Corp. Enter Partnership for Training," *New Pittsburgh Courier*, December 23, 1967.

104. "Gulf Oil Planning New OIC Service Station Exhibit for Tribune Show," *Philadelphia Tribune*, June 15, 1968.

105. "The Big Companies Venture to Help in the Civil Rights Effort," *Wall Street Journal*, June 14, 1968.

106. "Chase Bank Chairman New OIC Council Head," *New Amsterdam News*, January 25, 1969.

107. Memorandum, "Projected 1972 Funds from Corporations Represented on OIC Industrial Advisory Council," November 8, 1971, Box 1, Folder 14, OICA Records; Minutes of Budget and Operations Committee, 1973–1978, 1980, Box 2, Folder 17, OICA Records; National Technical Advisory Committee Meeting Minutes, March 6, 1975, Box 3, Folder 41, OICA Records; Report, "Highlights of the New OIC National Institute," April 22, 1969, Box 1, Folder 29, OICA Records.

108. Kenneth C. Laudon and Jane Laudon, *Management Information Systems: Managing the Digital Firm and E-Commerce* (Pearson, 1995).

109. Minutes of Budget and Operations Committee, 1973–1978, 1980, Box 2, Folder 17, OICA Records.

110. Report, "Highlights of the New OIC National Institute," April 22, 1969, Box 1, Folder 29, OICA Records.

111. Dan Bouk, *How Our Days Became Numbered: Risk and the Rise of the Statistical Individual* (University of Chicago Press, 2015); Sarah E. Igo, *The Averaged American: Surveys, Citizens, and the Making of a Mass Public* (Harvard University Press, 2008).

112. Minutes, OIC National Board of Directors Meeting, January 22, 1970, Box 1, Folder 4, OICA Records.

113. Aubry quoted in Jack Jones, "Self-Help Center in Minority Area of L.A. Fights to Survive," *Los Angeles Times*, November 17, 1968.

114. Jones, "Self-Help Center in Minority Area of L.A. Fights to Survive." Contesting views of accounting as a neutral, technical tool, critical scholars of accounting have stressed its entanglement with ideology and social hierarchies. See Tony Tinker, *Paper Prophets: A Social Critique of Accounting* (Prager, 1985); Anthony G. Puxty, *The Social & Organizational Context of Management Accounting* (Cenage Learning Emea, 1998); and Caitlin Rosenthal, *Accounting for Slavery: Masters and Management* (Harvard University Press, 2018).

115. Dunning, *Nonprofit Neighborhoods*.

116. Leonard N. Moore, *Carl B. Stokes and the Rise of Black Political Power* (University of Illinois Press, 2002).

117. Hatcher quoted in Countryman, *Up South*, 309.

118. Levy, *The Great Uprising*, 1.

119. Lyndon B. Johnson, "The President's Address to the Nation on Civil Disorders," July 27, 1967, online *The American Presidency Project*, https://www.presidency.ucsb.edu/node/238062.

120. FBI report, "Racial Disturbances," August 1, 1967, in *Civil Rights During the Johnson Administration, 1963–1969*, Part V, ed. Steven F. Lawson (University Publications of America, 1987), microfilm, reel 0035.

121. United States National Advisory Commission on Civil Disorders, *Report of the National Advisory Commission on Civil Disorders* (United States, Kerner Commission: U.S. G.P.O., 1968).

122. Dan Berger, *Captive Nation: Black Prison Organizing in the Civil Rights Era* (University of North Carolina Press, 2014), 67, 75–78, 96–97; Murch, *Living for the City*, especially chapter 6; Charles Earl Jones, ed., *The Black Panther Party [Reconsidered]* (Black Classic Press, 1998).

123. List and quote from Charles L. Sanders, "Industry Gives New Hope to the Negro," *Ebony*, June 1968.

124. Sanders, "Industry Gives New Hope to the Negro."

125. Sanders, "Industry Gives New Hope to the Negro."

126. Quote from Sanders, "Industry Gives New Hope to the Negro." See also James Mudge, "Hudson Group Asks State for $5.3 Million Riot Help," *Detroit Free Press*, August 25, 1967; "New Detroit Panel Submits Open-Housing Plan," *Detroit Free Press*, October 13, 1967.

127. On NAM's organizing in response to the Black freedom struggle, see Jennifer Delton, *Racial Integration in Corporate America, 1940–1990* (Cambridge University

Press, 2009), especially chapters 6 and 7; Frank J. Prial, "A 'New' NAM? Business Group Edges from Far Rights, Pushes Its Own Social Plans," *Wall Street Journal*, May 31, 1966.

128. "Convention Date Set by Urban Coalition; Co-Chairmen Named," *New York Times*, August 8, 1967. While focused on expanding private sector involvement in managing ongoing urban unrest, Urban Coalition members were not shy in requesting state resources, including issuing a statement calling on the federal government to "assume responsibility and act as the employer of last resort or . . . assure adequate income levels for those who are unable to work," a testament to the concerns of business leaders, who generally disapproved of social welfare, over further unrest. See Vincent J. Burke, "Urban Coalition Opens Drive for Million Jobs to Aid Ghettos," *Los Angeles Times*, August 25, 1967.

129. "The City: Detroit's Ditto," *Time*, June 13, 1969. For more on Ditto's work with the East Side Voice, see Joel Stone, "The Changing Face of Inner-City Activism," in *Detroit 1967: Origins, Impacts, and Legacies*, ed. Joel Stone (Wayne State University Press, 2017); Michael Stauch, "Wildcat of the Streets: Race, Class, and the Punitive Turn in 1970s Detroit" (PhD diss., Duke University, 2015), 177–84.

130. Stauch, "Wildcat of the Streets," 184–85.

131. Innis quoted in Victor Riesel, "Negro Lauds Nixon Over Kennedy," *The Palladium-Item and Sun-Telegram* (Richmond, IN), May 23, 1968. On CORE's embrace of Black nationalism and rightward turn, see Nishani Frazier, *Harambee City: The Congress of Racial Equality in Cleveland and the Rise of Black Power Populism* (University of Arkansas Press, 2017); Jennifer Montooth, "'Bridges to Dignity': Roy Innis, Conservative Black Power, and the Transformation of CORE, 1968–1998" (master's thesis, University of Maryland Baltimore County, 2017).

132. Brian D. Goldstein, *The Roots of Urban Renaissance: Gentrification and the Struggle over Harlem* (Harvard University Press, 2017), 120.

133. James Dowdy, "Harlem Commonwealth Council: A Business Success Story," *Review of Black Political Economy* 10, no. 1 (1979): 59–60.

134. Sylvan Fox, "Group In New York Scores First Gains in Harlem Area," *New York Times*, December 5, 1968.

135. Dowdy, "Harlem Commonwealth Council," 59–60; "Singer Shop 'Sings' In Harlem, N.Y.," *Pittsburgh Courier*, October 25, 1969; C. Gerald Fraser, "Antipoverty Unit Buys a Company," *New York Times*, August 5, 1972.

136. Charlayne Hunter-Gault, "New York's Black Leaders Now Focusing on Economics Not Protest," *New York Times*, September 30, 1977.

137. Ernest Boynton, "Sullivan Is Black Power," *Chicago Daily Defender*, January 4, 1969.

138. John Wilder and Art Peters, "Thousands Greet President at OIC and on Streets," *Philadelphia Tribune*, July 4, 1967.

139. Lyndon B. Johnson, "Remarks in Philadelphia at the Opportunities Industrialization Center," June 29, 1967, online at The American Presidency Project, https://www.presidency.ucsb.edu/node/238203.

140. *Comprehensive Manpower Act of 1969, the Manpower Act of 1969, and the Administrative Manpower Training Act of 1968, Hearings on H.R. 10908, H.R. 11620, H.R. 13472, December 10, 1969, Before the Select Subcomm. on Labor-Management Relations, Comm. on Education and Labor*, 91st Cong. 1–2 (1969) (statement of Hon. Robert N. C. Nix, A Representative in Congress from the State of Pennsylvania).

141. *Comprehensive Manpower Act of 1969, the Manpower Act of 1969, and the Administrative Manpower Training Act of 1968, Hearings on H.R. 10908, H.R. 11620, H.R. 13472, December 10, 1969, Before the Select Subcomm. on Labor-Management Relations, Comm. on Education and Labor*, 91st Cong. 1–2 (1969) (statement of Rev. Leon Sullivan, Founder of the Opportunities Industrialization Center).

142. 91 Cong. Rec. 34007 (1969).

143. *Comprehensive Manpower Act of 1969, the Manpower Act of 1969, and the Administrative Manpower Training Act of 1968, Hearings on H.R. 10908, H.R. 11620, H.R. 13472, December 10, 1969, Before the Select Subcomm. on Labor-Management Relations, Comm. on Education and Labor*, 91st Cong. 1–2 (1969) (statement of Rev. Leon Sullivan, Founder of the Opportunities Industrialization Center, Philadelphia, PA).

Chapter 4

1. Press Release, "Trip to Africa," February 14, 1969, Box 1, Folder 40, Opportunities Industrialization Centers International, Acc. 689, Special Collections Research Center, Temple University Libraries, Philadelphia, Pennsylvania (hereafter cited as OICI Records); Memorandum, "A Rendezvous with Rev. Leon H. Sullivan—The African Gathering: Report on Trip to Africa," May 7, 1969, Box 2, Folder 31, OICI Records.

2. OIC-Lagos Board to Sullivan, October 17, 1968, Box 8, Folder 38, OICI Records.

3. OIC/Africa Proposal: Administrative Phase, Submitted to the United States Agency for International Development, July 1969, OICI Records, Box 12, Folder 19.

4. Anna J. W. James, "Dr. Sullivan Hailed by Church Members After African Tour," *Philadelphia Tribune*, March 18, 1969.

5. Sullivan quoted in James, "Dr. Sullivan Hailed by Church Members After African Tour."

6. On the Back-to-Africa movement, see Claude Andrew Clegg III, *The Price of Liberty: African Americans and the Making of Liberia* (University of North Carolina Press, 2004); James Campbell, *Middle Passages: African American Journeys to Africa, 1787–2005* (Penguin Press, 2006).

7. The literature on twentieth-century Black internationalism has grown exponentially in recent decades, revealing the breadth and depth of Black Americans' engagement with the world. Foundational works in this regard include Brenda Gayle Plummer, *Rising Wind: African Americans and U.S. Foreign Affairs, 1935–1960* (University of North Carolina Press, 1996); Carol Anderson, *Eyes off the Prize: The United Nations and the African American Struggle for Human Rights, 1944–1955* (Cambridge University Press, 2003); Gerald C. Horne, *Black and Brown: African-Americans and the Mexican Revolution, 1910–1920* (New York University Press, 2004); Michael O. West, William G. Martin,

and Fanon Che Wilkins, *From Toussaint to Tupac: The Black International since the Age of Revolution* (University of North Carolina Press, 2009); Frank Andre Guridy, *Forging Diaspora: Afro-Cubans and African Americans in a World of Empire and Jim Crow* (University of North Carolina Press, 2010).

8. Brenda Gayle Plummer, *In Search of Power: African Americans in the Era of Decolonization, 1956–1974* (Cambridge University Press, 2012); Nico Slate, *Colored Cosmopolitanism: The Shared Struggle for Freedom in the United States and India* (Harvard University Press, 2012); Kevin Gaines, *American Africans in Ghana: Black Expatriates and the Civil Rights Era* (University of North Carolina Press, 2008). On Cold-War-era taming of Black internationalism, including the suppression of left-leaning activists and other critics of US policy, see Anderson, *Eyes off the Prize*; Penny Von Eschen, *Satchmo Blows Up the World: Jazz Ambassadors Play the Cold War* (Harvard University Press, 2006).

9. Martin Luther King Jr., "Letter from Birmingham Jail," April 16, 1963, reprinted in *The Atlantic Monthly* 212, no. 2 (1963): 78–88.

10. Jama Lazerow and Yohuru Williams, eds., *In Search of the Black Panther Party: New Perspectives on a Revolutionary Movement* (Duke University Press, 2006); Joshua Bloom and Waldo E. Martin Jr., *Black against Empire: The History and Politics of the Black Panther Party* (University of California Press, 2013); Sean L. Malloy, *Out of Oakland: Black Panther Party Internationalism During the Cold War* (Cornell University Press, 2017); Nikhil Singh, *Black Is a Country: Race and the Unfinished Struggle for Democracy* (Harvard University Press, 2005).

11. Stokely Carmichael and Ekwueme Michael Thelwell, *Ready for Revolution: The Life and Struggle of Stokely Carmichael (Kwame Ture)* (Simon & Schuster, 2005). See also Timothy B. Tyson, *Radio Free Dixie: Robert F. Williams and the Roots of Black Power* (University of North Carolina Press, 1999); Kevin Gaines, *American Africans in Ghana: Black Expatriates and the Civil Rights Era* (University of North Carolina Press, 2008); Seth Markle, *A Motorcycle on Hell's Run: Tanzania, Black Power, and the Uncertain Future of Pan-Africanism* (Michigan State University Press, 2017); Paul J. Magnarella, *Black Panther in Exile: The Pete O'Neal Story* (University Press of Florida, 2020); Andrew Ivaska, "Decolonizing Refugees: Exile and Political Possibility in 1960s Dar es Salaam," *Stateless Histories*, January 24, 2022, https://statelesshistories.org/article/decolonizing-refugees-exile-and-political-possibility-in-1960s-dar-es-salaam.

12. On Black American ambassadors and US diplomacy, see Von Eschen, *Satchmo Blows Up the World*; Mary Dudziak, *Exporting American Dreams: Thurgood Marshall's African Journey* (Princeton University Press, 2008); and Ashley Brown, "Swinging for the State Department: American Women Tennis Players in Diplomatic Goodwill Tours, 1941–1959," *Journal of Sports History* 42, no. 3 (2015): 289–309.

13. For a notable exception, see Jenifer Van Vleck, *Empire of the Air: Aviation and the American Ascendancy* (Harvard University Press, 2013), chapter 4.

14. My use of the term corporate imperialism builds on and extends forward in time work by historians like Jenifer Van Vleck, Nan Enstad, and Greg Mitman on the role of US corporations in shaping the contours of US imperialism, including through

the use of the technologies of race and gender to control labor. See Van Vleck, *Empire of the Air*; Nan Enstad, *Cigarettes, Inc.: An Intimate History of Corporate Imperialism* (University of Chicago Press, 2018); Gregg Mitman, *Empire of Rubber: Firestone's Scramble for Land and Power in Liberia* (New Press, 2021).

15. Biographical Note, Opportunities Industrialization Centers International, OICI Records.

16. Proposal to the Office of Private Enterprise, Bureau for Africa for Exploration of African Problems and Programs, September 1967, Box 12, Folder 22, OICI Records.

17. Unnamed OIC member quoted in Ibok Esema, "Rev. Leon Sullivan's OIC Mission Gets Warm Welcome in Nigeria," *Philadelphia Tribune*, August 11, 1970.

18. Sullivan quoted in Esema, "Rev. Leon Sullivan's OIC Mission Gets Warm Welcome in Nigeria."

19. For an overview of Pan-Africanism and its multiple and contested meanings, see Kwame Anthony Appiah, "Pan-Africanism," in *Africana: The Encyclopedia of the African and African American Experience*, ed. Kwame Anthony Appiah and Henry Louis Gates Jr., 1st ed. (Basic Civitas Books, 1999). See also Ronald W. Walters, *Pan Africanism in the African Diaspora: An Analysis of Modern Afrocentric Political Movements* (Wayne State University Press, 1997); Michael W. Williams, *Pan-Africanism: An Annotated Bibliography* (Salem Press, 1992); Ian Duffield, "Pan-Africanism, Rational and Irrational," *Journal of African History* 18, no. 4 (1977): 597–620; Immanuel Geis, *The Pan-African Movement: A History of Pan-Africanism in America, Europe, and Africa* (Africana Publishing Co., 1974); George Shepperson, "Pan-Africanism and 'Pan-Africanism': Some Historical Notes," *Phylon* 23, no. 4 (1962): 346–58.

20. Brandon Kendhammer, "DuBois the Pan-Africanist and the Development of African Nationalism," *Ethnic and Racial Studies* 30, no. 1 (2007): 51–71; Kwame Anthony Appiah, *Lines of Descent, W.E.B. du Bois and the Emergence of Identity* (Harvard University Press, 2014), 50, 63.

21. David Levering Lewis, *W.E.B. Du Bois: The Fight for Equality and the American Century, 1919–1963* (Henry Holt and Co., 2000), 58.

22. Keisha N. Blain, *Set the World on Fire: Black Nationalist Women and the Global Struggle for Freedom* (University of Pennsylvania Press, 2018), 5–6.

23. Malcolm X, "Memorandum to The African Summit Conference, the Second Conference of the Organization of African Unity," July 17, 1964, in *Malcolm X Speaks: Selected Speeches and Statements*, ed. George Breitman (Grover Press, 1965), 72–77.

24. On radical mid-twentieth-century Black (inter)nationalism, see Garrett Felber, *Those Who Know Don't Say: The Nation of Islam, the Black Freedom Movement, and the Carceral State* (University of North Carolina Press, 2020); W. Manning Marable, *Malcolm X: A Life of Reinvention* (Random House, 1973); Tyson, *Radio Free Dixie*.

25. Sullivan quoted in "Rev. Sullivan urges Nixon to back OIC," *Bay State Banner*, July 30, 1970.

26. Leon H. Sullivan, *Build, Brother, Build: From Poverty to Economic Power* (Macrae Smith Company, 1969), 179.

27. Agency for International Development, Opportunities Industrialization Centers, International, Audit Report No: 78–126, June 28, 1978, PDAA1.885, United States Agency for International Development Records.

28. Proposal for Training Submitted to the Government of Kenya from the Opportunities Industrialization Center National Institute, Inc., March 3, 1969, Box 12, Folder 21, OICI Records.

29. Proposal for Training Submitted to the Government of Kenya from the Opportunities Industrialization Center National Institute, Inc., March 3, 1969, Box 12, Folder 21, OICI Records.

30. Janine M. Ubink and Kojo S. Amanor, eds., *Contesting Land and Custom in Ghana: State, Chief, and the Citizen* (Leiden University Press, 2008); Sara S. Berry, *Chiefs Know Their Boundaries: Essays on Property, Power, and the Past in Asante, 1896–1996* (Heinemann, James Currey, David Philip, 2001).

31. "Rev. Sullivan Hailed in Africa," *Philadelphia Tribune*, July 21, 1970; "Rev. Sullivan urges Nixon to back OIC," *Bay State Banner*, July 30, 1970.

32. OIC Ghana, Monthly Report, April 1975, Box 7, Folder 1, OICI Records.

33. Charter of the Organization of African Unity, Box 3, Folder 22, OICI Records.

34. Executive Secretary of the Organization of African Unity to the United Nations, Memo No. GA/381/OUA/74, Box 3, Folder 22, OICI Records. See also Memo, Valfoulaye Diallo to Reverend Leon H. Sullivan, Subj: Discussion Guidelines for Meeting with OAU and African Representatives to the United Nations, January 16, 1975, Box 3, Folder 22, OICI Records; Correspondence, Valfoulaye Diallo to H.E. Dramane Quattara, Executive Secretary of the OAU, July 8, 1974, Box 3, Folder 22, OICI Records; and Correspondence, Leon H. Sullivan to H.E. Mr. Nzo Ekangaki, September 18, 1973, Box 3, Folder 22, OICI Records.

35. James Ferguson, *Expectations of Modernity: Myths and Meanings of Urban Life on the Zambian Copperbelt* (University of California Press, 1999); David Engerman, Nils Gilman, Mark H. Haefele, and Michael E. Latham, eds., *Staging Growth: Modernization, Development, and the Global Cold War* (University of Massachusetts Press, 2003); David Ekbladh, *The Great American Mission: Modernization and the Construction of an American World Order* (Princeton University Press, 2011); Allen Isaacman and Barbara Isaacman, *Dams, Displacement, and the Delusion of Development: Cahora Bassa and Its Legacies in Mozambique, 1965–2007* (Ohio University Press, 2013).

36. OIC/Africa Proposal: Administrative Phase, Submitted to the United States Agency for International Development, July 1969, Box 12, Folder 19, OICI Records.

37. Proposal for Training Submitted to the Government of Kenya from the Opportunities Industrialization Center National Institute, Inc., March 3, 1969, Box 12, Folder 21, OICI Records. On community development as an alternative to large-scale, top-down modernization projects, see Daniel Immerwahr, *Thinking Small: The United States and the Lure of Community Development* (Harvard University Press, 2015).

38. "OIC Program for Africa Is Launched by Rev. Sullivan: Trainees Coming from Ghana and Nigeria in '70," *Philadelphia Tribune*, November 18, 1969; Anna J. W. James,

"Dr. Sullivan Hailed by Church Members After African Tour," *Philadelphia Tribune*, March 18, 1969.

39. Fanon Che Wilkins, "The Making of Black Internationalists: SNCC and Africa before the Launching of Black Power, 1960–1965," *Journal of African American History* 92, no. 4 (2007): 467–90.

40. Markle, *A Motorcycle on Hell's Run*; Imamu Amiri Baraka, "Towards Pan-Africanism: Tanzania Independence Anniversary," *Black World* (March 1972): 67; Fanon Che Wilkins, "'In the Belly of the Beast': Black Power, Anti-Imperialism, and the African Liberation Solidarity Movement, 1968–1975" (PhD diss., New York University, 2001); Monique Bedasse, "'To Set-Up Jah Kingdom': Joshua Mkhululi, Rastafarian Repatriation, and the Black Radical Network in Tanzania," *Journal of African Religions* 1, no. 3 (2013): 293–323.

41. Forman quoted in Markle, *A Motorcycle on Hell's Run*, 53.

42. Markle, 57. For more on Black Americans providing technical assistance to postcolonial African nation-states, see Keri Lambert, "'It's All Work and Happiness on the Farms': Agricultural Development Between the Blocs in Nkrumah's Ghana" *Journal of African History* 60, no. 1 (March 2019): 25–44.

43. Despite an initial warm welcome, PASP soon found itself the target of government scrutiny and distrust. In one particularly revealing exchange, the Tanzanians responded to PASP codirector Fred Brooks's proposal to develop a three-hundred-acre lot as an "example" to the Tanzanians of how to manage a profitable farm, noting "Do we need an example?" In time, the Tanzanian government increasingly came to dislike the PASP volunteers, whom some perceived as threatening to take positions they had only recently acquired. Tensions continued to escalate, ultimately leading to PASP's dissolution coinciding with the government's rounding up of hundreds of Black Americans on charges of espionage for the CIA. See Andrew Ivaska, "Movement Youth in a Global Sixties Hub: The Everyday Lives of Transnational Activists in Postcolonial Dar es Salaam," in *Transnational Histories of Youth in the Twentieth Century*, ed. Richard Ivan Jobs and David M. Pomfret (Palgrave Macmillan, 2015), 202–4. See also Bill Sutherland and Matt Meyer, *Guns and Gandhi in Africa: Pan African Insights on Nonviolence, Armed Struggle and Liberation in Africa* (Africa World Press, 2006), 229.

44. Brad Simpson, "US Foreign Policy and the End of Development," in *The Cambridge History of America and the World*, ed. David C. Engerman, Max Paul Friedman, and Melani McAlister (Cambridge University Press, 2022); Michael Latham, *The Right Kind of Revolution: Modernization, Development, and U.S. Foreign Policy from the Cold War to the Present* (Cornell University Press, 2011).

45. Anne-Marie Angelo and Tom Adam Davies, "'American Business Can Assist [African] Hands': The Kennedy Administration, US Corporations, and the Cold War Struggle for Africa," *The Sixties: A Journal of History, Politics and Culture* 8, no. 2 (2015): 156–78.

46. Brendan M. Jones, "2 Trade Missions Emphasize Africa: Exceptional Opportunities are Detailed for Eastern and Western Areas," *New York Times*, May 29, 1960. See

also "Urge U.S. to Export; Trade More in Africa," *Chicago Daily Defender*, February 9, 1961.

47. US Department of Commerce, *Africa: Sales Frontier for U.S. Business* (US Government Printing Office, 1963).

48. Stephanie Decker, "Corporate Political Activity in Less Developed Countries: The Volta River Project in Ghana, 1958–1966," *Business History* 53, no. 7 (2011): 993–1017.

49. On US corporate profiteering from US Cold War investment in the Global South, see B. Alex Beasley, "Service Learning: Oil, International Education, and Texas's Corporate Cold War," *Diplomatic History* 42, no. 2 (2018): 177–203; Sarah Nelson, "A Dream Deferred: UNESCO, American Expertise, and the Eclipse of Radical News Development in the Early Satellite Age," *Radical History Review*, 141 (2021): 30–59.

50. Remarks of Senator John F. Kennedy to the National Council of Women, New York, New York, October 12, 1960, Papers of John F. Kennedy, Pre-Presidential Papers, Senate Files, Box 913, "National Council of Women, New York City, 12 October 1960," John F. Kennedy Presidential Library.

51. One of the earliest calls for a Marshall Plan for Africa came from the American Negro Leadership Conference on Africa (ANLC) in 1962. See Plummer, *Rising Wind*, 308.

52. Foreign Assistance Act of 1961, Pub. L. 87–195, 75 Stat. 424–2 (1961). See also Advisory Committee on Private Enterprise in Foreign Aid, *Foreign Aid Through Private Initiative* (Agency for International Development, 1965).

53. A number of these provisions built on and expanded measures implemented by the Economic Cooperation Act of 1948 and the Mutual Security Act of 1954.

54. Kwame Nkrumah, *Neo-Colonialism, the Last Stage of Imperialism* (Thomas Nelson & Sons, 1965), Introduction; While Nkrumah reserved much of his criticism in *Neo-Colonialism* for the West, other members of Ghana's government spoke out against the Soviet Union, which some viewed as imposing a white man's system on Ghanaians. Lambert, "It's All Work and Happiness on the Farms," 34–36.

55. Nkrumah, *Neo-Colonialism*, Introduction.

56. Declaration on the Establishment of a New International Economic Order, United Nations General Assembly, 6th special sess., resolution no. 3201–3202, May 1, 1974, United Nations Digital Library, https://digitallibrary.un.org/record/218450?ln=en&v=pdf.

57. Quinn Slobodian, *Globalists: The End Empire and the Birth of Neoliberalism* (Harvard University Press, 2020), 220. See also Charles Lipson, *Standing Guard: Protecting Foreign Capital in the Nineteenth and Twentieth Centuries* (University of California Press, 1985), 98; Noel Maurer, *The Empire Trap: The Rise and Fall of U.S. Intervention to Protect American Property Overseas, 1893-2013* (Princeton University Press, 2013), 350. For the most part, fears of widespread expropriations proved unfounded. Except for Tanzania, nationalization took place in only a few cases in Africa, including the partial nationalization of Ghana's gold mines and the wholesale nationalization of Zambia's

copper mines in the early 1970s. Many state expropriations, moreover, tended to target African migrants and Asian entrepreneurs, as opposed to Western businesses. See Marcelo Bucheli and Stephanie Decker, "Expropriations of Foreign Property and Political Alliances: A Business Historical Approach," *Enterprise & Society* 22, no. 1 (2021): 247–84; D. K. Fieldhouse, *Merchant Capital and Economic Decolonisation: The United Africa Company, 1929–1987* (Oxford University Press, 1994), 626–32; Stephen J. Kobrin, "Foreign Enterprise and Forced Divestment in LDCs," *International Organization* 34, no. 1 (1980): 65–88.

58. Sullivan quoted in James Cassell, "Money Now, Liberation Later, African Says at OIC Meeting," *Philadelphia Tribune*, September 11, 1973. See also "OIC's Rev. Sullivan Appeals for More Aid," *New York Amsterdam News*, August 8, 1970.

59. George Champion to Henry J. Galbraith, Asst. Genl. Manager, The Standard Bank Ltd., Nairobi, Kenya, Box 7, Folder 27, OICI Records.

60. Adom Getachew, *Worldmaking after Empire: The Rise and Fall of Self-Determination* (Princeton University Press, 2020).

61. *Texaco News* (January-March 1974), Box 21, OICI Records.

62. Waldemar Nielsen, William R. Cotter, Frank Ferrari, and Vivian Lowery Derryck, "A Short History of the African-American Institute," *Africa Report* 39, no. 5 (1994), 20.

63. Nielsen, Cotter, Ferrari, and Derryck, "A Short History," 22. See also "African-American Institute gets Grants Totaling $1,000,000," *New Pittsburgh Courier*, May 11, 1963.

64. William R. Cotter, President of the African-American Institute, to Anthony Forlenza, Vice Chairman Johnson & Johnson International, February 28, 1979, Harold R. Sims Papers, Box 14, Special Collections and University Archives, Rutgers University Libraries (hereafter cited as Sims Papers); William R. Cotter, President of the African-American Institute, to Stuart Christie, Vice Chairman Johnson & Johnson International, June 25, 1976, Sims Papers, Box 14.

65. This included adding business leaders to AAI's board of directors starting with John Harold Johnson of Johnson Publishing Co. Inc. and John B. M. Place, senior vice president of the Chase Manhattan Bank in 1963. See "African-American Institute Elects Five New Trustees," *New York Times*, May 20, 1963; William R. Cotter to Anthony Forlenza, Vice Chairman Johnson & Johnson International, February 28, 1979, Sims Papers, Box 14; Memo, R.P. Regimbal to J.J. Heldrich, March 5, 1976, Sims Papers, Box 14.

66. List of Participants, The African-American Conference, Maseru, Lesotho, November 29-December 2, 1976, Sims Papers, Box 14; Americans Planning to Attend the Lesotho Conference, African-American Institute, June 29, 1976, Sims Papers, Box 14.

67. Nielsen, Cotter, Ferrari, and Derryck, "A Short History of the African-American Institute," 23.

68. Memo, African-American Institute's Service to U.S. Corporations, Enclosure #1, Correspondence William R. Cotter to R.E. Sellars, Chairman Johnson & Johnson, September 3, 1975, Sims Papers, Box 14.

69. William R. Cotter to R.E. Sellars, Chairman Johnson & Johnson, September 3, 1975, Sims Papers, Box 14.

70. William R. Cotter to R.E. Sellars, Chairman Johnson & Johnson, September 3, 1975, Sims Papers, Box 14.

71. Rosemary E. Bachelor, "Where Do Commuters Go?: Public Relations Man from Scotch Plains Sports a Humble Tiger as His Teammate," *The Courier News*, September 7, 1968; "Avery is named PR manager of Humble's Northeastern Region," *Indianapolis Recorder*, January 11, 1969; Obituary of James S. Avery, Sr., DeMarco Funeral Homes, Inc., May 3, 2011, https://www.demarcofuneralhome.com/obituaries/James-S-Avery-Sr?obId=27857373.

72. "Dr. Leon Sullivan is Elected to G.M. Board," *Arizona Republic*, February 6, 1971; "Rev. Sullivan has big plans for his GM job," *Chicago Daily Defender*, January 13, 1971.

73. "Churchism is Dead! Jim McGraw Interview Dr. Leon Sullivan Founder of Opportunities Industrialization Centers," *Christianity and Crisis: A Christian Journal of Opinion* 31, no. 23, January 10, 1972 (emphasis in original), Box 25, Folder 5, Leon Howard Sullivan papers, Stuart A. Rose Manuscript, Archives, and Rare Book Library, Emory University (hereafter cited as LHS Papers).

74. E. Frederic Morrow, *Forty Years a Guinea Pig* (Pilgrim Press, 1980), 3.

75. Bayard Rustin, "From Protest to Politics: The Future of the Civil Rights Movement," in *To Redeem a Nation: A History and Anthology of the Civil Rights Movement*, ed. Thomas R. West (Brandywine Press, 1993), 232–35; Matthew J. Countryman, "'From Protest to Politics': Community Control and Black Independent Politics in Philadelphia, 1965–1984," *Journal of Urban History* 32, no. 6 (2006): 813–61.

76. Andrew DeRoche, *Andrew Young: Civil Rights Ambassador* (Rowman & Littlefield, 2003), 115–19.

77. Young quoted in "Business Aided by African Trip," *New York Times*, October 8, 1979.

78. "The Global Adventures of OPIC: Is Black Business Ready for the Third World?" *Black Enterprise*, March 1979.

79. Avant and Adams quoted in William J. Eaton, "American Blacks Optimistic About Business Opportunities in Africa," *Los Angeles Times*, September 26, 1979.

80. Eaton, "American Blacks Optimistic About Business Opportunities in Africa."

81. Binaisa quoted in Robert E. Johnson, "Andy's Mission Accomplished: Africans Ink Business Pacts Worth Over $1 ½ Billion," *Jet*, October 18, 1979. See also "The Global Adventures of OPIC"; "Pursuing the African Dollar," *Black Enterprise*, April 1981.

82. Dukes quoted in "Trade Mission Headed by Young Brings Results for U.S. Firms," *Business America*, September 1979.

83. Black quoted in "Trade Mission Headed by Young Brings Results for U.S. Firms."

84. Johnson, "Andy's Mission Accomplished."

85. Stephanie Decker, "Africanization in British Multinationals in Ghana and Nigeria, 1945–1970," *Business History Review* 92, no. 4 (2018): 710.

86. Compared to scholarship on US investment in Africa, US business in Latin America has garnered significantly more attention from historians, who have detailed its role as a site of American capitalist and imperial experimentation starting in the late nineteenth and early twentieth centuries. See, for example, Emily S. Rosenberg, *Financial Missionaries to the World: The Politics and Culture of Dollar Diplomacy, 1900–1930* (Duke University Press, 2003); Greg Grandin, *Empire's Workshop: Latin America, the United States and the Rise of the New Imperialism* (Henry Holt and Company, 2006); Greg Grandin, *Fordlandia: The Rise and Fall of Henry Ford's Forgotten Jungle City* (Macmillan, 2010). Latin America subsequently served as a reference point for a number of US corporations amid their post-WWII expansion into Africa. See R. A. Obudho, "A Comparative Study of the Political, Cultural, and Socio-Economic History of Africa and Latin America: Towards an Investment Strategy for Johnson & Johnson in Africa" (November 1975), Sims Papers, Box 10.

87. Obudho, "A Comparative Study."

88. "Johnson & Johnson Names H.R. Sims Vice-President," *Jet*, December 11, 1975.

89. Obudho, "A Comparative Study."

90. Obudho, "A Comparative Study."

91. Harold R. Sims to Foster B. Whitlock, Subj.: Trends and Early Warnings in Equity Participation Requirements and Practices (Public and Private) in Africa (Excluding South and Southwest Africa) and the Middle East, January 6, 1976, Sims Papers, Box 13; Report, Investment Laws, Regulations and Equity Participation in Africa and the Middle East, Prepared by Dr. R.A. Obudho, January 1976, Sims Papers, Box 13.

92. Harold R. Sims to J.J. Heldrich, Subj.: Support of Special Fund Request from the African-American Institute, March 24, 1976, Sims Papers, Box 14.

93. Year-End Activity Report 1974, Corporate Affairs Department, Harold R. Sims, Sims Papers, Box 14.

94. William R. Cotter to Stuart A. Christie, June 23, 1977, Sims Papers, Box 14.

95. John H. Heldrich to H.R. Sims, May 13, 1977, Sims Papers, Box 14. See also Mid-Year Report—Corporate Affairs Dep., June 15, 1977, Sims Papers, Box 14; Confidential Year-End Activity Report 1974, Corporate Affairs Department, H.R. Sims, 1/17/75, Sims Papers, Box 14.

96. Ferguson, *Expectations of Modernity.*

97. Kaunda quoted in "Loans Aren't Cure," *The Times of Zambia*, July 2, 1978, Sims Papers, Box 13.

98. H.R. Sims to D.E. O'Connell, Subj.: Report on Zambia—1978, August 10, 1978, Sims Papers, Box 13.

99. Memo, H.R. Sims to D.E. O'Connell, Subj. Report on Zambia—1978, August 10, 1978, Sims Papers, Box 13.

100. Harold R. Sims to The Hon. Siteke Mwale, June 1, 1978, Sims Papers, Box 13.

101. OIC Lagos, Annual Report 1976/76 Fiscal Year, OICI Records, Box 8, Folder 34.

102. OICI Records, Box 30, Folder 13.

103. In 1979–1980, OIC Sierra Leone achieved an 81 percent placement rate, placing 286 out of 353 trainees, while OIC Ghana achieved a 8 percent placement rate, placing 175 out of 225 trainees. See OIC International, Inc. Selected Statistics on Enrollment and Placement, Fiscal Year 1979–1980, OICI Records, Box 12, Folder 18.

104. Similar restrictions accompanied US support for the World Bank. See Patrick Sharma, "The United States, the World Bank, and the Challenges of International Development in the 1970s," *Diplomatic History* 37, no. 3 (June 2013): 572–604.

105. Simpson, "US Foreign Policy and the End of Development," 245–47. As part of this shift, Simpson notes that Congress imposed more conditions on US foreign assistance, including reporting on the human rights practices of recipient nations and fiscal responsibility.

106. Dan Morgan, "Humphrey Criticized on Aid Funding," *Washington Post*, February 13, 1975.

107. Sullivan quoted in Harry Amana, "Billions for Vietnam, While OIC and Africa Fight for $3 Million," *Philadelphia Tribune*, February 15, 1975.

108. Hubert H. Humphrey, "Sen. Humphrey on His Role in Aid Funding: Letters to the Editor," *Washington Post*, February 24, 1975.

109. *Hearings Before the Subcommittee on Employment, Poverty and Migratory Labor on Proposed Employment and Job Training Legislation, Feb. 27, Mar. 6, Apr. 3, 12, May 3–4, 1973*, 93rd Cong. (1973).

110. *Hearings Before the Subcommittee on Employment, Poverty and Migratory Labor on Proposed Employment and Job Training Legislation, May 4, 1973*, 93rd Cong. (1973) (statement of Dr. Leon Sullivan on Opportunities Industrialization Centers of America); See also *Hearings Before the Subcommittee on Departments of Labor & Health, Education, and Welfare and Related Agencies Appropriations on Elements of HEW and Labor Dept. FY75 Budget Requests, Part 7, May 8–10, 13–15, 17, 1974*, 93rd Cong. (1974); *Hearings Before the Subcommittee on Departments of Labor and Health, Education, and Welfare and Related Agencies on H.R. 15580, Part 7, July 11, 1975*, 94th Cong. (1975).

111. *Hearings Before the Subcommittee on Employment, Poverty and Migratory Labor on Proposed Employment and Job Training Legislation, May 4, 1973*, 93rd Cong. (1973) (statement of Dr. Leon Sullivan on Opportunities Industrialization Centers of America).

112. James A. Duff, Associate Director, United States General Accounting Office to Reverend Leon H. Sullivan, April 20, 1976, OICI Records, Box 3, Folder 28.

113. Elizabeth Schmidt, *Foreign Intervention in Africa: From the Cold War to the War on Terror* (Cambridge University Press, 2013); Odd Arne Westad, *The Global Cold War: Third World Interventions and the Making of Our Times* (Cambridge University Press, 2012), especially chapter 6; Thomas Borstelmann, *The Cold War and the Color Line: American Race Relations in the Global Arena* (Harvard University Press, 2003).

114. Nancy Mitchell, *Jimmy Carter in Africa: Race and the Cold War* (Stanford University Press, 2016), 53–54.

115. Kissinger quoted in *Hearings Before the Subcommittee on African Affairs and the Subcommittee on Arms Control, International Organizations and Security Agreements*

and the Committee on Foreign Relations, United States Senate, 94th Cong. 2nd Session (1976). See also Mitchell, *Jimmy Carter in Africa*, 37–57.

116. "Impressive List of Guests, Participants," *Philadelphia Tribune*, August 31, 1976.

117. "The Challenges of Africa," Secretary of State Henry Kissinger Address to Opportunities Industrialization Centers (OIC), Philadelphia, Pennsylvania, August 31, 1976, in *The African Foreign Policy of Secretary of State Henry Kissinger*, ed. Walton Hanes Jr., Robert Louis Stevenson Jr., and James Bernard Sr. (Lexington Books, 2007), 225.

118. Linn Washington, "OIC Refuses to Withdraw Invitation to Kissinger," *Philadelphia Tribune*, August 31, 1976. See also Hal Baron and Prexy Nesbitt, "Working Paper for an Alternative to Kissinger's Southern Africa Policy," Amilcar Cabral Collective, Campaign for a Democratic Foreign Policy, Kenneth K. Martin Southern Africa Collection [undated—late 1976 or early 1977].

119. Kenyatta quoted in Washington, "OIC Refuses to Withdraw Invitation to Kissinger."

120. Patrice Lumumba Coalition, "Southern Africa Must Be Free! USA Subversion Must Be Exposed!," Flyer, August 25, 1976, Kenneth K. Martin Southern African Collection, African Activist Archive Project, Michigan State University (hereafter cited as African Activist Archive).

121. Roderick D. Bush, *We Are Not What We Seem: Black Nationalism and Class Struggle in the American Century* (New York University Press, 2000), 7–8.

122. Adjoa A. Aiyetoro and Adrienne D. Davis, "Historic and Modern Social Movements for Reparations: The National Coalition for Blacks for Reparations in America (N'COBRA) and Its Antecedents," *Texas Wesleyan Law Review* 16, no 4 (2010)," 748.

123. Sullivan quoted in Washington, "OIC Refuses to Withdraw Invitation to Kissinger."

124. "Any Program Dealing with Jobs is Important to Black Americans," *Philadelphia Tribune*, July 3, 1976.

125. OICI Records, Box 30, Folder 13; OICI Records, Box 2, Folder 2.

126. OIC International, Inc. Selected Statistics on Enrollment and Placement, 1979–1980, OICI Records, Box 12, Folder 18.

127. Paul Lewis, "Billion-Dollar Stakes in Africa," *New York Times*, May 9, 1976. Specific country data with regard to Africa is difficult to come by in this period. As of 1976, the United States Department of Commerce quantified US direct investment in only four African countries, South Africa ($1.5 billion), Libya ($542 million), Nigeria ($238 million), and Liberia ($258 million).

128. Lewis, "Billion-Dollar Stakes in Africa."

Chapter 5

1. Norman Pearlstine, "GM and Its Critics: Auto Maker Resists Any Radical Overhaul, But Heeds Some Pleas," *Wall Street Journal*, March 24, 1971. See also James Mateja, "G.M. Offers Blacks Job Aid," *Chicago Tribune*, September 23, 1971; "Black Director of General Motors Makes Big Difference," *Oakland Post*, November 18, 1971.

2. Louis Martin, "The Big Parade: Rev. Sullivan Tackles GM Giants," *New Pittsburgh Courier*, January 23, 1971.

3. Louis Spade, "Blacks Winning Top Posts in Big Business," *Chicago Daily Defender*, January 9, 1971.

4. Leon H. Sullivan, *Moving Mountains: The Principles and Purposes of Leon Sullivan* (Judson Press, 1998), 1.

5. Alfred D. Chandler Jr., "Management Decentralization: An Historical Analysis," *The Business History Review* 30, no. 2 (1956): 111–74.

6. On Drucker's influence on management theory, see Daniel Immerwahr, "Polanyi in the United States: Peter Drucker, Karl Polanyi, and the Midcentury Critique of Economic Society," *Journal of the History of Ideas* 70, no. 3 (2009): 445–66; Nils Gilman, "The Prophet of Post-Fordism: Peter Drucker and the Legitimation of the Corporation," in *American Capitalism: Social Thought and Political Economy in the Twentieth Century*, ed. Nelson Lichtenstein (University of Pennsylvania Press, 2006).

7. A. Junn Murphy, "Making Managers in the U.S. Military: The Case of the Army Management School, 1945–1970" *Management & Organizational History* 15, no. 2 (2020): 154–68; Louis Hyman, *Temp: The Real Story of What Happened to Your Salary, Benefits & Job Security* (Viking, 2018); Angus Burgin, "The Reinvention of Entrepreneurship," in *American Labyrinth: Intellectual History for Complicated Times*, ed. Raymond Haberski Jr. and Andrew Hartman (Cornell University Press, 2018).

8. David Harvey, *A Brief History of Neoliberalism* (Oxford University Press, 2007).

9. See, for example, Nan Enstad, *Cigarettes, Inc.: An Intimate History of Corporate Imperialism* (University of Chicago Press, 2018); Elizabeth Esch, *The Color Line and the Assembly Line: Managing Race in the Ford Empire* (University of California Press, 2018); Greg Mitman, *Empire of Rubber: Firestone's Scramble for Land and Power in Liberia* (New Press, 2021). This book extends this line of inquiry forward in time, analyzing multinational corporations' role constructing a "post–Jim Crow/apartheid" racial order on an international scale.

10. See, for example, Kimberly Phillips-Fein, *Invisible Hands: The Making of the Conservative Movement from the New Deal to Reagan* (W.W. Norton, 2009); Kimberly Phillips-Fein and Julian E. Zelizer, eds., *What's Good for Business: Business and American Politics since World War II* (Oxford University Press, 2012); Benjamin C. Waterhouse, *Lobbying America: The Politics of Business from Nixon to NAFTA* (Princeton University Press, 2013).

11. An excellent illustration of this, and one with notable parallels to the struggle for Black inclusion, can be found in Margot Canaday's examination of LGBT workers' struggle for recognition within corporate America. This struggle, Canaday shows, occurred at multiple levels of the corporation, from the factory floor to newly created DEI offices. See *Queer Career: Sexuality and Work in Modern America* (Princeton University Press, 2023).

12. Reynolds Farley and Walter R. Allen, *The Color Line and the Quality of Life in America* (Russell Sage, 1987); Sharon Collins, "Black Mobility in White Corporations:

Up the Corporate Ladder but on a Limb," *Social Problems* 44, no. 1 (1997): 55–67. Nearly all Black directors appointed in the 1970s were men. Black women, who faced the double-burden of sexism and racism, were far slower in obtaining managerial positions. The first Black woman director of a Fortune 500 company was Patricia Robert Harris, who joined the boards of Scott Paper and IBM in 1971 and the board of Chase Manhattan in 1972. See Richard L. Zweigenhaft and G. William Dornhoff, *Diversity in the Power Elite: How It Happened, Why It Matters* (Rowman & Littlefield, 2006), 96. These early successes notwithstanding, in 1980, Black men comprised only 2.97 percent of all private-sector managerial positions, compared to 1.27 percent for Black women, 16.56 percent for white women, and 75.69 percent for white men. See Kevin Stainback and Donald Tomaskovic-Devey, "Intersections of Power and Privilege: Long-Term Trends in Managerial Representation," *American Sociological Review* 74, no. 5 (2009): 802, table 1.

13. "Rev. Leon Sullivan to Push for More Black Representation in General Motors Co." *Philadelphia Tribune*, March 9, 1971.

14. Jerry M. Flint, "A Black Director of G.M. Will Vote Against the Board," *New York Times*, April 9, 1971.

15. Sullivan quoted in "Episcopal Resolution Backed By Dr. Leon Sullivan of GM," *Oakland Post*, April 28, 1971.

16. Several sources credit activist and political theorist Saul Alinsky with pioneering the tactic of shareholder activism when he, in partnership with Rochester-area FIGHT, purchased several shares of Kodak as "tickets" to the company's 1967 shareholder meeting, where they protested racial discrimination. See Terry H. Anderson, "The New American Revolution: The Movement and Business," in *The Sixties: From Memory to History*, ed. David Farber (University of North Carolina Press, 1994), 178–79.

17. Julia C. Ott, *When Wall Street Met Main Street: The Question for an Investors' Democracy* (Harvard University Press, 2011); Heidi J. Welsh, "Shareholder Activism," *The Multinational Monitor* 9, no. 12 (1988), https://www.multinationalmonitor .org/hyper/issues/1988/12/mm1288_06.html; Stuart L. Gillan and Laura T. Starks, "A Survey of Shareholder Activism: Motivation and Empirical Evidence," *Contemporary Finance Digest* 2, no. 3 (1998): 3, 4, 10–34.

18. Following the Project for Corporate Responsibility decision, the average number of social-issue resolutions filed in the United States per year increased from just under a hundred in 1973 to approximately 275 in 1989. See Katherina Glac, "The Influence of Shareholders on Corporate Social Responsibility," *Economics, Management, and Financial Markets* 9, no. 3 (2014): 58. On the SEC's evolving rules related to shareholder activism, see Kyle Edward Williams, *Taming the Octopus: The Long Battle for the Soul of the Corporation* (W. W. Norton, 2024).

19. Eileen Shanahan, "13 in House Back Drive to Put Public Members on G.M. Board," *New York Times*, May 1, 1970. See also "'What's Good for U.S.' Posed at GM Annual Meeting," *Christian Science Monitor*, May 25, 1970; Barbara Gold, "New Protest: General Motors Undemocratic?" *The Sun*, May 17, 1970.

20. Jessica Ann Levy, "Black Power in the Boardroom: Corporate America, the Sullivan Principles, and the Anti-Apartheid Struggle," *Enterprise & Society*, 21, no. 1 (March 2020): 170–209; Williams, *Taming the Octopus*. Lizabeth Cohen likewise briefly discusses the links between Black activism and corporate social responsibility in *A Consumers' Republic: The Politics of Mass Consumption in Postwar America* (Vintage Books, 2003), 347–87.

21. Shirley Chisholm, *Unbought and Unbossed* (Houghton Mifflin, 1970), 170–71.

22. Chisholm quoted in Barbara Gold, "New Protest: GM Undemocratic?" *The Sun*, May 17, 1970.

23. Stokes quoted in Morton Mintz, "GM Responds to Charges of Job Discrimination," *Washington Post*, May 2, 1970.

24. Robert S. Brown, "Keynote Speech: The Need for Formulating a Black Economic Plan," paper presented at the National Black Economic Development Conference, Detroit, MI, Presbyterian Historical Society, Philadelphia, Pennsylvania, Records of the National Council of Churches, Box 35, Folder 14, Box 35.

25. Leon H. Sullivan, *Alternatives to Despair* (Judson Press, 1972), 88–89.

26. "UAW Chooses GM as Target for Strike: Woodcock Calls Midnight Walkout 'Quite Certain,'" *Los Angeles Times*, September 14, 1970; "4 Major Clashes Mark History of U.A.W.-G.M. Strikes," *New York Times*, September 16, 1970. On the links between the Black Power movement and labor activism in Detroit's automobile industry, see Heather Ann Thompson, *Whose Detroit? Politics, Labor, and Race in a Modern American City* (Cornell University Press, 2001), 103–27.

27. Exchange quoted in Nicholas von Hoffman, "'Responsibility' Kick Has Antisocial Consequences," *The Capital Times*, July 14, 1970.

28. Roche quoted in von Hoffman, "'Responsibility' Kick Has Antisocial Consequences."

29. Exchange quoted in William Serrin, "For Roche of G.M., Happiness Is a 10% Surcharge," *New York Times Magazine*, September 12, 1971. Similar disruptions occurred at over a dozen other shareholder meetings, including those of American Telephone, Bank of America, Boeing Aircraft, The Chase Manhattan Bank, Dow Chemical, General Electric, Gulf Oil, Honeywell, International Business Machines, and Union Carbide. See Phillip Blumberg, "The Politicization of the Corporation," *Faculty Articles and Papers* 386 (1971): 426, https://digitalcommons.lib.uconn.edu/law_papers/386.

30. By 1980, MEI had extended $3.8 million in financing to minority-owned companies. Using the start-up capital from MEI, these businesses borrowed an additional $20.8 million from other institutions, including the Small Business Administration. See "The General Motors Initiative," *The Black Monitor* 5, no. 6 (June 1980): 16, OICA Records, Box 24.

31. Louis Spade, "Blacks winning top posts in big business," *Chicago Daily Defender*, January 9, 1971.

32. Zweigenhaft and Domhoff, *Diversity in the Power Elite*, 91–93, 99.

33. On the sidelining of Black executives and managers within corporations, see Collins, "Black Mobility in White Corporations;" Zweigenhaft and Domhoff, *Diversity in the Power Elite*, 90–115.

34. According to Thomas Sugrue, between 1965 and 1970, 201 of the nation's 250 largest corporations created urban affairs programs, where only five had existed before 1965. See *Sweet Land of Liberty: The Forgotten Struggle for Civil Rights in the North* (Random House, 2008), 440. Long acknowledged by business professionals as one of the most important corporate assets, brands have only recently received substantive engagement from historians. See, for example, Roger Horowitz, *Kosher USA: How Coke Became Kosher and Other Tales of Modern Food* (Columbia University Press, 2016); Moreton, *To Serve God and Wal-Mart*. For an overview of the importance of brands by a nonhistorian, see Martin Kornberger, *Brand Society: How Brands Transform Management and Lifestyle* (Cambridge University Press, 2010).

35. Memo, Vice President Corporate Affairs, Corporate Staff, [circa 1972], Box 11, Sims Papers. E. Frederic Morrow similarly described his role as "representing the [Bank of America] on boards and in activities where a good corporate image was important" alongside "assistance on urban problems." See E. Frederic Morrow, *Forty Years a Guinea Pig: A Black Man's View from the Top* (The Pilgrim Press, 1980), 5.

36. Memo, "Consideration of Women's Discussion Groups and periodic Steering Committee meetings with upper management," September 27, 1974, Sims Papers, Box 11; Meeting Minutes, Special Meeting of the Council of Personnel Directors, November 20, 1972, Sims Papers, Box 11.

37. Roche quoted in "General Motors Names a Negro to Board, First Such Appointment in Auto Industry," *Wall Street Journal,* January 5, 1971.

38. Morrow, *Forty Years a Guinea Pig*, 2–3. See also Marylin Bender, "Blacks Snubbed in Business," *New York Times*, April 19, 1970.

39. "Rev. Leon Sullivan to Push for More Black Representation in General Motors Co.," *Philadelphia Tribune*, March 9, 1971.

40. Sullivan made $7,200 annually as a GM director. See Nick Thimmesch, "Leon Sullivan, a Black Boomer," *Chicago Tribune*, May 9, 1972. This was on par with director compensation at the time, which, according to a survey by Korn/Ferry International, amounted to $14,570 on average in 1980 ($6,860 in 1970 dollars) at publicly held corporations. It is important to note that director compensation varied widely across industries. In 1980, directors at Ford Motors, for example, received approximately $40,000 a year, compared to $73,000 at Texas Instruments. See Lydia Chavez, "Benefits of a Board member," *New York Times*, September 5, 1981.

41. Harold R. Sims to John Heldrich, Corporate Vice President for Administration, Johnson & Johnson, January 28, 1972, Sims Papers, Box 11.

42. Harold R. Sims, "The Quest for Corporate Social Responsibility: Altruism, Necessity or Opportunity?" *Contact* (Winter 1974): 34–41, Sims Papers, Box 14; Hon. Louis Stokes, "Corporate Social Responsibilities," *Monday*, February 10, 1975, Sims Papers, Box 14.

43. Richard W. Hull, *American Enterprise in South Africa: Historical Dimensions of Engagement and Disengagement* (New York University Press, 1990), 2, 19.

44. In the early twentieth century, nearly all of South Africa's petroleum was sourced by firms owned or controlled by Americans. See Hull, *American Enterprise in South Africa*, 123–24.

45. Other US companies active in South Africa in the early twentieth century include agricultural equipment manufacturer International Harvester, pharmaceutical manufacturer Merck, as well as Colgate-Palmolive Company and Gillette Company. See Hull, *American Enterprise in South Africa*, 138–40.

46. Hull, *American Enterprise in South Africa*, 250.

47. The literature on the anti-apartheid movement in the US is extensive, although weighted toward the 1950s and 1960s. See, for example, Francis Njubi Nesbitt, *Race for Sanctions: African Americans against Apartheid, 1946–1994* (Indiana University Press, 2004); Eric J. Morgan, "Into the Struggle: Confronting Apartheid in the United States and South Africa" (PhD diss., University of Colorado, 2009); Robert Kinloch Massie, *Loosing the Bonds: The United States and South Africa in the Apartheid Years* (Nan A. Talese, 1997); Donald R. Culverson, *Contesting Apartheid: U.S. Activism, 1960–1987* (Westview Press, 1999); Nicholas Grant, *Winning Our Freedoms Together: African Americans and Apartheid, 1945–1960* (University of North Carolina Press, 2017).

48. Eric J. Morgan, "The World Is Watching: Polaroid and South Africa," *Enterprise & Society* 7, no. 3 (2006): 520–49.

49. R. Joseph Parrott, "Boycott Gulf! Angolan Oil and the Black Power Roots of American Anti-Apartheid Organizing," *Modern American History* 1, no. 2 (2018): 195–220.

50. Douglas Robinson, "Episcopal Church Urges G.M. to Close Plants in South Africa," *New York Times*, February 2, 1971.

51. "Rev. Leon Sullivan calls for Business Boycott," *Sun Reporter*, March 20, 1971.

52. *U.S. Business Involvement in Southern Africa, Hearings before the Subcomm. on Africa of the H. Comm. On Foreign Affairs, Day 3*, 92nd Congress, First Session (1971) (statement of Rev. Leon Howard Sullivan, Board of Directors, General Motors Corp.).

53. Jerry M. Flint, "A Black Director of G.M. Will Vote Against the Board," *New York Times*, April 9, 1971.

54. John A. Mayer, Chairman of Mellon National Bank and Trust Company to Leon Sullivan, February 22, 1971, LHS Papers, Box 1, Folder 4.

55. Black banking executive quoted in Sharon M. Collins, *Black Corporate Executives: The Making and Breaking of a Black Middle Class* (Temple University Press, 1997), 58.

56. Collins, *Black Corporate Executives*, 62.

57. Anonymous Black bank manager quoted in Edward D. Irons and Gilbert W. Moore, *Black Managers: The Case of the Banking Industry* (Praeger, 1985), 82.

58. Anonymous Black bank manager quoted in Irons and Moore, *Black Managers*, 53.

59. Concern for the role prominent Black Americans play with regard to corporate image continues through the present, as evidenced by revelations regarding payments

received by Reverend Al Sharpton from several companies in exchange for him refraining from speaking about racism at their companies. See Isabel Vincent and Melissa Klein, "How Sharpton gets paid to not cry 'racism' at corporations," *New York Post*, January 4, 2015, http://nypost.com/2015/01/04/how-sharpton-gets-paid-to-not-cry-racism-at-corporations/.

60. John A. Mayer, Chairman of Mellon National Bank and Trust Company to Leon Sullivan, February 22, 1971, LHS Papers, Box 1, Folder 4.

61. "General Motors and South Africa," October 16, 1972, Presentation by Mr. E.M. Estes at the "Council on Religion and International Affairs" Seminar, LHS Papers, Box 51, Folder 9.

62. Oliver S. Crosby, Director Southern African Affairs, U.S. Department of State, to Leon Sullivan, Itinerary for South Africa Trip, October 13, 1972, LHS Papers, Box 1, Folder 7; Sullivan, *Moving Mountains*, 32.

63. Oliver S. Crosby, Director Southern African Affairs, U.S. Department of State, to Leon H. Sullivan, Itinerary for South Africa Trip, October 13, 1972, LHS Papers, Box 1, Folder 7.

64. Alan de Kock to Leon H. Sullivan, LHS Papers, Box 54, Folder 2.

65. Ron Nixon, *Selling Apartheid: South Africa's Global Propaganda War* (Jacana Media, 2015), 2.

66. Sullivan, *Moving Mountains*, 41.

67. Keletso Atkins, "The Black Atlantic Communication Network: African American Sailors and the Cape of Good Hope Connection," *Issue: A Journal of Opinion* 24, no. 2 (1996)," 23–25; Erlmann, "A Feeling of Prejudice."

68. James T. Campbell, *Songs of Zion: The African Methodist Episcopal Church in the United States and South Africa* (Oxford University Press, 1995); Robert Trent Vinson, *The Americans Are Coming! Dreams of African American Liberation in Segregationist South Africa* (Ohio University Press, 2012).

69. Sullivan, *Moving Mountains*, 44–45, 48.

70. Sullivan, 50.

71. J.M. Cornely to Leon H. Sullivan, February 21, 1977, LHS Papers, Box 54, Folder 6. See also Hull, *American Enterprise in South Africa*, 280.

72. Sullivan, *Moving Mountains*, 48–49.

73. Hull, *American Enterprise in South Africa*, 346.

74. "New York OIC Honors IBM's President Cary," *New York Amsterdam News*, November 2, 1974.

75. Leon H. Sullivan to Mt. T. J. Barlow, President and Chief Executive Officer, Anderson Clayton & Company, March 26, 1976, LHS Papers, Box 54, Folder 3; S. Prakash Sethi and Oliver F. Williams, *Economic Imperatives and Ethical Values in Global Business: The South African Experience and International Codes Today* (Kluwer, 2000), 3.

76. Sullivan, *Moving Mountains*, 49. See also Harry Amana, "Rev. Sullivan, U.S. Firms Hold Secret Meeting on S. Africa's Racist Policies," *Philadelphia Tribune*, March 13, 1976.

77. "General Motors Names a Negro to Board, First Such Appointment in Auto Industry," *Wall Street Journal*, January 5, 1971.

78. James W. Wilcock, Chairman and Chief Executive Joy Manufacturing Company to Leon H. Sullivan, January 3, 1977, LHS Papers, Box 54, Folder 6.

79. Nesbitt, *Race for Sanctions*; Culverson, *Contesting Apartheid*.

80. Frank T. Cary to Leon Sullivan, November 19, 1975, LHS Papers, Box 54, Folder 2.

81. Sethi and Williams, *Economic Imperatives and Ethical Values in Global Business*, 10.

82. Robert E. Terkhorn, Vice President Citibank, to Sullivan, February 22, 1977, LHS papers, Box 54, Folder 6.

83. William Tavolareas, President Mobil Oil Corporation to Leon Sullivan, February 18, 1977, LHS Papers, Box 54, Folder 6.

84. Simon Stevens, "'From the Viewpoint of a Southern Governor': The Carter Administration and Apartheid, 1977–81," *Diplomatic History* 36, no. 5 (2012): 843–80; Massie, *Loosing the Bonds*, 407–9.

85. Helena Pohlandt-McCormick, *"I Saw a Nightmare . . .": Doing Violence to Memory: The Soweto Uprising, June 16, 1976* (Columbia University Press, 2005).

86. Marshal Murrell to Sullivan, February 14, 1978, LHS papers, Box 54, Folder 7.

87. Leon H. Sullivan to Mr. T. J. Barlow, President and Chief Executive Officer, Anderson Clayton & Company, March 26, 1076, LHS Papers, Box 54, Folder 3.

88. Virginia B. Smith, President Vassar College, to Leon Sullivan, February 16, 1978, LHS Papers, Box 54, Folder 7; Valerie Reilly, Program Director, Los Angeles World Affairs Council, to Leon H. Sullivan, June 12, 1987; Michael J. Brassington, Executive Director, The Commonwealth Club of California, to Leon Sullivan, August 6, 1987, LHS Papers, Box 4, Folder 6; E. Lockwood, Chairman European Advisory Council, General Motors, to Mr. Mogens Pagh, Chairman, The East Asiatic Co. Ltd. June 15, 1977, LHS Papers, Box 54, Folder 6; Press Release, "Sullivan Calls London Conference of World's Multi-National Companies to Pressure Changes Against Apartheid in South Africa," November 20, 1980, LHS Papers, Box 55, Folder 9.

89. "A Business Response to Apartheid," *Washington Post*, March 5, 1977. See also Thomas E. Mullaney, "12 Big U.S. Concerns in South Africa Set Equality in Plants," *New York Times*, March 2, 1977; "11 Large U.S. Companies Planning Reforms in S. Africa Operations," *Los Angeles Times*, March 2, 1977; Wayne Green, "Racially Neutral Policies in South Africa in Jobs Promised by 12 Major U.S. Firms," *Wall Street Journal*, March 3, 1977.

90. Roy Wilkins, "Wilkins Speaks: Sullivan's S. Africa coup," *Afro-American*, March 26, 2977.

91. Dramane Ouattera, Ambassador, Executive Secretary of the OAU, to Leon Sullivan, February 10, 1977, LHS Papers, Box 54, Folder 6.

92. J. R. Humphrey, "Our Readers Say Firms Help South Africa," *Afro-American*, April 2, 1977.

93. Prexy Nesbitt quoted in Cheryl Devall, "Universities Continue Focus on South Africa," *Bay State Banner*, April 19, 1979.

94. Culverson, *Contesting Apartheid*, 103; David L. Hostetter, *Movement Matters: American Antiapartheid Activism and the Rise of Multicultural Politics* (Routledge, 2006), 37.

95. Leon H. Sullivan to Tim Smith, Director Interfaith Center on Corporate Responsibility, April 11, 1977, LHS Papers, Box 54, Folder 6.

96. Moose quoted in "State Dept. endorses 'Sullivan Principles,'" *New York Amsterdam News*, June 2, 1979.

97. Edward B. Fiske, "South Africa is New Social Issue for College Activists," *New York Times*, March 15, 1978.

98. Biondi, *The Black Revolution on Campus*, 250–51.

99. Parrott, "Boycott Gulf!" On TransAfrica, see Nesbitt, *Race for Sanctions*, especially chapter 5.

100. Anne Rutledge, Assistant to the VP of Finance and Staff Assistant to the Committee on Social Responsibility in Investments, to Sullivan, October 25, 1977, Box 54, Folder 6; Open Letter from Ad Hoc Committee on the Sullivan Six Principles, LHS papers, Box 54, Folder 7.

101. Leon H. Sullivan to Donald Brown, Vice President of Finance at the University of Minnesota, December 28, 1978, LHS papers, Box 54, Folder 9. See also "University May Sell Stock as a Gesture for Human Rights: Ohio State Wants Three Firms to Support the Sullivan Principles in South Africa," *Wall Street Journal*, November 13, 1978.

102. Phillips-Fein and Zelizer, *What's Good for Business*; Phillips-Fein, *Invisible Hands*; Waterhouse, *Lobbying America*.

103. Peter Fortune to Leon H. Sullivan, December 18, 1978, LHS papers, Box 54, Folder 9.

104. On the Wiehahn Commission, see Alan Rycroft and Barney Jordaan, *A Guide to South African Labour Law* (Juta, 1992); Sonia Bendix, *Industrial Relations in South Africa* (Juta, 1996); Alex Lichtenstein, "'We Do Not Think That the Bantu Is Ready for Labour Unions': Remaking South Africa's Apartheid Workplace in the 1970s," *South African Historical Journal* 67, no. 2 (2015): 113–38; Alex Lichtenstein, "'We Feel Our Strength Is on the Factory Floor': Dualism, Shop-Floor Power, and Labor Law Reform in the Late Apartheid South Africa," *Labor History* 60, no. 6 (2019): 606–25. Drawing a direct connection between the Wiehahn reforms and the Sullivan Principles, Mattie C. Webb notes that the initial Wiehahn report "adopted much of the same language as the Sullivan Principles." See "'An Exercise in the Art of the Possible': Waging a Battle Against Apartheid in the South African Workplace," *Enterprise & Society* 25, no. 2 (2024): 336.

105. Statement of Principles Industry Support Unit Inc., August 8, 1979, LHS papers, Box 55, Folder 1.

106. Sethi and Williams, *Economic Imperatives and Ethical Values in Global Business*, 69.

107. Anonymous chief executive quoted in D. Reid Weedon Jr. to James W. Rawlings, Vice Chairman, Union carbide Africa and Middle East Inc., March 15, 1979, LHS papers, Box 54, Folder 12.

108. Henry Ford II to Hon. Charles Diggs, Jr., February 13, 1978, LHS papers, Box 54, Folder 7.

109. Arthur D. Little Inc., *Report on the Signatory Companies to the Sullivan Principles*, 1 (Arthur D. Little, 1978), African Studies Collection, University of Cape Town.

110. Sullivan quoted in "Sullivan's Evaluation: Statement of Principles' Program Helping Black South African Workers," *Philadelphia Tribune*, December 8, 1978.

111. Leon H. Sullivan to Bishop Donald George Ming of AME Church in Cape Town, May 24, 1978, LHS papers, Box 54, Folder 8.

112. Arthur D. Little Inc., *Report on the Signatory Companies to the Sullivan Principles*, 1 (Arthur D. Little, 1978), African Studies Collection, University of Cape Town.

113. Terry Myers to Sullivan, November 22, 1978, LHS papers, Box 54, Folder 9.

114. Webb, "'An Exercise in the Art of the Possible.'"

115. Board Meeting Minutes, International Council for Equality of Opportunity Principles, December 10, 1979, quoted in Sethi and Williams, *Economic Imperatives and Ethical Values in Global Business*, 100.

116. Sethi and Williams, *Economic Imperatives and Ethical Values in Global Business*, 106–8.

117. Sethi and Williams, *Economic Imperatives and Ethical Values in Global Business*, 88; Patricia Arnold and Theresa Hammond, "The Role of Accounting in Ideological Conflict: Lessons from the South African Divestment Movement," *Accounting, Organizations and Society* 19, no. 2 (1994): 111–26.

118. Marshae Murrell to Sullivan, February 14, 1978, LHS papers, Box 54, Folder 7.

119. M. C. Roux, W. L. Nkuhlu, W. H. Thomas, C. W. Manona, and M. G. Whisson, *The Sullivan Principles at Ford: Audit 2* (South African Institute of Race Relations, 1981).

120. Elizabeth Schmidt, *Decoding Corporate Camouflage: U.S. Business Support for Apartheid* (Institute for Policy Studies, 1980), 25–26.

121. Thomas N. Todd quoted in Nathaniel Sheppard Jr., "Rights Leaders at Odds on Whether Corporate Seats Pose a Conflict," *New York Times*, July 4, 1978.

122. Nesbitt, *Race for Sanctions*, 103.

123. Randall Robinson, "Testimony before the Subcommittee on Africa and International Economic Policy and Trade," *Issue: A Journal of Opinion* 9, no. 1/2 (1979): 17–20.

124. Sullivan quoted in "Tough talk on Blacks," *Philadelphia Daily News*, September 5, 1980.

125. Sullivan quoted in Carl Rowan, "Students lead drive against U.S. firms in South Africa," [circa June 1978], Sims Papers.

Chapter 6

1. "NAFCOC President Tells Overseas Business . . . Disinvestment No Good for Black Progress," *African Business* (April 1974), National Library of South Africa-Cape Town (hereafter cited as *African Business*).

2. Steve Biko and Millard W. Arnold, *Black Consciousness in South Africa* (Vintage Books, 1979); Gail M. Gerhart, *Black Power in South Africa: The Evolution of an Ideology* (University of California Press, 1978); Tom Lodge, *Black Politics in South Africa since 1945* (Longman, 1983); C. R. D. Halisi, *Black Political Thought in the Making of South African Democracy* (Indiana University Press, 1999), especially chapter 4; Daniel Magaziner, *The Law and the Prophets: Black Consciousness in Southern Africa, 1968–1977* (Ohio University Press, 2010).

3. Leslie Anne Hadfield, *Liberation and Development: Black Consciousness Community Programs in South Africa* (Michigan State University Press, 2016).

4. Nigel Gibson, "Black Consciousness 1977–1987: The Dialectics of Liberation in South Africa," *Africa Today* 35, no. 1 (1988): 6; Andy Clarno and Salim Vally, "The Context of Struggle: Racial Capitalism and Political Praxis in South Africa," *Ethnic and Racial Studies* 46, no. 16 (2023): 3425–47; Robert Fatton Jr., *Black Consciousness in South Africa: The Dialectics of Ideological Resistance to White Supremacy* (State University of New York Press, 1986).

5. "NAFCOC President Tells Overseas Business."

6. William Beinart, Peter Delius, and Stanley Trapido, eds., *Putting a Plough to the Ground: Accumulation and Dispossession in Rural South Africa, 1850–1930* (Raven Press, 1986); Colin Bundy, *The Rise & Fall of the South African Peasantry* (James Currey, 1988).

7. Samuel M. Motsuenyane, *A Testament of Hope: The Autobiography of Dr. Sam Motsuenyane* (KMM Review Publishing, 2011), 18–19.

8. "United Nations and Apartheid Timeline, 1946–1994," *South African History Online: Towards a People's History*, https://www.sahistory.org.za/article/united-nations -and-apartheid-timeline-1946-1994.

9. Garth Mason, "The Moral Rearmament Activist: P.Q. Vundla's Community Bridge-building during the boycotts of the Witwatersrand in the mid-1950s," *Journal for the Study of Religion* 28, no. 2 (2015): 154–80.

10. Thelma quoted in Motsuenyane, *A Testament of Hope*, 31.

11. Sheila May Susan Keeble, "The Expansion of Black Business into the South African Economy with Specific Reference to the Initiatives of the National African Federated Chamber of Commerce in the 1970s" (PhD diss., University of the Witwatersrand, 1981), 16.

12. George M. Fredrickson, *White Supremacy: A Comparative Study of American and South African History* (Oxford University Press, 1981).

13. The role played by white Americans in the development of South Africa was extensive and wide-ranging. On white American missionaries in southern Africa, see, for example, Richard Elphick and Rodney Davenport, eds., *Christianity in South Africa:*

A Political, Social, and Cultural History (David Philip; University of California Press; James Currey, 1997); C. Tsheloane Keto, "Race Relations, Land and the Changing Missionary Role in South Africa: A Case Study of the American Zulu Mission, 1850–1910," *The International Journal of African Historical Studies* 10, no. 4 (1977): 600–27; Arthur Fridjof Christofersen, *Adventuring with God: The Story of the American Board Mission in South Africa* (Inanda Seminary, 1967). More recently, scholars have expounded on the role of white American engineers and industrialists, including their work informing the particular forms of racialized labor that emerged in South Africa's mining sector. See Stephen Tuffnell, "Engineering Inter-Imperialism: American Miners and the Transformation of Global Mining, 1871–1910," *Journal of Global History* 10, no. 1 (2015): 53–76; Charles van Onselen, *The Cowboy Capitalist: John Hays Hammond, the American West, and the Jameson Raid in South Africa* (Jonathan Ball, 2017); Megan Black, *The Global Interior: Mineral Frontiers and American Power* (Harvard University Press, 2018), 43–44; Mark Hendrickson, "Advance Agent of Expanding Empires: George F. Becker and Mineral Exploration in South Africa and the Philippines," *History and Technology* 35, no. 3 (2019): 237–65.

14. Thomas Borstelmann, *Apartheid's Reluctant Uncle: The United States and Southern Africa in the Early Cold War* (Oxford University Press, 1993).

15. Carol Anderson, *White Rage: The Unspoken Truth of Our Racial Divide* (Bloomsbury Books, 2016).

16. For an excellent account of racial liberalism and its limitations, see Lani Guinier's "From Racial Liberalism to Racial Literacy: *Brown v. Board of Education* and the Interest-Divergence Dilemma," *Journal of American History* 91, no. 1 (June 2004): 92–118. Guinier defines racial liberalism as a set of ideals that "helped fashion the legal strategy of the biracial elite" through "emphasiz[ing] the corrosive effect of individual prejudice and the importance of interracial contact in promoting tolerance" (95). See also Mark Brilliant, *The Color of America Has Changed: How Racial Diversity Shaped Civil Rights Reform in California, 1941–1978* (Oxford University Press, 2010); Charles W. Mills, "Racial Liberalism," *PMLA* 123, no. 5 (2008): 1380–97. On South African apartheid and American liberal internationalism, see Ryan M. Irwin, *Gordian Knot: Apartheid and the Unmaking of the Liberal World Order* (Oxford University Press, 2012). While neither engage the term directly, Mary L. Dudziak and Carol Anderson likewise offer helpful accounts for understanding how this dynamic played out in the context of US international relations, including highlighting the role of Black Americans and anti-colonial leaders in pressuring US officials regarding American race policy. See Mary L. Dudziak, *Cold War Civil Rights: Race and the Image of American Democracy* (Princeton University Press, 2011); Carol Anderson, *Eyes Off the Prize: The United Nations and the African American Struggle for Human Rights, 1944–1955* (Cambridge University Press, 2003).

17. Memo, United States-South Africa Leader Exchange Program, Inc., United States—South Africa Leader Exchange Program Records, 1955–2003, AG3237, Historical Papers, The Library, University of the Witwatersrand, Johannesburg, South Africa (hereafter cited as USSALEP Records), B1.

18. "My General Impressions and Observations on My Visit to the United States as an Exchangee of the United States-South Africa Leader Exchange Program," June 1, 1960, USSALEP Records, G2.6, Individuals-Motsuenyane. See also Motsuenyane, *A Testament of Hope*, 54.

19. Motsuenyane, *A Testament of Hope*, 54.; Jacob Mawela, "Dr Sam and Mrs Jocelyn Motsuenyane's 95th and 90th Birthdays Celebration," *Soweto Life*, March 9, 2022, https://sowetolifemag.co.za/dr-sam-and-mrs-jocelyn-motsuenyanes-95th-and-90th-birthdays-celebration/.

20. Sam Motsuenyane to Dr. F. Loescher, November 18, 1959, USSALEP Records, G2.6, Individuals-Motsuenyane.

21. Motsuenyane, *A Testament of Hope*, 57.

22. "My General Impressions and Observations on My Visit to the United States."

23. On Durham's Black Wall Street, see Quincy T. Mills, *Cutting Along the Color Line: Black Barbers and Barber Shops in America* (University of Pennsylvania Press, 2013), 99; Walter Weare, *Black Business in the New South: A Social History of the North Carolina Mutual Life Insurance Company* (Duke University Press, 1993), 51–81, 268–69, 278.

24. Motsuenyane, *A Testament of Hope*, 69.

25. Memo, United States-South Africa Leader Exchange Program, Inc., USSALEP Records, B1; "Assistance to Small Traders in Community and Economic Development," USSALEP Records, H6.

26. Pamphlet, USSALEP Records, H6. Black American businessmen, too, participated in this exchange, including, notably, John Wheeler, President of the American Farmers and Mechanics Bank. See USSALEP Records, N1.1.

27. Frank Andre Guridy, *Forging Diaspora: Afro-Cubans and African Americans in a World of Empire and Jim Crow* (University of North Carolina Press, 2010).

28. Robert Trent Vinson, *The Americans Are Coming! Dreams of African American Liberation in Segregationist South Africa* (Ohio University Press, 2012), 28, 129.

29. Joseph Lelyveld, "Children of African Dissident Live With Rep. Young Family," *New York Times*, December 18, 1976.

30. Brenna Wynn Greer, "Selling Liberia: Moss H. Kendrix, the Liberian Centennial Commission, and the Post-World War II Trade in Black Progress," *Enterprise & Society* 11, no. 2 (2013): 303–26; Guridy, *Forging Diaspora*, 16, 25, 72, 78–79, 151–94; Tiffany M. Gill, *Beauty Shop Politics: African American Women's Activism in the Beauty Industry* (University of Illinois Press, 2010), especially chapter 4.

31. "25 Years Ago: Historic Gathering Became Milestone in Black Endeavour," *African Business* (July 1989).

32. Ramusi quoted in Keeble, "The Expansion of Black Business," 253–54.

33. "One Economy for All—Ntsanwisi," *African Business* (March 1977).

34. "Your Business and You—S. Nyamakazi," *African Business* (March 1978).

35. Motsuenyane, *A Testament of Hope*, 55–56.

36. On Atlanta's Black and white governing coalition, see Clarence Stone, *Regime Politics: Governing Atlanta, 1946–1988* (University Press of Kansas, 1989).

37. "My General Impressions and Observations on My Visit to the United States as an Exchangee."

38. "My General Impressions and Observations on My Visit to the United States as an Exchangee."

39. Gerhart, *Black Power in South Africa*; Lodge, *Black Politics in South Africa since 1945*; Arianna Lissoni, Jon Soske, Natasha Erland, Noor Nieftagodien, and Omar Badsha, eds., *One Hundred Years of the ANC: Debating Liberation Histories Today* (Wits University Press, 2012); Stephen Ellis, *External Mission: The ANC in Exile, 1960–1990* (Oxford University Press, 2012).

40. Magaziner, *The Law and the Prophet*, 5–6.

41. South African Department of Statistics, *South African Statistics* (International Publications Service, 1980), 17.

42. Holly E. Reed, "Moving Across Boundaries: Migration in South Africa, 1950–2000," *Demography* 50, no. 1 (2013): 71–95.

43. Deborah Posel, for example, has situated consumption and efforts to regulate it at the heart of South Africa's racial order. See "Races to Consume: Revisiting South Africa's History of Race, Consumption and the Struggle for Freedom," *Ethnic and Racial Studies* 33, no. 2 (2010): 157–75. Building on Posel, in 2015, the journal *Critical Arts: South-North Cultural and Media Studies*, published a special issue highlighting a growing body of scholarship on the topic. See Mehita Iqani and Bridget Kenny, eds., "Consumption, Media and Culture in South Africa: Perspectives on Freedom and the Public," special issue of *Critical Arts* 29, no. 2 (2015). See also Jean Comaroff and John L. Comaroff, *Of Revelation and Revolution*, vol. 2, *The Dialectics of Modernity on a South African Frontier* (University of Chicago Press, 1997); Sarah Nuttall, "Youth Cultures of Consumption in Johannesburg," in *Youth Moves: Identities and Education in Global Perspective*, ed. Nadine Dolby and Fazal Rizvi (Routledge, 2008): 151–78. Whereas much of the aforementioned scholarship focuses on the relationship between consumerism, colonialism, and modernity, Tina Campt, Brenna Wynn Greer, and others emphasize the ways consumption and material culture served as a bridge, linking Black people across the African diaspora. See Tina Campt, *Image Matters: Archive, Photography, and the African Diaspora in Europe* (Duke University Press, 2012); Greer, "Selling Liberia."

44. Keeble, "The Expansion of Black Business," 9–11.

45. Masekela quoted in Keeble, 28.

46. Keeble, 25–26. Mention of the Afrikaners' history of economic development through business organization and the adoption of protective measures permeated the pages of NACOC's monthly magazine, *African Business*.

47. "Koornhof's suggestion rejected," *Rand Daily Mail*, June 4, 1969, quoted in Keeble, "The Expansion of Black Business," 69.

48. Keeble, 172.

49. Thembisa Waetjen, *Workers and Warriors: Masculinity and the Struggle for Nation in South Africa* (University of Illinois Press, 2004), 40–43; Cherryl Walker,

"Gender and Development of the Migrant Labour System, c. 1850–1930," in *Women and Gender in Southern Africa to 1945*, ed. Cherryl Walker (David Philip, 1990): 168–96.

50. Clive Glaser, *Bo-Tsotsi: The Youth Gangs of Soweto, 1935–1976* (Heinemann, 2000).

51. "Black Businessmen Suffer Most During Riots: Presidential Policy Statement 1977," *African Business* (June 1977).

52. "Best of Both Worlds," *African Business* (March 1978).

53. Scholars of Africa have aptly problematized the concept of tradition and/or custom, both of which were widely contested by Africans amid attempts by European colonial powers and local elites to assert control over local communities. See, for example, Martin Chanock, *Law, Custom, and Social Order, the Colonial Experience in Malawi and Zambia* (Cambridge University Press, 1985); Dorothy Hodgson, *Once Intrepid Warriors: Gender, Ethnicity and the Cultural Politics of Maasai Development* (Indiana University Press, 2001); Sara S. Berry, *Chiefs Know Their Boundaries: Essays on Property, Power, and the Past in Asante, 1896–1996* (Heinemann, James Currey, David Philip, 2001); Janine M. Ubink and Kojo S. Amanor, eds., *Contesting Land and Custom in Ghana: State, Chief, and the Citizen* (Leiden University Press, 2008). Still, one should avoid, as Carolyn Hamilton counsels, viewing "African tradition" as invented by European colonists. See *Terrific Majesty: The Powers of Shaka Zulu and the Limits of Historical Invention* (Harvard University Press, 1998).

54. "Bophuthatswana Beauty," *African Business* (April 1979).

55. Keeble, "The Expansion of Black Business," 168.

56. NAFCOC Financial Report, *African Business* (June 1975).

57. "Beauties on Parade," *African Business* (July 1979).

58. "Grooming Those Beauties," *African Business* (May 1982).

59. "Businessmen Want Co-operation but No True Partnership Without Policy Change," *African Business* (July 1977).

60. "NAFCOC Auditors Report for the Year Ended February 1977," *African Business* (June 1977).

61. In addition to associate membership at the national level, NAFCOC also established associate membership at the regional level. The first branch to accept associate members was NAFCOC's Inyanda Chamber of Commerce. See Kwandiwe Kondlo, *A Legacy of Perseverance: NAFCOC: 50 Years of Leadership in Business* (KMM Review Publishing Company, 2014), 44.

62. "Financial Report—S.P. Kutumela," *African Business* (July 1980).

63. "Nafcoc News: Meeting with Associates," *African Business* (December 1978).

64. In statistics revealing of the disregard shown by police for Black life, a subsequent government investigation into the causes of the uprising, known as the Cillie Commission, found that police used 50,000 rounds of ammunition against youth protesters in Soweto, the East Rand, and the Cape Peninsular, killing a total of 284 protesters, and injuring another 2,000. These numbers, moreover, are widely believed to be gross underestimates of the bodily toll of police violence in the weeks during and

following the Soweto Uprising. See Archie Mafeje, "Soweto and its Aftermath," *Review of African Political Economy*, no. 11 (Jan–Apr 1978): 18.

65. Indeed, the uprising and the police response led many youth to flee the country, providing a fresh wave of new recruits for the movement in exile.

66. "Black Businessmen Suffer Most During Riots." The riots contributed to a drop in NAFCOC membership, and the fear of violence led many traders to stop paying membership fees. See Keeble, "The Expansion of Black Business," 157.

67. "Two win top business titles," *African Business* (February 1978). Part of the cost to businesses derived from the practice, also common in the US, whereby township residents destroyed customer records used by business managers to track consumer credit during the unrest. See Deborah James, *Money from Nothing: Indebtedness and Aspiration in South Africa* (Stanford University Press, 2014), 103–4.

68. Motsuenyane, *A Testament of Hope*, 69–70.

69. One example of these kinds of early African financial schemes was the Natal Bantu Cooperative Society founded in 1949. See Kondlo, *A Legacy of Perseverance*, 12.

70. P. G. Gumede, Inyanda Annual Report, *African Business* (June 1975).

71. "Building Financial Institutions by Self-Help—Dr. Motlana Suggests New Role for NAFCOC in Conference Speech," *African Business,* (June 1979).

72. Leon Sullivan quoted in "Oh Man, You Better Change Your Ways Faster . . . !!" *African Business* (October 1980).

73. Keeble, "The Expansion of Black Business," 248–50.

74. "Proposal for Participation in African Small Business Development Center," Sims Papers, Box 13.

75. "Proposal for Participation in African Small Business Development Center."

76. Report on South Africa Trip—1976, March 7, 1977, Sims Papers, Box 10.

77. Kondlo, *A Legacy of Perseverance*, 70–71.

78. Harold R. Sims to Dr. J. DeBeer, May 2, 1977, Sims Papers, Box 10.

79. Keeble, "The Expansion of Black Business," 248–50.

80. Memo, Maximizing the Performance of U.S. base Multinationals in South Africa in the Development of a Non-European Business Leadership Class in South Africa, Johnson & Johnson, September 2, 1977, Sims Papers, Box 13.

81. Letters of Endorsement for Constance Ntshona, Sims Papers, Box 22.

82. Harold R. Sims to Mr. Lester Gagnon, Ethnor Ltd, May 27, 1977, Sims Papers, Box 22.

83. Kodak's actions were indicative of a broader trend among white-owned South African companies, which expanded their share of the African market during the 1960s and 1970s. See Anne Mager, "The First Decade of 'European Beer' in Apartheid South Africa: The State, the Brewers and the Drinking Public, 1962–1972," *Journal of African History* 40, no. 3 (1999): 367–88; "Changing Trade Trends in the Motor Industry," *African Business* (January 1978).

84. "Trading in Photography," *African Business* (September 1978).

85. "Tom Molete-Manager," *African Business* (March 1977).

86. "Speakout: The Alternative Push by Tom Molete," *African Business* (November 1986).

87. Dr. G. M. E. Leistner, "The Road Ahead for Black Business," *African Business* (June 1979).

88. S. M. Motsuenyane, "Presidential Policy Statement 1979," *African Business* (June 1979).

89. Dr. J. J. Fouché, "Free Enterprise—Equal Opportunity for All—J.J. Fouché," *African Business* (February 1977).

90. "Meeting with the Minister," *African Business* (September 1977).

91. Bethany Moreton, *To Serve God and Wal-Mart: The Making of Christian Free Enterprise* (Harvard University Press, 2009); Angus Burgin, *The Great Persuasion: Reinventing Free Markets since the Depression* (Harvard University Press, 2015); Quinn Slobodian, *Globalists: The End of Empire and the Birth of Neoliberalism* (Harvard University Press, 2020).

92. George Marais, "Strategy for Successful Black Business Community—Keynote Address," *African Business* (June 1978).

93. "Open White trading areas to Black businessmen," *African Business* (November 1977).

94. "Annual Conference Final Resolutions," *African Business* (August 1979).

Chapter 7

1. Meeting Minutes of the OIC Executive Council, November 6, 1980, OICA Records, Box 2, Folder 60.

2. Minutes of the OIC National Technical Advisory Committee Meeting, November 21, 1980, OICA Records, Box 3, Folder 51. On racism and US tax politics, see Andrew W. Kahrl, *The Black Tax: 150 Years of Theft, Exploitation, and Dispossession in America* (University of Chicago Press, 2024).

3. Minutes of the OIC Executive Council Meeting, May 30, 1981, OICA Records, Box 2, Folder 61; Robert M. McKee, Special Agent-in-Charge, Philadelphia Regional Investigations Office, Office of the Inspector General Investigations (Fraud) to Elton Jolly, Executive Director, Opportunities Industrializations Center Inc., February 2, 1981, OICA Records, Box 2, Folder 61.

4. Minutes of the OIC Executive Council Meeting, May 30, 1981, OICA Records, Box 2, Folder 61.

5. Sullivan quoted in "Sullivan Rips 'Safety Net,'" *Philadelphia Daily News*, April 2, 1981.

6. George Derek Musgrove, *"We Must Take to the Streets Again": The Black Power Resurgence in Conservative America, 1980–97* (forthcoming). Recent years have seen a rise in scholarly interest in the 1980s, revisiting and challenging entrenched narratives of the 1980s as one of Black political decline. See, for example, Joshua Guild, George Derek

Musgrove, Benjamin Talton, Keeanga-Yamahtta Taylor, and Leah Wright Rigueur, eds., "The Black 1980s," special issue, *Journal of African American History* 108, no. 3 (2023); Dan Berger, *Stayed on Freedom: The Long History of Black Power Through One Family's Journey* (Basic Books, 2023); Austin McCoy, "No Radical Hangover: Black Power, New Left, and Progressive Politics in the Midwest, 1967–1989" (PhD diss., University of Michigan, 2016).

7. "The biggest Black nationalist effort of the early Reagan years," historian Dan Berger notes, the NBIPP garnered attention from Black revolutionaries within and beyond the borders of the US, including in Grenada, where two of the organization's founding members, Zoharah Simmons and Ron Daniels, represented the party at the festivities celebrating the second anniversary of the Caribbean island's socialist revolution. See Dan Berger, *Captive Nation: Black Prison Organizing in the Civil Rights Era* (University of North Carolina Press, 2014), 262–64, 267–71.

8. Jesse Jackson quoted in Art Harris, "Jesse Jackson Preaches a New Politics to the Alabama Legislature," *Washington Post*, May 25, 1983.

9. Jackson quoted in "NUL Conference Highlights: Atlanta mayor Andrew Young says Reagan doomed to fail," *Afro-American*, August 14, 1982.

10. Wendell Rawls Jr., "Mayoral Primary in Atlanta Contains Symbols for Civil Rights Movement," *New York Times*, October 5, 1981.

11. Jessica Ann Levy, "Selling Atlanta: Black Mayoral Politics from Protest to Entrepreneurism, 1973 to 1990," *Journal of Urban History* 41, no. 3 (2015): 420–43.

12. Hooks quoted in Patrice Gaines-Carter, "Coretta King talks to NAACP of nonviolence," *Miami News*, July 1, 1980.

13. Jackson quoted in William Raspberry, "PUSH, Coke Agreement: Pact Could Have Historic Impact," *Memphis Press-Scimitar*, September 8, 1981.

14. N. D. B. Connolly, "A White Story," *Dissent*, January 22, 2018, https://www.dissentmagazine.org/blog/neoliberalism-forum-ndb-connolly/.

15. William O. Tome, "Black leaders pushing a boycott against the Coca-Cola Co.," United Press International, July 23, 1981, UPI Archives, https://www.upi.com/Archives/1981/07/23/Black-leaders-pushing-a-boycott-against-the-Coca-Cola-Co/5754364708800/; "Blacks and Coke," *The Skanner*, July 29, 1981.

16. Raspberry, "PUSH, Coke Agreement: Pact Could Have Historic Impact"; W. Manning Marable, "Reaganism, Racism, and Reaction: Black Political Realignment in the 1980s," *Black Scholar* 13, no. 6 (1982): 10.

17. Coca-Cola President Donald R. Keough quoted in Raspberry, "PUSH, Coke Agreement: Pact Could Have Historic Impact."

18. "Accord Ends Coke Boycott," *New York Times*, August 11, 1981; "Coke to Aid Black Areas: 'Rights,' Boycott Called Off," *The Christian Science Monitor*, August 12, 1981.

19. Marable, "Reaganism, Racism, and Reaction," 10.

20. Raspberry, "PUSH, Coke Agreement: Pact Could Have Historic Impact."

21. Thomas Oliver, "Coke Earnings Climbed 14 Percent In '81," *Atlanta Constitution*, March 4, 1982.

22. Carl Ware to Earl T. Leonard Jr., July 25, 1984, Subj.: Herb Schild, *The Atlanta Journal/Constitution*, Box 27, Folder 5, Carl Ware papers, Archives Research Center, Atlanta University Center, Robert W. Woodruff Library (hereafter cited as Ware papers).

23. Memo from Carl Ware to Earl T. Leonard Jr., July 25, 1984, Subj.: Herb Schild, *The Atlanta Journal/Constitution*, Ware papers, Box 27, Folder 5.

24. Sandy Boyer, "Divesting from Apartheid: A Summary of State and Municipal Legislative Action on South Africa," American Committee on Africa (March 1983), African Activist Archive, https://kora.matrix.msu.edu/files/50/304/32-130-CB5-84-al .sff.document.acoa000587.pdf.

25. Beverly Barnes, "Atlantans Protest Policies in Southern Africa," *Atlanta Constitution*, April 1, 1982.

26. "Divestiture Sought for Pension Funds," *Atlanta Constitution*, June 22, 1982; "Divesting from Apartheid: A Summary of State, Municipal Legislative Action on S.A.," *Atlanta Voice*, May 14, 1983.

27. Phillip H. Wiggins, "Company Earnings; Coca-Cola Advances by 2.1%," *New York Times*, April 28, 1982.

28. "Coca-Cola in South Africa," *The Africa Fund* (January 1986), African Activist Archive, http://kora.matrix.msu.edu/files/50/304/32-130-F43-84-al.sff.document .af000217.pdf.

29. Earl T. Leonard Jr. to Claus Halle, May 18, 1983, Re: State Representative Tyrone Brooks, South Africa Legislation, Ware papers, Box 38, Folder, 8.

30. Carl Ware to Ray Renaud, May 11, 1983, Re: Meeting with Brooks (May 10), Ware papers, Box 38, Folder, 8.

31. Amanda Joyce Hall, "Students Are the Spark: Anti-Apartheid in the Long 1980s," *Journal of African American History* 108, no. 3 (2023): 369–97; Amanda Joyce Hall, "Black Students and the U.S. Anti-Apartheid Movements on Campus"; Martha Biondi, *The Black Revolution on Campus* (University of California Press, 2012).

32. Kevin Houston quoted in Lauren E. Moran, "South to Freedom?: Anti-Apartheid Activism and Politics in Atlanta, 1976–1990" (PhD diss., Georgia State University, 2014), 37.

33. Moran, "South to Freedom?," 38–39.

34. Brenda Mooney, "For Emory, Past and Present, Things Go Better with Coke," *Atlanta Constitution*, November 9, 1979.

35. The gift put Emory's endowment, at $268 million, on par with prominent universities such as Columbia ($294 million), Rice ($255 million), and Washington University in St. Louis ($230 million). See Tyrone D. Terry, "Woodruff Gives Emory $100 million," *Atlanta Constitution*, November 9, 1979.

36. James T. Laney to Jon Gunnemann, Re: Advisory Committee on South Africa, September 10, 1985, the President: President's Advisory Committee on South Africa records, Box 1, Emory University Archives, Stuart A. Rose Manuscript, Archives, and Rare Book Library, Emory University (hereafter cited as Emory University, President's Advisory Comm. on South Africa records).

37. James T. Laney to Jon Gunnemann, Re: Advisory Committee on South Africa, September 10, 1985, Emory University, President's Advisory Committee on South Africa records, Box 1.

38. Kristen Mann to Jon Gunnemann, Re: South Africa Review Committee, September 22, 1985, Emory University, President's Advisory Committee on South Africa records, Box 1.

39. Jackie Irvine to Jon Gunnemann, Re: Report of the Subcommittee on Emory's Economic Ties to South Africa, Emory University, President's Advisory Committee on South Africa records, Box 1.

40. Tom Bertrand to Advisory Committee on South Africa, Subcommittee on Emory/South Africa Economic Ties, October 22, 1985, Emory University, President's Advisory Committee on South Africa records, Box 1; Report of the President's Advisory Committee on South Africa, May 1986, Emory University, President's Advisory Committee on South Africa records, Box 1.

41. Tom Bertrand to Gunnemann et al., November 6, 1985, Emory University, President's Advisory Committee on South Africa, Box 1; Jon Gunnemann to Members of South African Advisory Committee, January 16, 1986, Emory University, President's Advisory Committee on South Africa records, Box 1.

42. Emory University Consolidated Portfolio, October 1985, Trusco Capital Management, V. Jere Koser, Group Vice President to Bradley Currey, November 4, 1985, Emory University, President's Advisory Committee on South Africa records, Box 1.

43. "Meeting the Mandate for Change: A Progress Report on the Application of the Sullivan Principles by U.S. Companies in South Africa," USSALEP Records, L18.

44. Sullivan quoted in "Business: Sullivan to World's Corporations: 'Shape-Up or Ship Out' of S. Africa," *Philadelphia Tribune*, September 19, 1980. See also Caryle Murphy, "U.S. Firms Pressed on S. African Code," *Washington Post*, September 7, 1980.

45. Sullivan quoted in Aaron Epstein, "Leon Sullivan sees Apartheid Ebbing," *Philadelphia Inquirer*, October 22, 1979.

46. Joan Specter, "Socking it to S. Africa . . ." *Philadelphia Inquirer*, May 21, 1982; Jane Eisner, "Phila. Council Considers Sale of Investments," *Philadelphia Inquirer*, April 6, 1982.

47. Specter, "Socking it to S. Africa." See also Boyer, "Divesting from Apartheid."

48. On the CBC's role advocating divestment, see Nesbitt, *Race for Sanctions*, 74–80, 124, 132, 137; Culverson, *Contesting Apartheid*, 59–61, 69–72, 92, 102, 134.

49. A Bill Directing the President to Exercise Authorities Contained in the International Emergency Economic Powers Act to Issue Regulations Prohibiting Investment in South Africa, H.R.1392, 98th Cong. (introduced February 17, 1983); A Bill Requiring United States Persons Who Conduct Business or Control Enterprises in South Africa to Comply with Certain Fair Employment Principles, Prohibiting Any New Loans by United States Financial or Lending Institutions to the South African Government or to

South African Corporations or Other Entities Owned or Controlled by the South African Government, and Prohibiting the Importation of South African Krugerrands or Other South African Gold Coins, H.R. 1963, 98th Cong. (introduced February 25, 1983).

50. Solarz quoted in Joan Mower, "Demos see Political Gain by Challenging Apartheid," *The Californian*, November 21, 1983.

51. Vernon Jarret, "U.S. Continues to Ignore Apartheid," *The Parsons Sun* (Parsons, KS), November 3, 1983.

52. *Hearings on International Economic Policy and Trade of the Committee on International Relations, Before the Subcommittees on Africa and House of Representatives*, 95th Cong., 2nd Session (statement of William R. Cotter, President of the African-American Institute).

53. "South Africa: Questions and Answers on Divestment," American Committee on Africa, , Oliver Tambo Papers, African National Congress Archives, University Libraries, University of Fort Hare, Alice, South Africa (hereafter cited as Tambo Papers), [circa November 1985] 073/0779/14.

54. "Reverend Leon Sullivan's Statement on the Republic of South Africa," Emory University, President's Advisory Committee on South Africa records, Box 1.

55. Leon H. Sullivan, "Give the Sullivan Principles Two More Years," *Washington Post*, May 28, 1985.

56. Richard W. Hull, *American Enterprise in South Africa: Historical Dimensions of Engagement and Disengagement* (New York University Press, 1990), 337–38.

57. An Act to Prohibit Loans to, Other Investments in, and Certain Other Activities with Respect to, South Africa, and for Other Purposes, Pub. L. No. 99–440, Stat. 1086 (1986).

58. Message to the House of Representatives Returning Without Approval a Bill Concerning Apartheid in South Africa, Ronald Reagan Presidential Library & Museum, https://www.reaganlibrary.gov/archives/speech/message-house-representatives-returning -without-approval-bill-concerning-apartheid.

59. "Reverend Leon Sullivan's Statement on the Republic of South Africa," Emory University, President's Advisory Committee on South Africa records, Box 1.

60. Press Release, "U.S. Company Signatories Pledge Increased Effort on Behalf of Sullivan Principles in South Africa," June 3, 1987, Emory University, President's Advisory Committee on South Africa records, Box 1.

61. A key exception to the ban on new investments by US nationals in South Africa was investments made to firms owned by Black South Africans.

62. Mark Pendergrast, *For God, Country, and Coca-Cola: The Definitive History of the Great American Soft Drink and the Company That Makes It* (Basic Books, 2000), 364. See also William E. Schmidt, "Coca-Cola Fills Atlanta With A Celebration of Its Centennial," *New York Times*, May 9, 1986.

63. John Kirby Spivey, "Coke vs. Pepsi: The Cola Wars in South Africa during The Anti-Apartheid Era" (master's thesis, Georgia State University, 2009), 32.

64. Goizueta quoted in Holly Planells, "Coke won't pull out of South Africa," United Press International, May 9, 1986, UPI Archives, https://www.upi.com/amp/Archives /1986/05/09/Coke-wont-pull-out-of-South-Africa/7063515995200/.

65. Bart Elmore, *Country Capitalism: How Corporations from the American South Remade Our Economy and the Planet* (University of North Carolina Press, 2023).

66. On activist struggles against apartheid in Atlanta, see Winston A. Grady-Willis, *Challenging U.S. Apartheid: Atlanta and Black Struggles for Human Rights, 1960–1977* (Duke University Press, 2006).

67. Connie Green and Keith Herndon, "Coke to sell its assets in South Africa," *Atlanta Constitution*, September 18, 1986.

68. Curtis quoted in Michael Isikoff, "Coke to Sell All Holdings in S. Africa," *Washington Post*, September 18, 1986.

69. Connie Green, "Coke Getting Out of South Africa," *Atlanta Journal*, September 17, 1986; Spivey, "Coke vs. Pepsi," 32–33; Bill Sing, "Coca-Cola Acts to Cut All Ties with S. Africa," *Los Angeles Times*, September 18, 1986.

70. John D. Battersby, "U.S. Goods in South Africa," *New York Times*, July 27, 1987.

71. Keough quoted in John Gorman, "Coke to Leave S. Africa," *Chicago Tribune*, September 18, 1986.

72. Ware quoted in Kathleen Teltsch, "Coca-Cola Giving $10 Million to Help South Africa Blacks," *New York Times*, March 24, 1986.

73. Lowery quoted in John Gorman, "Coke to Leave S. Africa," *Chicago Tribune*, September 18, 1986. See also Lowery's comments in Green and Herndon, "Coke to sell its assets in South Africa."

74. Young quoted in Isikoff, "Coke to Sell All Holdings in S. Africa." Among others who praised Coca-Cola's "divestment" was Rev. Jesse Jackson, who described the EOF as "a victory for those who want to get profits from the South African oppressors and give contributions to the apartheid opposers." See Jackson quoted in Teltsch, "Coca-Cola Giving $10 Million to Help South Africa Blacks."

75. "News Desk: Black Businessmen Aim for 30% Coke Share," *African Business* (February 1987).

76. Carl Ware, *Portrait of an American Businessman: One Generation from Cotton Field to Boardroom* (Mercer University Press, 2019), 140.

77. "Black Retailers to Buy Coke Shares," *African Business* (April 1987).

78. "News Desk: Plan to Revive Pepsi Plant," *African Business* (February 1988).

79. "Investments: Could Disinvestment Give Meaning to the Concept of Black Economic Empowerment?" *African Business* (July 1989).

80. Gcabashe quoted in Spivey, "Coke vs. Pepsi," 34.

81. Spivey, 36–38.

82. Desmond Tutu to Carl Ware, April 10, 1989, Ware papers, Box 28, Folder 3.

83. Desmond Tutu to Carl Ware, April 10, 1989, Ware papers, Box 28, Folder 3.

84. While a member of the SACP and read in Marx, Mandela, like other African communists, remained an Africanist first, committed to African liberation over

class revolution. Such a commitment sometimes put him in conflict with the white-dominated SACP. See Paul S. Landau "The ANC, MK, and 'The Turn to Violence,'" *South African Historical Journal* 64, no. 3 (2012): 538–63; Paul S. Landau, "Controlled by Communists? (Re)Assessing the ANC in its Exile Decades," *South African Historical Journal* 67, no. 2 (2015): 222–41.

85. Tom Lodge, "Mandela and the Left," *Journal of Southern African Studies*, 45, no. 6 (2019): 1069.

86. "While His ANC Counterpart Draws Lessons," *Daily World*, March 5, 1985, A. Philip Randolph Education Fund, David Jessup Papers, Emory University, Stuart A. Rose Manuscript, Archives, and Rare Books Library (hereafter cited as Jessup Papers), Box 20, Folder African National Congress.

87. Carol Anderson, *Eyes Off the Prize: The United Nations and the African American Struggle for Human Rights, 1944–1955* (Cambridge University Press, 2003); Kevin Gaines, *American Africans in Ghana: Black Expatriates and the Civil Rights Era* (University of North Carolina Press, 2008); Mary L. Dudziak, *Cold War Civil Rights: Race and the Image of American Democracy* (Princeton University Press, 2011); Thomas Borstelmann, *The Cold War and the Color Line: American Race Relations in the Global Arena* (Harvard University Press, 2003).

88. "While His ANC Counterpart Draws Lessons."

89. On the ANC's reliance on the Soviet Union, see Irina Filatova and Apollon Davidson, *The Hidden Thread: Russia and South Africa in the Soviet Era* (Jonathan Ball, 2013).

90. Ron Nixon, *Selling Apartheid: South Africa's Global Propaganda War* (Jacana Media, 2015).

91. Oliver Tambo to Sidney Poitier, June 5, 1987, Tambo Papers, 010/0074/7; Mark Gevisser, *Thabo Mbeki: A Dream Deferred* (Jonathan Ball, 2007), 169–70; Eric J. Morgan, "Into the Struggle: Confronting Apartheid in the United States and South Africa" (PhD diss., University of Colorado, 2009), 98–152. On the ANC's role constructing Mandela as an icon and symbol of the movement, see Elleke Boehmer, *Nelson Mandela: A Very Short Introduction* (Oxford University Press, 2008); Deborah Posel, "'Madiba Magic': Politics as Enchantment," in *The Cambridge Companion to Nelson Mandela*, ed. Rita Barnard (Cambridge University Press, 2014).

92. Howard Rosenberg, "TV Review: A Timely Apartheid Docudrama," *Los Angeles Times*, June 18, 1987; "Hollywood is Hot for Mandela Saga," *San Francisco Chronicle*, October 2, 1986, 20.

93. Ron Krabill, *Starring Mandela and Cosby: Media and the End(s) of Apartheid* (University of Chicago Press, 2010).

94. "Rights Gained for Film About Winnie Mandela," *New York Times*, August 19, 1986; "Personalities," *Washington Post*, August 19, 1986.

95. "Breaking the Barrier of Silence: Thousands Join Campaign to Unlock Apartheid's Jail," *American Committee on Africa Action Newsletter*, no. 24 (Winter 1987–88), Tambo Papers, 073/0779/3.

96. Dali Tambo to Camille Cosby, Tambo Papers, 010/0077/1.

97. Jessica Carney Smith, ed., *Encyclopedia of African American Business* (Greenwood Press, 2006), 807; "Introduction and Summary," Summary of Coca-Cola's Response to South African Divestment Campaign, circa 2006, Ware papers, Box 28, Folder 4.

98. "Interview with Nelson Mandela at first press conference given to local and foreign journalists by Mandela on his release from prison," February 13, 1990, Speeches by Nelson Mandela, http://www.mandela.gov.za/mandela_speeches/1990/900213_release .htm.

99. "Ending Apartheid in South Africa: Grassroots pressure helps produce change," American Friends Service Committee, Peace Works, http://peaceworks.afsc.org/ending -apartheid-south-africa; Spivey, "Coke vs. Pepsi," 36–37.

100. Neville Isdell with David Beasley, *Inside Coca-Cola: A CEO's Life Story of Building the World's Most Popular Brand* (St. Martin's Press, 2011), 115, 141–42.

101. "Mandela Tour Organizers Say They Reject Coke's Offer to Help," *AP News*, June 13, 1990; "Mandela Aides Bar Coke Bid: The African . . ." *Chicago Tribune*, June 14, 1990; Eleanor Randolph, "Mandela's Stops During U.S. Tour Reflect ANC Political Concerns," *Washington Post*, June 17, 1990, https://www.washingtonpost.com/archive/politics /1990/06/17/mandelas-stops-during-us-tour-reflect-anc-political-concerns/f41a84a3 -4aa5-462f-abc3-fc2a9213bb58/.

102. Deborah Marshall quoted in Ron Taylor and Joseph Albright, "Atlanta Opens Heart to Mandela: 50,000 Cheer ANC Leader at Stadium," *Atlanta Journal-Constitution*, June 28, 1990.

103. Makhathini quoted in Randolph, "Mandela's Stops During U.S. Tour Reflect ANC Political Concerns."

104. Lewis quoted in Randolph, "Mandela's Stops During U.S. Tour Reflect ANC Political Concerns."

105. Sheila Poole and Ernie Suggs, "'Welcome Home:' Mandela's 1990 Visit to Atlanta Rained Adoration," *Atlanta Journal-Constitution*, December 5, 2013; Neil Barsky and Asra Q. Nomani, "NWA in Talks to Operate, Buy Trump Shuttle," *Wall Street Journal*, March 8, 1991; Matt Viser, "Donald Trump's Airline Went from Opulence in the Air to Crash Landing," *Boston Globe*, May 27, 2016; "Special Friday Flashback: When Trump Ran 'The Shuttle,'" *Airways Magazine*, January 20, 2017.

106. Nicholas Kaplan, "Major Landlord Accused of Antiblack Bias in City," *New York Times*, October 16, 1973.

107. Tracy Wilkinson, "Trump Takes Mandela Under His Wing," *Los Angeles Times*, June 25, 1990; Deborah Hastings, "FBI Spied on Nelson Mandela During His First U.S. Trip: Report," *New York Daily News*, May 28, 2014.

108. Diane E. Lewis, "Mandela to Visit Boston During A Tour of US," *Boston Globe*, May 23, 1990; Interview by Carmen Fields with Themba Vilakazi and Janet Levine, *Ten O'Clock News*, June 20, 1990, Boston TV News Digital Library, https://bostonlocaltv.org /catalog/V_NQB2FPGOZ5V3Q38.

109. Photograph, Themba Vilakazi addressing a rally on Boston Common, April 4, 1986, African Activist Archive, https://africanactivist.msu.edu/image.php?objectid= 210-809-903; Leaflet, The Case for Pension Fund Divestment from South Africa, Boston Coalition for the Liberation of Southern Africa papers, African Activist Archive, https://africanactivist.msu.edu/document_metadata.php?objectid=210-808-8930; "A group of Boston University students say a decision . . . ," United Press International, October 11, 1985, UPI Archives, https://www.upi.com/Archives/1985/10/11/A-group-of-Boston-University-students-say-a-decision/8639497851200/.

110. Newsletter, *Fund For a Free South Africa* 1, no. 1 (January 1988); Themba Vilakazi, Fund for a Free South Africa Progress Report, Miloanne Hecathorn Papers, African Activist Archive, https://africanactivist.msu.edu/document_metadata.php?objectid= 210-808-5972.

111. Vilakazi, Fund for a Free South Africa Progress Report.

112. Poster, "First National Bank of Boston means Oppression in South Africa and Cutbacks for Boston"; Leaflet, "Boycott First National Bank!!," Boston Coalition for the Liberation of Southern Africa, circa 1979, Boston Coalition for the Liberation of Southern Africa papers, African Activist Archive, https://africanactivist.msu.edu/document _metadata.php?objectid=210-808-4130.

113. "Bank of Boston cuts off loans to South Africa," United Press International, March 25, 1985, UPI Archives, https://www.upi.com/Archives/1985/03/25/Bank-of-Boston-cuts-off-loans-to-South-Africa/6692480574800/.

114. FNBB Advertisement in Fund for a Free South Africa, "A Tribute to Nelson Mandela, June 23, 1990, 20, Private Collection of Willard Johnson, African Activist Archive, https://africanactivist.msu.edu/record/210-849-27708/.

115. "Address by Nelson Mandela at Options for Building an Economic Future Conference convened by the Consultative Business movement attended by South African business executives," May 23, 1990, Speeches by Nelson Mandela, http://www .mandela.gov.za/mandela_speeches/1990/900523_econ.htm.

116. On Mandela's embrace of business, see Colin Bundy, "The Challenge of Rethinking Mandela," *Journal of Southern African Studies* 45, no. 6 (2019): 1008–9.

117. "Address by Nelson Mandela at Options for Building an Economic Future Conference convened by the Consultative Business movement attended by South African business executives," May 23, 1990.

118. "Address by Nelson Mandela on Signing of Statement of Intent to Set Up a National Capacity for Economic Research and Policy Formulation," November 23, 1991, Speeches by Nelson Mandela, http://www.mandela.gov.za/mandela_speeches/1991 /911123_intent.htm.

119. "Address by Nelson Mandela at Options for Building an Economic Future Conference convened by the Consultative Business movement attended by South African business executives," May 23, 1990.

120. "Message by Nelson Mandela to USA Big Business," June 19, 1990, Speeches by Nelson Mandela, http://www.mandela.gov.za/mandela_speeches/1990/900619_bus.htm.

Many of the ideas expressed by Mandela were reiterated in the ANC's Reconstruction and Development program, which elaborated on the party's commitment to a "mixed economy" approach with government focused on the provisioning of social welfare, while also ensuring conditions necessary for private enterprise to thrive.

121. Draft of Report on Visit to South Africa, June 9–19, 1984, Prepared by Carl Ware, Ware papers, Box 28, Folder 5.

122. "Introduction and Summary," Summary of Coca-Cola's Response to South African Divestment Campaign, circa 2006, Ware papers, Box 28, Folder 4.

123. Motlana quoted in Hans Pienaar, "Doctor, Activist and Businessman Motlana Gave Life to Healing Apartheid's Wounds," *Cape Times*, December 2, 2008.

124. "President Nelson Mandela Visits U.S.; Seeks Business for South Africa," *Jet*, October 17, 1994.

125. Sullivan quoted in Vincent Thompson, "Sullivan: Economic Freedom as Important as Political Freedom," *Philadelphia Tribune*, April 29, 1994.

126. Kendall Wilson, "Sullivan Makes Triumphant Return to S. Africa," *Philadelphia Tribune*, September 2, 1994.

127. Donna Bryson, "Coke to Resume Business in S. Africa," *Seattle Times*, June 18, 1994.

128. Nelson Mandela to Carl Ware, July 28, 1993, Ware papers, Box 28, Folder 3.

Chapter 8

1. George Raine, Tupper Hull, and Eric Brazil, "L.A. Under Siege: Looters Hit Downtown Stores; Troops Deployed," *San Francisco Examiner*, April 30, 1992; "Los Angele Erupt After Officer Acquitted," *Cincinnati Post*, April 30, 1992; Linda Deutsch, "L.A. Explodes in Anger: Nine killed; Fires, Looting Sweep City," *Capital Times* (Madison, WI), April 30, 1992.

2. While LA garnered the most media attention, it was far from the only city to experience an urban uprising in this period. Similar rebellions in the Mount Pleasant neighborhood of Washington, DC, and Crown Heights in New York City preceded the LA riots, each occurring following a violent incident involving a Black victim.

3. Clinton quoted in Robert Pear, "Clinton Tours City's Damaged Areas and Chides Bush," *New York Times*, May 5, 1992.

4. "Platform: Alternatives to College: What's Out There?," *Los Angeles Times*, June 7, 1993.

5. Clinton quoted in Pear, "Clinton Tours City's Damaged Areas and Chides Bush." See also Robert Pear, "Clinton, In Attack on President, Ties Riots to 'Neglect,'" *New York Times*, May 6, 1992. Clinton's championing of empowerment politics and entrepreneurship fits with Lily Geismer's assessment of Clinton's and other New Democrats' belief in the market's ability to achieve traditional liberal goals of equality and social justice alongside economic growth and profits. See *Left Behind: The Democrats' Failed Attempt to Solve Inequality* (Public Affairs, 2022), 8–10, 144–145.

6. Various Black Economic Empowerment policies defined Black people in South Africa differently. At its broadest, the term Black included anyone discriminated against under apartheid, including Indians, Coloured, and other non-white people. A narrower categorization defined Black as people of African descent.

7. In addition to the various programs and policies promoting Black economic empowerment, the 1990s and early 2000s also witnessed an explosion in the discourse on Black empowerment as demonstrated by searches for the term "black empowerment" across multiple databases, including ProQuest (Newspapers, Books, Journal Articles), Google N-grams (Books), and Newspapers.com (Newspapers). This discourse, notably, resisted monopolization by any particular political party or organization, taken up by a variety of actors, ranging from Louis Farrakhan to George W. Bush Jr., who imbued the term with different meanings. Still, promoters of Black empowerment shared a general commitment to self-help and Black entrepreneurship reflecting the simultaneous rise of neoliberalism and "free markets."

8. Kit Konolige, "Rev. Sullivan to Retire: Leaving Pulpit to Aid Disadvantaged Youths and the Hungry," *Philadelphia Daily News*, January 6, 1988; Vanessa Williams, "Sullivan Retiring as Zion Pastor," *Philadelphia Inquirer*, January 7, 1988.

9. Harper quoted in Joe B. Warrick, "Author of 'Sullivan Principles' Retires," United Press International, January 7, 1988, UPI Archives, https://www.upi.com/Archives/1988/01/07/Author-of-Sullivan-Principles-retires/7514568530000/.

10. Sullivan quoted in Williams, "Sullivan Retiring as Zion Pastor."

11. Estimated attendance at the first African-African American Summit ranged between 1,000–2,000 attendees. Among those countries that sent official delegations were Cote d'Ivoire, Botswana, Burkina Faso, Gambia, Guinea-Bissau, Uganda, Morocco, Zaire, Gabon, Lesotho, Niger, Sao Tome and Principe, Senegal, Sierra Leone, Togo, Zambia, Benin, Cameroon, Ghana, Guinea, Mali, Nigeria, and Tanzania. Intermingling with Africans at the summit was a large delegation of Black Americans, including Benjamin Hooks, Joseph Lowery, Coretta Scott-King and Dorothy Height. See Official, Registered Delegation at the First African African-American Summit, Abidjan, Cote D'Ivoire, April 17–19, 1991, LHS papers, Box 19, Folder 7; Press Release, African Summit Launches Dual Citizenship Plan, LHS papers, Box 19, Folder 8; Niara Sudarkasa, "African Summit: Forming New Bonds," *Focus* 19, no. 7 (July 1991): 5, LHS papers, Box 19, Folder 8.

12. Reverend Leon H. Sullivan speaking at the Third African-African American Summit in Dakar, Senegal, 1995, posted June 21, 2012, by the Sullivan Foundation, YouTube, https://www.youtube.com/watch?v=ah_ugqyUkUo.

13. Robert Lensink, *Structural Adjustment in Sub-Saharan Africa* (Longman, 1996).

14. Thomas M. Callaghy, "Debt and Structural Adjustment in Africa: Realities and Possibilities," *Issue: A Journal of Opinion* 16, no. 2 (1988): 11–18.

15. Press Release, African Summit Launches Dual Citizenship Plan, LHS papers, Box 19, Folder 8.

16. Elmer Smith, "A Natural for U.S. Blacks: Rev. Sullivan Urges Help for Sub-Saharan Africans," *Daily News*, January 29, 1991, LHS papers, Box 19, Folder 8.

17. Daniel Geary, Camilla Schofield, and Jennifer Sutton, eds., *Global White Nationalism: From Apartheid to Trump* (Manchester University Press, 2020). These appeals to racial identity coincided with and ran counter to simultaneous pronouncements that claimed the 1990s the decade of multiculturalism. See Roger Hewitt, *White Backlash and the Politics of Multiculturalism* (Cambridge University Press, 2009).

18. Press Release, African Summit Launches Dual Citizenship Plan.

19. Declaration of Principles and Actions, The First African/African American Summit on the Development of Sub-Saharan Africa and the Strengthening of America's Support for the Region, LHS papers, Box 19, Folder 9; Niara Sudarkasa, "African Summit: Forming New Bonds," *Focus* 19, no. 7 (July 1991): 5, LHS papers, Box 19, Folder 8.

20. Declaration of Principles and Actions, The First African/African American Summit on the Development of Sub-Saharan Africa and the Strengthening of America's Support for the Region.

21. Press Release, African Summit Launches Dual Citizenship Plan.

22. Among the list of companies that joined the support group were Citicorp, Merck & Co., and General Motors.

23. 1st African-African American Summit Invitation Letter, May 4, 1992, LHS papers, Box 19, Folder 6; Greg DeYonker to Leon H. Sullivan, May 4, 1992, LHS papers, Box 19, Folder 19.

24. Mandela, Sullivan, and author quoted in Askia Muhammad, "Mandela: Blacks Must Unite Throughout World," *New Pittsburgh Courier*, August 30, 1997.

25. Sullivan quoted in William R. Macklin, "Expanding His Quest for Equality," *Philadelphia Inquirer*, October 31, 1999, LHS papers, Box 61, Folder 3.

26. Announcement of the Global Sullivan Principles, November 2, 1999, LHS papers, Box 61, Folder 3.

27. Announcement of the Global Sullivan Principles.

28. On the consumer and public interest movement behind these protests, see Paul Adler, *No Globalization Without Representation: U.S. Activists and World Inequality* (University of Pennsylvania Press, 2021).

29. The Global Sullivan Principles, February 1, 1999, LHS papers, Box 61, Folder 3.

30. The term "crisis," as Benjamin Holtzman notes, while easily and regularly deployed as hyperbole by those with racist, sexist, and other kinds of anti-democratic agendas, at other times reflected the sentiments of urban residents concerned with the very real crises, including "aging housing, unstable municipal budgets, a declining industrial economic base, rising welfare rolls, dilapidated parks," etc., afflicting late twentieth-century urban America. See *The Long Crisis: New York City and the Path to Neoliberalism* (Oxford University Press, 2021), 1.

31. Kimberly Phillips-Fein, *Fear City: New York's Fiscal Crisis and the Rise of Austerity Politics* (MacMillan, 2017); Destin Jenkins, *The Bonds of Inequality: Debt and the Making of the American City* (University of Chicago Press, 2021).

32. The interplay between racialized policing, mass incarceration, and austerity politics has features prominently in recent scholarship on the carceral state, including in a special issue, "Historians and the Carceral State," ed. Kelly Lytle Hernández, Khalil Gibran Muhammad, and Heather Ann Thompson, of *The Journal of American History* 102, no. 1 (June 2015).

33. Bradley quoted in Jane Fritsch, "Riots in Los Angeles," *New York Times*, May 4, 1992.

34. William Julius Wilson, "Imagine Life Without a Future," *Los Angeles Times*, May 6, 1992.

35. On the rise of free ports, tax havens, and other special economic zones, see Dara Orenstein, "Foreign-Trade Zones and the Cultural Logic of Frictionless Production," *Radical History Review* 109 (2011): 36–61; Vanessa Ogle, "Archipelago Capitalism: Tax Havens, Offshore Money, and the State, 1950s–1970s," *American Historical Review* 122, no. 5 (2017): 1431–58"; Quinn Slobodian, *Crack-Up Capitalism: Market Radicals and the Dream of a World Without Democracy* (Metropolitan Books, 2023).

36. Ronald Reagan, "Message to the Congress Transmitting Proposed Enterprise Zones Legislation," March 23, 1982, Ronald Reagan Presidential Library & Museum, https://www.reaganlibrary.gov/archives/speech/message-congress-transmitting -proposed-enterprise-zones-legislation; W. Manning Marable, "Reaganism, Racism, and Reaction: Black Political Realignment in the 1980s," *The Black Scholar* 13, no. 6 (Fall 1982): 2.

37. Kevin D. Bird, "Bringing New Life to Enterprise Zones: Congress Finally Takes the First Step with the Housing and Community Development Act of 1987," *Washington University Journal of Urban and Contemporary Law* 35, no. 1 (1989): 109–27.

38. Rooted in empire, special economic or enterprise zones gained prominence during the late twentieth and early twenty-first centuries amid conservative efforts to safeguard private capital from national politics, including government regulation and democracy. See Ogle, "Archipelago Capitalism;" Slobodian, *Crack-Up Capitalism*

39. Tananarive Due, "Louis Farrakhan: Many Blacks Listening to Nationalist Leader," *Kenosha News* (Kenosha, WI), August 7, 1994; Peggy Landers, "Islam's Message Draws Praise, Ire for Being Militant," *Salt Lake Tribune*, August 13, 1994.

40. Clinton quoted in "Transcript of Clinton's Address to a Joint Session of Congress," *New York Times*, February 18, 1993, A20.

41. Debate over the Omnibus Budget Reconciliation Act, as well as the EZ/EC's inclusion in it, was hotly contested and prolonged. It was, notably, New York Congressman Charles Rangel, a prominent member of the House Ways and Means Committee and the Congressional Black Caucus, who helped shepherd the bill through, despite initial hesitancies with regard to the success of the concept, including ensuring social

grants remained a part of the 1993 legislation. See Sarah F. Liebschutz, "Empowerment Zones and Enterprise Communities: Reinventing Federalism for Distressed Communities," *Publius* 25, no. 3 (1995): 123–24.

42. While official program language utilized the race-neutral language of "depressed areas," the Empowerment Zones program had a strong association with Black America, with six out of the nine initial zones located in cities with Black majorities.

43. Larry Copeland, Lea Sitton, and Larry Fish, "Envisioning Empowerment: Poor Vie for Slice of Federal Aid," *Philadelphia Inquirer*, March 28, 1994.

44. Fact Sheet: Empowerment Zones and Enterprise Communities, Domestic Policy Council, Carol Rasco, and Issues Series, "EZ/EC [Empowerment Zones/Enterprise Communities]," December 21, 1994, *Clinton Digital Library*, https://clinton.presidential libraries.us/items/show/18412.

45. Geismer, *Left Behind*, 150–51.

46. Fact Sheet: Empowerment Zones and Enterprise Communities.

47. Fact Sheet: Empowerment Zones and Enterprise Communities.

48. Copeland, Sitton, and Fish, "Envisioning Empowerment."

49. Copeland, Sitton, and Fish, "Envisioning Empowerment."

50. Leon H. Sullivan, *Build, Brother, Build: From Poverty to Economic Power* (Macrae Smith Company, 1969), 57–58.

51. On the multiple waves of arson, including arson-for-profit, in Black and Brown communities, see Bench Ansfield, "The Crisis of Insurance and the Insuring of the Crisis: Riot Reinsurance and Redlining in the Aftermath of the 1960s Uprisings," *Journal of American History* 107, no. 4 (2021): 899–921; Dylan Gottlieb, "Hoboken Is Burning: Yuppies, Arson, and Displacement in the Postindustrial City," *Journal of American History* 106, no. 2 (2019): 390–416.

52. Alston quoted in Anthony S. Twyman, "The Jump Street Blues," *Philadelphia Daily News*, April 10, 1995. On Jim Crow nostalgia, see Michelle R. Boyd, *Jim Crow Nostalgia: Reconstructing Race in Bronzeville* (University of Minnesota Press, 2008).

53. Needle quoted in Twyman, "The Jump Street Blues."

54. Sheila Simmons, "N. Phila., 7 Years into Plan," *Philadelphia Daily News*, March 19, 1993.

55. Joseph P. Blake, "North Philadelphia Revitalization Gets a Starting Point," *Philadelphia Daily News*, February 22, 1989.

56. Sheila Simmons, "N. Phila., 7 Years into Plan," *Philadelphia Daily News*, March 19, 1993.

57. Lea Sitton, Craig R. McCoy, Larry Copeland, and Dwight Ott, "Hope and Skepticism on Federal Aid Zones," *Philadelphia Inquirer*, July 11, 1994.

58. Simmons, "N. Phila., 7 Years into Plan."

59. "How the Plan is Shaking Out: Cecil B. Moore Avenue Business Corridor," *Philadelphia Daily News*, March 19, 1993; Twyman, "The Jump Street Blues." On the late-twentieth-century rise in Black tourism and its discontents, see Danielle Wiggins, "'Save Auburn Avenue for Our Black Heritage': Debating Development in Post-Civil Rights

Atlanta," *Journal of African American History* 107, no. 1 (2022): 79–104; Christopher Coady, "New Orleans Rhythm and Blues, African American Tourism, and the Selling of a Progressive South," *American Music* 37, no. 1 (2019): 95–112; Elizabeth Grant, "Race, Place, and Memory: African American Tourism in Postindustrial City," in *African American Urban History since World War II*, ed. Kenneth L. Kusmer and Joe W. Trotter (University of Chicago Press, 2009).

60. Temple's expansion into North Philadelphia is but one example of what Davarian Baldwin has described as the rise of Univer-cities, in which colleges and universities have come to play a driving role in facilitating and perpetuating urban inequality. See *In the Shadow of the Tower: How Universities Are Plundering Our Cities* (Public Affairs, 2021).

61. Twyman, "The Jump Street Blues."

62. Nelson quoted in Twyman, "The Jump Street Blues."

63. Twyman, "The Jump Street Blues."

64. "OIC 30 Years and Going Strong," *Philadelphia Daily News*, October 7, 1994.

65. Larry Copeland, "A Hotel Equipped for Learning," *Philadelphia Inquirer*, May 9, 1991.

66. "Sullivan Expected to Visit Groundbreaking for Center," *Philadelphia Inquirer*, May 15, 1994.

67. Rosland Briggs, "A Food Distributor's Move is a Neighborhood's Win," *Philadelphia Inquirer*, March 24, 1999; Thomas J. Brady, "Incentives and Merger Keep Furniture Distributor in City," *Philadelphia Inquirer*, April 20, 2002.

68. "The Coca-Cola Company announced Monday the sale of part . . ." United Press International, July 19, 1983, UPI Archives, https://www.upi.com/Archives/1983/07/19/The-Coca-Cola-Company-announced-Monday-the-sale-of-part/4925427435200/.

69. "Lawyer, Dr. J Take Over Coke Bottling Firm," *Los Angeles Times*, December 19, 1985, https://www.latimes.com/archives/la-xpm-1985-12-19-fi-30555-story.html.

70. Coca-Cola Senior Vice President Tomas Orenstein quoted in "Lawyer, Dr. J Take Over Coke Bottling Firm." The pattern of 51/49 (or 52/48) share agreements is discussed in Chapter 5, Empowering Africa.

71. Sheila Simmons, "Local Bottling Firm Adds Some Pop," *Philadelphia Daily News*, June 22, 1989.

72. John F. Morrison, "Obituary: J. Bruce Llewellyn, pioneering executive," *Philadelphia Inquirer*, April 9, 2010; Jeffrey McKinney, "45 Great Moments in Black Business—No. 19: J. Bruce Llewellyn and Dr. J's $100 Million Coke Bottling Franchise," *Black Enterprise*, December 22, 2017.

73. Simmons, "Local Bottling Firm Adds Some Pop." On McDonalds's sponsorship of Black community uplift, see Marcia Chatelain, *Franchise: The Golden Arches in Black America* (W. W. Norton, 2020).

74. Peter Binzen, "For North Philadelphia, Coca-Cola is it," *Philadelphia Inquirer*, May 18, 1998.

75. Wilson quoted in Binzen, "For North Philadelphia, Coca-Cola is it."

76. This number was actually up from 11 percent prior to Llewellyn taking over the plant. See Binzen, "For North Philadelphia, Coca-Cola is it."

77. Peter Nicholas, "Empowerment Zone at Center of Probe by FBI," *Philadelphia Inquirer*, March 16, 1999.

78. Ledyard King, "Cumberland Loses Out on Aid Shortfall: Empowerment Zone Designation Brought Hope, But Little Money," *Daily Journal* (Vineland, NJ), September 23, 2000; John Bebow, "Probe Targets Empowerment Zone," *Detroit News and Free Press*, February 11, 1996.

79. Stephen Ohlemacher, "Inner City Job Rates Continue to Decline Despite Federal Help," *Lansing State Journal* (Lansing, MI), November 29, 2005. Other researchers concluded the Philadelphia EZ program was responsible for a mere 1,700 new jobs between 1994 and 2000. See Jennifer Brown, "Ad Agency Thrives on Being Different," *Sentinel* (Carlisle, PA), September 1, 2000.

80. Denise Clay, "Mandela to come for the 4th," *Philadelphia Tribune*, May 21, 1993.

81. William J. Clinton: "The President's News Conference with President Nelson Mandela of South Africa," October 5, 1994, online at The American Presidency Project, https://www.presidency.ucsb.edu/node/218275.

82. "President Nelson Mandela Visits U.S.; Seeks Business for South Africa," *Jet*, October 17, 1994.

83. Sullivan quoted in Vincent Thompson, "Sullivan: Economic Freedom as Important as Political Freedom," *Philadelphia Tribune*, April 29, 1994. See also Kendall Wilson, "Sullivan Makes Triumphant Return to S. Africa," *Philadelphia Tribune*, September 2, 1994.

84. "Ferraro Says Pepsico Will Sell Plant in South Africa," *Los Angeles Times*, May 15, 1985; "News Desk: Plan to Revive Pepsi Plant," *African Business* (February 1988); Adrian Croft, "Black Group Tries to Revive Pepsi Africa," *The Globe and Mail*, March 22, 1988.

85. Anthony Ramierez, "Pepsico Out of South Africa Following Failure of Bottler," *New York Times*, April 12, 1990; John Kirby Spivey, "Coke vs. Pepsi: The Cola Wars in South Africa during The Anti-Apartheid Era" (master's thesis, Georgia State University, 2009), 30–40.

86. Sinclair quoted in Glenn Collins, "Pepsi and South Africa To Get Together Again," *New York Times*, June 7, 1994.

87. Jay Matthews, "New Investment Age in S. Africa: Pepsi Teams with African Americans in Returning to Country," *Washington Post*, October 4, 1994; Glenn Collins, "Pepsi and South Africa To Get Together Again," *New York Times*, June 7, 1994.

88. Mthembu quoted in Collins, "Pepsi and South Africa To Get Together Again." See also Nelvis Qekema, "A Tribute to Cde Khehla Mthembu by Cde Nelvis Qekema," *Azapo Tributes*, July 13, 2021, https://azapo.org.za/2021/07/13/a-tribute-to-cde-khehla-mthembu-by-cde-nelvis-qekema/. Mthembu's path from anti-apartheid activist to business executive proved a common one, pursued by many Black Consciousness, ANC, and trade union activists, including, most notably, President Cyril Ramaphosa.

89. Liz Sly, "Pepsi's Return to the New S. Africa Turns Sour," *Chicago Tribune*, December 19, 1994, https://www.chicagotribune.com/news/ct-xpm-1994-12-19-94121 90172-story.html; Bill Keller, "Corporate Foe of Apartheid Finds Reward Elusive," *New York Times*, December 9, 1994.

90. Mathlejoane quoted in Sly, "Pepsi's Return to the New S. Africa Turns Sour."

91. Keller, "Corporate Foe of Apartheid Finds Reward Elusive."

92. Sly, "Pepsi's Return to the New S. Africa Turns Sour"; Paul Taylor, "Pepsi Returns to S. Africa is Troubled," *Washington Post*, November 20, 1994.

93. Sly, "Pepsi's Return to the New S. Africa Turns Sour."

94. Nelson Mandela, State of the Nation Address, House of Parliament, Cape Town, South Africa, May 24, 1994, South African Government, https://www.gov.za/news /speeches/president-nelson-mandela-1994-state-nation-address-24-may-1994. In addition to extreme rates of unemployment, one of the biggest challenges facing the ANC in the early 1990s was the country's debt. As part of the negotiations surrounding the transition to democracy, ANC leaders agreed to take on a sizeable portion of the nation's debt, which, by the early 1990s, had reached exorbitant levels, at one point exceeding 46 percent of GDP, amid the Afrikaaner Nationalist Party's efforts to hold onto power. See "Apartheid Debt Settled," *News 24*, September 3, 2001, https://www.news24.com/Fin24 /apartheid-debt-settled-20010903. See also Léonce Ndikumana and James K. Boyce, *Africa's Odious Debts: How Foreign Loans and Capital Flight Bled a Continent* (Bloomsbury Academic, 2011), 88.

95. Nelson Mandela, State of the Nation Address, House of Parliament, Cape Town, South Africa, May 24, 1994.

96. The choice of Metropolitan Life (Metpol) was fitting given the company's history of selling insurance to Black South Africans. At the time of the transfer, 50 percent of Metpol's business stemmed from selling insurance to Black South Africans, while another 30 percent came from sales to Coloured South Africans. See Grietjie Verhoef, *The Power of Your Life: The Sanlam Century of Insurance Empowerment, 1918–2018* (Oxford University Press, 2018), 184.

97. Donald G. McNeil Jr., "South Africa Blacks Lose Control of Black Empowerment Company," *New York Times*, August 6, 1999.

98. Roger Southall, "Ten Propositions About Black Economic Empowerment in South Africa," *Review of African Political Economy* 34, no. 111 (2007): 73–75.

99. The past several decades have given rise to an extensive literature on the ANC's program of Black Economic Empowerment. While acknowledging BEE's success—including, most notably, in fueling the expansion of a Black business class—the literature has underscored BEE's failure to engender the kind of large-scale economic transformation demanded by South Africans. See Duncan James Randall, "Prospects for the Development of a Black Business Class in South Africa," *Journal of Modern African Studies* 34, no. 4 (1996): 661–86; Okechukwu C. Iheduru, "Black Economic Power and Nation-Building in Post-Apartheid South Africa," *Journal of Modern African Studies* 42, no. 1 (2004): 1–30; Dume Gqubule, *Making Mistakes, Righting Wrongs: Insights*

into Black Economic Empowerment (Jonathan Ball, 2006); Southall, "Ten Propositions about Black Economic Empowerment in South Africa"; Stefano Ponte, Simon Roberts, and Lance van Sittert, "'Black Economic Empowerment', Business and the State," *Development and Change* 38, no. 5 (2007): 933–55; Bill Freund, "South Africa: The End of Apartheid and the Emergence of the 'BEE Elite,'" *Review of African Political Economy* 34, no. 114 (2007): 661–78; Roger Tangri and Roger Southall, "The Politics of Black Economic Empowerment in South Africa," *Journal of Southern African Studies* 34, no. 3 (2008): 699–716.

100. O'mano Emma Edigheji, *The Evolution of 'Black Economic Empowerment' in South Africa: From the Lenses of Business, the Tripartite Alliance, Community Groups, and the Apartheid and Post-Apartheid Governments (1985–1999)* (National Labour and Economic Development Institute, 2000), 3–4. See also Sipho Sibusiso Maseko, "Black Bourgeoisie in South Africa: From Pavement Entrepreneurs to Stock Exchange Capitalists" (PhD diss., University of the Western Cape, 2000).

101. "Joe Manchu: The Power of Networking," *Black Enterprise (SA)* 11 (1987).

102. Tsitsi D. Wakhisi, "African-American Settlers Flock to South Africa," *The Crisis*, July 1994, 40.

103. Kevin Gaines, *American Africans in Ghana: Black Expatriates and the Civil Rights Era* (University of North Carolina Press, 2008).

104. Juliet E. K. Walker, "Neocolonialism in the African Diaspora?: Black American Business Competition in South Africa," in *Black Business and Economic Power*, ed. Alusine Jalloh and Toyin Falola (University of Rochester Press, 2002).

105. Wakhisi, "African-American Settlers Flock to South Africa."

106. Mandela quoted in Wakhisi, "African-American Settlers Flock to South Africa," 17–18.

107. Cassandra Hayes, "Can a New Frontier Boost Your Career," *Black Enterprise*, May 1995.

108. Thurow quoted in Walker, "Neocolonialism in the African Diaspora?," 545.

109. Hazlewood quoted in Hayes, "Can a New Frontier Boost Your Career."

110. Mohammad Amir Anwar, "White People in South Africa Still Hold the Lion's Share of All Forms of Capital," *The Conversation*, April 24, 2017, https://theconversation.com/white-people-in-south-africa-still-hold-the-lions-share-of-all-forms-of-capital-75510.

111. George W. Bush, Remarks at the Leon H. Sullivan Summit in Abuja, July 12, 2003, in *Public Papers of the Presidents of the United States: George W. Bush, 2003, Book II* (US Government Printing Office), 865–67.

112. Remarks by President Obama at the Global Entrepreneurship Summit, United Nations Compound, Nairobi, Kenya, The White House, Office of the Press Secretary, July 25, 2015, https://obamawhitehouse.archives.gov/the-press-office/2015/07/25/remarks-president-obama-global-entrepreneurship-summit.

113. The Reconstruction and Development Programme, Building the Economy, March 1, 1994, African National Congress, Policy Documents, https://www.anc1912

.org.za/policy-documents-1994-the-reconstruction-and-development-programme -building-the-economy/.

114. Mbeki quoted in "SA needs black bourgeoisie: Mbeki," *IOL*, November 20, 1999, https://www.iol.co.za/news/politics/sa-needs-black-bourgeoisie-mbeki-20213.

115. Judith Evans, "Baltimore's Dawn of an Urban Renaissance: Empowerment Program Pays Off in Jobs and Hope," *Washington Post*, November 2, 1996; Charles B. Rangel, "Harlem Empowerment Zone Embraces People and Business," *New York Times*, April 24, 1995.

116. Donald G. McNeil Jr., "Once Bitter Enemies, Now Business Partners: South African Blacks Buy into Industry," *New York Times*, September 24, 1996; "S. Africa Firm's Sale is Landmark Deal," *Los Angeles Times*, August 29, 1996.

117. Hugh Dellios, "Empowerment or Money Grab?," *Chicago Tribune*, September 29, 1996; Robert J. Lopez, "A Federally Funded Empowerment Zone Is Good News for L.A., but Its Limited Size Will Exclude Many Needy Areas," *Los Angeles Times*, November 7, 1993; McNeil Jr., "South Africa Blacks Lose Control of Black Empowerment Company."

118. Recent scholarship has revealed the persistence of the racial wealth gap in the US and South Africa. See, for example, Elise Gould, "Black-White Wage Gaps Are Worse Today Than in 2000," Working Economics Blog, Economic Policy Institute, February 27, 2020, https://www.epi.org/blog/black-white-wage-gaps-are-worse-today-than-in-2000/; National Bureau of Economic Research, "Exploring 160 Years of the Black-White Wealth Gap," *The NBER Digest* (August 2022): 1–6; Antony Sguazzin, "South Africa Wealth Gap Unchanged Since Apartheid, Says World Inequality Lab," *Time*, August 5, 2021; Grieve Chelwa, Mashekwa Maboshe, & Darrick Hamilton, "The Racial Wealth Gap in South Africa and the United States," *Review of Political Economy* 36, no. 2 (2024): 423–40.

Epilogue

1. "Leon Sullivan, 1922–2001," *Arizona Daily Star*, April 30, 2001.

2. Claudia Levy, "Civil Rights Crusader Leon Sullivan Dies," *Washington Post*, April 26, 2001.

3. Jackson quoted in Jacques Billeaud, "Civil Rights Leader Praised for Unifying Spirit," *Arizona Daily Star*, May 2, 2001; F. Finley McRae, "World, U.S. Leaders Eulogize Rev. Leon Sullivan," *Los Angeles Sentinel*, May 3, 2001.

4. Associated Press, "Activist Leon Sullivan Dies," *The Record* (NJ), April 26, 2001.

5. Kanya quoted in Jacques Billeaud, "Civil Rights Crusader Eulogized as Visionary," *Courier-Post* (Camden, NJ), May 2, 2001.

6. Annan quoted in Kendall Wilson, "Dr. Leon H. Sullivan Built a Legacy," *Philadelphia Tribune*, April 27, 2001.

7. "Ex-UN Envoy Andrew Young Replaces Leon Sullivan As Summit Chair," *Jet*, August 20, 2001; "Daughter, Former Greensboro Colleague Carry On Leon Sullivan's Legacy," *WFMY News*, May 24, 2003, https://www.wfmynews2.com/article/news/local /daughter-former-greensboro-colleague-carry-on-leon-sullivans-legacy/83-404089021.

8. Opportunities Industrialization Centers of America, https://oicofamerica.org/; Opportunities Industrialization Centers International, https://oici.org/.

9. Stephen Williams, "OIC of America launches expanded national Sullivan Training Network," *Philadelphia Tribune*, August 7, 2023; "Sullivan Training Network," OIC of America, accessed July 9, 2024, https://oicofamerica.org/sullivan-training-network/.

10. Obama quotes in "Obama's Early Morning," *Temple News* (Temple University, PA), October 14, 2008, https://temple-news.com/obamas-early-morning/.

11. The 2008 recession disproportionately affected Black Americans. By comparison, between December 2007 and December 2009, the nation's overall unemployment rate rose from 4.9 percent to 10 percent, while the white rate climbed from 4.4 percent to 9.3 percent. See Associated Press, "Advocates Want More for Black Unemployed," *NBC News*, December 22, 2009, https://www.nbcnews.com/id/wbna34539582.

12. Associated Press, "Advocates Want More for Black Unemployed."

13. Obama quoted in Associated Press, "Advocates Want More for Black Unemployed."

14. Keeanga-Yamahtta Taylor, *From #BlackLivesMatter to Black Liberation* (Haymarket Books, 2019).

15. "Fact Sheet: The American Jobs Act," Press Release, September 8, 2011, The White House, President Barack Obama, Office of the Press Secretary, https://obamawhitehouse.archives.gov/the-press-office/2011/09/08/fact-sheet-american-jobs-act; Barack Obama, Fact Sheet: American Job Training Investments—Skills and Jobs to Build a Stronger Middle Class, April 16, 2014, online at The American Presidency Project, https://www.presidency.ucsb.edu/node/308867.

16. Barack Obama, Press Release—"We Can't Wait: The White House Announces Federal and Private Sector Commitments to Provide Employment Opportunities for Nearly 180,000 Youth," January 4, 2012, online at The American Presidency Project, https://www.presidency.ucsb.edu/node/351738.

17. "Remarks by President Obama at the Global Entrepreneurship Summit," United Nations Compound, Nairobi, Kenya, The White House, Office of the Press Secretary, July 25, 2015, https://obamawhitehouse.archives.gov/the-press-office/2015/07/25/remarks-president-obama-global-entrepreneurship-summit.

18. Calvin Butler, Ron Peterson, and Ronald Daniels, "A commitment to 'BLocal' in Baltimore," *Baltimore Sun*, April 7, 2016.

19. Tracy Jan, Jena McGregor, and Meghan Hoyer, "Corporate America's $50 billion promise," *Washington Post*, August 23, 2021.

20. Manthata and Bam quoted in Andrew Maykuth, "Recalling the effect of Sullivan Principles," *Philadelphia Inquirer*, April 29, 2001.

21. Broad-Based Black Economic Empowerment Act 53 of 2003 (South Africa).

22. Broad-Based Black Economic Empowerment Amendment Act 46 of 2003 (South Africa).

23. Roger Southall, "Ten Propositions about Black Economic Empowerment in South Africa," *Review of African Political Economy* 34, no. 111 (March 2007): 67–84;

Roger Tangri and Roger Southall, "The Politics of Black Economic Empowerment in South Africa," *Journal of Southern African Studies* 34, no. 3 (2008): 699–716.

24. "Mbeki Approves Empowerment Act," *Mail & Guardian* (Johannesburg, South Africa), January 9, 2004.

25. Tutu quoted in "Tutu Warns of Poverty 'Powder Keg,'" *BBC News*, November 23, 2004, http://news.bbc.co.uk/2/hi/africa/4035809.stm.

26. "Transcript of Nelson Mandela Annual Lecture 2015," University of Johannesburg, October 3, 2015, Nelson Mandela Foundation, https://www.nelsonmandela.org/news/entry/transcript-of-nelson-mandela-annual-lecture-2015.

27. "South Africa Most Unequal Country in the World: Report, International Center for Transitional Justice," International Center for Transitional Justice, March 10, 2022, https://www.ictj.org/node/35024#:~:text=South%20Africa%20is%20the%20most,World%20Bank%20report%20has%20said; Victor Sulla, Precious Zikhali, and Pablo Facundo Cuevas, *Inequality in Southern Africa: An Assessment of the Southern African Customs Union* (World Bank Group, 2022), http://documents.worldbank.org/curated/en/099125303072236903/P1649270c02a1f06b0a3ae02e57eadd7a82.

28. Greg Grandin, *Fordlandia: The Rise and Fall of Henry Ford's Forgotten Jungle City* (Macmillan, 2010); Nan Enstad, *Cigarettes, Inc.: An Intimate History of Corporate Imperialism* (University of Chicago Press, 2018); Gregg Mitman, *Empire of Rubber: Firestone's Scramble for Land and Power in Liberia* (New Press, 2021).

29. Ryan M. Irwin, *Gordian Knot: Apartheid and the Unmaking of the Liberal World Order* (Oxford University Press, 2012).

30. Francis Njubi Nesbitt, *Race for Sanctions: African Americans against Apartheid, 1946–1994* (Indiana University Press, 2004).

31. Jones quoted in TaRhonda Thomas, "OIC Celebrates Decades of Creating New Opportunities," *6ABC News*, September 1, 2023, https://6abc.com/opportunities-industrialization-center-philadelphia-block-party-today-oic-darlene-jones/13726347/.

32. Business Partners Limited, "30 Years On, Entrepreneurs are Making the Most of SA's Enduring Miracle," *Biz Community*, April 24, 2024, https://www.bizcommunity.com/article/30-years-on-entrepreneurs-are-making-the-most-of-sas-enduring-miracle-786922a.

33. Taylor Telford, "2024 Might be Do-or-Die for Corporate Diversity Efforts. Here's Why," *Washington Post*, December 27, 2023, https://www.washingtonpost.com/business/2023/12/27/dei-affirmative-action-legal-challenges-corporate-america/.

34. While there are indications that global inequality—between countries—has decreased, inequality within most countries remains high and, in many cases, has expanded in recent decades. In the US, for example, from 1983 to 2016, the share of aggregate wealth going to upper-income families increased from 60 percent to 79 percent. During that same period, lower-income family wealth decreased from 7 percent to 4 percent. See Juliana Menasce Horowitz, Ruth Igielnik, and Rakesh Kochhar, "Trends in Income and Wealth Inequality," Pew Research Center, January 9, 2020, https://www.pewresearch.org/social-trends/2020/01/09/trends-in-income-and-wealth-inequality/;

See also "Nine Charts about Wealth Inequality in America," Urban Institute, April 25, 2024, https://apps.urban.org/features/wealth-inequality-charts/. Some of the lowest incomes and levels of wealth, moreover, continue to be seen in the Black world, including Africa. See Lucas Chancel, Thomas Piketty, Emmanuel Saez, and Gabriel Zucman, "World Inequality Report 2022," World Inequality Lab, wir2022.wid.world.

35. Danilo Trsis and Matt Saenz, "Economic Security Programs Reduce Overall Poverty, Racial and Ethnic Inequities," Center on Budget and Policy Priorities, July 1, 2021, https://www.cbpp.org/research/poverty-and-inequality/more-than-4-in-10-children-in-renter-households-face-food-andor; World Bank, *The State of Social Safety Nets* (World Bank, 2018), http://hdl.handle.net/10986/29115.

INDEX

urban renewal, 63, 69, 76, 274n41
US Agency for International Development
    (USAID), 7, 12, 99, 103–5, 107–8,
    119–21, 124
US Bureau of International Commerce
    Africa Division, 107
US Department of Commerce, 107

Vance, Cyrus, 143
Vilakazi, Themba, 207
Virginia Jubilee Singers, 28–29, 139
Volta Aluminum Company (VALCO), 107
Volta River Project, 107
Vundla, Phillip Qipu, 161–62

Walker, Juliet E.K., 235
Wall Street Journal, 89, 126
Ware, Carl, 187–89, 191–92, 200–01, *202,
    205–6, 211, 212,* 213. *See also* Coca-Cola
War on Poverty, 5, 11, 65, 71–73, 78–82,
    85, 94, 96, 215, 275n48. *See also* John-
    son, Lyndon B.
Washington, Booker T., 10, 17–22, 25–26,
    30–31, 255n5. *See also* racial uplift
    politics
The Washington Post, 120, 145, 194, 239
Weedon, D. Reid, Jr., 149–51
Western Union Telegraph Company, 86
West Virginia State College, 22–23
Wheeler, John, 164
White, Walter, 37
white flight, 43, 53, 69, 72, 264n19
Wiehahn Commission, 148, 299n104
Wilberforce Institute, 18, 28–31
Wilcock, James W., 141
Wilkins, Roy, 145
William Penn Foundation, 225

Williams, Ken, 135
Wilson, Ian, 231
Wilson, James Q., 47
Wilson, Ronald, 228
Winn Dixie, 189–90
women's empowerment, 10, 83, 133–34,
    172, 212, 214, 242–43, 253–54n34
Wood, Thomas A., *114*
Woodland Job Training Center, 87–88, *88*
Woodruff, Robert, 199
Woodson, Carter G., 22
Woodward, Samuel L., 84
World Bank, 117, 217, 244, 290n104

Ylvisaker, Paul, 73–74
Young, Andrew: 1979 trade mission and
    113–16, *115*; on cooperation with the
    private sector, 184–85; on divesting, 200;
    Leon H. Sullivan Foundation and, 240;
    as a proponent of Black empowerment,
    116; Sullivan Principles and, 143; as US
    ambassador to the United Nations, 113
Young, Whitney, 132
Young African Leaders Initiative, 236,
    241
Youth Opportunities Unlimited, 214

Zambia, 29, 104, 116, 118–19, 122
Zion Baptist Church. *See* Sullivan, Leon
    Howard
Zion Gardens, 76
Zion Investment Associates (ZIA), 70, 75.
    See also Progress Investment Associates
Zion Non-Profit Charitable Trust (ZNPCT),
    75
Zulu Christian Industrial Institute. *See*
    Ohlange Institute

ACKNOWLEDGMENTS

What a journey! Writing this book has taken me to many places across the US and South Africa and more years than I care to admit, during which I have accumulated numerous debts.

First and foremost, thank you Bob Lockhart, who early on took an interest in this project and has remained a steadfast supporter ever since. This book and I are immeasurably better because of your keen insights, meticulous editing, and kind words of encouragement. My sincere thanks also to the Politics and Culture in Modern America series editors. Tom Sugrue, Matt Lassiter, and Margot Canaday all offered their astute feedback at a crucial stage in this project's development, encouraging me to think more broadly about Black empowerment's place in the wider landscape of US political culture. Toward the end, Matt and Keisha Blain each graciously took time to read the full manuscript and offered additional comments. Thank you for your time and insights. Any remaining shortcomings are mine alone.

It is one of the highest honors to have people you admire engage with your work. My deepest gratitude to Robert Trent Vinson, Vesla Weaver, Sara Berry, Bethany Moreton, Paul Kramer, Michael Hanchard, Josh Guild, and two anonymous readers for their careful readings of the entire manuscript. This is a much better book because of your input. Adam Ewing, Marcia Chatelain, and Alex Beasley likewise read and provided valuable feedback on various portions of the manuscript, for which I am very grateful.

Over the years I have had the privilege of presenting portions of this work at multiple workshops, seminars, and conferences. Thanks to the participants in the Washington, DC, African American Studies Works-in-Progress Seminar, the Centre for African Studies Seminar at the University of Cape Town, the Boston Seminar on Modern American Society and Culture, the Movements and Directions in Capitalism Program Workshop at the University of Virginia, the Johns Hopkins University Department of History Seminar, the Hagley Research Seminar, and the Hagley Work in Progress Seminar on the

History of Race and Business for their perceptive questions and comments. Some of my greatest insights came from discussions with audiences at the German Historical Institute, the Walter P. Reuther Library Archives of Labor and Urban Affairs, Atlanta University Center Robert W. Woodruff Library, Princeton University, Colgate University, Harvard University, Lehigh University, and Franklin & Marshall College.

I would not be the scholar I am today without my teachers. At Emory University, Joe Crespino, Matthew Payne, and Bobbi Patterson helped nurture my love for research and writing, while also modeling engaged and engaging pedagogy. The idea for this book originated while completing a master's degree at the University of Chicago. Thank you to my professors there, including Tom Holt, Leora Auslander, and Jane Dailey, for opening my eyes to new ways of thinking about race, gender, politics, and the city. A special note of thanks to my master's thesis advisor, Jim Sparrow, who first helped me believe I was onto something in probing the intersection between racial politics and entrepreneurship in late twentieth-century America.

The years I spent as a doctoral student at Johns Hopkins University were truly formative. Thanks to Sara Berry, Ron Walters, Todd Shepard, Toby Ditz, Tobie Meyer-Fong, Liz Thornberry, Katie Hindmarch-Watson, Casey Lurtz, Jessica Marie Johnson, Mary Ryan, Martha Jones, Lou Galambos, Lester Spence, and the late Pier Larson, for their wisdom, guidance, and support. Some of my greatest teachers at Hopkins were my classmates. Thank you to Paige Glotzer, Amira Rose Davis, Mo Speller, Morgan Shahan, Jessica Keene, Ayah Nuriddin, Franziska Strack, Jennie Grayson, Rebecca Stoli, Sara Rahnama, Julia Cummiskey, Emma McGlennen, Misha Mintz-Roth, Yonaton Glazer-Eytan, Mimi Stewart, Brandi Waters, and Meredith Gaffield for pushing me to be a better scholar and supporting me with your friendship. My deepest gratitude is reserved for my co-advisors. Angus Burgin made me a more precise thinker and writer, while demonstrating what it means to repeatedly go above and beyond for one's students. Nathan Connolly holds a singular place in my intellectual development. This book would not exist without you. Thank you for opening my eyes to the world.

Multiple trips to South Africa were critical for my understanding of Black empowerment's multiple roots and routes. Thank you to everyone at the Centre for African Studies at the University of Cape Town and especially Lungisile Ntsebeza for providing me with an intellectual home away from home. While in South Africa, I likewise benefited from conversations with Anne Mager,

Keith Breckenridge, Catherine Burns, Stephen Sparks, Bernard Dubbeld, and Kelly Gillespie, who generously shared their insights on South African history and politics with me. My ability to navigate South Africa—literally and figuratively—was further made possible by an incredibly generous and brilliant group of friends and comrades. Laura Phillips, Luke Spiropoulos, Rahma Leuner, Maya Schkolne, Simon Mayson, Vinayak Bhardwaj, Laura Pascoe, John Haffner, Thuto Thipe, Tara Weinberg, and the entire Weinberg family, my deepest gratitude for your warm hospitality and friendship. Enkosi kakhulu. Ndiyabulela.

Multiple fellowships and grants gave me the space and time to refine my ideas and write. Thank you to the German Historical Institute, which awarded me a fellowship in International Business History. A special thank you to Roger Horowitz and Carol Lockman for their hospitality and engagement during the year I spent in Wilmington as the Jefferson Scholars/Hagley Library Dissertation Fellow in Business and Politics. The same fellowship brought me to the University of Virginia, where Brian Balogh assembled a venerable group of scholars and public intellectuals to discuss history and the urgent need for public engagement, as head of the national fellows program.

I was privileged to spend a year as a postdoc in the Department of African American Studies at Princeton, surrounded by some of the most brilliant and generous scholars I have ever met. My sincere gratitude to Josh Guild, Eddie Glaude, Tera Hunter, Naomi Murakawa, Keeanga-Yamahtta Taylor, Ruha Benjamin, Reena Goldthree, and Wallace Best, for your incisive comments and encouragement. At Princeton, I likewise benefited from discussing my ideas with various people in the History department, including Jacob Dlamini, Alison Isenberg, and Kevin Kruse. Thank you for your contributions to this project.

A second postdoc at the University of Virginia facilitated my return to Charlottesville, where I profited from the generosity and probing questions of numerous individuals. In the History department, my sincere thanks to David Singerman, Justene Hill Edwards, Claudrena Harold, Sarah Milov, Kevin Gaines, Penny Von Eschen, and William Hitchcock. Thanks also to my fellow CLEAR Lab members: David Singerman, Shan Aman-Rana, Michael Gilbert, Daniel Gingerich, Deborah Hellman, Vineet Kapoor, Sandip Sukhtankar, Sylvia Tidey, and Jan Vogler. A special note of gratitude to Andrew Kahrl: Some of my fondest memories from that year, before COVID hit, include evenings spent discussing politics and activism at gatherings you helped facilitate.

I joined the faculty of Purchase College, State University of New York, in January 2021. Despite a challenging start, forced to teach my first classes via Zoom from my living room in Richmond, I have since had the pleasure of becoming acquainted with what makes Purchase the "cultural gem of the SUNY system." This includes my colleagues in history and the humanities. Many thanks to Christian Bailey, Leandro Benmergui, Laura Chmielewski, Rachel Hallote, Lisa Keller, Renqiu Yu, Sarah Warren, Emiliano Diaz, Gaura Narayan, Amy Beth Wright, Anna Ozbek, Mariel Rodney, Elise Lemire, Kerry Manzo, Sharon Zechowski, Paul Kaplan, Leah Springer, Odile Delgado, and all the humanities faculty and staff for welcoming me to Purchase. A special note of gratitude for our fearless leader, Aviva Taubenfeld, and my faculty mentor, Jennie Uleman, for their assistance, helping me navigate the challenges of being a new faculty member. To Shaka McGlotten, Krystal Perkins, Paula Halperin, Rudolf Gaudio, Diana Cassells, Sam Galloway, and all my colleagues in Global Black Studies, your commitment to our students and to making Purchase a more equitable and just place is a source of inspiration.

Megan Rossman was the first colleague I met in person after I moved back to New York City, and one of my principal guides to campus. Our friendship, including co-teaching a course on history and media together, as well as playing softball, has been a highlight of the last few years. Thanks for helping me feel at home on campus and in the city.

To all of my students, thank you for inspiring me with your questions, ideas, and perseverance in the face of so many obstacles. This work would have little meaning if not for you.

As I write these acknowledgments, our nation's libraries and archives are under attack. This is a tragedy of enormous consequence, not least for the people who work tirelessly, often for little pay, to preserve our shared history and make it accessible for contemporary and future generations. My deep appreciation goes out to the archivists and librarians at Temple University Special Collections; NYU's Tamiment Library and Robert F. Wagner Labor Archives; the New York City Municipal Archives; Columbia University Special Collections; the Schomburg Center for Research in Black Culture; the African Activist Archive at Michigan State University; Harvard University's Divinity School; the General Motors Heritage Center; Rutgers University Special Collections and University Archives; the US National Archives in College Park; the Library of Congress; the National Archives and Records Service of South Africa; the National Library of South Africa; the University of Cape Town African Studies Library; the Historical Papers at the University of the Witwatersrand; the University of Fort Hare; and the Mayibuye Archives at the University of the Western Cape. I owe a special thanks to Emory University's Stuart A. Rose Manuscript, Archives, and Rare Books Library; Atlanta University Center Robert W. Woodruff Library; the Hagley Library; and the Walter E. Reuther Library, Archives of Labor and Urban Affairs at Wayne State University for providing me with travel grants to help cover the cost of research. In addition to those already mentioned, this book was made possible with grants from the Society for Historians of American Foreign Relations, the Center for Global Inquiry + Innovation at the University of Virginia, and the SUNY Joint Labor Management Committee.

Writing this book has been a labor of love, one that I could not have sustained without the support of my academic communities, including Alex Beasley, Julia Ott, Louis Hyman, Shennette Garrett-Scott, Derek Musgrove, Heather Ann Thompson, Tim Gilfoyle, Pedro Regalado, Destin Jenkins, Ben Holtzman, Dylan Gottlieb, Mike Glass, Bench Ansfield, Lindsay Keiter, Anne-Marie Angelo, Jeanette Estruth, Amy Zanoni, A.J. Murphy, Emily Connolly, Joan Flores-Villalobos, Lizzie Ingleson, Sarah Sklaw, Sarah Snyder, Chris Dietrich, Brad Simpson, Peter Cole, Amanda Kleintop, Brandon Winford, Danielle Wiggins, Austin McCoy, Josh Davis, Andy Holter, Emma Park, Aaron Jakes, Atiba Pertilla, Alexi Garrett, Amanda Gibson, and too many others to name. Thank you for creating the space for me to feel at home within the academy. Your insights have enriched my thinking and your camaraderie kept me going through the many hurdles associated with being an academic.

Finally, to my friends and family, whose love has sustained me over the years. Misa Appeltova, Billy Kelly, Brandy Houser, Maria Town, Betsy Cohen, Emily Hootkins, and Christina Dill, thank you for lending a sympathetic ear and/or a couch to crash on following a long day in the archives. A special note of gratitude to my ride-or-die Allie Ettenger: Our friendship means the world to me. I was lucky to attend graduate school in the city where I grew up and where my family still lives. Brian, Amee, and Sonia, I cherish time spent with you, whether on the playground or around the dinner table. I was inspired to become a historian, in part, by my dad, Peter Levy, whose love for teaching and writing history helped convince me this was a path worth pursuing. To my mother, Diane Krejsa: Your intellect and drive are an inspiration, and you a model of how to navigate this world as a strong, successful woman committed to both their family and their career. I only hope I can be a role model to Julia the way you have been for me.

Paulina, there is no one who knows more the sacrifices I have made to complete this book and who has sacrificed so much to support me and my career over the years. Through multiple moves and jobs, to caring for our cats Beetle and Tosca in their later years while I jetted off to yet another conference, to tending to Julia so I could finish writing, this book would not exist without you. Most of all, thank you for loving me. Your love is the greatest gift of all, and my greatest joy comes from the privilege of sharing this one precious life with you and Julia.